TOUCHED THE AFRICAN SOUL

Compiled by
Gloria Cunningham
Lois Okerstrom

Edited by
Lois Okerstrom, Helen Erickson, Martha Fosse

Quiet Waters Publications
Bolivar, Missouri
2001

For information contact:
    Quiet Waters Publications
    P.O. Box 34, Bolivar MO 65613-0034.
    E-mail: QWP@usa.net.
For prices and order information visit:
    http://www.quietwaterspub.com

ISBN 0-9663966-9-3
Library of Congress Catalog Card Number 98-065154
BV2090.C86

Credits include:
    Olan Mills – for photographs.
    World Bible Publishers – For quotes from NRSV Bible.
    Vuga Press – for Sketches.
    George Woods – for maps.
    Phil Grey – for illustrations from *Kwendi Gusome*, published by Vuga
        Press, Tanzania.
    "Lift High the Cross" – George W. Kitchin and Michael R. Newbolt,
        ©1974 Hope Publishing Co., Carol Stream, IL 90188. All rights reserved. Used by permission.
    Contributors (photos) are Lore Heidel, Ruth Fryhle, Louise Faust,
        Lois Okerstrom, Gloria Cunningham.
    Front Cover – Photos by Gloria Cunningham, design by John Hiebert.
    Back Cover – Photo by Robert Houser, www.roberthouser.com.

IN GRATEFUL MEMORY
of our women missionary colleagues who, as Tanzanian
Christians say, "have moved" to their Eternal Home; and
in dedication to our many Tanzanian Christian sisters with
whom we are one in faith.

IMPORTANT NOTICE TO OUR READERS

The first edition of *Touched by the African Soul* was self-published in 1998 by the sixty-two authors included in this book. The three thousand copies we were able to have printed sold out swiftly, and we used the total net proceeds to establish a scholarship fund for Tanzanian women in higher education.

We are exceptionally pleased that *Quiet Waters Publications* is reprinting our book and donating eight percent of the sales price of each book to our established scholarship fund. However, we need your help and your additional contribution for expanding our scholarship fund to help more of these young women. You may send a tax-deductible check to the administrators of this fund at this address:

Lutheran Community Foundation
625 Fourth Ave. So.
Minneapolis, MN 55415
(612) 340-4110

On the "memo line," please write: *Touched by the African Soul Fund.*

We give you our sincere thanks, as will each young woman whom you have helped with your kindness and generosity. Bless you!

CONTENTS

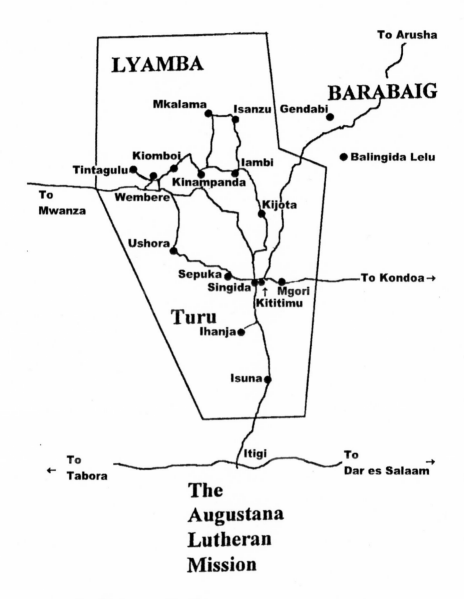

LYAMBA

BARABAIG

To Arusha

Mkalama Isanzu Gendabi

● Balingida Lelu

Kiomboi

Tintagulu
Kinampanda

Iambi

To
Mwanza

Wembere

Kijota

Ushora

Sepuka
Singida

To Kondoa →

Mgori
Kititimu

Turu

Ihanja

Isuna

Itigi

To
Tabora

To
Dar es Salaam →

The
Augustana
Lutheran
Mission

One inch = ca. 40 miles

NOTE

So you thought a *safari* was a hunting trip! Well, as you will read, a *safari* is *any* journey or trip.

Swahili words used in these stories are printed in italics with translation in parentheses, immediately following their use. Swahili is a marvelous language: you write it exactly as it sounds (no *k*nives or *k*nees or *p*neumonia), and you read and pronounce it as it is spelled! Normally, each syllable ends in a vowel.

Swahili vowels are pronounced as shown below, with examples taken from the stories:

a - like the a in f*a*ther *panga* (machete); *safari* (trip)

e - like the e in f*e*rry; th*e*m *Jembe* (hoe)

i - like the e in f*ee*t, b*e*; *Swahili*; *bibi* (lady, miss)

o - like the o in f*o*r, *moto* (fire); *polepole* (slowly)

u - like the u in d*u*rable, mbutu (a long horn)

oo - is two syllables: a lengthened "o" sound, *njoo!* (come!)

The accent in Swahili words is normally on the next to the last syllable, as in *"Karibu !"* (Welcome!), pronounced: Ka-RI-bu.

"Karibuni !" (Welcome!, plural), pronounced: Ka-ri-BU-ni.

Njoo! = NjO-o! (Come! -singular); njooni = njo-O-ni (Come! -plural)

FOREWORD

From the beginning, women like Mary Magdalene and Priscilla carried the Good News of Jesus Christ from the open tomb outside Jerusalem to the Mediterranean world, to Africa and Asia, to the ends of the earth. Often their roles were narrowed and restricted by church tradition and local contexts. This might have limited the scope of their influence.

Yet the women God called into the mission of Christ were not bound in their vision and commitment to serve. They found countless ways to witness whether their role was formally sanctioned or if it developed informally around the edges of mission and church, or within the home life of the missionary family and out the kitchen door.

The title of this collection of memories and stories of sixty-two missionary women is an apt one. "Touched" is an appropriate modifier for women's approach to life in mission.

Characteristically, the missionary woman was open and vulnerable to the daily touch of her new neighbors and friends. With a divine calling she connected compassionately with people at their human level and at the level of the "soul." She wept with local women when their babies died. She served as mediator, witness and friend when cultural practice separated male missionaries from communication and relationships with local women. She lived the faith, taught the faith and persevered out of a personal faith that embraced her whole being.

In this collection of women's stories, progress is made in the critical and mostly neglected task of collecting the perspectives and experiences of missionary women. Their stories often are absent in the documentation and writing of the official histories of the mission agencies and churches. These women who served in what is now the Evangelical Lutheran Church in Tanzania have made a significant contribution in preserving the memory of their experiences. Our thanks go out to them for participating in this crucial endeavor.

Bonnie L. Jensen, Executive Director,
Division for Global Mission, ELCA

PREFACE

One of the sixty-two writers of these stories was asked, "How have your years in Tanzania affected your life?" She answered, "It affects *everything*— what I think about, what I pray about, what I read, what I buy or don't buy, what I save, my use of time, even customs or language I still want to use." She, along with the rest of the writers, was truly TOUCHED BY THE AFRICAN SOUL.

"What did the missionary *wives* do in Africa?" That question was casually asked by one of the women visiting us one day as we were all sitting around a table drinking coffee. Hours later, that question motivated us to reflection and sparked the beginnings of the imagining of this book. It was one of God's astonishing surprises that this book came to be! At first, we had only thought to include the stories of the wives who went along with their husbands. Then we realized that the story of the women in the missionary field is complete only by including the single women missionaries. Together we all served on the former Augustana Lutheran Field in central Tanzania.

The short stories in this book all emerged from the lives of sixty-two Lutheran women missionaries in the central area of Tanzania (formerly called Tanganyika) in East Africa. We were wives of teachers, pastors, doctors or agriculturalists. We were also single women who worked as secretaries, nurses, literacy workers and teachers. Although we are not professional writers, we all share a love for Africa, its people, culture, customs and language. As we wrote and shared our ideas, frustrations, and prayers, and then as we offered our monetary contributions for publishing the book, the teamwork and bonding we enjoyed were typical of the spirit of our mission family. The stories in this book fondly embrace some 50 years in time, from the early 1940's until 1996.

Although the book is not intended to be a historical account, it may be appropriate to include a few historical facts so that the reader may better understand the context of some of the stories. American mission work began among the Lyamba (also called Iramba or Ilyamba) people in 1926 when George N. Anderson, Herbert Magney, and Ludvig Melander, all pioneer Lutheran missionaries, walked 280 miles south from the northern

Kilimanjaro region in order to convey God's message. Through evangelism, education, and medical work, the message of God's love through Christ spread to the neighboring Turu and then to the Barabaig peoples.

In 1958, the church that emerged from that mission work became autonomous as the Lutheran Church of Central Tanganyika. In 1963, it became one of the synods/dioceses of the newly formed Evangelical Lutheran Church of Tanzania (ELCT). Today the ELCT is a vital, growing church of approximately 2.5 million members. The Central Diocese and its mission sites, where these stories take place, number about 85,000 in 55 congregations.

We are deeply indebted to our Tanzanian sisters and brothers with whom we lived and worked, and with whom we have so many shared memories. We continue to interact in many ways with our African friends, through visits, prayers, traditional mail, and now also through *email*. We continue to be inspired by their faith and fortitude, the "soul" of Africa's people.

Special thanks to all the authors and to our very fine editorial staff for volunteering their valuable expertise. This includes *Lois Okerstrom*, who did the editing for the wives' manuscripts, plus the final editing/proofing of the entire book; and *Helen Erickson* and *Martha Fosse*, who co-edited the manuscripts written by the single women. We also want to express our heartfelt gratitude to *Ray Cunningham*, who good-naturedly agreed to undertake the compiling on computer of all the stories which make up this book.

We especially wish to thank *Rev. Bonnie Jensen*, former missionary to Ethiopia, now Executive Director of the Division of Global Missions, ELCA, who wrote the Foreword, emphasizing the seldom-acknowledged, but crucial part women have played in missions.

The utmost of gratitude goes to *our Lord and Saviour Jesus Christ* Who called and enabled each of us who served in Tanzania, and Who continues to call us all to go into all the world and share the Good News with all people.

The writers hope that these stories of Africa will touch your life, whether it be through their inspiration, their faith, their joys, their grief, or even through their humor.

Gloria Cunningham and Lois Okerstrom
Compilers

OF MOONS AND TUNES AND SHINING NIGHTS

Beatrice Beyerhelm

"'Twas the night before Christmas" … Actually, it was two days before Christmas and I wasn't ready.

The magical tricycle, the gift from the grandparents in Illinois for two-year-old Carl David, the long-awaited tricycle, was held hostage at the post office in Singida, thirty miles away, by the coming of the rainy season. The grass was green and lovely, the trees were leafing out, but the roads were bottomless clay pits, waiting to suck in any vehicle. We couldn't get the trike for Christmas. There was no way.

I had a few small presents—a couple of matchbox cars and a Noddy book for Carl David (Noddy's car always said "Parp, Parp" and Carl David liked that), a stuffed dog made out of sewing scraps for five-month-old Christopher, and a British mystery paperback for my husband, Carl. Shopping at the Indian *dukas* (stores) in Singida was limited - a few British things, a few East Indian things. The available gift wrap, for some reason I never understood, came only in orange, for me a Halloween color, not a Christmas wrap at all. But it would have to do.

A Christmas tree would make it Christmas. This was the day to go off to the *pori* (bush forest) right after lunch, find a somewhat green tree without too many thorns, cut it down, and carry it home.

Carl and I were more ready for Christmas this year than last, our first in Tanganyika. Being still pretty shaky with language and suffering culture shock, we had tried to do an American Christmas, but there weren't any props for it—no snow, no cold, no turkey, no Marshall Fields, not even Sears. I was saved from despair only by the sound of some familiar carol tunes at church and by the moon which I knew shone not only on us at our isolated mission station at Ushora but also on our home in Lemont, Illinois, half a world away.

This second Christmas I was in somewhat better shape. I knew enough not to put candy shot on my Christmas cookies. Last year my African guests, encountering the strange, hard objects on the cookies, politely spit them out into the corners of the dining room, a flurry of ball bearings bouncing on the floor.

This second Christmas, after a long dry season, Carl and I had come to appreciate the Tanganyikan weather pattern and to celebrate it in our Christmas card:

The Advent wind cries…
Repent,
Prepare ye,
Bow down.
The Christmas rain comes…
Quieting,
Cleansing,
Renewing.

But I still needed a tree to make Christmas real for me. And I wasn't about to get one that day.

While we were eating lunch, the medical assistant from the dispensary came by, stood at the door in his white shorts and shirt with his stethoscope hanging around his neck. "I have a patient who needs to get to the hospital today. Can you take him?"

I knew the mission pickup was the only vehicle for miles around and we were frequently called on to take people to the hospital, but today my heart cried, "No, we're going for a tree."

Carl calmly said, "Sure, we'll be ready in fifteen minutes."

"OK, Beatrice," I said to myself. "Adapt. A trip to the hospital at Kiomboi means a chance to visit with some other Americans, for the kids to play in English, to see somebody else's Christmas decorations, taste their Christmas cookies. It can be a family outing."

But the roads were sure to be terrible. The trip, 35 miles, was a pleasant jaunt in good weather but would be one of life's "maybes" today. I had been around long enough to know how to pack—diapers, sweaters, blanket, food. There were sweet rolls left in the breadbox. I filled a canteen with milk and the thermos with tea.

The patient was able to sit up so he rode in the front of the pickup with Carl. The children and I settled in on the assorted bags and boxes in the covered back of the truck. I wished we had a four-wheel drive vehicle but Ushora was still on the waiting list to get one.

The first part of the trip featured slithering and sliding. I could see Carl's shoulders hunched over the steering wheel as he tried to keep the truck on the road. Carl David thought it was fun, shouted "Whee" while I prayed.

To divert the children and keep me calm we sang—Jingle Bells, Up On the Housetop, Silent Night, Away in a Manger, and *Mungu ni Pendo* (the "Jesus Loves Me" of the Tanganyikan church).

We were doing well until we came to the Kironda River. The river runs at the bottom of a deep, narrow valley. Normally the water was only a few inches deep and we could cross easily on a cement drift.

But that day the Kironda was racing and roaring. Carl pulled the truck over to the side of the road and we got out.

"What now?" he asked. "Do you think it's going up or coming down? It hasn't rained yet today."

The water was tearing stones and mud from the bank as it flew by our feet. It didn't look at all like the flood was slowing down.

"The high road is thirty miles farther and it's bound to be chewed up by the Singida-Kiomboi lorry traffic," Carl continued anxiously.

"Maybe we could wait a while and see what happens?" I suggested. "It's only two."

So we decided to wait.

We sat on some nearby boulders. When the boys got antsy, we skipped stones. We floated stick boats. We built sand castles. We recalled being stuck in snow storms at Christmas. We nervously watched our patient sitting stoically in the truck.

An English Ford came along with the son-in-law of the Italian who operated a rather run-out gold mine on the opposite side of the river. We exchanged news while he also waited.

An Indian lorry arrived. The Sikh driver took one look, backed up, and headed for the longer route.

At four we had "high tea" with sweet rolls and milk.

The river showed no sign of going down. This could take all night.

When Mr. Bicchieri, the gold mine owner, came to the opposite bank to see if his son-in-law had arrived yet, he called out, "I don't think this river is going to be passable before morning. You all want to come over to my house to spend the night?"

But we needed to get to the hospital.

So Mr. B. threw across a rope which we tied to our truck while his son-in-law waded home through the neck-deep water.

We turned around and started the long trek to Kiomboi.

When night fell I was grateful for the sweaters. The boys and I snuggled together in my grandmother's old patchwork quilt. As the full moon rose, Chris dozed off. Carl David said, "Tell me again about Christmas, about Baby Jesus."

So together we told about a family with no place to sleep, some kind people who took them in, friendly animals, wonderful music in the sky, angels and shepherds.

"And it was Christmas," Carl David said sleepily, "Christmas."

Then he slept and I rode in silence, past the African compounds, catching sight of evening fires, hearing the voices of children and parents talking and laughing, the sound of cattle lowing and distant drums beating, and thought about God finding a place to be born in every country and town and every time.

I knew Carl must be getting very tired of fighting to hold the truck on the road, to ride the ridges of the ruts and not slip into the wallows. God was good. We arrived safely at Kiomboi about ten p.m., deposited the patient at the hospital, and went in search of a place for us. Missionary hospitality is always warm and soon we were eating scrambled eggs and drinking coffee with the missionary doctor's family who took us in.

The next morning we started home. Deciding to risk the short route, we found the Kironda, as Mr. Bicchieri had predicted, behaving nicely in its banks, and crossed easily.

Noon. Home again. Christmas Eve. Still no tree.

Carl was beginning to panic. He didn't have a Christmas sermon finished and the church wasn't decorated yet.

He hurried to find the axe, get the station evangelist, and set off to cut palm branches for the church.

I put the boys down for naps. Self pity set in. "Here I am. No tree for Christmas, no decent presents, no proper wrapping paper, no help from Carl. There just won't be any Christmas," I pouted.

Then I glanced at the bushes in the back yard. Ah-ha! I got the kitchen butcher knife, whacked off a few branches, wired them together and called it "Christmas Tree"—not Scotch pine, more weeping willow, but "Christmas Tree"!

I stuck it in a bucket of sand, put it in the living room, and hung our few decorations on it. I wrapped the presents in the orange paper and hid them under my bed. I was as ready as I was going to get.

At the village Christmas Eve service the church was lit by candles and a kerosene lantern or two. Night services are rare in a land of lions and leopards and long distances to walk, but Christmas Eve is a special night.

As I worshipped in the dim church I began to realize that this year I not only knew the tunes to the carols but I could also sing the Lyamba words. I could hear, really hear, the words of the Christmas story. When the evangelist prayed the Christmas Eve collect, "You made this holy night shine," I knew he meant this night in this place. I learned a new carol, an African lullaby for the *Mwana Mwelu* (the Holy Child). I looked around me lullaby for the *Mwana Mwelu* (the Holy Child). I looked around me and saw people whose names I knew and who knew my name. I saw the baptismal font where my child had been baptized.

And I sang *Shekulu Waza Nantende*, Joy to the World, joy to Lemont, Illinois, and to Ushora and to all the places between. Joy to the world, the Lord is come!

Carl and I walked home in the moonlight, sleeping Christopher tied on my back, Carl David hopping between us. A bicycle bell sounded in the distance. "Santa!" Carl David shouted and raced for bed to be safely asleep before Santa's arrival.

Carl went into the study to polish his Christmas Day sermon. I put our gifts under the tree, made a cup of tea, and settled in to quietly watch the Advent candles burn down.

About eleven Carl came out of his office stretching and said, "Well, it's almost Christmas."

I smiled and replied, "And I'm ready."

Beatrice Beyerhelm *is the wife of Pastor Carl Beyerhelm. They served in Tanzania from 1955 to 1964 living at Ushora and Kinampanda in the Central Region and then at Makumira Seminary.*

Carl David was eight months old when they arrived in Tanzania. Christopher, Mary and Ruth were born there. Carl and Bea are presently retired in Iowa City, Iowa.

FROM HONEYMOON TO BUBONIC PLAGUE

Elaine L. Palmquist

World War II had just finished when my husband, Marvin, and I began our honeymoon journey to Tanganyika Territory, East Africa, on the "Gripsholm." This Swedish ship was one of the first allowed to carry passengers after the war. It darted back and forth through the Mediterranean Sea. I vividly remember the sunken ships with their masts sticking out of the water near Naples, Italy. We spent the first two days in Alexandria, Egypt, but the bed bugs had taken over our beds so thoroughly that we had to sleep in the bathtub. So we decided to move on to Cairo.

Our traveling companion, Ms. Vivian Gulleen, finally found passage down through the Red Sea and took our heavy luggage with her. Marv and I were able to take the "Cooks Tour" up the Nile River, requiring some twenty transfers, from train, bus, river boat and lake steamer.

The first hundred miles was on a train, from Cairo to Aswan. The train windows were tinted and we found ourselves crossing a hot, dry desert. We were given bottled water, but it had an odd taste, like mineral water. We forced ourselves to drink it.

From Aswan we continued by boat. We found a small pamphlet describing the different people living along the Nile River. We wondered whether these people were similar to those with whom we would work. Our boat captain often stood on the bridge and shot crocodiles lying on the bank. We both thought it was a tragic waste.

On this trip we stopped periodically for wood, which was used to fire the steam boilers of the ship, and on one occasion the lower deck was piled high with green bananas for a settlement up-country. At Wadi Haifa the chief invited us to a local wedding. We were fascinated by the indigenous music and dancing, to say nothing of their near nudity!

We tried to study Swahili along the way, but made little progress. In the evening we often climbed to the top deck of one of the barges and played hop scotch for exercise.

When we neared Juba the boat became stuck on a sand bar and in desperation the captain finally had to radio ahead to Juba for a light launch to rescue the passengers. Marv asked the captain as we were leaving, "How long will you be stuck here?"

With a shrug he replied, "Until the rains come upcountry, raise the water level here and set me free."

After a few days' stay at a hotel in Kampala, Uganda, we boarded a lake steamer, and when we docked at Mwanza we realized we were finally in our country of destination, Tanganyika. We boarded a train to Singida for the last leg of our journey. We had saved our last clean clothes to meet Pastor Occie and Doris Rolander and Pastor Melander. On this very chilly morning I wore a thin cotton sun dress and Marv had on a white shirt and white shorts. Those meeting us wore heavy wool sweaters!

During our language study there were some major adjustments. Marv was eager to use what little Swahili he knew, so he asked an African young man to light a fire in the wood-burning cook stove. Before long smoke began pouring out into the living room and when we ran into the kitchen, we discovered he had built a fire on the stove rather than in the stove. *Jikoni* can be understood as either "in" or "on the stove." After that, we explained carefully that the fire was to be *ndani (inside)* the stove. This young man was fascinated by the clean oven where peanuts could be roasted without burning them.

Moving to the Wembere plains left us with no transportation other than our legs. The area had a very scattered population of some 25,000 people. In contrast to the plateau above, the plains were hot and dry. The air was very still except when occasional wind made dust whirls blow high into the sky. At first, however, I was having a really fun time opening our trunks, seeing our wedding gifts again and trying to set up our first home. I sewed curtains and drapes for the many windows.

But then loneliness set in. Marv was often gone. He would climb the 1,000-foot escarpment behind our house and walk the twenty-two miles round-trip to Kiomboi where he was vice-pastor. The waterfall a quarter mile from our back door caused our house to shake when in full flood. I worried about Marv having to cross that same river up on top before he could return home again.

An elementary school and a medical clinic had been built and a medical worker, already trained to use a microscope, was able to diagnose malaria from a blood slide. A midwife was available, but losing her eyesight. On one occasion I was called to help a teenager, named Anna, give birth to a baby girl. She and I became very good friends. Her first request was "Mama, I am eager to learn to knit and sew for my baby. Will you help me?"

Soon I had a group of young girls and their mothers sitting on our verandah, chatting in the Lyamba language and trying desperately to thread a needle or cut cloth with my pinking shears. What impressed me was that they often held the yarn with their toes. Anna said it was because their hands were already busy. They were far better pupils than I was a teacher. Iowa farm women from near my home sent us packages of colored chicken feed sacks and yards of flannel to make simple garments. This was one avenue of friendship I continued into our second term of service. Our daughter, Annette, helped by putting fussy babies in her doll buggy and kept them happy while their mothers sewed.

I was glad I could have a short Bible study while the women were sewing. Some of the women would say to Juliana, a school teacher, "Tell Mama I do not understand her Swahili." Juliana would quickly translate what I had said into the Lyamba language. They would nod in agreement and their faces would light up with new hope. One of those mothers was especially eager to be baptized. I remember she chose the name *Tyatawelu*, which means "I follow the light."

Marv had twenty-two bush schools to supervise and once he received a motorcycle it seemed as though he was never home. So one day I took a pillow and tied it to the saddle seat of his cycle. I rode with him all the way to Kiomboi, forty-four miles round-trip via the lower road.

I soon had another job, paying teachers' salaries and giving out school supplies. Each school received a tennis ball to play with, and when it was worn out they would receive another, but only after bringing back the broken pieces.

For Mark's birth in June, 1947, we traveled 80 miles from Wembere to Iambi Hospital. Our good friend and cook, Zakayo Msengi, accompanied us. As it often happened, our car became stuck in the mud. With no thought for his own safety, Zakayo offered to walk to Iambi Hospital through lion country to get us some food and hot coffee. In the dark he became lost in the bush and came struggling back to the car just before dawn, soaking wet from the rain and very weary. We finally made it to the hospital later that morning.

I was so eager to show our newborn son to our African friends, I brought him to the outdoor worship service in his new perambulator. We had no church building large enough to accommodate all our parishioners so we worshipped under a large wild fig tree at a beautiful stone altar. When the African children saw me coming out of our house, they followed closely as they had never seen a white baby. They were soon talking and giggling about his very pink skin and his lack of hair.

The conversations at our sewing groups soon began referring to a dreaded disease called *tauni*, bubonic plague. There had been a good harvest and with grain spilled on the ground, the rats had multiplied and infested the homes. On one trip to the Tintigulu Leprosarium, it became dark before Marv returned home. The lights of the car evidently attracted the rats to the road and he could feel them squishing under the tires as he drove along. We ordered many rat traps, but they were little better than nothing.

Then the rats began to die and the infected fleas which carried the plague found a new host, the human body. The symptoms were similar to malaria with a very high fever so at first it was difficult to diagnose. Then the bubo glands in the groin and underarms became tender and would begin to swell. In the final stages the capillaries under the skin would hemorrhage and turn dark, hence the term "black death."

The first ones to die were the patients at the leprosarium. The evangelist, Natianota Lyanga, reported a number of patients had bled to death while they were sleeping. The rats had chewed on an insensitive leprous body part, severed a blood vessel, causing the patients to die in their sleep. We could hear the wailing of the mourners and the drums beating the death dances.

Dr. Stan Moris insisted we leave immediately as Mark was beginning to crawl. We had stored corn in our attic and the rats would roll the ears of corn across the floor and wake our baby. Soon our entire area was quarantined. Marv was allowed to enter the area to bring medical supplies and pay salaries. When he passed the road block he was sprayed with kerosene to kill the fleas.

Finally Dr. Moris and my husband took a can of cyanide powder down to our house in an attempt to kill the rats. They placed a key in each door lock and a wet newspaper on the floor of each room. They held their breath and poured the cyanide on the newspaper and closed and locked each door. Later that evening we read in *Time* magazine of a house in America that had exploded when a similar treatment had been done. We prayed earnestly this would not happen to our home.

In order to try to control the rat population, each individual in the quarantined area was required to bring to the local sub-chief the tails of 70 rats every day. This meant that a family of seven had to kill 490 rats! The people later told us it only took about two hours each morning to fill this quota.

After the plague subsided and we were allowed to return to our home, we could see the area was very dry and the rains were late in coming. We experienced a severe famine. The leprosy patients were hit hardest because they could not travel to find food and they had only small gardens. Finally in desperation to keep them from starving to death, Marv used money from a "Christmas cheer fund" to purchase five tons of corn which gave a bit of relief. Each head of a household could receive one tuna fish-sized can of corn per day per person. It didn't fill their stomachs when ground into cornmeal but kept some alive until the next harvest.

The lower road was still impassable so the corn was delivered to the top of the escarpment. The leprosy patients walked the five miles to our station and climbed the escarpment to receive this ration. They did so without complaint. Marv wanted to give a week's supply, but Natianota Lyanga objected, saying, "They are so hungry, they would grind the week's supply and eat it all in one day." Some of the corn did spill on the ground, so the women agreed that each day one of them could pick up the loose kernels.

Another tragedy was that many had eaten even the seed corn they had expected to plant the next season. Then they had to travel far from home in search of both food and seed.

Our second term of service was far different than the first at Wembere. We were placed at the large hospital station of Kiomboi. So we moved from the plains to the plateau, from relative remoteness to a busy, but still rural center. I was honored to help teach one class at Kiomboi Nurses' Training Center.

Then next to my sewing classes, I became involved in Sunday School work. Each Saturday two African girls helped me hectograph pictures for the children to color, illustrating the Bible story for that Sunday. Each Sunday I also taught the congregation a new hymn before our worship service began. Kiomboi was a fulfilling and extremely busy era of our lives.

Remembering that first honeymoon and our first days on the Wembere plains, we took a second one 37 years later, returning to visit our first home. There we participated in a most memorable six-hour service, reminiscing and celebrating with the people.

The power of the Gospel had changed them forever.

Elaine Bexell Palmquist *graduated from Swea City High School, Minnesota, attended Gustavus Adolphus College in St. Peter, MN, for one year and then entered Bethesda School of Nursing, Minneapolis, MN, graduating in 1943. She is an R.N.*

In 1944, Elaine married Marvin A. Palmquist, a Lutheran seminarian. After Marvin's ordination, they were commissioned in August 1945 for missionary service in Tanganyika, East Africa.

Together, Marvin and Elaine served the church at Wembere Mission Station, 1946-1950. During furlough, 1951, Elaine attended the University of Minnesota. From 1951 to 1956 Marv and Elaine served at Kiomboi Mission Station.

Their three children are Mark Robert, born in Iambi Mission Station, East Africa, 1947, who died in 1991; Annette Eileen, born 1950, Minneapolis, MN; and Daniel Marvin, born 1960, Hastings, MN.

GIVE ME THE "SIMPLICITY" LIFE
Edna Dibble

My hobby was—and still is—sewing. When we lived at Kiomboi I was delighted to have the use of a Singer machine which was powered by a foot-treadle so I could use it when the station's electricity was shut down—which was most of the daytime hours unless the doctors were in surgery down at the hospital. Lois Austin had a complete set of Simplicity patterns which she generously loaned to the seamstresses on the various stations. I quickly became the Kiomboi dressmaker and was both honored and humbled when a dress that I had made for Nurse Jean Myklebust was used for her burial.

The "Hollywood Tailor Shop" in the village of Kiomboi was my nearest competitor. You could walk in there, look at a Simplicity pattern book, and point to the garment you wanted made. Then the tailor would "size you up," and in a week or so your new outfit was ready. And it always fit!

One afternoon while working in the kitchen, I looked out and saw Petro, the young man who worked with me in our home, running up the path to the back door. He was quite excited as he said, "Mama, I have a sewing job for you!"

"What's that?" I asked.

"I've just bought a dress for my wife. I got it at Bibi (Miss) Ruth Halvorson's thrift sale."

"But, Petro, your wife is a size 18 and this dress is only size 10. I don't have any material that matches it."

"That's all right. Just use anything you can find to make it bigger!"

Fortunately the dress had a deep hem which I was able to remove and insert in the sides as gussets. Of course, after doing that, Petro was sure I could do *anything* on the sewing machine.

NEVER AGAIN !

"Don't *ever* ask me to go on another hunting trip!"

I greeted Birney, my husband, with those words when he came back to where he'd left me standing watch over a dead impala.

We were spending the weekend at a village called Chem-chem down on the plains north of the Lyamba Plateau. We had an impala on the ground and were getting ready to field dress it when our son Eric spotted a small herd of eland running through the bush a couple of hundred yards away.

"Stay with the impala, will you, Edna?" Birney said. "Maybe we can get a shot at one of those eland." He took off in the Land Rover with Eric and our daughter Barb.

Almost as soon as he drove away a vulture circled low, and then another, and another, until there were dozens of them swooping down at me where I stood waving my arms and jumping up and down to protect the impala (myself?). Others stood in a circle around me, pacing back and forth, fighting amongst themselves, darting in toward me. They never attack live people, I kept telling myself. Do they?

So when the family finally came back—seemingly hours later—I said firmly, "Never again."

Until the next time.

YES, WE HAVE NO BANANAS, BUT DO WE HAVE BEANS !

"Dad, what happened to our front yard?" Eric asked excitedly.

"And look across the road," Barb said. "Everything's been dug up."

"Oh, no!" I said, "Godson's been at it again!"

We had just returned to Kiomboi from a weekend hunting on the Wembere plains. As we neared our home we could see that, indeed, our gardener, Godson Makala, had gone overboard with planting kidney beans. Our front yard, the patch of weeds across the road, as well as our large *shamba* (garden) all had been dug up and planted with beans.

A month later, we kept Augustana School, Kiomboi Hospital, ourselves and Godson's family supplied with kidney beans for one whole season.

GOT A BEE IN YOUR BONNET?

"Mom, come quickly!" shouted both Barb and Eric. "Dad's running around in circles and we don't know what's wrong with him."

I knew Birney was harvesting the honey that a swarm of bees had made in a container which Dr. Denny Lofstrom had placed on the roof of the house when he lived here. But Birney was well-covered with a poncho, gloves, hat, scarf, and his snorkel mask. So surely he'd be well protected.

However, when I saw him running about and slapping at his head and face I realized a bee had gone down the hole where the snorkel fits into the mask. It was buzzing about inside the mask. He was afraid to take off the mask because he was surrounded by the bees. He continued to fight the one in his mask, where it was buzzing right in front of his eyes.

Finally, the bees flew off and he was able to take off his mask. And we recovered most of the honey and it was delicious!

Edna Dibble, *R.N. While at Kiomboi, Edna worked in the preemie nursery, taught English in the School of Nursing, and had music classes at the school for missionary children. Her husband Birney is a surgeon.*

The Dibbles were in Tanzania for two short-term periods of a year and a half each: 1962-63, 1967-68.

They have two children, Eric and Barbara.

WHEN THE HEART SAYS HOME

Helen Erickson

It was my first Sunday in Tanganyika (now Tanzania); in fact my first Sunday in a Lutheran church in the past six months. The young Lyamba man kneeling at the altar rose, turned to the congregation and sang:

"Mwelu, mwelu, mwelu, Shekulu wa maumbi
Nsii tulu ijulile uuza waakue."

My heart warmed as the well-remembered call to worship continued. The words he sang had no meaning for me that day—that would come later—but on this day, the melody sang to me the words I had known since childhood:

"Holy, holy, holy is the Lord of hosts
The whole earth is full of his glory."

Until that moment I had not recognized how much I had been missing the whole fabric of life of which this call to worship had been so integral a part of my being.

For despite the faltering economy in our land, life in rural mid-America had been solid, predictable and in most ways, safe. Or had it only seemed so? It had certainly contrasted with the past six months of rootless wandering, a member of our group making bookings, one "leg" at a time, for our journey to Tanganyika. In wartime, no ongoing reservations could be guaranteed.

"We" at the start of travel were two single women, Ruth Holmer (now Friberg) and myself. After three months of exploring Portugal and pleading with the travel agents to find us passage on a ship going around the South African Cape, our party of missionaries of the Augustana Synod had grown to ten people. The groups of missionaries from other persuasions had grown proportionately.

All these people were vying for space on any ship going that way. Quite likely, German U-boats busy on that route explained why no passenger ships were being sent there. Taking a more direct route to East Africa through the Mediterranean Sea and Suez Canal was out of the question in

1944. Situated between North Africa and Italy, it was a military lake; passenger vessels were simply not permitted to enter.

Meanwhile, Portuguese ships continued plying their Atlantic routes, bringing ever more missionaries to fill Lisbon's hotels and pensions. The waiting was not unpleasant; there were many things to see, learn and enjoy. Our forays to castles and other ruins gave us a growing list of places to take newcomers arriving on future ships. But under all the activity lay the knowledge that we were not where we belonged and wondering whether and when we would reach that place.

Risk was inherent in our situation; one could not forget the torpedoing of the Egyptian ship Zamzam just three years earlier. Nineteen of our Augustana missionaries had been among the 300 people dumped into the South Atlantic (including a mother and her six little ones).[*] Yet miraculously, no life had been lost. Risk, yes, but tamed by the strong conviction that this was God's call and He could be trusted to care for us regardless of where the road might take us.

The call had been so compelling: With the onset of World War II, the German missionaries in Tanganyika had been interned, their fields left without experienced leadership. The six American missionary pastors of the Augustana Synod's tiny field in central Tanganyika were trying to give supervisory help in six other mission areas, all older and larger than ours, formerly staffed by 170 Germans. The needs were desperate. The cry went out from the "orphaned" fields: "Come and help us!"

I had heard this cry for help when it came to our U.S. churches. Slowly, inexorably, a long-held suspicion that God may be calling me to missionary service became galvanized into an undeniable conviction that propelled me, with some reluctance, into the office of the Augustana Synod's Missions Director, Dr. S. Hjalmar Swanson.

What followed that visit remains with me today as a faded collage of impressions: mission board, immunizations, passport, visas, packing lists for household and personal needs. Wartime: cooking utensils hard to find (metal went to making munitions), train connections, and finally, the ship.

Our ship, flying the flag of neutral Portugal, sailed the Atlantic fully lit to inform both the Axis and our Allies that we were not engaged in conflict with anyone. With German submarines prowling in the hidden depths, it was reassuring that we were advertising our neutrality; yet memories of the Zamzam near-disaster were never completely absent from our minds.

---

[*] Eleanor Anderson, *Miracle at Sea: The Sinking of the Zamzam and Our Family's Astounding Rescue* (Bolivar, MO: Quiet Waters Publications, 2000).

So one must face the question: Was I fearful? Worried about those U-boats? In truth, there was a "What if…" scenario often playing in my mind, particularly when we saw Nordic-looking civilian men in our hotels from time to time and wondered, "Are they some sort of agents?" There was a sort of curiosity, but I have no memory of the curiosity spawning worry as such. For this I can only thank the kind God who guarded my thoughts from such an invasion—even as He has promised to do. The whole situation was simply an ever-present fact of life.

A more tangible "fact" perhaps inscribed itself at a deeper lever—the sense of not belonging, of being transients. Our ten from Augustana were but a drop in the bucket of the whole picture. We were just an anomalous, non-moving mass fretting over the delays, asking each other, "Will we ever get there?" Perhaps thinking, "Will we be where we belong when we do arrive?" And yet there was always the undergirding conviction that we were in God's care: He has called, He will do it.

For most of our Augustana group, the stay in Portugal ended when, on Thanksgiving Day, 1944, we began the first of three voyages that would take us around the Cape to Beira, up to Mombasa and back to Dar es Salaam. Eventually, we reached Singida by train and rejoiced that our days of rootlessness were ending.

Pastor Ludwig Melander—whom we came to know and love as Uncle Lud—had driven to Singida to meet us and provide transportation for the Rolanders and me to Iambi. Others in our group had other destinations.

This first exposure to roads in rural Africa was somewhat revealing. Years later I heard Occie Rolander claim I had announced, "This is a road? The track around our back forty is better!"

The welcome from Dorothy Anderson, our hostess at Iambi, was warm and genuine that Saturday afternoon when we arrived, dusty and eager.

And now it was Sunday morning, my first in Tanzania. I was hearing the call to worship sung in the Lyamba language and it came like nourishment for a hunger I hadn't recognized. I felt as though I had come home. I had come to a place where I belonged. I had been convinced all along (against my will at first) that it was God's call that sent me on this journey. Being welcomed to worship in my new home with *"Mwelu, mwelu, mwelu"* was an extra gift, a special affirmation of love, a "Welcome home!"

EPILOGUE

Years later, I would rejoice with my Tanzanian brothers and sisters for the new Swahili liturgy their pastors had produced—both words and music.

With the church growing and producing its own pastors, translated liturgies (music as well as words) from American and European sending churches were no longer needed—nor, for that matter, appropriate. But the translations had served as an introduction and a bridge in the early days when the whole gospel message was just taking root in the country. It also served as a bridge for this new missionary from the Augustana tradition before she had taken root in the country!

Helen L. Erickson *was born and schooled in Forest Lake, MN. One year at Gustavus Adolphus College and the three-year course at the Swedish Hospital School of Nursing in Minneapolis, MN, prepared her for an RN. Two years in staff nursing posts in Minneapolis and Los Angeles, CA, preceded attendance and graduation from the Lutheran Bible Institute in Minneapolis and commissioning in 1944 by the Augustana Lutheran Church as a missionary nurse to Tanganyika.*

After a term in general nursing administration at Iambi Mission Hospital, her furlough was devoted to earning a B.S. in Nursing Education at the University of Minnesota. This proved to be important for rapidly developing needs in Tanganyika. Among the burgeoning programs in medical education of that time were schools of nursing. Accordingly, the Kiomboi Nurses' Training Centre was opened during her second term. Helen directed this centre for some years.

During her next furlough, Helen was introduced to linguistic analysis via the Summer Institute of Linguistics. Meanwhile, on the field more progress was being made in analyzing and mastering the many local languages of the country. For most Tanganyikans of that day, Swahili was a second language; communication was much more effective in the "tribal" (local) language. If missionaries could master the local language as well as Swahili, the national language, they could work more effectively and directly with local people, especially those who had not been to school.

During Helen's next term, doors opened to work on this problem for a time. She was assigned to language-literature work in Lyamba, and during her next furlough, opportunity for related studies led to an M.A. in Linguistics.

Again the study prepared for a need, albeit not the need originally envisioned: she was asked to open a language school for new missionaries to learn Swahili before beginning their work assignment. Peter continued at this post for twelve years. She expresses gratitude to her sending church for its forward-looking policies of preparing its missionaries to be ready for changing needs in the countries in which they serve. Retired in 1983, she lives in Richfield, MN.

AT OUR OWN RISK

Ida Marie Jacobson

"The government officials have given us permission to return to Wembere." Marvin Palmquist, missionary pastor of the Wembere congregation, brought me this electrifying news at Ushora where I was living then.

Marv and his wife, Elaine, had been displaced persons during the height of the epidemic of bubonic plague in the Wembere area. Marv had been allowed to enter the quarantined area occasionally to check on things but he had not been permitted to stay. After language study I had been assigned to be a parish worker at both Ushora and Wembere, but to live at Wembere. However, because of the epidemic I, too, was displaced.

They explained, "If you agree to join us, we will move back to live. However it would be entirely at our own risk."

The date, May 20, 1948, stands out in my memory. It brought a night of soul-searching: "Am I really willing to face the risks involved? I could continue working at Ushora until the plague is over. Is this really God's will?"

The next morning I had my answer: "I will go!"

Many times we turned to Psalm 91 for encouragement during those difficult days. *'You who live in the shelter of the Most High, who abide in the shadow of the Almighty, will say to the Lord, "My refuge and my fortress; my God, in whom I trust." For he will deliver you from the snare of the fowler and from the deadly pestilence.'* (Psalm 91:1-3). It was in these promises in God's Word that we trusted.

We were told that if a full twenty-one days passed with no new case, the epidemic would be over and the quarantine could be lifted. At times when nineteen or even twenty days had passed, everyone was hopeful that it was over. Then we would hear the death wails again or hear of an outbreak in another village.

When it was over after almost a year of quarantine church statistics revealed that in some chapels seventy-five percent of the Christians were missing! Some had run away but many had died. At that time there was no specific antibiotic to cure the disease. Presently, if victims are administered streptomycin or other powerful newer antibiotics quickly enough, they can survive.

GOD'S PROTECTION

The house I was to live in at Wembere was not ready. The building contractor and his workers could not come to finish the job because of the plague. So I lived with the Palmquists for a year. Marv had built a bedroom in the attic with mud brick walls and a hardboard ceiling laid above the walls. Bats loved to live in the dark space between the ceiling and the roof. It was too hot to be in my room during the day, so I would bring down all needed items in the morning and not go back until after dark when it cooled off a bit. I often forgot my flashlight upstairs in the morning, even when I had batteries for it, so at night I would run up the stairway in the dark. I knew just where to find my kerosene lamp and matches.

One night I was running up the stairs as usual when I was stopped short just three steps from the top. No matter how hard I tried, my legs refused to go another step. I listened but could hear nothing! I tried to look up but that night it was very dark.

Puzzled, I argued with myself. "I can't hear a thing. Why can't I take another step?" I went downstairs and scolded myself soundly and tried again." When I got to the third step from the top, I could go no farther. Some people are slow learners. I tried a third time but did not succeed.

Defeated, I returned downstairs again and asked the Palmquists if I could borrow a lamp for a few minutes. Up the stairs I went again holding the light in front of me. There at the head of the stairs, an eight-foot long cobra was coiled, poised to strike! If I had been allowed to go one step farther any of those three times, I could have been killed. Do we have guardian angels? I certainly believe we do.

My yells of "*Nyoka!* Snake!" brought Marv and Elaine running. The snake apparently began to get nervous. As it started to uncoil and slither away, Marv placed a club firmly on its tail (thus disabling it from re-coiling again) and ordered, "Elaine, hold this tight so I can shoot the snake!" By this time, I was shaking so hard that I had to hold the lamp in one hand and the lamp chimney with the other.

Bang! Bang! The sound echoed throughout the house. We were missing a tile in the roof, but the snake was dead!

Then I realized that I had been living in close proximity with the snake for at least three days. I had been rejoicing that the bats which lived above my ceiling had disappeared, not realizing that I had had the company of a far more dangerous creature!

JUST ENOUGH WATER

After a year of quarantine the plague finally was over, but then a new difficulty arose: a severe drought. Eighteen months passed with only one rain. During that time the land looked as if it had been swept with a gigantic broom.

By now I was living in my own home. The rainwater cistern had been built but there was no rain to fill it. We had to go farther and farther up the river near the waterfall, now a mere trickle, to get water for household use. So did all of the people in nearby villages, which created a new problem. Some people would bathe and wash clothes in the few small ponds where water was still available. Drinking and cooking water tasted soapy no matter how long you boiled it. "Where could I get some clean water?" I asked as I prayed.

One day I was taking a walk along the side of a steep gully near my house. To my surprise, I found a spot where the soil looked damp. There had never been water there before. I dug a bit with a stick and found a tiny spring. The next day we carefully dug a small basin in which to collect the water. That small spring provided just enough clean water for drinking and cooking until the first rain came. Then it disappeared, and we could never find it again.

A SON RESTORED

When I came home one afternoon during the famine, there stood a man holding one of the most malnourished children I have ever seen. It was so skinny, it could have been used for an anatomy lesson on the human skeleton.

The man pleaded, "I have brought you my son. His mother starved to death while she was trying to nurse him and keep him alive. He is now two and one-half years old and has never walked. Would you please take him?"

"He is dying," I replied.

"He has no chance to live if he stays with me," the father said. "The only thing we've had to feed him since his mother died a month ago is *makapi* (the husks of millet) cooked into a gruel. Maybe he would have a chance to live if you would take him."

"And if he dies?"

"I'm giving him to you." I didn't think it possible that this little boy could live, but I couldn't refuse the father's pleading. Perhaps he would have a chance to live if he had good care and careful feeding, but I had grave doubts.

I was away from home much of the time on school supervision trips, so I went to the dispensary and asked the midwife if she could help me. I would provide food, clothing, a crib, and other needs, if she could help with his daily care.

A big box was transformed into a crib and I made a mattress and sheets. The little boy was so weak he could only whimper. If we fed him too much too quickly he would die, so for many days he was fed a special formula with a medicine dropper, a few drops every hour. Finally, he got strong enough to take an ounce of milk from a bottle, then two ounces. How we rejoiced when he could drink a full eight ounces, and when we could gradually add porridge and other foods.

As he gained strength, he could finally sit up in his crib and play with some toys. Then he learned to creep and after many months he took his first steps and began to talk. After nine months, adequate rain brought the famine to an end and food was available again. I called his father, who lived in a remote village, to come to see his son, now a healthy three-and-one-half-year-old. I said, "Now you can take Yohana home."

He hesitated. "I gave him to you and he is alive because you cared for him."

"But I choose to give him back to you now." I could see in his eyes that he really wanted the child, but he was hesitant to take back a gift. "He is your son, and I have chosen to give him back to you."

Finally, he went off rejoicing with Yohana in his arms. I know that Yohana attended school and finished class six, an unusual accomplishment at that time. Then I lost track of him as I was moved elsewhere.

BUSH SCHOOL SURPRISES

One of my responsibilities as a parish worker was to train and supervise teachers for some forty "bush schools." The purpose of these schools was to give more children a chance to learn the rudiments of reading, writing, arithmetic, and Bible. The teachers of these schools had only three or four years of education themselves. They were expected to bring the children up to a standard two (second grade) level so they could compete for a place in standard three at a registered primary school. Books and materials were scarce. Children sat on mud brick benches or on seats made of poles. They wrote on slates or on a sandy spot cleared on the ground.

I enjoyed walking or biking to these schools to help the teachers and children. Often I had to hire a guide to help me find the school. These guides usually chose to be paid with bars of soap or brown sugar.

One day as we were walking through tall grass, my guide said, "Often there are rhinos on this path. If one comes, quickly climb a tree." Luckily for me, we met no rhinos as those trees had long thorns!

Another day I had biked five miles on a track and depended on finding a guide at a milk depot to help me find my way on a narrow path through the bush. Strangely, no one volunteered. Several times I was given this terse advise, "There's the path. Just keep going and you will find the school. There is only one path."

"Strange," I thought, "people are usually more friendly and helpful than this."

When I arrived at the school, the teacher asked, "Who guided you here?" When I told him I had no guide, he said, "You are not going to go back to the road alone. I will go with you when school is over."

I always had to be aware of how the children were learning to read. If I tested them with their school readers, some children would look at the picture on the page and recite the whole page while looking at the ceiling. They had memorized the whole book!

At this school, however, it appeared that the children really could read, but when I wrote words on the blackboard, they failed. What was wrong? I watched closely as the teacher called the children up to his desk to read. Aha! I recognized the problem. I quietly removed the blackboard from the wall and turned it upside down. Now they could read every word. When they read for the teacher, they stood in front of him with the book facing him. The whole school had learned to read, but upside down!

Later, I learned why I couldn't recruit a guide. A man-eating lion had killed and eaten a person in that area only a few days before!

GOD'S ASSIGNMENT

Zebadayo, age 19 years, had just completed the teacher training course at Kinampanda and was awaiting his first assignment. As a rule, young teachers were sent to established schools, but Zebadayo was sent to a Muslim community to open a new school. He later told us about his first night there.

When he came with his loads, there was no one to greet or help him except the evangelist and his wife. That night when he went to bed, he could not sleep. Doubts filled his mind. "Can I really do the job here? I'm too young. Will people really accept me and send their children to school? I don't think this is the place for me." His thoughts went round and round.

Finally, he lit his small kerosene lamp and took out his Bible. "God please show me if this is your place for me." His Bible fell open to Isaiah 41:10,

"Do not fear, for I am with you; do not be afraid, for I am your God. I will strengthen you, I will help you. I will uphold you with my victorious right hand." He read the words over and over again. Now he had his answer. He was not alone; God was with him and would enable him. He blew out the light and slept soundly. He did succeed in starting the new school.

FROM TRACKS TO WORDS

How would you get the concept of *reading* across to children who had no contact with books before they came to school? Their tribal language had no word for "read." That was the challenge facing a young teacher whose school I was visiting. He had carefully taught the children some basic oral vocabulary in the Swahili language. He had also taught them to understand simple pictures. *Now* he wanted to teach them to read. He wrote the appropriate word under each picture and told his pupils to *read* the word.

The children looked puzzled, "You're telling us to 'read.' What's that?" He tried his best to explain it in their language, but to no avail.

When the children went out for recess, we discussed the problem, and a likely solution, but the teacher was so discouraged that he said, "Will you please try?"

When the children came in, we started a discussion about what they could see at a waterhole in the morning. "The animals who drank there during the night have left. Could you tell what animals had been there?"

"Oh, yes," they said.

"How would you know? Could you tell the difference between the tracks of a goat and a dikdik?" I used examples of other tracks that would be somewhat similar.

"Oh, yes, anybody could do that," they said confidently.

Then I replied, "Words and letters are like that. If you look at them carefully, you won't need the pictures because you'll recognize the tracks." They got the point. As I wrote words on the blackboard, the children would compare them with the words beneath the pictures. Soon they were able to recognize the 'tracks' without the pictures and were really reading.

Ida Marie Jacobson *grew up on a farm near Montrose, SD. After a year of college, she taught in rural schools for three years. She graduated from Lutheran Bible Institute, Minneapolis, MN, and then attended St. Cloud Teachers' College, St. Cloud, MN.*

Ida Marie was commissioned in 1947 by the Augustana Lutheran Church as a missionary teacher to serve in Tanganyika. Her first assignment was as a parish worker at Ushora and Wembere; then she taught at Kinampanda Teachers' Training College.

Her next assignment as an Education Assistant found her traveling thoughout the district, supervising primary schools and essentially living in a Land Rover rather than a tent, from Monday through Friday.

Later, Ida Marie was moved to Arusha to work in the Christian Education Department of the Evangelical Lutheran Church in Tanzania.

Her last assignment was in Leadership Training, at Morogoro Junior Seminary, until her retirement in 1991 after 44 years.

Thanks to the mission policies of the Augustana Lutheran Church and later the Lutheran Church in America, she was able during her furloughs to complete studies at the University of Minnesota for a B.S. in Education and an M.A. in Teaching English as a Second Language.

SOUNDS FROM KINAMPANDA GRAND CENTRAL

Joyce Anderson

It was our first child, Pamela, who asked our missionary friend, Marian, if she knew that everything had its own music. Suddenly we all became intensely aware of our unusual but typical African surroundings: the absolute silence at times, the breeze blowing through the tall dry grass, the crying hyena, the cough of the lion outside our bedroom, and the call of the golden crested cranes as they migrated north over our home.

I also remember the chatter of the *kanga* (guinea fowl), the ringing of the school bell to waken the boys for breakfast and later for classes, the laughter of those so eager to learn, the cheers from the football field, the chatter and rattle from the lorry that came twice a week with mail and vegetable baskets for each missionary family. They were from Mr. Ruhl who lived forty miles away in Singida, our main center in the district.

Sharing these sounds with us often during the mid-forties were the other mission families at Kinampanda: Dr. George N. Anderson and his wife Annette, and Vivian Gulleen and Marian Halvorson. My father-in-law, George Anderson, was the pastor of the Kinampanda Church and General Director of all Lutheran missionary work in Tanganyika. Vivian served on the teaching staff at Kinampanda Teacher Training Center (KTTC), and my husband, Paul, was the principal of the Center. Marian helped George in his work as director.

There were very special sounds: the shuffle of feet and soft murmuring of Christians who walked as far as forty miles to celebrate communion at an open air service under a blazing hot sun, young students singing the Hallelujah Chorus. This was something new to many Africans. It required many rehearsals and produced a glorious ending.

An unusual noise not far from our front door involved a whistle. The sound of the whistle set the pace for the thirty or more individuals who were setting out on a salt safari. Each person carried a small bag of grain and a big stick because they might have to deal with lions. They would find the salt in a dried lake bottom many miles from Kinampanda. This salt expedition was a happy event with much laughter and calling to each other.

Something quite memorable occurred during the first months we spent in Kinampanda. There was a very puzzling and unpleasant sound "over our heads" while visiting with Dad one evening. We heard a slow sliding sound in the attic. We talked about it and finally decided that there must be a rat dragging something toward the water tank area. The sound repeated itself quite often but our many investigations revealed nothing.

One day our outside worker called Paul to tell him that a cobra had earlier crawled out of the shed and headed toward our house at a good clip. The snake disappeared into a hole in the outside wall of the house. We spent the rest of the day and several weeks to come waiting for our friend, the cobra, to appear.

Then one day I, being very large with child, was lying on the bed for my afternoon rest. I heard an overhead sound coming from the far side of the house, all the way across the attic, settling on the floor above my head. Bells rang in my head. This had to be a long snake, so, being the brave gal that I was, I called my kitchen staff. I told them the story and sent them, and whomever else they could find, upstairs to remove the creature.

They moved boxes, trunks and suitcases and found nothing until they came to the next to the last trunk. It had sprouted a tail that stuck out about six inches. This brought real action. All the helpers ran to the other side of the attic and called for me to bring the gun to kill the cobra. I declined (I'm not that good a shot). Can you imagine the noise there would have been on the corrugated *mabati* (metal) roof? There was enough of a racket when they used bows and arrows that banged off the floor into the stone walls and then the roof.

Pam and I were at the table having lunch when Yosia, our cook, came to us with a very dead and dripping six-foot cobra draped over an arrow that he had used to kill the uninvited guest. There was a path of blood across the living room floor and out the kitchen door. We were very glad that our carpet was red.

Another memory from our early days in East Africa was the harsh buzz of a six-inch wide column of soldier ants marching through our bedroom when I had settled down for a quiet evening. Soon the sound reached the hallway. Grabbing a flashlight I saw, to my horror, thousands of the ants coming at a good pace through the outside wall. I opened the patio door and used a table leaf as a barrier to them. Fortunately these large ants are blind so when they hit the board they turned and walked out onto the patio and disappeared into the night.

Snakes and ants—now what next? The low rumble of an earthquake could come at any hour, day or night. It would come creeping up the valley from south to north, shaking dishes and pictures, giving us a quiet speechlessness until the quake moved past.

A common sound among the Lyamba people—DRUMS! There was drumming among our school children and out in the community. The word *suka* (death dance or funeral) was a word we learned early. The death dance could go on for days and nights. The sad beat of the drums was haunting and not easily forgotten. One wonders what they were saying. Were they pleading to their god, frightening evil spirits, or just finding release in time of sorrow?

The rain dance had a different sound. They told me that I was privileged because I was the first white woman to witness the pleading for rain done by *Mtemi* (Chief) Kingu in the fall of the year. They invited several of us to the chief's compound to witness the dance. I remember two types of horns and also the drums. One horn is made from the horn of a *kongoni* (hartebeest) and the other, the *mbutu*, is a long cylinder of wood hollowed out with a hole near one end (as in a flute). The blast from these horns as the chief walked through the compound was harsh, but it compelled attention. He led his followers past the vats of native beer, not too clean but potent, and the cooking fire. As the men marched around and the *Mtemi* prayed for rain, the drums beat, the horns blew, and the women sang with a shrill high-pitched crying out sound called ululating. The men circled the compound in step with the drumbeat as the women sang. They gave us permission to take a few movies that are, sadly, without sound.

The crunch of bicycle tires brought Pam to tell me that Daddy was home for morning tea and thirty minutes of family time. Often there was a *hodi* (an announcement that someone wants to come in) at the door from one or more of the school staff who would gather to talk business and sip tea with us. Our wonderful house staff kept the wood-burning stove and teapot hot all day long. One day Pam announced that we didn't have to have a special prayer for tea because Grandpa had said that the breakfast prayer lasted until lunch. We let Grandpa explain that one.

Grandpa was a quiet soft-spoken man whom Pam enjoyed watching in his office. I think his pipe had a special attraction, and she would sit by him and pretend to read while he puffed away. I used to marvel that he would let her play while he labored over the tremendous task of uniting and supervising the entire Lutheran Mission of Tanganyika. This was no small job considering that all of the paperwork had to go by slow mail to his fellow missionaries, to British government officials and to the mission board back in the United States.

What a difference there would have been if telephone service had been available! The patience required and restraint demanded were very taxing and Dad found little time for anything but grinding away at the monumental task. Marian, Grandpa's right hand "man," was invaluable to him and the work. No one knows how much material they sent out of his office. He was always under pressure. Grandma was there for him, but he was often forced to neglect her. Sometimes she had to remind him to take the regular late afternoon walk that they always enjoyed.

With all of this work to do we set aside the hour before sunset for activities like biking. Marian and Vivian joined us when they could. It was good for all of us to get out into the countryside. This was especially true when the rainy season was beginning, bringing plants to life, and surrounding us with beauty. We never did find the plant that smelled like boiled potatoes after the first rain. After six long months of dry season, oh, what a relief it was to feel the first drops! Psychologically, we were more than ready for a break. The dryness was especially hard on our eyes and sinuses.

A mission station only few miles away rarely had a visitor of European or American background, but not so at Kinampanda, with its training school and General Director's office. With a building program also going on, there was a continual round of company. I found myself constantly planning meals and trying new recipes with our wonderful staff of three brothers who pitched in and covered for one another whenever needed.

We needed help just to feed missionary visitors passing through and also government officials at times, not to mention our own relatives from the United States. There were months when most of our salary went for food. I was disappointed when I learned that I could not have a garden. I had counted on that activity as primary, but it was not to be. Kinampanda is dry most of the year.

A very welcome sound was the purr of a diesel-powered generator that Paul installed, giving the school and each of the three mission houses two lights that could be used simultaneously. I shall never forget the light in the eyes of Gerson, our wonderful house- helper, when we gave him an electric iron to use. He was so thrilled that he insisted on staying to finish the ironing though it meant walking home through lion country after dark. He had served in the army (World War II) and Gerson was a delight to have around because he was so happy to be home.

The youngest brother, Natanaeli, was a real pal to Pam; he played with her after finishing his tasks. Pam, with her pet baboon, gave him much joy. They climbed trees and chased Pam's pet with great shrieks of pleasure.

Yosia, our cook, was tops in every way. We were never caught short no matter how many unexpected guests showed up for meals or tea. Also, before the guests left we would help them check their petrol supplies and water. The petrol (gasoline) came in metal *debes* (five-gallon containers) and was quite expensive.

Wampuka, a kind young lady who helped with Pam the first year, later had five daughters and named them Joyce, Pam, Judy and Gail. How flattering that was for us!

Abraham Lincoln said that a wife should stay home and fry lamb chops and the husband should make the living and the decisions. My father-in-law did not tell me this, but he believed it. So I felt no guilt staying home and being Mom. I could not have had this wonderful opportunity to entertain so many travelers had I stayed in the United States. In Tanganyika I could stay home and be a wife to a great guy and a Mom to three treasures.

It was not unusual to have guests in our home, but the visit of my parents with the "oohs" and "ahs" of two sets of grandparents over their African-born grandchildren, Judy and Gail, was music that will never be erased from our memory.

God is relentless in His giving and sharing. While I have never had the feeling of a special call, I have experienced miracles that could only have been His love being poured out to me. Thank you, God for allowing me to be a part of this great work.

Joyce H. Anderson *was born in St. James, Minnesota, in 1923, to Harry and Minnie Wenstrom. After junior high school in West Palm Beach, Florida, she returned to St. James where she graduated from high school in 1941.*

Joyce attended the University of Minnesota and Gustavus Adolphus College. She married Paul E. Anderson in 1943. She and Paul were both students at the Kennedy School of Missions, Hartford, CN, 1944-45, and their first child, Pamela, was born in Hartford.

In 1946 Joyce and her family traveled to East Africa where they lived at Kinampanda Mission Station until the fall of 1950. Two daughters, Judy and Gail, were born to Joyce and Paul during the Africa years.

From 1951-1978 Joyce lived as a Lutheran pastor's wife in Waterbury, CN; New York City and Miami, FL. Daughters Wendy and Heidi were born during this time.

Since 1978, Joyce and Paul have lived in retirement in north Georgia and south Florida.

GROWING THROUGH PAIN

Louise Anderson Olson

Through the thick fog of anesthetic numbness I could see my husband's face blurred and indistinct, and I knew that something was very wrong. Tears, yes, tears on Howie's face and squeezes on my hand—what was he saying? "Our baby was stillborn, Lou, there was nothing the doctor could do to save him."

Every fiber in my body wanted to scream, "No! God knew this baby was already dedicated to Him. God wouldn't take the baby we've prayed for, for so long. No, no, no!" I didn't scream, and instead there came a quiet peace, in spite of tears and not of my will, but a feeling of strength, of being held in the loving arms of God.

Forty-eight years have passed, and still I feel the angel wings of God's comforting messengers, pushing back this incredible pain of bereavement, changing it into an experience of God's grace and blessing. It took many years to fully realize that our loss was a tool in God's hands to make both Howard and me better "instruments of God's peace."

At first I wanted the members of our Kijota congregation to comfort me, to come and weep with us, to speak God's words of comfort and hope. It didn't happen just the way I'd expected. Slowly I saw that we had joined a big group of people who had already experienced bereavements and losses of many kinds. They understood. But it was I who needed to share the joy of the angels who had carried me through dark days, the strength of the Good Shepherd whose rod and staff took us through the valley of the shadow of death. And as I was able to share these things with African friends and neighbors, I myself was comforted too and grew in the knowledge of God's love and care.

Two years later, one of the many precious speeches at our farewell to the Kijota congregation was given by teacher Loti Filipo, dear friend and co-worker. Quoting from Psalm 126, he remembered our little grave: *"May those who sow in tears reap with shouts of joy! Those who go out weeping, bearing the seed for sowing, shall come home with shouts of joy, carrying their sheaves."*

What a promise and a hope later fulfilled! The dear women of the congregation, led by Mama Maria, presented me with a beautiful hand-made fertility doll, appropriately named "Maria" to express their loving prayers for us as a couple. How empathetic and loving! I still have the doll and we have four wonderful (now grown) children.

TEAM WORK

Seven years later, when our son, Howie Joe, was 4½ years old, in the middle of our second term we received news at Kijota of a six-member World Literacy Team coming to Kinampanda for a Literacy/Literature Conference. Howard would be involved, and so it seemed would I.

"Who, me? Chief cook and bottle washer?"

"Yes, you. But you won't be alone; there are many experienced helpers." Helpers: that meant a team, and I like being part of a team. So I said "Yes" to the request to head up a hostessing committee for this three-month literacy conference.

The six experts would be Wes and Roslyn Sadler, literacy workers in the Lutheran Church of Liberia; Chesley Baity of the World Health Organization in Switzerland; Phil Gray, artist/illustrator in World Literacy and Jim Carty, journalist, both from the U.S.; Enoch Mulira of the Community Development office of Uganda; and Mr. Horace Mason of the Social Development Department, assigned by the Tanganyikan government to work with the World Team and the missions represented in the Christian Council of Tanganyika.

The goal was no less than a frontal attack on illiteracy through the production of primers and readers in Swahili, Lyamba and Turu. Literacy and literature were to be Siamese twins, tools of evangelism, public health and personal growth. To be part of such a mission, even if my domain was to be in the kitchen and laundry room—well, it was easy to say "Yes," because I wouldn't be alone!

How many times in the forty or so years in Africa did I not find myself gratefully dependent on kind and helpful, capable African helpers who got me through hostessing conferences, committees, language guests, and days when I was too sick to do anything in the kitchen!

Now at Kinampanda, preparations included boiling drinking water in 44-gallon metal drums over outdoor fireplaces. (I cringe now when I think of how many trees had to be cut to get firewood to boil water and milk, to stoke the wood stoves where all the bread, rolls, cakes, muffins, pies and cookies were prepared from scratch and the sadirons heated to keep our guests' clothes neat.) I brought along my eggless recipes, for getting enough eggs for baking and for breakfasts was an uncertain thing. I found out that though other fruit might run out, we had plenty of wonderful bananas.

Rev. Jim Carty enjoyed writing for his home newspaper in Tennessee about bananas on cereal, banana bread, banana cake, banana fritters, bananas in fruit salad, bananas baked—you get the idea!

Towards the end of the three months, at the time when about forty-five African and missionary delegates from the Northern, Usambara, Eastern, Southern, and Lake Provinces of Tanganyika joined those from our Mission at the Literacy/Literature planning course, some of the Committee planned a closing and farewell.

"Be sure you're there, Lou, with Howard and Howie Joe." Many evenings I was folding clothes from the laundry done that day and sometimes hunting for a missing sock, or I'd be planning more menus after checking on supplies.

"Yes, I'll be there." To my great surprise and immense delight, when it was my turn to be thanked, I was given a beautiful scroll-like certificate of a Master's Degree in the Culinary Arts and a huge chef's hat—all great fun. I accepted it, but in my heart I knew that it was the team of cooks, sweepers, laundry people, not to mention the wood cutters and the dish washers who deserved the thanks and praise of us all!

I WAS A CULTURAL OUTSIDER

Greta Mugaluli's friendly greeting was always music in my ears, but one day the words that followed were really intriguing: "Come with me to watch the circumcision rite of passage of many young girls over at Ibrahim's house."

"Will I, an outsider, be allowed to watch?"

"Well, you're a woman," she countered, "but if anyone asks if you've been circumcised, just say 'Yes' and it will be okay."

Well, I wasn't going to say "yes" to such a question, for just thinking of female clitoridectomy was frightening and totally repugnant to me. Yet here were Christian girls of the Ihanja congregation, ages between perhaps ten and fifteen, joining other girls of their age group to undergo this Turu ritual of long antiquity, referred to as "mutilation" in other corners of the world, and also by the Lyamba people right next door. So I went with Greta, prepared to be thrown out, if anyone discovered I'd never been mutilated.

Oh my, what an experience! My white face stood out in that crowd of Turu women, and I was stared at with surprised looks, but no one threw me out. (Maybe it was just as well that I didn't understand one old woman's Turu—I answered with a mixture of Swahili and English and a friendly smile.)

Hazy skies, dry season wind and dust, bare fields long after harvest, a dried goat skin on the ground near a *minyara* hedge, low flat-roofed pole and mud plaster houses in the background, adult women everywhere—where were the young girls? What could they be thinking?

The venerable "practitioner" checks the sharpness of her trusty old razor blade, an improvement over the flint knife of olden times, and quietly the first girl appears in the doorway of one of the houses, led by several adult women to where the dried goat hide is positioned on the bare ground. If I recall correctly, she wears only a loin cloth which is removed, and then she lies down submissively. Four women each take a leg or arm and hold her fast, spread-eagled. Greta tells me that the mothers threaten their daughters with severe twisted pinches, if they show fear or try to pull away. They are also extolled to be brave and are praised with ululation if they don't resist or cry out.

Before I can realize what's happening, the first girl is finished. There's no fanfare or seeable ritual, no sterilization of blade or washing of hands before or after. Nor is there awareness of hygienic risk from the dust, whipped up by the dry season wind, nor of re-use of the blade over and over. There seems to be no regard for the pieces of flesh cut off; they're tossed aside.

But small gourds of clarified butter are provided by each mother to apply a soothing unguent to the wounds of each daughter. I wasn't close enough to see the operation, nor could I bear to watch each girl's face—not all could endure the operation silently—and for many nights thereafter I heard again and again the screams of those children.

There was a celebratory atmosphere among the older women, and as each girl recovered somewhat from the pain and shock, anointed by the ghee, she was encouraged to take a few steps, legs far apart, to sway with the dancers and singers. This was done to prove her courage and ability to endure pain, but also because music has a soothing power, and the socializing is a sharing of women's pain and fortitude.

At least one of these girls developed an infection and the reopening and cleansing of the wound must have been twice the suffering of the first operation. Greta wanted me to see first hand what Turu girls experience and perhaps to speak out against this ancient and cruel custom. I disappointed her, for changing such a deeply ingrained custom must be done from within.

The first Turu pastor, Yohana Sima, was one of the first to declare publicly that he would not have any of his daughters undergo this operation. The girls, however, fear that no Turu man will marry them if they are not circumcised, so such a big change must be made by both men and women, and education is the hope for bringing about these changes.

Midwives attest to the increased pain and danger in childbirth caused by scar tissue for those who have been "mutilated," not to mention the sexual pleasure denied these women. Blessings on all who fight for future generations, keeping the good in all the rites of passage, but protecting young girls from needless and harmful pain and suffering.

THE GREAT DAY OF FREEDOM

Political independence for our beloved, adopted country of Tanganyika was attained on December 9, 1961. Julius Nyerere, the father of his country, prepared carefully for this event. There was not a single incident of violence anywhere, and four days later he could leave the country for the United Nations knowing that independence had been achieved without bloodshed.

In Singida District there were a hundred extra police officers on duty. In our Mission we had a 24-hour radio monitoring system to call Singida if any disturbance occurred. Three ambulances were on constant call. The Public Works Department had commandeered a fleet of vehicles in case of emergency. The King's African Rifles troops could be airborne, standing ready at Tabora. A special constable was placed at Kiomboi, and Kititimu was on hourly police patrol. All missionaries were to be at stations with radio contact, with emergency fuel supplies at hand, and were advised to do little traveling and no hunting whatsoever during the four-day celebration. All churches and mosques had prayers the day before independence.

At Ihanja, Pastor Zephania Gunda preached; a teacher spoke on the rule of the Germans; my husband, Howie, spoke on the rule of the British; and Pastor Doug Lundell of the Ihanja Bible School spoke on the achievements of TANU (Tanganyika African National Union).

On December 9, as the new black and gold and green flag reached the pinnacle of the flag pole, what loud shouts of joy and gratitude were heard! In the local courthouse a big poster proclaimed, *Uhuru na Kupendana* (Freedom and Love for Each Other). The TANU slogan was *Uhuru na Kazi* (Freedom and Work), so this was a new and special twist. Tanganyika had shown the world what real integration and a multi-racial society can be. Blessings on this nation!

Louise Anderson Olson was born February 1, 1927, at Marangu Teachers' Training Center, PO Moshi, Tanganyika, to pioneer Augustana missionaries, George and An-

nette Anderson. The family moved that same year to Ruruma in Singida District where Louise grew up.

Louise was home-schooled through 9½ years except for grades 4 and 5 in St. Paul, MN. She graduated from West High School in Minneapolis in 1943 and then attended Augustana College in Rock Island, IL, 1943-1946. During their first furlough in 1952, Louise graduated from Augustana College with a transcript of credits earned from correspondence courses from the University of Chicago and from courses at the Hartford Seminary Foundation.

Further education during one furlough was at a community college in California and a course in Teaching English as a Second Language at U.C., Berkeley. In addition, she enjoyed taking various classes at three different seminaries where Howard was teaching: at Pacific Lutheran; at Makumira, Tanzania; and at Wartburg in Dubuque, IA.

Louise was married on June 17, 1946, in St. Paul, MN, to the Rev. Howard S. Olson, who was on a call from the Board of World Missions of the Augustana Lutheran Church to serve in the Singida District of central Tanganyika.

Although Louise had grown up among the Lyamba people, after their language study at Kinampanda she and Howard were stationed among the Turu people. For their sixteen years on this field, they served at Kijota, Isuna and Ihanja.

After their year's furlough, 1963-64, they moved to the Lutheran Theological College, Makumira, and stayed there until 1988. For the next three years Howard taught a variety of courses at Wartburg Seminary, and Louise assisted in the Office of International Students. Their final retirement in 1991 brought them to Sun City Center, Florida, where they now reside.

Louise says, "I feel a great debt to my dear parents for the faith they taught in word and example, as well as the love for Africa and its people which they imparted to me. I'm grateful to missionary colleagues, and most of all to the African sisters and brothers who have blessed my life. All praise and thanks to our God who always leads us with blessings too many to count, and to Jesus, our Shepherd and Friend, whose Spirit enables and empowers!"

WEAVINGS

Ruth E. Fryhle

"Our lives are but fine weavings that God and we prepare
Each life becomes a fabric planned and fashioned in His care...
Not till the loom is silent and the shuttles cease to fly
Shall God unroll the canvas and explain the reason why..."

Sometimes we are privileged to have God unroll the canvas before the loom is silent. This is a tale of the spinning of "threads of gold and silver" which began in 1952.

As a young architectural designer in my mid-twenties, I had spent several years executing plans of luxury estates for the wealthy of the Northeast. To keep my value system in balance, I vacationed at youth conferences held by the Augustana Lutheran Church where inspiration came from great preachers like Dr. Wilton Bergstrand and Dr. George Hall.

One year at such a gathering at Colgate University, a clear inner voice said, "You've got to do more with your life." Several exploratory contacts were made and a year later a call came from the national headquarters of the Augustana Lutheran Church in Minneapolis. "There is a need to establish a Department of Church Architecture—would you be interested?"

The time of testing began. Could I, Ruth Anderson, give up a lucrative salary, good friends and family, and my church to move halfway across the country to frigid Minnesota? While struggling with this question, another letter came from headquarters saying, "Sorry, the department cannot be established this year because of lack of funds." *Then,* experiencing keen disappointment at this news, I realized how much I really wanted to accept this challenge.

Fortunately, pressure for guidance in remodeling old and building new churches continued to increase so money was found to begin the new department. In March 1952 my new "Green Hornet" Chevy and I drove through high winds and sub-zero temperature to begin two of the most wonderful years of my life. The warmth, the caring, the fun and the Christian fellowship experienced among the staff at Augustana Headquarters defies description. Working in partnership with the Rev. Carl Sandgren to form the new department was challenging and exciting—especially after "P.S." (Pastor Sandgren) suffered a heart attack and the New Jersey new-comer was left to run the office and also travel the country to meet with building committees. Many times in my travels during those pre-feminist days, I was greeted with "What is *she* doing here?"

An old frame house which housed World Mission activities stood next to the impressive Gothic-style stone headquarters office at 2445 Park Avenue. Tucked away on the second floor of the old house was my office and draw-ing board. One of my earliest assignments was a request to draw plans for a school for missionaries' children to be called Augustana School and located at Kiomboi Mission Station in Tanganyika, East Africa. "It sounds interest-ing," I thought, "but how do they build over there—with grass and mud? It seems I've got a lot to learn before designing can begin!"

By a stroke of good timing, the Rev. Ruben Pedersen, a seasoned mis-sionary who also had a talent for building, happened to be home on fur-lough and willingly spent hours with me describing the materials, methods and conditions for construction in Africa.

There was an urgency to complete these plans so it was with great relief that, after carefully checking all notes and dimensions to make sure there were no errors, I filled in the title box and with a flourish wrote in the fin-ishing date—April 21, *1951* rather than *1952!* This seemingly inconsequen-tial mistake was to create quite a brouhaha on the mission field in Tanzania.

Eventually, having made a long journey, the roll of plans arrived at the Kinampanda office of the mission president, Dr. George N. Anderson. A committee meeting in progress in his home was interrupted to examine the drawings. There was great curiosity to see the plans, but there was dismay also. Why? Because construction had already begun at Kiomboi on a build-ing to house the school, designed by a committee on the field and being constructed under the able supervision of Pastor Marvin Palmquist. To compound the dismay, someone noticed that the drawings were dated *1951!* "What in the world is the matter with the people back in the States? These plans were urgently needed—*and they've been ready for a whole year and never sent to us!!!*

Despite the annoyance he must have felt, Dr. Anderson sent the plans to Marvin at Kiomboi. Marv's initial reaction was, "These plans are too late. Too much work to change things now." So he tossed them aside, un-opened. But a persistent little genie would not let him ignore them for long, so one morning he spread them out on his dining room table. Marv writes in his memoirs: "They were simply beautiful! Without a moment's hesita-tion, I hopped on my bike and rode pell mell over to the building project. 'Stop, stop everything!' I shouted. The contractor must have thought I'd lost my marbles! 'Come, I want to show you something new.'"

It was obvious that the new design would costs more than the price contracted with Lachman Singh, even after the front veranda and the large central fireplace between dining and fellowship areas were eliminated. However, Marv writes, "The next morning I made a quick trip to Kinampanda
to consult with Dr. Anderson and we agreed that we should make the
change immediately, even if it cost more. We never regretted the decision."

The many threads of this story came together years after the event. In-
credibly, half a world away from me but present at the disrupted Kinampanda committee meeting when my drawings were scrutinized, was the
man I would marry one day!

That summer of 1952 shocking news was received at headquarters in
Minneapolis. I came down from my office one noon to find the secretaries
and Dr. Hjalmar Swanson, director of World Missions, in great consterna-
tion. A telegram had just been received saying that the Tore Fryhle family
was flying home from East Africa on a medical emergency. Eleanor Fryhle
had been diagnosed with advanced breast cancer and they would be going
to Mayo Clinic. I was shown pictures of this fine family of three and felt
struck by the probable tragedy they were facing. Their little blond boy,
Allan, in his sailor suit, looked so vulnerable. Then Eleanor died.

As the months went by, I became more and more engrossed in my work
and my relationships at HQ. But then one day, at the weekly chapel service
for the staff, Pastor Tore Fryhle gave the message and I knew I had to meet
this fascinating man. The story of how this was accomplished, our unusual
courtship and wedding, followed by a romantic voyage to Africa, is a colorful and beautiful part of our family tapestry. But that is another whole story!

We arrived in Dar es Salaam in November 1954, drove a load of pineap-
ples upcountry to the completed Augustana School at Kiomboi Mission
Station, enrolled our son Allan as a student and enjoyed an American
Thanksgiving dinner with all of the missionary children in their home away
from home. Our Allan lived many months of each year in this building with
which his new mom had been so involved even before we two had met.
Real life can be stranger than fiction.

During his absence from the mission field, Tore's work as Education Secretary had been ably carried on by Marian Halvorson. As quickly as possible, we got settled into our home in Singida so that he could resume his
responsibilities. Although this residence was in a small town with many Indian shops and the seat of the British District Government, this city girl
looked around at the parched fields surrounding the house and the structure of grey cement blocks and felt as if she had been sentenced to four
years on the moon! Wisely, my husband let me buy all the paint I wanted in
order to brighten up both interior and exterior and, by adding plenty of
elbow grease, our house soon became our home.

It was a privilege during my first year in Africa to design two churches in Turuland, one at Kijota and the other at Sepuka. It was especially gratifying because they were to serve local congregations. Both churches seated about 1000 people. The challenge was to provide a way to baptize and/or commune at least 50 people at one time and thus shorten services that were usually two or three hours long. Although different in style and concept, the answer in both churches was a central altar that allowed the family of God to gather *around* it.

The threads from this part of the weaving went both forward and backward in time. The Kijota church was a memorial to the sister of Pastor Howard Olson, who had recently drowned. The Sepuka church was to become a tribute to Pastor David Henry, under whose supervision it was constructed, and who was later killed in an automobile accident in the States.

A classroom building was desperately needed at Augustana School to augment the dormitory/dining facility. Now another thread from my past went into the weaving. My initial architectural training in a New York City firm specializing in schools proved helpful. This classroom unit was fun to design as I was now familiar with wind, rain and sun conditions and had an ample site on which to maximize the environmental setting.

There was a problem, however. Once again the facilities needed outstripped the budget allowed. It seemed that the only possible solution was for Marv to become the de facto builder, to which he reluctantly agreed. Apparently I could be an audacious taskmaster. Marv still occasionally reminds me that I insisted he tear out some uneven height steps—not only once, but *three* times! Is it any wonder that patient Marvin Palmquist became a golden thread in my weavings?

One of the classrooms was designed with a stage at one end which also doubled as a worship center. It was here that Allan was confirmed by Pastor Ray Cunningham and where our second son, Craig, was baptized later by Tore's good friend, the Rev. Oscar Rolander, during his visit from New York on behalf of the National Lutheran Council.

To make the school fully functional, additional plans were needed for a Laundry/Service Unit, a Teachers' Residence and a Headmaster's Residence. The first two were done in 1955 and the last came off the drawing board in April 1957.

My third year on the mission field was especially busy. Iambi Hospital wanted a new Administration and Surgical Unit and we also assessed the use of the existing buildings and reassigned functions. A similar overall look was taken at Ruruma Girls' School. Wembere requested a new building for inpatient leprosy care. Kiomboi station also needed a girls' dormitory and a girls' bathroom for the Nurses Training Center. There was no shortage of work!

One tiny building at Kiomboi became especially dear to us. It was called the Sick Bay for Missionaries—two patients' rooms, an attendant nurse's room, a bathroom, a delivery room and a scrub room—and it was built within shouting distance of the residence for the missionary nurses. Could it be that the desirability of having such a facility became obvious to the medical staff during the weeks in 1956 when I had to occupy a room in the nurses' residence due to a severe kidney infection?

A year later, when I was eight and a half months pregnant, Dr. Viola Fischer advised that we drive the sixty miles of rough roads between our home in Singida and Kiomboi to await the birth of our baby in proximity to the mission hospital. The Sick Bay was erected but not yet finished, so Tore spent the waiting time installing water pipes and also a buzzer system to the nurses' residence. Together we painted the bathroom and the patients' rooms.

On Sunday morning, September 1, 1957, just as the sun came over the horizon and etched into my memory forever the vision of a silhouetted fan palm that I could see through the window in the delivery room, our son Craig made his appearance. What a privilege it was to be the very first patient and to deliver the first baby to be born in this mini-hospital. It was like giving birth to a building and a baby boy simultaneously.

During the mid-50's the mission's leprosy program experienced many changes brought about by government policy, budget, personnel, and rapid changes in treatment as well. The site for a new leprosarium was chosen at Iambi. Working with Dr. Stanley Moris, an overall plan was developed and a home designed for the lay supervisor, agriculturalist Roly Renner. The residence was the only segment of the scheme that I saw finished before we left for America.

Mission work was moving ahead in another new area as well. Pastor Harold Faust and Louise were ready to move to Barabaig to undertake pioneer work in that tribe. It was a pleasure to work with these friends to plan as comfortable living conditions as possible at this remote station. One of my very last safaris was to go by bus with many other missionaries to a service of dedication at Barabaig while Tore stayed at home to care for our baby.

Enjoying the role of full time mother and caring for Craig substantially reduced the amount of time I spent at the drawing board during the final year of our term. However, two buildings, which I never got to see, were eventually built in conjunction with Kiomboi Hospital. At an angle to one side of the old hospital, we planned a new Obstetric-Gynecological Unit consisting of two long wards with fifteen and eleven beds respectively, as well as semi-private rooms, a nursery, labor room, clinic, doctors' offices and ancillary facilities. Opposite this unit was the site for the Memorial Chapel.

The Memorial Chapel had been in the dreams of many people during our entire term. Many missionaries had given their lives in their love of God and the Africans, and this unique little worship center was in remembrance of them. It had a special poignancy for our family. Eleanor Fryhle, as well as Tore's sister Ruth Uhlin, were among these saints. Of course, personnel at Kiomboi had changed over time, but Fred Malloy, then housefather at Augustana School, was a gifted builder. Photos and verbal accounts have shown the care he gave to implementing this dream.

From the States we continued to be involved by sending a golden dossal curtain and one of my watercolor paintings entitled "The Hand of God" to be used in the little prayer room. The painting represented several races and most of the faces were intended to resemble people who lived in our section of Tanzania at that time. It was to this chapel that the hospital workers came for prayer and meditation before beginning their day's work as the hands of God.

The decades have passed. Joys and sorrows have filled the lives of those of us who served in world missions. Through it all we have remained one big family woven together by our common love of our Lord, Jesus Christ, and his people in Africa.

"We may not always see just how the weavings intertwine,
But we must trust the Master's hand and follow His design,
For He can view the pattern upon the upper side,
While we must look from underneath and trust in Him to guide."
Author Unknown

Ruth E. Fryhle, *(nee Anderson), born in Nyack, NY, spent most of her life in Bergenfield, NJ. Working in NYC, she attended night school at Grand Central School of Art and later Columbia University, School of Architecture. Called by the national office of the Augustana Lutheran Church in Minneapolis to help establish a Department of Church Architecture, she continued night courses in architecture at the University of Minnesota.*

She met and married the Rev. Tore Fryhle. While serving a term with him in Tanganyika, she designed twenty-one mission buildings. On return to America, she served two terms on the LCA Commission on Church Architecture. Continuing as a consultant, she produced two educational films to guide churches in the building process.

Before retiring, she conducted seminars nationally for the architectural society Interfaith Forum on Religion, Art and Architecture.

The Fryhles had three children: Allan (deceased), Craig and Corinne. Watercolor painting, church involvement and travel fill retirement days.

"BUT GOD ..."

BEGINNING AN AMERICAN SCHOOL

IN RURAL TANZANIA

Mildred G. Anderson

The preparations were many. We had made large purchases of supplies un-available in East Africa and we had been given many items. We had packed cream separators, butter churns, kerosene lamps and lanterns. There were glass jars for canning fruit and vegetables. We packed a case each of all kinds of cake mixes, jello flavors and a case of soap and Fels Napha for the laundry. We even brought a case of lye in case we would have to make our own soap when the original supply was depleted.

We had carefully chosen the curriculum, the Houghton-Mifflin materials for elementary schools with which we were familiar and packed the books.

Why all of this buying and packing? My husband Art (Pastor Arthur L.) and I were to establish a school for missionaries' children in Tanganyika, East Africa. It had been named "Augustana School" in honor of the na-tional church body which sent the missionaries whose children we would teach. It was 1952.

Our first impression of Augustana School consisted of twine attached to stakes, indicating where the foundation was to be dug. As we looked at the unfinished school, I kept thinking of the architect's plans with the building completed and trees and shrubbery planted nearby. These drawings, with articles about the proposed school had been published in our national church magazines. Reality was far removed from these idealistic plans!

I thought, "The youngsters will be disappointed when they come for the first term and see this unfinished structure."

We had two months of language study as guests of Bill and DeLois Ja-cobson at Wembere Mission Station. Then on February 1, 1953, Pastor Marvin Palmquist drove down the 1000-foot escarpment road, which he had constructed while pastor there, to bring Art and me to Augustana School and Kiomboi. Marv was unusually cheerful as he greeted us with *"Jambo!* (Hello!) *Habari?* (How are you?) Guess what??"

"Our barrels and crates are at Kiomboi!" I exclaimed.

"Yes, thirty-five barrels and five crates arrived at Kiomboi this very morning. They're waiting to be unpacked at Augustana School."

"What perfect timing!" I responded. "Only two weeks until the opening day."

And what rejoicing as we thanked Bill and DeLois Jacobson and said, "Farewell until we see you at Augustana School. You must have the first cup of coffee served at the school!"

What a joy to see again the things we had packed the previous summer at the Bethel Lutheran parsonage in Duluth, Minnesota!

"What are we going to do first, Art?"

"Mildred, I don't know exactly, but we will do all we can with what we have to work with."

It was a miracle to see the superstructure of the school when two months ago all we could see were the stakes and twine where the foundation was to be. Yet there was still concern because there were no doors, no windows, no furniture, no desks, no beds, no chairs.

"Pastor Marvin, perhaps we should telegraph the parents to keep the children at home until further notice, " Art questioned

Confident, faithful, always optimistic Marv replied, "Art, you have lived in Africa only two months. Don't worry, it will all work out just right."

A few more days went by. Doors and windows were now being installed, but no sign of furnishings which we had carefully designed several months previously for the Indian carpenters in Singida, sixty miles away.

One evening, Art and I were walking to the pastor's house where the Palmquists lived, for he was the pastor of the entire station in addition to supervising all the building construction.

Art said to me. "I'm not going to mention this to Marvin but I must draft the telegrams tomorrow informing the parents not to send their children. We cannot start school without the basic furniture."

"But God…" How many times would we have the delightful surprise of divine intervention and exclaim, *"And my God will satisfy every need of yours according to his riches in glory in Christ Jesus."* I've lost count.

Late that very night a lorry (truck) pulled into the mission station and parked next to our bedroom window. Never before or since has a lorry ever parked so close. Art and I were aroused from sleep. Straining our eyes to peer through the darkness, we saw that the lorry was filled with desks, chairs, beds. Everything we would need to provide for Augustana School to open on schedule! In his mind's eye Art could see a huge banner attached to the side of the lorry (meant just for him) which stated, *"Oh you of little faith!"*

Truly God's banner over us and the Augustana School was *"Love."*

That was almost forty-five years ago, but still vivid in the archives of my mind. And so went the following years: miracle following miracle. Yes, an overabundance of miracles showered on us by the generous hand of Almighty God to show His goodness and His faithfulness to His children.

On February 16, 1953, as the last mosquito net was being tied, a large van drove into the school grounds. Several children bounded out and raced wildly to the front door exclaiming, "O boy, O boy!" Never before or since have we seen children so excited about coming to school. They didn't see the part of the building which was still unfinished. They had arrived at *their* school and that was enough.

We started with twelve students. Art and I were the staff. We were the houseparents; we were the teachers. The school would grow to more than sixty students during our tenure, and a staff of eight. Fifteen separate nations were represented in the student body.

My main responsibility was the kitchen, the laundry and the cleanliness of the facility. I could never have accomplished this without the support of Art, of course, and the faithful assistance of the African staff. I experienced real teamwork with everyone.

The kitchen had the glorious aroma of bread baking every other day. One day Art said, "Jonas is such a good painter. Maybe he could mix bread as well as he mixes paint." So I taught Jonas to assist me with the baking when the liquid needed for a batch of bread totaled twenty-one cups. I just could not knead such a mass of dough. The nearest bakery was 300 miles away. Jonas proved invaluable.

Teofilo was our chief *dobi* or laundry worker. He, too, proved invaluable. I operated the two Maytag washing machines which had gasoline-powered engines. I was the only one who used them because first, I didn't want anyone to get their hands caught in the attached wringer and secondly, we couldn't risk having anything happen to the machines.

One African employee said, "There's one thing that the Americans can't make."

Art replied. "I'm sure there are many things that Americans can't do, but what did you have in mind?"

The man answered, "Americans cannot make anything that we can't break!"

That certainly appeared to be true as someone reported a broken anvil and we had a cast iron skillet that was broken. We experienced that the greatest amount of breakage were the handles of sadirons. (A sadiron lives up to its name. It is placed on the wood or coal range and is picked up and used with a detachable handle.) Art had ordered a gross (144) of these. My mother had one handle which lasted her whole life and is still in good repair. I still don't know why Art ordered so many; providentially, we needed them all as the supply was dwindling rapidly toward the end of our term.

One day Teofilo attended a sale at some place far away from Kiomboi. The children's clothes displayed for sale looked strikingly familiar to him. He began to examine the clothes and immediately identified them as belonging to the students at Augustana School. The thief must have made his move when the clothes were hung out to dry. Teofilo returned to the school with the stolen goods. I was so proud of him. He and I always saw to it that the children left school with nothing but clean clothes in their suitcases.

An ear-piercing, clamorous sound exploded from the temporary dining room one day just before the children were to come to their noon meal. I ran to the dining room to find it in shambles. An old demented man had caused quite a ruckus. He was parading around the dining area shouting unintelligible noises, sporting a woman's red felt hat and nothing else. Nasanya, our faithful kitchen helper, hurriedly fetched a blanket to wrap up the intruder. Nasanya also gave him food and accompanied him home. He had emptied all the water glasses—a wet mess!

Before our three big underground cisterns were constructed, we relied on our water holes in the *shamba* (garden) where we grew most of our fruits and vegetables. We had no warning of our impending shortage until the day the water carriers came to the classroom where Art was teaching.

"The water in the *shamba* is gone. Where shall we go for water now?"

Any place, but especially equatorial Africa, is a very bad place to run out of water. What to do next? We did what we always did. We dialoged with our Heavenly Father.

One child queried, "How will we catch the water that God is going to send?" It was decided that we place all our fifty-five gallon barrels under the gutters all around the school building. Then we prayed for rain.

"Did it rain?" someone asked once when I told this story.

"Remember it was still the dry season. There had been no sign of the coming rain."

But God! Did He ever make it rain! It poured down while we were having our evening devotion with the children. One of the pleasures of life is the sound of rain on the roof, but the sound of this downpour on a metal roof was the thrill of a lifetime. The witness of a miracle!

"Let's thank the Lord!" several children exclaimed together, but one of our older students said, "There are no words to express what I feel!"

Every one of our barrels was filled to the brim. The words of Jesus still thrill me, *"Everyone who drinks of this water will be thirsty again, but those who drink of the water that I will give them will never be thirsty. The water that I will give will become in them a spring of water gushing up to eternal life.*" Our water problem has been solved forever!

We had music at the school, lots of it! Several missionary wives gave of their time and talents to teach piano.

But practice time was hard to coordinate. Pupil Chris Nelson asked me one morning, "Aunty Mildred, how can I get more time for practicing the piano?"

"What can we do, Chris? We have only four pianos and many students taking lessons. The hours available are all filled."

"I wake up early," Chris responded. "May I practice as soon as I wake up?"

Chris was permitted to start practicing when the rising bell rang at 6:30 a.m., the time it was light enough to move about without using the electric generator. Chris must have dressed and walked to the lounge in the dark, because as soon as the rising bell stopped, we could all hear the "prelude of the day" begin.

We celebrated every birthday with a special dinner, and of course, there was always a birthday cake, made with one of those many cake mixes brought with us from the States. I tried to cook the favorite food of the birthday person. When I asked David Hedman what he would especially like, I was greatly surprised when he said, "Liver."

His sister, Mary, said, "Well, I don't like liver, but I'll eat it if that is what David wants." The rest of the children just groaned!

Tasks were endless at Augustana School, but there was always time for a loving hug and a smile and an encouraging word.

Each Sunday we had a worship service in English in the school chapel, and then joined with the Kiomboi community at the large Kiomboi Church.

One Sunday as we were walking back to the school from the service, the boys said to Art and me, "Did you see Irene give her beads away at church?"

Winifried and Irene Bohringer had come to our school from East Germany. They had left their home with just the things they had on their persons. Irene had a pretty blue dress which was kept for Sunday and special occasions.

In answer to the boys' question, I'm afraid that my first thought was, "Now why would she do that?" Those beads looked as if they had been made for Irene and they just matched her Sunday dress.

Back at the school, Art and I went to the kitchen to get the noon meal on the table. Soon little Irene came running in and she was up in my arms, as was her custom.

In her beautiful German accent, Irene asked me, "Did you see that poor, blind woman in church today? I sat right in front of her. I asked myself, 'Why should she be so poor and I be so rich?' So I just turned around and put my beads in her hands."

We gave Irene a big hug as tears welled in our eyes. Nothing more was said of the incident. Long after this we celebrated Irene's birthday. She was opening her presents and one package was from her "big sister," Mary Hedman. There in a box lay a string of blue beads almost exactly like the ones Irene had given away.

As we thought of these acts of unselfish love, the new beads took on a special brilliance. They sparkled like diamonds in the African sun. Precious little Irene continued to drop things in peoples' hands. When we visited that family in 1958 in Germany, each day when Irene came from school, she brought us a tiny pitcher or a vase as a gift.

It would be impossible to relate all the incidents that occurred at Augustana School. The school functioned because there was trust and teamwork involving each member of the team, both our American and African staff. Most of all there was the intervention, time and again, of our gracious and powerful God.

Jesus said, *"I am the vine, you are the branches. …apart from me, you can do nothing."*

Someone wrote, "If you are going to attempt to do something for God, attempt something so big that if He doesn't intervene, you will absolutely fail." That is exactly how it happened: "But, God…"

A friend asked me, "Would you do it again?"

I answered, "In a heartbeat, dear friend, in a heartbeat!"

Mildred G. Anderson *was born and reared on a farm near Longmont, Colorado. She received her elementary and high school training in Erie, CO, and higher education at Elmhurst College, Elmhurst, IL.; Denver University, Denver, CO; Baker University, Baldwin City, KS; and the University of Northern CO at Greeley, CO.*

Mildred served as a teacher in Longmont, CO, then as parish worker at Holy Trinity, Duluth, MN; First Lutheran Church, Ault, CO; and Emmanuel at Hoisington, KS.

Overseas service began in 1952 when she and her husband, Pastor Arthur LeRoy Anderson, established the Augustana School for missionaries' children at Kiomboi, Tanganyika, East Africa. Her role there was teacher, housemother and hostess, supervising and working with the staff.

After her African experience she volunteered as parish worker at First Lutheran Church, Ault, CO; in Dacca, East Pakistan and Emmanuel Lutheran Church in Hoisington, KS, where she also served as full-time secretary.

FROM A SMALL BEGINNING

Margaret R. Peterson

KIOMBOI HOSPITAL

"Mama, can't you have some classes for us?"

This plea was one Dr. Moris and I heard many, many times. A need with which we ourselves often wrestled and said, "Oh, for more trained staff" at this young mission hospital located at Kiomboi in central Tanganyika.

The year was 1941, barely thirteen years after the first missionaries from America arrived. The hospital was built under the direction of Dr. Hobart Johnson and added to by his successor, Dr. Stanley Moris. It was funded by the Women's Missionary Society of the Augustana Lutheran Church, one of the predecessor bodies of the ELCA. Built in the shape of a quadrangle with an inner court surrounded by wards, it accommodated many patients. The small outpatient clinic was a separate building. On any given day there were up to forty inpatients and two to four hundred outpatients.

Nasola Mtindi and Petro Msengi, the first dressers trained by Drs. Johnson and Moris, were taught to cleanse, apply ointment and wrap bandages on the many who had tropical ulcers caused by poor nutrition, poor sanitation and poor care. Both dressers and aides (young women) had minimal primary education, barely able to read or use Swahili, the official language of the country.

"Mama, can't we have classes? We want to know more about diseases! What causes them? And about our bodies and ourselves. We want to understand how to heal the many who come to us."

For us, it was curative treatment that took precedence over preventive health care. Time was not available for teaching how to treat various ailments, to recognize causes of illnesses or determine why they were ill.

But the *cry* was there: "*—teach us, have classes!*"

"Tumbo linauma" (my stomach hurts); *"Kiuno kinauma"* (my back hurts); *"Miguu inauma"* (my legs hurt); or *"Mtoto ni moto"* (my child is hot) were all too familiar complaints of those arriving at the hospital.

Nasola, the dresser who served as laboratory technician, became quite adept in diagnosing many of the people's illnesses by using the monocular microscope, affectionately known as the "one eye." He readily recognized the malaria parasite, the tapeworm, the hookworm and other microscopic parasites—illnesses that were exacerbated by poor hygiene, lack of nutritional food, and carried by mosquitoes or other insects.

One day we heard a loud cry from Nasola, "Mama, look what came from America, a large two-eye microscope. I can use both eyes now!" His excitement was felt all over the hospital.

World War II was beginning to cause a scarcity of medicines. Quinine for treating malaria was nearly gone. We began searching around for alternative medicines. The chino tree's bark gave us totaquine; the brewed eucalyptus tree leaves became an expectorant; soda bicarbonate was used for abdominal distress; sulfur ointment was used for scabies and tropical ulcers.

The painful tropical skin disease *yaws* could be treated with six injections. Often after two injections the patient felt better so did not return for the much needed last four of the series.

Petro suggested, "Let's charge a shilling for the six treatments, then when they complete the series, we will return the shilling." His strategy worked! Yaws is seen no more.

Four miles from Kiomboi Hospital was a small colony for people with leprosy, quite common at the time. The dressers went to a village called Mkeo to give thick chaulmoogra oil shots that were very painful. With the advent of new medicines and dedicated nurses and doctors, specialists in leprosy management, leprosy is almost eradicated—but that's another story in itself.

Today smallpox is a thing of the past worldwide. But our dressers had been known to give up to 3,000 vaccinations in one day in outpatient clinics or in village centers.

The workday at the hospital started with the staff (dressers, aides, nurses, cooks, doctors, and laundry workers) meeting in the chapel for *sala* (devotions). Members of the staff led these as they testified to their Christian faith. As we left *sala* and proceeded to the day's work we heard the repeated question, "When are we going to have time to have regular classes?"

During hospital rounds, Kiula, a patient, was asked what was wrong. She responded, "My head hurts."

Nasola drew blood, examined the slide under the microscope and reported, "Yes, she has malaria."

Assistants to the doctors needed more training in sterilization and needed answers to the many whys: Why do we do this? Why do we do that? Why? Why? Why?

Again the cry, "Mama, we need some regular classes!"

The next stop was at the outpatient clinic, to which many had walked two to ten miles to have dressings changed, to be diagnosed, given medication or encouragement. The "African Ambulance" was often a bed carried upside down with a blanket tied to its legs to serve as a canopy or just a blanket tied to two poles and carried by four men.

Esta came running, "The baby just came and is doing well!" Mama Salome Lyuki, the midwife, had done the delivery. She was among the first Christians of the Lyamba people and became a matriarch of the tribe. Her contributions to Kiomboi Hospital are unsurpassed. Drs. Johnson and Moris taught her to deliver babies, to recognize difficulties in labor, and principles of infant care. Mama Salome developed the idea of having a special washroom for ceremonial washing after delivery according to their tribal customs.

Mama Salome obtained help from Paramount Chief Kingu to instruct his sub-chiefs to get help for women who were in difficult labor, to carry them to the hospital. She trained other widows to go into the "bush" to help women who couldn't make it to the hospital. (According to their custom, they would not permit a young unmarried girl to help mothers in labor or to deliver babies.) These Christian older widows were trained in the rudiments of hygiene and deliveries. They were given a box containing scissors to cut the umbilical cord, a string to tie cord, bandages, a bottle of Lysol and a basin. They reported to the hospital every month or two. They tied knots in a piece of string to signify how many deliveries they had; they were paid fifty cents (about seven cents in U.S. money) for every delivery!

By the end of hospital rounds and outpatient services, there was no fixed slot for class time. The complaint was still being heard, "We want some formal classes!"

Using my nursing notes from home, I tried to spend evenings putting some anatomy and physiology, medical and surgical nursing, and obstetrical notes into some form of understandable language. It was difficult to adapt them to the culture and language. There were many laughs as they tried to understand my notes and my Swahili. But it was a beginning as we tried to find an hour and a classroom. We made a stricter schedule, and taught more in the clinical setting rather than in the classroom. But in time it bore fruit.

As the whole educational system grew, more adequately prepared candidates became available for training in health professions as well as in education and other fields. Years later, I was involved in the School of Nursing for Grade B nurses at Kiomboi.

Today there are certified midwives, registered nurses, teachers of nursing and medical doctors lecturing, practicing and researching. Many diseases have been wiped out, the death rate decreased, infant mortality rates lowered, hygiene practiced and tropical ulcers nearly eliminated.

I am most grateful to have been part of these experiences in the early forties along with Ruth Safemaster Flatt and Edythe Kjellin. And now what a joy to be blessed by God with enough years of life to see these changes.

A SHOPPING TRIP: TANGANYIKA STYLE

Learning to drive on Tanganyika's "paved highways" in an old Chevy, driving on the left side of the road with the steering wheel on the right, was an experience!

My driving lesson began when we planned a trip to Singida, the "metropolis" having a couple of grocery stores, located about sixty miles from Kiomboi. Before undertaking such a safari, we carefully surveyed our needs, as petrol (gas) was in short supply. Our hospital supplies were low: blankets, soap, medical supplies that had been sent by rail from Dar es Salaam were waiting at the railhead, Kinyangiri. We knew there were some mission boxes sent from the USA in Singida. Household items were also depleted, so we determined that the safari was necessary.

We filled our canteens with boiled water and a thermos with coffee. Cookies and sandwiches were packed in baskets. I began to learn how to drive twenty to thirty miles an hour over dirt, and over rough, grassy roads. We picked up our supplies and after lunch with the Zeilingers, new missionaries in the Singida area, we started our return trip. But with a light rain falling, we were reminded: *the rainy season had begun!*

About twenty miles along the way, we came to a roaring stream. Earlier it was dry and we had driven over it. On the opposite bank there was *mbuga* (depthless mud). We waited for the rain to stop and the stream to go down, but it kept on raining. Thus our only recourse was to spend the night in the *pori* (woods). I had been in Tanganyika only three weeks—so I was quite apprehensive and frightened.

The sun was just setting. There is no twilight only four degrees from the equator. There are 12 hours of day and 12 hours of night. We had to stay in the car. The canvas curtains were fastened down to keep out the rain and the lions who might be roaming around.

To keep warm, we wrapped ourselves in the blankets we had just purchased for the hospital. These also helped to protect us from the mosquitoes. It was rather close quarters in the front seat for Dorothy Anderson, Edythe Kjellin and myself, but we were ready for the night. Martin Olson and Daudi Msengi sat or tried to lie down among the supplies in the back seat. I thought we should have some fresh air and was about to pull up one of the canvas curtains, when Marty said, "No! The hungry lions might come and take a bite of your nose!"

We had devotions, thanked God for His protecting care and that we had a place to stay out of the rain. The evening and night hours were filled with memory games, trying to name the capitals and the largest cities of each state, quoting nursery rhymes, and when exhausted, yielded to a good sleep.

Just as the sun sets suddenly, daylight comes suddenly. The rain stopped after dumping on us six and a half inches in six hours; that rushing stream was now only a trickle. We put on our boots, pushed the car across the stream and were on our way.

We thought the worst was over and with a "Hurrah," we were on our way back to Iambi. The dirt roads were slick but Marty's good driving skill got us the twenty miles to Kinyangiri, the railhead. In this tiny village we were most grateful for the hot tea and biscuits which the Indian merchants served us.

Our freight had come this far by rail, including my Montgomery Ward order. Surprisingly, despite shortages due to the war, there were bags of sugar and flour, other available groceries and personal supplies which were most welcome. *But* this gave our vehicle a heavier load!

After another fifteen miles there was another river which was wider and the current was faster than the previous one. Any way we tried we encountered another river. The high water had even carried away a bridge we were counting on. No one wanted to spend another night in the car. The only alternative left was to walk back to Iambi.

Three and a half hours of sunlight remained but we expected a full moon. Our food intake was skimpy, but we did have a chunk of meat and some potatoes. Daudi made us a good fire and we had a steak fry. The tin of fruit salad was left, but we decided that would be good to take with us on our walking *safari!*

What a sight—Marty wearing his hip boots; the rest wore rain boots. Carrying our canteen of water and the tin of fruit, off we went. Daudi led the way brandishing a large stick. We three came next and Marty took up the rear carrying a gun.

My thoughts went rampant. Could I do this? We stopped every hour for five to ten minutes to drink some water and swallow some of the fruit salad. At one point I said, "I don't think…."

Marty quickly said, "Do you prefer to stop in one of the huts along the way, together with the bugs, mosquitoes, etc.?"

We stumbled on—across more streams over which Marty, with his hip boots, had to carry us one at a time. After more than six hours, we saw the roof tops of Iambi. We made it through grass, mud, cornfields, and water and more water.

Now, how was that for a couple of greenhorns? We survived muscle aches, blisters, hunger, earaches and a memory that survives the dimming effects of years.

Margaret Peterson was born and schooled in Bridgeport, Kansas. After high school, she attended Bethany College in Lindsborg for two years, then continued her professional education at the School of Nursing at Trinity Lutheran Hospital in Kansas City, MO.

She was commissioned for service in Tanganyika in 1939 at the national church convention in Lindsborg, KS. She traveled with another new recruit, Dorothy Anderson, on a Japanese steamer, taking two months for the journey to Singida, Tanga- nyika.

Margaret was stationed at Kiomboi all the years she spent in the country (1940 to 1963). She constantly sought opportunities for improving the quality of medical care in the district. When, in 1953, a nursing course was opened at Kiomboi, it could fairly be credited to Margaret's prodding.

Attending Peabody College for Teachers, Nashville, TN. during furlough, she earned the credits for a B.S. in Public Health Nursing and brought back to Kiomboi a zeal for preventive medicine. On her next furlough she earned an M.A. in Education at Peabody.

After resigning from mission service in 1963, she became a public health nursing supervisor in Wichita, KS. She climaxed her career as Associate Professor of Public Health Nursing at Kansas Medical Center, Kansas City, KS.

In retirement she has been active in her church and community; in the St. James congregation in Kansas City, she was coordinator for LAOS Academy, a well-defined study program for congregations, aimed at bringing one's faith into action during the week. She has since retired in Lindsborg, KS.

THE RAIN BROUGHT THE GIRLS
Marian A. Halvorson

"If your God wants our girls to come to school, let him prove it! Tell him to send rain now while we sit here!" The Tanzanian elder of the Turu tribe challenged the school supervisor and me at the Parent-Teacher meeting we had called to try to persuade them to send their daughters, as well as their sons, to school. The sixty-five to seventy parents clapped their hands in agreement. They knew he had asked for the impossible! It was mid-August and in that part of Tanzania, there was no rain from the middle of April until mid or late October.

But Andrea, the school supervisor, answered at once: "No problem…we'll just ask Him to do that." He bowed his head and prayed a short prayer, then went on talking about the benefits of sending girls to school.

"Andrea," I thought to myself, "do you really think God will change the seasons like that? Be reasonable!" The sky was clear, no sign of a cloud, but what happened?

In less than ten minutes black clouds scuttled overhead, and the rain was pouring down! The gathered assembly packed themselves into an empty classroom. The old man stood up again. "Your God wants our girls to come to school. They will come."

No more PTAs were necessary on that subject. The news of rain in August spread quickly to every area, and whenever we went to visit primary schools in Turuland after that, at least a third of the pupils in the first grade were girls!

LITERACY AND THE LIGHT

The Lutheran Church had just begun our area-wide adult literacy program among the Lyamba people of central Tanzania. In a class that had been meeting only a month, a gray-haired elder was already reading Book 3. I said, "You knew how to read when you joined this class, didn't you?"

"I didn't know 'a' from 'z'," he replied quickly, "but the light is right here in my eyes. It must get into my mind, into my heart, into my arms and legs. Then I'll be able to read!" His arms pointed to his head, heart, arms and legs as he talked. He knew already that reading had to be life-changing. We had many evidences of that during those years.

One day, in another class, I sat with a young mother. As she was reading the pages to me, she turned abruptly and said, "Wait a minute, I have a question."

"Yes?"

"What does a mother do when her heart tells her she must become a Christian?"

"Mother, you listen to your heart and obey it."

"But my husband will beat me. He hates Christians. He drinks and threatens me."

Her voice was becoming louder and others in the class were listening. Before I could answer, a father, formerly Muslim, but now converted to Christianity, spoke up. "Mother, I'll give you some advice. When he scolds you, don't answer back. When he beats you, prepare his food more quickly than ever before. Then he'll know it's a good thing to become a Christian!"

The reading class had become a sharing-Jesus group. Whether that mother became a Christian, I don't know, but seeds were sown which could and did often bear fruit.

After visiting other literacy classes, I picked up a young father whom I had seen in one of the groups. When I asked his name, I knew he was not a Christian. At the time of baptism, new Christians normally chose a new name to denote their new life in Christ.

"You are Makala Msengi? Have you ever thought about becoming a Christian?"

"Oh, don't you know? I've been a catechumen for over a year now and I'll be baptized this fall."

"How did that come about?" I asked.

"Our teacher not only taught us in class. He came to our home. When we were sick, he prayed for us. Many times he explained to us very carefully about Jesus dying for our sins, and coming out of the grave. Then last year, when the certificates were given out at the local court, you told us that God had given us new light in our eyes, and we had to choose how we used that light. I said to myself, 'Yes, I've been reading all this time. Now I must choose.' "

So he, like many others, had chosen the way of life and light.

GOD'S SAINT—YAKOBO NTUNDU

One afternoon during the very first literacy class session at our station, one of the earliest Christians, Yakobo Ntundu, walked the 11 miles from his home in Ruruma to find out what was going on. After class, he came up to me and said, "I've taught many people to read at Ruruma."

"You have?" I answered. "What books did you use?"

"Books? *We didn't have any books in those days—only the Swahili New Testament.*"

"Then how did you teach people to read?"

"That's easy! I just picked out words that started with each letter of the alphabet. They learned the letters and how they joined with others to make words and sentences!"

Then he continued: "When I was the first evangelist at Ruruma, I'd go to the places where the men sat around drinking beer. I always carried my little slate (blackboard) with me. First I'd ask, 'What are you drinking?'

"'*Pombe*,' they'd answer. So I'd write '*pombe*' on the slate and ask them to listen to the two parts: '*po*' and '*mbe*'. Then I'd put two '*po*'s on the board and ask 'what is this word?' Someone would say '*popo*' (bat).

"Then I'd show them how to build '*embe*' (mango) and say, 'Look, in a few minutes you have learned three words with five letters! In Swahili there are only 24 letters to learn. If you'll stop drinking long enough to get the bats from your belfry (using the Lyamba equivalent!), you could learn to read very quickly.' I always got a good group to come to read, and many of them became the first Christians."

That day Yakobo took our new books home. Later we heard he would walk to the prison, six miles away, several times a week to teach reading and share with them the good news of Jesus Christ.

When I moved to the station where he lived, he would often come to our home in the late afternoon and talk about the early days when he first became a Christian. He was just a young boy of 13; the first Germany missionary, Rev. Everth, (from Leipzig Mission, Germany) had taught him to read. He often traveled with him over all of Lyambaland on preaching missions.

"Pastor Everth was sure that Jesus was coming back very soon," he'd say. "It was the beginning of the first World War so he walked all over the area until his shoes were so worn out he had to tie on the soles. His clothes were so worn out they were just rags. He would preach and preach, and thousands of Lyamba people would come. Before he'd leave any preaching place he would call upon those who wanted to come for baptism and receive Jesus, to form long lines for baptism! I remember some evenings, when the sun was going down, we'd be so tired, but there were still several hundred in the baptism line.

"What he didn't know," Yakobo added, "was that most of those people thought the government had sent him to perform this ceremony, so they all lined up and took other names—Yoshua, Elijah, Matthew, Daniel, Elizabeti, Maria—but before he could get them together and teach them what their baptism really meant, he was interned and later sent back to Germany."

"How then did you learn what Christianity really meant?"

"About that time we heard from one of our men who had been sent to the Marangu Teachers' Training Center, Daudi Kidamala, that some missionaries from America had come to replace the interned missionaries from Germany. In fact, one of the American missionaries walked all the way from Marangu and even came to Ruruma—Rev. Ralph Hult. But he left and didn't return to Lyamba-land. So three of us, who had been baptized by Rev. Everth, walked to Marangu—all 350 miles—to plead with the Americans there to come to Lyambaland. It was a long, tiresome and dangerous journey, but eventually some Americans came—Rev. George Anderson, Rev. Herbert Magney, Rev. Ludwig Melander and one doctor—Dr. Bertha Anderson."

Then Yakobo told us how one of their shamans had prophesied that some light-skinned people would come bringing a book with the message of the true God. We were to receive them and believe their message. So he explained, "We *knew* that Rev. Everth and those who came from America had been sent to us by God."

The missionaries soon learned that there were hundreds of people in Lyambaland with Christian names, but little knowledge of what Christianity could mean to them. Classes were started and continued for several years before the very first congregation in Lyambaland was organized at Ruruma.

In August 1929, 86 new Christians were baptized and the 65 adults and 75 children who had previously been baptized by Rev. Everth were confirmed. All the newly baptized and confirmed Christians brought cows, sheep, goats and chickens to be sold, providing funds to build the first church at Ruruma.

Yakobo lived until he was past 90. That old first church in Lyambaland, then in use for over 70 years, was in sad disrepair. But funds were being collected to build a new church. The day Yakobo got word that the foundation was in, he clasped his hands and prayed like Simeon, "Lord, now you can take me home." That afternoon he died.

Now the work of the Holy Spirit is bearing fruit, and we know that among the lay evangelists there are many saints like Yakobo Ntundu.

Marian A. Halvorson *was born in Proctor, MN. She studied at Bethany College, Lindsborg, KS, and at Pacific Lutheran University, Tacoma, WA, and was awarded an honorary doctorate by the latter. She was commissioned as a missionary by the Augustana Lutheran Church in 1946.*

Her first term was spent as secretary to the General Director of all Lutheran missions in Tanganyika. Then for seven years Marian headed the Lyamba Adult Literacy Program of the Lutheran Church, Central Synod.

For the following 26 years she was a consultant for adult literacy programs in twenty African countries, under the auspices of the National Christian Council, World Literacy and Christian Literature (later Intermedia).

Marian retired in 1987 and lives in Mt. Vernon, WA.

CONTRASTS IN COLOR

Marie Matsen

Africa was a pleasant surprise! We had a long eventful journey to Africa in the fall of 1945. World War II had just ended. There had been countless delays and frustrations. We had not been able to journey with scheduled travel companions because our name had been misspelled on papers from Africa. Two months after leaving our homes, we arrived at Singida, Tanganyika.

Very soon, brilliant color greeted us in East Africa. It was the rainy season and the foliage was lush and green. There were beautiful and brilliantly colored birds. Flowers of many varieties bloomed at every turn. There were lavender jacaranda trees, fragrant frangipani (plumeria) shrubs with white and yellow-throated wax-like blossoms, and bright orange flamboyant trees. There were painted daisies, lupines, spreading poinsettia bushes, pink oleander bushes, red hibiscus, and lilies of various kinds.

When the first rains came the clouds were awesome, almost frightening in their blackness. But after a heavy rain storm for a few hours, the grayness disappeared and it was bright and sunny for the rest of the day.

Music very quickly began to add another dimension of color to our lives. I shall never forget the first Sunday worship service at the church at Iambi, where we were to have language study for six months. I couldn't understand a word, but the hymns were dearly familiar. Oh, how these Africans loved to sing! It was sheer joy to hear them.

Very soon, I was giving lessons on the reed organ to three of Iambi's teachers and playing for some of the church services. The congregation learned new songs quickly. I was always amazed at the innate ability the African has for music. Their harmonies were so interesting and different. It seemed everyone could sing and most in harmony. I never heard a monotone there. They added several innovations to their music, such as the ululation (trilling) by the women, an indication of joy and emotion.

Teacher Loti's 4th grade students sang Handel's "Hallelujah Chorus" with more precision than many adult groups I've heard in the United States. In both large and small groups the people sang at almost every occasion. When they worked in the fields they worked in rhythm and sang songs to the beat of the hoeing.

While at Iambi, four of us missionaries formed a quartet that sang at different events. Later a women's trio and a missionary chorus were formed, which I directed. The missionary chorus made a recording of the anthem "Lost in the Night" in Swahili for the Board of World Missions to distribute in the States. Later I taught music to the children of missionaries at Augustana School. These things added to the kaleidoscope of music in my life in Tanzania.

And then, the color of language and of customs! One day I was teaching our cook, Yonatani, to make cookies. In the process I noticed him and another helper smiling at each other. "What did I say wrong now?" I asked them.

"Mama, you asked Yonatani to crawl in the oven. We think you mean to put the cookies in the oven!"

There was a large screen window between the kitchen and our eating area. Several times we saw the house-helpers leaning on their elbows and watching us eat with those strange utensils of knife, fork and spoon. The cook asked me one day why we always had fruit first at the morning meal and last at the evening meal. I really couldn't give him a good answer.

When we first arrived at Ushora, we were in a sea of black faces. One day I met Yonatani's father. He had some of the same facial expressions and smile as my grandfather in America. From then on I never noticed a difference in color, but just the character as it shone through various personalities.

Our place of service was at Ushora Mission in the southwest corner of our field among the Lyamba people; we also worked with Turu people at a nearby station. We were the first resident missionaries in a long time, and we were warmly welcomed by the people. They were friendly and considerate and seemed genuinely glad to have us there to be their friends and to help them. Our house-helpers had to be trained; we found people who learned fast and were loyal and faithful friends during our two terms of service at Ushora. These workers were surely among the brightest of colors in our Africa kaleidoscope!

MAMA, GET YOUR GUN!

There were some gray areas too! Snakes were not uncommon at Ushora! They seemed to like the attic in our house and several times we found snake skins which had been shed in the attic. Two puff adders wanted to take up residence in our house one time. My husband, Thor, killed them with a piece of kindling wood while I was "screaming silently" at the other end of the room.

We had a trumpet vine across the front of our house. One Sunday after church I was returning to the house with baby Luther in the buggy. I went to unlock the door and heard a "s-s-st." I heard it again, looked up, and saw a green mamba snake in the vine above the door. We slowly backed up and enlisted the help of Africans who were passing by. They threw rocks at it and it went its way. The trumpet vine soon came down.

One day I saw a green mamba snake in a large tree beside the house. "Mama, get the gun!" someone shouted. Thor was off on safari, so I got his 22-rifle and some bullets and emptied the gun on that poor snake. I watched him fall from the tree, dead. That news probably traveled fast on the "African Internet!"

Our part of Africa had many kinds of animals. We often saw zebra and giraffe on our safaris between Ushora and Kiomboi. Our four children played a game of counting how many animals they could see on a trip. Thor did some hunting for our meat supply. We enjoyed the taste of impala, wildebeest and eland. Our Tanganyikan neighbors were always glad when he went hunting as it meant they would get some meat also. I could always tell when he was returning from a hunting trip as these neighbors started to come to the station long before he arrived, to get their share of the meat!

We frequently heard lions at night. One evening we heard them in our front yard. We quickly closed the door and windows and soon they were gone. When the children were still in the toddler stage, Rudia, their *ayah* (nursemaid) would put them in the baby buggy and take them for a walk around the mission grounds in the afternoon.

One day Rudia was bringing Luther back to the house from the main road. They saw an animal sitting in the road. It looked at them; they looked at it. Rudia did not recognize the animal. She brought Luther back to the house. That evening around the campfire at her home, Rudia told her family about the animal she had seen. Her father told her to bring him to the spot the next morning and he'd examine the tracks. He found it to be a lion's tracks. God's protecting hand followed us all our days in Africa!

We usually had an annual visit of *siafu* (driver ants) at our house. We were always on the lookout for them outdoors near the house. We would spread hot coals and ashes from our wood-burning stove around their paths, and in the house we spread pyrethrum powder around all doorways. Driver ants were dangerous and could cause suffocation if they got into one's throat. They would eat most anything in their path and really cleaned the house of bugs—and food.

Another gray part of life at Ushora had to do with a notorious thief in the area.

Gunda had been in and out of prison in the Central Province town of Dodoma several times. Ushora was his home and in his younger years he had worked for the missionary living there at the time. He knew the house well.

One night he paid us a visit. He cut the screen in the kitchen door, came in and did his "work" while we slept through the whole thing. He raided the office and stole mission money and our personal money. He took kitchen towels, pots and pans, sheet and pillow and blanket from Luther's buggy. I had just baked cookies that day and he emptied the cookie jar too! After that we had expanded metal mesh put over the windows.

Gunda paid us one more visit during our second term. I was home alone with the children. Thor was at a meeting at another station. I awoke in the middle of the night and heard the French doors to the living room open. I asked, "Who is it? Who is there?" (I had been told by older missionaries to make a lot of noise and thieves would run away). I kept hollering and started to look for whoever was there.

I then heard a skirmish at the hooked door on the porch. My adrenaline was working overtime and I was very alert. I realized I had nothing to protect me. Thor had taken the gun with him, as he often shot an impala on his way home for our meat supply. I thought of a butcher knife in the kitchen, but realized the thieves would be far more adept with a knife than I was. By this time they were out and gone.

A house-helper was sleeping in another room, but had not awakened. I called him and he came. Our children had also slept through it all. About this time I realized what danger I had been in and shook like a leaf from head to toe.

The house-helper and I stayed up the rest of the night looking at scrapbooks and pictures. The next morning when other workers came and saw what had happened, the news spread fast.

Before long some of the church elders and others came to see me and hear the story. They asked me, "Mama, if you had a gun, would you have shot the thieves?"

I said, "No, I could never do that. But I might have shot in another direction to scare them."

Elder Marko said, "That's why they rob you. In the old days if someone stole, his hand was cut off, so we didn't have robberies. They know you won't hurt them."

I had visitors all day long, including the local chief of the area and the government police from Singida. Eventually Gunda was caught. Some of our stolen goods were found in his possession. I was called to testify in court in Singida.

As we came into the courtroom the judge was ushered in. He was a British judge with black robes and a long, curled, moth-eaten looking white wig, just like the pictures of British magistrates in England. I identified our belongings that Gunda had stolen. The judge asked me, "Did you see the accused face to face?"

"No," I replied, "just his back as he was trying to escape."

Gunda was acquitted because I did not see him face to face, but later he was found guilty of other crimes and sent back to prison again. I was glad this never happened again in our home. God's protecting hand was ever with us.

THE TRAVELING BASKET

The Executive Secretary of the Lutheran World Federation, Dr. Fredrik Schiotz, visited our mission field. As he toured most of our Lyamba and Turu stations, we all wanted to feed him as well as possible. The missionary hosts in the first home he visited had ordered a large ham from Dar es Salaam, on the coast, for the occasion.

Wherever Dr. Schiotz went, a basket of food was also sent with him from station to station. If the succeeding hosts didn't have meat on hand, they could use the ham, fruit, or whatever else was sent along in the basket. This visitor remarked afterwards about the delicious meals he had on the field and especially the good ham he had at some of the stations. He didn't know that these seldom-seen precious varieties of food had traveled with him.

At our house we made potato chips the day before his arrival. He was amazed at "potato chips in the heart of Africa!" We also packed a lunch for him when he left and included the rest of the chips. When we met Dr. Schiotz again on our furlough in the States, he remembered us and remarked, "I'll never forget those potato chips in the heart of Africa!"

"RUDIA, WHERE ARE YOU ?"

Our four children, Luther, Karen, Paul and Sandra were born in Africa. All of them had a happy relationship with an *ayah* (nursemaid) when they were small. That freed me for sewing classes with the African women and teaching some music. Luther identified very closely with his *ayah*, Rudia.

After five years in Africa we went home to the United States for a year's furlough. What a joy to be with family again! But Luther soon learned he had some additional "bosses."

One day his grandmother admonished him for something and then I came in and did the same. About that time, Luther stood in the middle of the room and cried, "Rudia, where are you?"

Rudia was, of course, thousands of miles away, but we were all glad to see her upon our return to Tanzania.

VIEWS FROM THE PORCH

Our screened-in porch at the front of the house had many uses, as play area for the children, sometimes as eating area, and always a place to view the passing scene of people.

I was out on the porch with the children one day when a funeral procession passed by the house. A small child of one of the local teachers had died. First came the elderly non-Christian grandmother dressed in a loincloth shouting and ranting to the heavens and screaming. Behind her came the African pastor, the mother and father carrying their child wrapped in a blanket, and then their Christian friends and relatives. They were all singing "Safe in the Arms of Jesus." At this time of tremendous sorrow, they were able to know that their child was safe in the arms of Jesus.

I thought, "What a picture of the fruits of God's Word in this area of the world." We came that these people might know the love of God through Jesus Christ and the hope of eternal life, that God would meet them at every corner and give them strength and peace to carry on.

Our days in Tanzania were happy ones. We made deep friendships with the people, and we have many cherished memories of those days. We learned much from the Tanzanian people and their customs. We are grateful that God called us to service among them and rejoice that today the church there is strong and growing.

Marie Matsen *was born at Hordville, NE. A graduate of Hordville High School and Luther Junior College, Wahoo, NE, she became a high school music teacher. She also worked in different clerical positions.*

Marie married Thor Matsen, September 8, 1944. In June 1945, Thor was ordained as a pastor in the Augustana Lutheran Church and commissioned as a missionary to Tanganyika. Marie and her husband served as missionaries in Africa from 1945 to 1956, living at Ushora Mission Station. Four children were born to this family: Luther, Karen, Paul and Sandra.

Upon returning to the States, Thor and Marie served churches in Sheridan, WY; Hobart, IN; and Louisville, KY.

Thor and Marie retired in 1984 and now live in Portage, WI.

NEW LIFE

Louise Faust

The sun was going down. I paused by my bedroom window to watch the muted golds in the sky merge into orange, then deeper red. A refreshing breeze crept through the open window, heralding the return of the cool tropical evening and my favorite time of day.

The shrill ring of the army telephone on my desk shattered the stillness announcing, I assumed, a crisis at the mission dispensary where the companion phone was located.

I was right. Yoeli's voice clipped off the news.

"Qwarsan and Maria are here with their son, Peter. He's the three-year-old. He's unconscious. Maria wants you to come."

Yes, Maria would want me to come, I thought as I hung up the phone. Perhaps even Qwarsan would too, if it seemed the beckoning finger of death was reaching out to touch his son.

I had had many conversations with gentle Maria since her baptism three years ago. I pulled on a sweater, remembering our first talk.

"What are we going to do about my husband?" she asked. Her brown eyes conveyed the anxiety she felt. "For years Qwarsan told me if I wanted to go to church I would first have to pass his *fimbo*."

How well I knew what that meant: a beating with the rod-like walking stick all rural Tanzanian men carried. It was a strong, slender stick that could alternately serve as a shepherd's staff, a sure defense against snakes, a weapon to fell birds for food, or a rod to keep errant wives in line.

Maria continued, "Sometimes he beat me. Sometimes not. Whatever happened, I kept on going back to church. One day he agreed I could be baptized, but *never* any of the children, he said, and certainly not himself."

She had patted the pregnant protrusion of her abdomen.

"I want so much for this one to be baptized," she said. "What can we do?"

"Maria," I remembered telling her, "God says in His Word that if two people are agreed on a thing and pray for it according to His will, it *will* happen. "We'll pray about this together, you and I."

Hurrying now toward the dispensary with keys, flashlight and stethoscope in hand, I remembered the day I had laid Maria's newborn son in her arms.

"I want his name to be Peter," she had whispered.

And so he was named. Qwarsan had reluctantly agreed to his baptism. "But only this child," he had warned. "No more."

Entering the pediatric ward, I found Maria bent over the unconscious form of their son. Qwarsan stood ramrod straight at the foot of the bed. The stern features of his brown face were handsome. His checkered *shuka*—a four-yard piece of material many African tribesmen wear as an outer garment, or sometimes their only garment—was thrown, toga fashion, over one shoulder. He nodded, acknowledging my presence.

Peter lay sprawled on the blanket, his head turned to one side, eyes closed as though he were sleeping. His usually active legs were still. I touched his forehead, then his body. His skin was cool. No temperature there. I pried open his eyes and shone the flashlight directly into them. Pupil reaction a little sluggish, I thought.

"What happened?" I asked.

"He was all right this morning," Maria volunteered. "He played hard with the others. But this afternoon he laid down on his mat in the corner and..."

Qwarsan picked up the narrative. "He said his head hurt. He went to sleep but he hasn't awakened."

I applied the stethoscope to the youngster's chest. The heart beat was regular and strong. I rolled the limp form over and listened to his chest in back. Breath sounds were clear.

Yoeli, my African helper, whose expertise was with the microscope, appeared at my side.

"All blood tests are normal," he said.

"No malaria?" I queried.

"I didn't see it in the slide."

"Or relapsing fever?" I named the two tropical diseases most apt to fell people in their tracks in the severe form.

Yoeli shook his head.

"We'll treat him anyway," I said. "Start the intravenous fluids. I'll get the chloroquine and penicillin injections," naming the specific drugs for the two diseases.

I turned to the parents. Maria was weeping. Qwarsan stood straight and unsmiling. What was he thinking? I wondered. Does he feel Peter's baptism may have caused this illness? I knew full well this could happen.

Aloud I said, "We must take him to a hospital. The closest one is the Makiungu Catholic Hospital. It's but half the distance to our own mission hospital in Kiomboi. We should go right now, but we can't. The headlights are out on the car." I indicated the blackness outside the paned windows of the ward. "Now it's night."

I covered Peter with a blanket. "Maybe he will respond to the medicine. I hope so. But we can't diagnose his sickness here. So we will have to go in any case. One of you will have to go with me."

Qwarsan spoke firmly.

"I'll go. Maria will stay with the other children."

"All right then, we will leave at the second crow of the cock—as soon as it is light enough to see the road."

The grey light of pre-dawn found Peter no better. When I backed the Land Rover to the ward veranda, Qwarsan was ready. He loaded his walking stick, his *furushi* (a small bundle of clothes), a bag of corn flour and cooking utensils into the back of the car.

I eyed the 1500-foot escarpment to the west that rose as steep sides of the Rift Valley in which we lived. There was a short cut out there. It was usable only in the dry season and that was just starting. I knew pouring rains had gouged the road. It was rutted, twisting, turning—very steep in spots— unused recently as a road. Could we get through? It would save twenty miles and at least two hours in traveling time.

I voiced my thoughts to Qwarsan, then said, "What do you think? Should we try it?"

"I don't know. The ruts are bad..." But I saw a gleam of hope in his eye.

I entered the dispensary room. Maria, shrouded in a heavy *shuka* as protection against the cold morning air, was holding Peter's limp body in her arms, crooning the haunting African melody of her child's song, composed at his birth. Tears splashed off her cheek onto the boy's closed eyelids, running in rivulets down his face toward his open mouth.

"Mama—Mama," she moaned as she rocked, "Pray for my baby."

I made a snap decision.

"We'll try the escarpment road," I said.

I discontinued the intravenous fluids. Gently Qwarsan lifted Peter from Maria's arms. Wrapping him in his own *shuka*, he carried the limp bundle to the car and seated himself on the front seat of the Land Rover.

"He loves Peter too," I thought.

Rattling down the road, I mentally reviewed my options. The long way around would be longer, but safer. But Peter needed hospital help fast.

It didn't take long to reach the turn-off. Now, as I paused there, the ribbon of main road stretched invitingly before me. What should I do? I was familiar with the 4-wheel drive. I had often used it in the mud or on steep main road inclines. But on this hand-hewn track, chopped from the craggy escarpment, I had always been the passenger, never the driver.

Perhaps I should go back for Hal. Though busy with his own rigorous schedule, my husband often made medical trips for me, but only when I asked him. Should I go back to ask him now?

Qwarsan looked at me quizzically. The dawn was bright around us. I glanced down at Peter's still form half-buried in his father's *shuka*. Maria's words, "Pray for my baby," echoed in my mind. I turned onto the escarpment road.

On the level ground, traveling was not too difficult, though the track was rough and hard to find in the overgrowth. At the base of the escarpment, we began our ascent. The road was clearly visible now, but in terrible shape. The heavy rainfall, using the course of least resistance, had formed rivers to gouge ruts and holes. We were bounced and buffeted as we forged ahead, hitting one rut, missing another.

But there was no turning back. Shifting into a lower gear, the car growled and groaned, bouncing up the steep slope, around the hairpin turns.

"We're almost at the top now," I said to Qwarsan. "Just one more sharp incline and bad turn. If we make that, we've made it."

I shifted into the lowest gear. The car churned forward with a determined growl. Pressing the accelerator to the floor, I jerked the wheel to the left to make the sharp turn.

Qwarsan and I looked at each other in horror. I slammed on the brake and pulled the emergency. My mouth was dry. "Oh God! What do we do now?"

Qwarsan lay his unconscious son on the seat and stepped out of the car to assess the damage.

"We're hung up," he said tersely. Gingerly I stepped out of the car. In making the blind turn I had not been able to see the road was washed away, leaving a tree root completely exposed. It was on that the rear axle was jammed, leaving the right wheel spinning free. The rest of the car leaned slightly to the left.

I looked around. There was no sign of human life. I knew this area. No one lived nearby.

Qwarsan was busy gathering stones and chunks of wood to shore up the exposed wheel. Remembering Peter, alone and unconscious in the car, I climbed back in beside him.

Terror clutched at my throat and twisted my gut. Glancing backward, the ascent had been at a 45-degree angle. A vision flashed before my eyes of the car slipping backwards, then rolling side over side with Peter and myself being thrown around inside, helpless as rag dolls.

I jerked myself back to reality. This would never do. Qwarsan appeared at the window, his hand on the open window frame.

"All right now," he said. "I have used stones and logs to pack the wheel as best I can. I'm the only one here, so I'll have to both lift and push. Give it all you've got and let's pray to God for help."

I was too busy concentrating on my next action to be surprised at this unusual statement from Qwarsan. But I certainly agreed with his words. For a brief moment Qwarsan and I were one in still another common purpose. I covered his hand with mine.

Aloud I said, "Father, God we need your help. We need your strength. Help us now!"

"*Ndio,*" Qwarsan said in agreement. "Yes."

Qwarsan scurried to his position at the back of the car and braced himself against it, both hands under the bumper.

I glanced at Peter lying on the seat. The rise and fall of his chest was the only sign that life continued. I tried to tuck the *shuka* in which he was wrapped between the seats to act as a brace through the next rough maneuver, for my hands would not be able to hold him.

"Now!" I shouted out the window. I released the brakes and clutch together and felt the car begin to slip backward. I jammed the gear into the lowest range and accelerated the gas. Dirt flew and rocks clattered as the support system began to give way. The back wheel clawed at the logs, the other wheels clutching at the steep incline. Suddenly the car bolted forward, bouncing viciously, then victoriously as all four tires bit into the hillside.

We were free! I did not pause in acceleration and thrust forward until I reached more level ground.

Qwarsan arrived panting and disheveled to climb onto the seat beside me. Peter again in his arms, we continued our journey.

We traveled in silence for awhile. Then Qwarsan spoke.

"Mama," he said. "That was not my strength that lifted that wheel off the root."

"I know," I said.

Peter had not responded in any way to the rough ordeal we had just been through. He just as passively endured the transfer to a hospital cart when we reached the hospital. He was promptly wheeled away.

After speaking with the doctors and nurses, I left Qwarsan standing under the plaster gaze of the statues of Jesus and Mary in the foyer of the hospital. I returned to our station by the longer route.

For a week Maria kept a daily vigil, watching for someone bringing word from her husband and son. We often talked together. We continued in our mingled prayers for Qwarsan and for God's will to be done in the life of little Peter.

One day as we stood on our steps, we saw a lone figure trudging across the valley from the escarpment road. It was Qwarsan.

Maria's feet flew to meet him. I was close behind. But Qwarsan's arms were empty. He carried only his walking stick, the bundle of clothing and cooking utensils in his hand. He told us that Peter never regained consciousness, although the doctors worked very hard and tried everything they knew.

"Yesterday he just stopped breathing," he said.

Maria was sobbing quietly. My arm was around her.

"Mama," Qwarsan said calmly, "where is Pastor? I want to see him. I have decided to become a Christian."

Apparently noting my startled look, Qwarsan leaned on his walking stick and went on with his story.

"When Peter died, I just stood there. I didn't know what to do. I couldn't possibly bring his dead body with me on the bus—even if I had money for a ticket. To walk home with his body on my back would be fifty miles and too far. Just then a man touched me on the shoulder.

"I am a Christian and a member of the church here," he said. "It is our policy to help with the burial of strangers who die at the hospital. Your son had a Christian name. He will be given a Christian burial."

Qwarsan went on. "When the grave was dug, the priest, a nun and a few others came. They sang songs and the priest said a prayer. Then they gave me the money for my bus trip home."

Qwarsan's stern features had softened. A hint of a smile tugged at his lips.

"Mama, I want to see Pastor. Will I find him at home?"

I nodded.

Qwarsan laid his walking stick and bundle at his wife's feet and continued his trek toward the house alone.

Maria looked at me through her tears.

Her brown eyes reflected sharp grief over the loss of her son—yet mingled there were seeds of joy that another, still held in her heart, had been reborn.

AN AFRICAN NIGHT'S ADVENTURE

The wipers flick-flacked the last few drops of rain from the windshield. The late afternoon sun, struggling for a final look at her world through slate-grey clouds, slanted orange rays into the rivulets of water running down the road. I tried to avoid the deep ruts in the middle and the drainage ditches on the sides of the ribbon of mud that lay before the Jeep.

The Barabaig man sitting behind me clutched a spear in one hand. With the other he tapped my shoulder.

"Here," he said. "Turn here."

I looked for a road. There was none. There wasn't a cow trail or even a native footpath. As far as I could see there was only a wall of forest, wet and dripping.

I had left our mission station an hour earlier in the company of this man and Danieli, who was frequently my translator and guide. The Barabaig man had told me that his wife was desperately ill. Would I bring her to our dispensary for help?

So for an hour we had been slipping and sliding over the muddy road, grateful at least for the track. Now he asked me to leave it for the forest with no path.

"I'll lead the way," he offered helpfully. He sprang out of the Jeep. His carriage was that of the typically tall, muscular Barabaig man. He wrapped his brown-fringed cloth about him, flinging one end over his shoulder, toga-fashioned. He seized his spear and walking stick.

"Come," he said. "It isn't far."

It is never far. Experience had taught me that my conception of measuring a long distance and that of the Barabaig were usually totally different.

"What shall I do?" I asked Danieli.

He shrugged. "I suppose we had better follow him. If his wife is as sick as he says she is, she won't be able to walk."

I humped the Jeep over the ruts and through a wider place in the drainage system. Our friend was disappearing into the forest. I tried to follow as best I could, weaving about through the trees. Eventually we came to a narrow path. For a time the driving was easier as we played follow the leader through the African forest. But dusk was deepening fast. It would soon be night.

I snapped on the headlights. The myriad of dark tree trunks stood like shining black sentinels in the circle of light. The branches reached out tentacle arms as we swept past them. I stopped the car. I had lost the path.

"I can't drive farther." I said to Danieli. "We could get hopelessly lost in these woods. I'm not sure we aren't already."

I turned off the headlights. Danieli and I got out of the car. We stood for a moment trying to adjust our eyes to the unaccustomed darkness.

The night was full of an undercurrent of noises. Cicada hummed. Frogs croaked from their damp domain in the undergrowth. Bush babies gave an occasional wild shriek from the trees. I looked up. A few stars peeked through the clouds. The rain had stopped. Our guide had disappeared. We were alone in the forest. I had no idea where we were.

Danieli halooed several times. Finally a voice called from a long way away.

"What did he say?" I asked Danieli.

"He said we should go to our right and we'll find the path. Just keep on that, and he'll meet us later."

I marveled at the instinct of this man who could know from the sound of our voices on which side of the path we were lost and give us instructions to find it again. True to his direction we found the path.

Danieli carried only a walking stick. He had left his spear behind. As we walked along with only a frail flashlight beam to show the way, he said, "*Tutakosa simba wapi hapa?*" (How can we miss running into a lion here?)

I stopped. "Is this lion country here?"

"Very much so," he assured me.

I peered into the dark forest around me. My small flashlight and Danieli's walking stick seemed small protection against a roving lion.

"Perhaps we had better go back to the car," I suggested.

"No, let's go on. God is watching over us," he said. I gave silent tribute to his faith as we continued our single-file march.

We came around a bend in the path. A large bush fringed the trail. I froze as a sudden fierce growl erupted from the bush.

"What was that?" I whispered.

"Leopard," he said briefly.

Once again I asked inanely, "What shall we do?"

"We'll go on," he said. "God will take care of us."

Although less confident than he, I started. We gingerly skirted the bush, giving it wide berth. All was silent.

A few yards farther on we came to a gully. It's sides were steep and rocky. The narrow bed at the bottom was less than six feet wide. Overhead bush branches and vines were entwined.

"A perfect leopard's lair," I thought.

We scrambled up the other steep embankment. There we met our Barabaig friend and his wife. She was obviously acutely ill. She was burning with fever and so weak she could scarcely stand.

"Once we get back through this gully we'll have to carry her," I told Danieli.

We returned down and then up the steep banks as quickly as we could with our ill patient. Snatching at vines, we pushed and pulled her to level ground above the chasm.

As I straightened up, I heard a strange thundering sound. I turned around to see a wall of water crashing down the dry canyon through which we had just walked. Of course the accumulated rain at the top of the escarpment would do that, I told myself. I watched in fascinated horror as the water thundered, splashed, and swirled.

I glanced at Danieli, but he had already turned his back on it. He was busily helping to prepare a litter on which to carry the sick lady. Once more I looked at the treacherous water that covered the dry bed where we had stood moments before. A minute later and we would have been trapped.

"God is watching over us indeed," I thought.

Then I turned to join the others.

Louise Faust *was born August 9, 1923. She was a graduate of Rock Island High School in 1941 and the Lutheran Hospital School for Nurses in 1947. She married Harold Faust on October 18, 1947.*

After his ordination in 1948, Harold and Louise traveled to Tanganyika, East Africa to begin 26 years of missionary service for the Board of World Missions of the Augustana Lutheran Church in America. Eighteen of those years were spent working with the Barabaig, a tribe hitherto untouched by evangelistic outreach.

The Balangida Lutheran Mission station was opened in 1957. Louise served as a volunteer nurse in the dispensary that eventually grew to have 30 in-patient beds.

Five children were born to the Faust union: Mark, Ann, Linda, Stephen, and David.

The Fausts returned to the United States in 1975. Harold served 11 years in ministry at Our Saviour's Lutheran Church in Iron Mountain, MI. Louise continued working as a registered nurse at the local hospital until their retirement in 1987.

CUSTOMS IN CONFLICT

Doris Rolander

World War II was not over in 1944 when my newly ordained pastor husband, Oscar Rolander (Occie), and I set out for Tanganyika Territory, East Africa. We spent almost six months traveling from Philadelphia to Dar es Salaam. It took two weeks on a small Portuguese ship to cross the Atlantic Ocean. Two and a half months elapsed as we waited in Lisbon for passage to Beira, Portuguese East Africa, a voyage of six weeks. After a month in Beira, passage was secured to Mombasa, Kenya, and then we waited for another ship back to Dar es Salaam.

Having missed the weekly train to Singida, we had a chance to see Dar es Salaam. The beautiful crescent-shaped harbor was dominated by the spires of the Lutheran and Catholic churches. Between the churches were little shops dealing in spices, exotic fruits, fabrics, artifacts and furnishings. We were dazzled by the diverse population of Africans and Indians, Arabs and Somalis. Africa seemed like a very long way from Everett, Washington.

Study of the Swahili language for us took place at Iambi Mission Station situated among the Lyamba people. Occie and I occupied one of the large houses on the station. One of the first nights at Iambi I was alone in the house since Occie was at a meeting with Marty Olson, the resident missionary. At midnight I was awakened by the tolling of church bells, somehow a truly disturbing sound. I had to wait until breakfast time to learn why the bells had tolled so mournfully and so long. Two Lyamba women had been murdered by young men from the neighboring Barabaig tribe. A wrist had been removed from each victim to serve as a trophy, a custom to prove the manhood of the perpetrators.

Some weeks later the High Court of Dar es Salaam sent a judge to Iambi to try the case. The large screened porch of our house was used for a court room. The judge was formally garbed in traditional British robes which included a full white wig. Since the tribal leaders would not cooperate in disclosing the identity of the assassins, the whole tribe was penalized. They were ordered to provide a number of cattle to the Lyamba people.

Some weeks later it was early in the morning when we heard the beating of drums. We were told this was a death dance, a tribal way of mourning the passing of a member of the clan. By following the sounds we came at last to a circle of huts enclosed by a high hedge. Inside this area we could see the fresh mound of earth where a body had been buried. Here some men were beating drums and others blowing horns, hollow bamboo poles six or more feet in length, from which they produced loud beeps. As they blew their horns they danced and swung their horns menacingly. Most of the persons appeared to be in a trance from the hypnotic effect of the music and no doubt the drinking of a considerable amount of their homemade beer. The dancers were hard at work shimmying and occasionally leaping up into the air. We marveled at the control with which they constantly moved the muscles of their backs up and down. Loud wailing contributed by the women added to the confusion within the courtyard.

After language study at Iambi we were sent to Singida to expand the work among the Turu people that had been begun by Lud Melander. Lud was a much loved older pastor who uniquely blended fun with piety, delighting and instructing his audiences of young and old with violin playing and Bible verse quoting. In his later years he married a fellow missionary, Esther Olson. She with her accordion and he with his violin made quite a team.

Our mode of transportation, which had been a BSA motorcycle, was greatly improved when we acquired an ex-military one-ton Ford pickup. Soon we were able to set up a tent at Ihanja, some twenty miles from Singida, for some longer visits. During this time we made arrangements to get a Right of Occupancy permit from the government to establish a mission station in that area. Once that permission was granted, we built a little sun-dried mud brick, thatched-roof, three-room house with an open porch, outdoor kitchen and outdoor latrine. We had monthly meetings with the bush school teachers and evangelists. Occie instructed the evangelists while I met with the teachers. When checking the attendance records from the bush schools, I was always saddened to note the number of times I saw the notation "*amekufa*" (he has died).

Lyamba Christian men and their families were recruited to establish bush school/chapels at various places in Turuland. At each site mud and wattle buildings with flat mud roofs were erected to serve as chapel and school room. For seating, poles were supported on forked sticks providing seats six inches high. On occasion a teacher reported "A goat has chewed up our blackboard!" In later years proper school buildings were erected, using sun dried bricks. The teachers and evangelists walked many miles every month to Ihanja to get instructions and supplies.

For the big church festivals, teachers walked with all their people to Ihanja. Here we were fortunate to have a large baobab tree under which we set up a temporary altar and placed our portable pump organ. Children from each of the dozen or so bush schools took turns singing a song or two that they had learned. We made a game out of trying to identify which carol or hymn they were singing. Often part of the melodies got lost from the time the teacher learned the song until they taught it to their pupils. After some hours of greetings, worship, sermons and lots of singing, it was time for a feast. A cow or two was butchered and "barbecued" to feed the hungry crowd. Brown sugar, which came in an unrefined solid chunk, was hacked into small pieces and distributed to the children as a special treat.

Although hardly qualified in any medical sense, we found ourselves practicing first aid, applying sulfa salve on open, running sores and giving quinine to those with malaria. We encouraged the building of latrines. In order to get more vitamin C into their diet, we distributed seeds for tomatoes and string beans.

While at Ihanja I had one of my painful learning experiences. Some Turu women were still bare-breasted and wearing cow hide skirts. Babies were carried on the mother's back in a goat skin pouch. If a wife was having a problem becoming pregnant, it was the custom for her to carry a fertility doll on her back as if it were a baby. This was a gourd decorated with beads.

The Turu women with whom I was visiting spoke no Swahili and I didn't speak Turu. The women were admiring a doll that one woman was displaying. I took it into my hands to admire it. When I tried to return it to the owner, she refused to accept it.

A lot of unpleasant talk took place so I sought a teacher who could translate for me. I learned that the woman with the doll thought I had put a curse on her, so I needed to make some kind of reparation such as giving her my sun helmet or my glasses to cancel the curse. I felt that I could not give in to her demand since it would indicate that I had indeed put a curse on her. I have always felt uneasy about that decision and wished that I had had a better understanding of their traditions.

Ihanja was the place where we had our first baptism of Turu people. At the time of the baptism one of the women stood up and said, "We have something we wish to tell you. No longer can we follow some of our old customs." The silence was deafening as the women proceeded to disclose details about their practice of female circumcision, clitoridectomy. The Turus were a matriarchal tribe which meant the women were direct and aggressive, quite in contrast to the Lyamba women who were more shy and reluctant to speak out. The Holy Spirit had led the women to feel the need to renounce openly the practice of female circumcision. To do this they revealed what these practices had been.

Among other things young girls were taught that a lion would attack them if they failed to observe the teachings of their elders. The women showed us that by stretching a wet chamois over a clay pot and then twirling a stick on the taut surface they could mimic a lion's roar. They talked about cutting off the clitoris, keeping the girls in a dark hut for healing and weeks of instruction. All this took place when the girls were about twelve years of age. When they taught the girls about their bodies they used a couple of beans to symbolize the ovaries; some fine chain, the fallopian tubes; and an egg, the uterus. The men were truly amazed hearing these things, since the women had always kept these matters secret.

As a consequence of this revealing of tribal secrets, the women were brought before the local Turu chief, Misanga, and declared guilty of disloyalty to the tribe. Their punishment was to bring cows to the chief, the cows to be slaughtered for a feast for the people. The hides were to be cut into little pieces to be distributed to everyone to acknowledge the women's admission of their guilt.

When the women refused to bring cows to the chief they were sentenced to jail in Singida. Meanwhile their families were being persecuted by people who damaged their homes by lifting up and shaking the poles that held up the flat mud roofs. Others came into their courtyards and dug shallow graves, thus putting a curse on them. Life was truly difficult for these early Christians.

When the women were brought to the court of the local British District Commissioner in Singida, we learned to our dismay that he took the side of the Turu Chief. The women again refused to accept their punishment so they were sent by train to Dodoma to be tried by the Provincial Commissioner. Since the train went only once a week, and Occie had not been informed of their departure, it was necessary for him to ride his motorcycle to Dodoma, over 100 miles away, so he could be with the women for their trial. Fortunately in this court, wiser heads prevailed, the sentence was lifted and religious liberty guaranteed.

News was coming to Singida that there were "lion killings" in outlying Turu areas. At times we saw men coming to the government headquarters bringing corpses wrapped in cow hides suspended from poles. The coroner at the government office could see that the victims had been attacked with metal claws, not lion claws. Yet, witnesses swore that they had actually heard and seen lions. The people were terrified. For three shillings, the price of a hoe, someone whom an adversary wanted out of the way could be murdered. A government anthropologist was sent to Singida to study the phenomenon of lion killings. This would help the local officials deal with this difficult situation.

It was daybreak when I heard a *"hodi"* (a call) at our door. I recognized the voice of our teacher, Elisha Kilupi. "Mama, can you come and help my wife, Uswili? She delivered her fifth and sixth babies alone, but now she is in trouble. Please, come now!"

I had never delivered a baby nor had even given birth myself, but I couldn't refuse a request to help. I set off through the millet fields single file behind Elisha. As we reached his hut, he disappeared and I joined the women who were with Uswili. Having just come into the dark hut from the blinding African sun I could see nothing.

After a moment or two, a woman nudged me and gently said, "Mama, you are standing in the coals of the fire." My heavy shoes had prevented my being aware of the situation!

Having located Uswili in the darkness, I did the only thing I knew how to do: I prayed fervently. Soon there was great excitement and I was handed the baby. Someone cut the umbilical cord. We tore some strips off my cotton slip to do the tying. I got credit for delivering the baby and always felt a special relationship to little Solomon.

Singida was located at the end of a railroad spur north from the town of Manyoni so we often had a number of guests. Saturday mornings a house-helper would climb up the large rocks near our house to watch for the arrival of the weekly train so we could have breakfast ready for the arrivals. One morning he came to the house very excited and declared, "The train has come, but it is just the head. I don't know where the body or tail are." Because the train had been running out of firewood and water, the engine had come in without the cars. After some delay securing wood and water, the engine was off to bring in the cars with loads and passengers.

To say that we were missionaries to the Turu is true, but the real missionaries were the Lyamba teachers and evangelists and their wives. They had to overcome the language barrier. They had to adapt to different customs. It was especially difficult for the women since the Lyamba did not practice female circumcision, nor was their tribe matriarchal as were the Turu.

However, when we saw the Lyamba and Turu people coming to the Communion Table together, it was a dramatic indication of reconciliation and acceptance of their differences. God had indeed worked a miracle!

This miracle was made personal for us at the farewell we experienced at the small Ihanja bush school. At the farewell service in the chapel/school one of the Turu women stood up, adjusted the baby on her back and began to speak.

"We have always known that God created the world and us, but we thought God had forgotten about us. We put offerings on the graves of our ancestors hoping they would intercede for us. We are so thankful that you came to tell us that God loved us so much he sent His Son Jesus to show us the way. Now we know that God has not forgotten us and that He does love us. Thank you for coming and thank you to the people so far away who sent you here."

This testimony alone gave value to every day we had spent with the Turu people!

Doris Rolander *lived her early years in Everett, WA. She holds a B.S. degree in Home Economics and a Smith-Hughes Teaching Certificate from the University of Washington, Seattle, WA. She taught Home Economics for some years.*

Doris married Oscar Rolander, who was ordained and commissioned in June 1944 by the Augustana Lutheran Church to serve in Tanga-nyika Territory among the Turu people, 1944-1949. He also taught at Kinampanda Teachers' Training Center, 1950-1953.

Doris and Occie have three children: Thomas Alan, born at Kiomboi Hospital, 1948; John Stanley, born in St. Peter, MN, 1950; and Ruth Elizabeth, born in Princess Elizabeth Hospital in Nairobi, Kenya in 1951. Health problems prevented Doris and Occie from returning to Africa.

MKALAMA: PLANS FOR HOPE

Greta Ekstrand Mathewson

It had been a bleak community without hope, only a place to die. That was the reputation of Mkalama Leprosarium until the Augustana Lutheran Mission took over its management. People afflicted with Hansen's Disease had tried to eke out a living on that rocky hillside, and sought the comfort obtained from living with others having the same isolating disease.

Being a new recruit from Canada and having language study completed, I was assigned to the Mkalama Leprosarium as a nurse. My home, however, would be at Isanzu Mission Station, eight tortuous miles from Mkalama. To save time, energy and fuel traveling that distance twice a day, I would stay alone in a small one-room rest house from Monday to Friday, returning to Isanzu only for the weekend.

My first Sunday, Edythe Kjellin, part-time nurse at Mkalama, walked with me to the church. The words that rang in my heart as we saw patients come from all directions was *"I was glad when they said unto me, 'Let us go into the house of the Lord.'"* (Psalm 122:1)

Eileen Fossel, my predecessor, drove the pickup truck to the hospital so that the blind and crippled could crawl into the back and get a ride to the church. Others were led along the way, with a stick to help if they were blind. Some had only stubs remaining on their hands; most of their fingers had been absorbed due to neglected injuries. The feet of many were wrapped in bandages because of ulcers.

The children from the school played their fifes and drums while they entered the church. Nalingigwa Mpya, the evangelist, led the service of singing and short talks. His face beamed with joy though his hands and feet were crippled.

From the back of the church came Mama Marta, physically blind, but a shining light to the others. She hobbled down the aisle with the aid of a stick.

"Where is the new nurse?" she asked. And soon she stood before me speaking in the Lyamba language using John 3:16, and then leading in prayer.

Again the children sang while the people came and gave me 149 eggs, a chicken and a lamb. They had sacrificed in order to give. What a humbling experience! I was truly overwhelmed.

My mentor and teacher for my orientation was Edythe, whom I later called "Edy." Not only was she an excellent nurse and teacher, but she became a wonderful friend who was multi-talented. Among her several hobbies were photography, astronomy and growing roses. At Isanzu she would gaze at the stars at night and name many of them. Her photographs were masterpieces.

At Mkalama, Edy instructed patients to become capable laboratory technicians. She held prenatal classes, well-child clinics and hand therapy sessions. Edy was a certified midwife, and had many babies named after her.

Edy loved special occasions and always made them memorable for us. At Christmas a thorn tree was garlanded to make a lovely Christmas tree. Flowers always decorated our table. Devotional times were special as we read God's Word together and prayed with our co-workers at Mkalama and Isanzu.

Because of the stigma attached to it, leprosy separates from families and friends, even though it is not highly contagious. The two major types of leprosy, the lepromatous and the tuberculoid, share characteristics of diminished sensation in hands and feet, copper-colored skin lesions and loss of eyebrows.

Several drugs have been developed for treatment. A combination of certain drugs, also highly effective for treating tuberculosis, may actually cure leprosy if diagnosed and treated early. To take these drugs with the regularity required, leprosy patients need to remain at the place of treatment for an extended time. Side effects need to be monitored. Deformity can be prevented by using measures such as the wearing of sandals to prevent injury of feet that have become insensitive to pain. Patients with insensitive hands can use hotpads to prevent burns when handling hot earthen pots.

During the time I was at Mkalama, there was one full-time nurse and one part-time nurse to care for 450 patients. There were 30 hospital beds and an out-patient clinic for 75 tuberculoid cases. The doctor in charge came twice a month to examine patients and to re-evaluate treatment. Bone surgery, nerve stripping, enucleations (eye removal), and amputations were also performed during the doctor's visits. No patient was discharged until his condition had been inactive for at least two years.

The need for better facilities became increasingly evident. We needed better food and water sources, and physicians living on-site for closer patient supervision. We needed expanded opportunities for physical therapy and occupational therapy.

We had a vision of new arts and crafts for those patients who were able and interested. There would be sandal-making from tires, instruction in growing better crops and caring for animals. Patients could learn to sew, knit, make baskets and pottery. Developing skills in sisal rope-making, tin-smithing, and basic carpentry would help to increase the patients' feeling of self-worth and assist them to find financial independence.

The American Leprosy Inc. of New York had supported the work at Mkalama and now, together with the help of BELRA (British Empire Leprosy Rehabilitation Association), it was interested in building a new leprosarium. A leprosy specialist was sent to Mkalama and affirmed that it was no longer adequate.

To certify the real need in the area, Dr. Stanley Moris said, "Greta, we need to know specifics! We have to go to Mgori and inspect 2 000 people there. I requested the *Mtemi* (sub-chief) there to call in his people for examination."

But, instead of 2 000, we were faced with 15 000 people who came to be examined. Medical guidelines from BELRA state that 1 000-1 500 examinations are possible in one day. How were we to deal with 5 000 each day for three days?

Dr. Moris requested that I examine the women. We knew that direct sunlight is preferable for leprosy examination and we soon discovered that the examining rooms were too dark. But I had brought two bolts of white cloth with me, so we wrapped them around trees to make two enclosures. At 9:00 a.m., we began examining the great lineup of people, each with an identification card prepared by eight busily-writing clerks.

Even so, women crawled in under the cloth instead of waiting their turn, resulting in a packed enclosure with no room for examining. I requested, "*Mtemi*, please have the women leave the enclosure."

So we started over. The examination consisted of searching for signs of leprosy on the whole body, and feeling ulnar nerves to determine if there was any enlargement. The second day was much better organized and we finished by 4:00 p.m. We had closely examined 5 000 people, with the survey results revealing about four percent of the area's population diagnosed with leprosy.

Our vision for a new leprosarium became a reality after my departure. No longer did Marta and others need to stumble on the jagged rocks and break open their ulcers. Water was plentiful so they could improve their personal hygiene. Many craft and literacy classes helped to enhance the dignity and self-esteem of the patients. God had heard our prayers and opened the way. God's promise through Jeremiah had been experienced again: *"For surely I know the plans I have for you, plans for your welfare...to give you a future with hope."* Jer. 29:11

Throughout my stay in Mkalama, the prayers of family and friends back home in Canada, as well as the prayer partners in many church congregations, sustained, guided and strengthened me, and, I trust, helped others to see God's love. Equally, the prayers, support and friendship of African and American fellow-workers buoyed me. In my heart I can still see Mkalama and all its people.

Greta Ekstrand Mathewson *was born in Calgary, Alberta, Canada. After highschool, she attended a business college and then the School of Nursing at Calgary General Hospital. She was a student at Lutheran Bible Institute in Minneapolis, MN, 1952 to 1953, while serving also as school nurse and assistant matron.*

Greta served on the Augustana Lutheran Mission Field in Tanganyika, from 1953 to 1957. She met and married Bill Mathewson, an agriculturist, and lived in various parts of Tanzania until 1965. They now reside in North River, Nova Scotia, Canada.

EXPERIENCING GOD'S GUIDANCE AND LOVE

Dorothy E. Hanson Lofgren

AND I ASKED GOD, "WHY?"

Have you ever questioned God's goodness? I remember so clearly Dr. Merle Sjogren coming into my room at Kiomboi Hospital and sitting down by my bed, just after David was born.

"Dottie," he said softly, "your little baby was born without a right foot."

I had held David, even before the cord was cut, and I hadn't noticed! I cried! I felt very much alone, since it was early Sunday morning, and my husband, Melvin, was preaching at Ruruma, and didn't even know he had a son. And I asked God, *"Why?"*

And God answered immediately by bringing into my mind the verses from John 9, *"Rabbi, who sinned, this man or his parents, that he was born blind?"*

Jesus words came as the answer to all my questioning. *"Neither this man nor his parents sinned; he was born blind so that God's works might be revealed in him."*

A messenger had been sent on foot the eight miles to our Ruruma station and Mel was told, "You have a son! But please see the doctor before you go in to see Dottie."

By the time Mel arrived, it was okay. God had answered and I believed. I can't deny that a "dart" has pierced my heart, when I have seen that little stump sticking out from beneath his sheet, or watched David *hop* down to the Indian Ocean, while his friends *ran* down and plunged in.

But God has kept his promise. David has skied, played tennis, basketball and soccer. He climbed Mt. Kilimanjaro. Today he has a lovely wife and four precious children. He is a doctor, certified in Family Practice, and he loves the Lord. Can't you picture him with a patient faced with an amputation, or parents being told of a birth defect, as he pulls off his prosthesis and tells how good God has been to him?

When your time of questioning comes, trust God. He'll be there to see you through.

CLOSED FOR THE DAY

One of the things I did in Africa, for which I was totally unprepared, was to become a "supplier of meat" for a number of missionary homes. It just happened that we knew of an African in the Ruruma area who would buy cows, butcher them, and sell us meat.

Twice a week, Yosiah came to the house with beef—the two back legs, two front legs, steaks from along the spine, and meat to grind from the neck. The rest of the meat was sold to people of the village. Without our orders, he could not have disposed of a whole cow, since our villagers had very little cash, and seldom ate meat. Usually greens, peanuts, or beans accompanied the millet porridge which was their staple diet.

"Runners" from five stations arrived on foot with meat orders from the missionaries at those stations. Two of them, who came from stations that were a long day's walk away, arrived the evening before. I would sit by a table outside, with the orders and a kitchen scale, and as I read out each order, my African helper would cut the roasts, meat for grinding, meat for steaks, and soup-bones that were requested. We would weigh out the proper amount, keeping track of what each missionary received. I then paid Yosiah for his meat, and billed each missionary home.

But in early August, 1952, I was not in my "meat-shop." The announcement that went out to all the missionaries was a picture of an African meat-shop with meat hanging on hooks in the window. "Closed for the day" read the sign on the outside of the shop. David had been born that day. Having my baby had taken precedence over my meat-shop.

COIN HELD BETWEEN THE PALMS OF HIS HANDS

We hadn't been at Ruruma very long when I accompanied Melvin to the small Mkeu Leper Colony which was part of our parish. Melvin was conducting services that Sunday. He and I were the only *well* adults at that service.

In our African churches, rather than passing a collection plate, people walked to the front of the church and placed their offerings on the altar. Often, the offerings consisted of "in kind," rather than of money. After church, the eggs, chickens, grain, vegetables or fruit would be sold, to get money for the church's ministry. But this particular day, I watched intently as people came to the front to give their thank-offerings. I had not had much contact with people with leprosy (Hansen's disease), so as I observed the disfigured faces, I also noticed the missing fingers and toes, the sores and ulcers on their arms and legs.

As I watched, I became amazed—some, who had no fingers, came up to the altar, with coins held between the palms of their hands, and dropped them into the offering basket by spreading their hands. My heart cried out, "What have you to be thankful for?" And then, I was silenced as I remembered that they, like me, were God's children, and had been given forgiveness, salvation and eternal life just as I had. The question was, "Was *I* thankful?"

I shall never forget that first visit to a leprosy colony, and the sight of people, who had no fingers or toes, holding a coin between the palms of their hands, and dropping it on the altar, because they *were thankful!*

MOST OF THE GROUP COULDN'T READ

"Mama, won't you start a Bible Study for the women in our church?" one of the women from our Ruruma congregation asked me. "We know so little about God's Word."

How could I ignore a plea like that? In our large congregation, there might be many who would respond. But then I began to get practical. How could I teach them? Most of the women understand only Lyamba. When I'd tried to converse with them, our conversation would usually go like this: *"Wela! Welileyani? Mmm. Ee. Mmm. Songela. Kukakiona! Mulamu."* Translated, that would be: "Good morning! How are you? Well...Yes...Well. Thank you. I'll be seeing you. Good-bye." That was all I knew of their language; I spoke only Swahili. How could I teach them? Besides, most of the women could not read.

But I began to pray about this request. Then an idea came. Why not use the women who knew both languages, and could read? I could teach them first, and then they could be the leaders for small group discussions at church. But would the women come?

The women did come—again and again. Each month, I met first with a smaller group of women who could read, and we studied the life of a woman of the Bible. We looked for specific things as we went over the Scripture passages, and the women took notes.

What did we fail to understand? What did we learn today that we had not known before? What did God tell us that we should do? Did God tell us not to do something? Which verse is our favorite verse? It was a blessed time of fellowship for us.

On Wednesday, we divided the women into groups of thirty, and each leader found a place for her little group. Since the majority of women could not read, the leader introduced the woman of the Bible they were going to study. Then one verse at a time, she read them the scripture passages, pausing at each verse to let them ask questions, explain something that they had just learned; share with the others something they noticed that God was asking them to do or not to do. And at the end they shared their choice of a favorite verse.

When time was up, we all met together again, and the leaders of each group shared the things they had discovered together. Through an interpreter, I answered questions that had not been answered and summarized the lesson. It *was* possible to give these women, who could not read, the joy of engaging in Bible study together.

1100 PUPILS AND 54 TEACHERS

Eileen Nelson, a teacher at the Ruruma Girls' Middle School, ran into our house one Sunday shouting, "Dottie, we've got to do something about the Sunday School." Then she went on to explain. "I was just over to church and I found two classes, with 102 children in one class, and more than 80 in the other. An elder was standing in front of each group 'preaching.' We've got to do something!"

So we sat down to pray and to think. Starting a Sunday School wasn't quite like doing it in the U.S.A. We had children—lots of them. It wouldn't be too hard to organize them into classes. But trained teachers? Lesson books for teachers and pupils? Visual aids? Teachers' helps? Project materials for the pupils? Some way to train them? All of these were missing. It seemed we had our work pretty well cut out for us.

"It'll be easy to get teachers for our younger children," Eileen suggested. "We can use the students at the Girls' Middle School here. We can train them well, give them the chance to feel the joy of teaching right here at Ruruma, and then when they finish school and go back to their villages, they will be ready to start Sunday Schools wherever they live." We began to get excited!

"And we can meet in the Primary School," I suggested. "There are four rooms there; we can use one for each department. Our 80 pre-schoolers will make four classes for Room One; the 120 primary children could be another four classes in Room Two, and we'd still have two rooms for the older children and youth. Why not have a class in each corner?"

But where would we get teaching materials? Eileen and I realized we'd have to produce those ourselves, by putting Bible stories into language that would be appropriate for children, and then making lesson plans in Swahili to go with those stories.

Eileen agreed to work on Nursery/Beginner material, and I would concentrate on the Primary. We'd somehow have to keep a week ahead of our classes, so as to provide training for the teachers. I'd also have to prepare materials for training teachers. Were we attempting too much? But what better way to use our time and energy than to help children know Jesus!

That following Saturday, I faced our first group of eight girls, eager to know how they could help. Eileen and I each had one lesson plan ready. I demonstrated how they might tell the story, and we went over the rest of the lesson plan for that first Sunday. I could tell they would eagerly await another training session.

As we made our way over to the school the following Sunday, we wondered: "Would the children be afraid of us? Would the little ones leave their brothers or sisters?" But we had no problem in dividing the children into classes, and soon we had groups of children sitting in semi-circles on the floor, with their happy teacher telling them a story. How attentive they were!

Things changed rapidly. By the third Sunday, we had prepared handwork for over 200 children. The teachers had requested more time for Sunday School, so it was lengthened to one hour and a quarter. We began cutting out and mounting leaflet pictures to be used as visual aids.

As the number of children grew, new teachers joined the training class. Mature members of the congregation were found to teach the Intermediates and Juniors. We began making our own flannelgraph sets. As evangelists in the out-station chapels began to hear of the Sunday School work, they requested training for their teachers, so they could begin Sunday Schools, too. It wasn't long before one out-district had ten teachers with 215 children. On one Sunday two new Sunday Schools were opened in out-district settings. In just a few months, we had nine Sunday Schools in our parish.

"Eileen," I asked her one Sunday, "Do you remember the Sunday when you ran into our house and said 'We've got to do something about Sunday School?' "

"I've been thinking about that," was her reply.

"Do you realize," I continued, "that we have gone from 182 children with two teachers that first Sunday, to over 1100 children with 54 teachers in just a little over a year? I still have to pinch myself to see if I am dreaming."

"I find it hard to believe, too," Eileen replied. "These folk were really ready for this new phase of advancing the Kingdom. I can't help but believe that this was God's time for Sunday School."

Truly God had given the increase.

THREE GIRLS AT THE DOOR

"Hodi!" It was about 1:30 p.m. and I had just gotten the two boys settled for their afternoon naps, anticipating my own rest period.

But I had to respond to that *"Hodi!"* I could tell by the voice that called out that traditional greeting, that there was a child at the door. I hurried to see who it was. There stood, not one, but three little girls, their arms full of the muslin school bags.

"Teacher sent us," they said with big smiles, as they handed me a note. Recognizing the teacher's name, I knew that these girls had come a long way. They had brought their schoolbags for me to inspect, so that they could get the supplies needed for their next project.

Panties were to be the next project. We had three sizes of panties; the teacher had already measured her girls, and told me what she would need. Twenty-three had already been cut, but they needed three more. And I needed to cut eight more drawstrings, as well. So I inspected each bag, their bright dark eyes eagerly watching to see if I was pleased. I cut the additional items, then quickly jotted off a long note to their teacher, giving instruction for sewing the simple panties. It was about 3 p.m. when I sent the girls off on their six-mile walk back to school.

There were 116 girls in our ten schools who were learning to sew. Most of these girls had never held a needle in their hands before. Now after practicing hand-sewing a straight seam on small squares of cloth, they were making themselves school-bags and panties. If time still remained, they would sew baby gowns or dresses for tiny tots. Then next year, they would go on to skirts and blouses. I had met with their teachers, and explained the projects.

Now I had to keep ahead of the girls, and cut out the items that were needed for each school.

As I went wearily towards my bedroom, I realized that another school would come tomorrow, and I would need to have 30 more pairs of panties cut by then. But the girls were learning to sew!

I remember another very special *"Hodi"* at our door. Lidia and Kilie stood there with big smiles on their faces. "Mama," Lidia said, "we've finished our outfits. We wanted to come and show them to you." They were dressed in blue jumpers, flowered blouses, (made from feed-sacks which had come from America), and I knew that underneath they had panties and slips, all of which they had made for themselves in school. They looked so smart, and they were so happy!

After I had examined everything, as I knew they wanted me to do, Kilie spoke, "Mama, we want to say thank-you. Thank you for all your work in preparing all these things, so that we could learn to sew. We'll think of you every time we make something for our families." And with another big smile, the girls turned to return to their village.

WHERE IS MAMA?

Most of our water came from the Ruruma River, a couple of blocks from our home. During much of the year, it was a dry river bed. But we were always able to find water below the surface when we dug a hole. It was really nice clear water, filtered by the sand. But we always boiled any water for consumption. The Africans used water holes in the same area for their livestock and water for home use.

We hedged our water-hole with branches of thorns, so cows couldn't get in and dirty it. Water was drawn from our hole and put into five-gallon tins, and then pushed up to our house, about a block away, on a little two-wheeled cart. There it was dumped into a 55-gallon steel drum (the kind in which we had shipped all our things to Africa), and by means of a hand-pump, moved up into the two steel drums in the attic of our home.

It really made for a rather ingenious water system. Having the water stored in the attic made sufficient pressure to flush our toilet. A pipe running through the firebox of our woodstove in the kitchen gave us a steady source of warm water for bathing and dishes.

One day, about mid-afternoon, Mel, I and the boys had returned from a long safari, tired and dusty, and we found that the faucets were dry. We had hired a man to keep our water supply full, and to cut our wood for the stove, but something must have happened. We really needed water to clean up.

So Mel took the car to the river to get water, while I started supper and got the children settled down. He was on his knees beside our waterhole, scooping up the shallow, clear water at the bottom of our two-foot deep hole, and pouring it into five-gallon tins. It was a slow job! While he was getting the water, some women came to the river.

"*Mchungaji* (Pastor)," they called, "why are you getting water? Where is mama? Don't you know that it's a woman's job to draw water?"

Mel had thought the women would be pleased that he was helping me. Instead, he was rebuked! The implication was that I should have been there at the river. There was a rather fine line of division of labor in an African household. The man did not draw the water for his home; that was woman's work. But I was grateful on that warm, tiring day for a very helpful husband.

NEEMA, NEEMA, NEEMA TU !
(BY GRACE, BY GRACE, ONLY BY GRACE !)

On the morning of the 30th Anniversary celebration of the Central Synod Lutheran Church in 1956, I was gazing down towards our Ruruma River, thankful that there was no visible water in our river. I had waded through that river when we had come home from safari and found the river full of water; we had to leave our Jeep on the other bank. I had often stood amazed at the river's edge after a rain in the area, and watched as a wall of water quickly moved down our river, filling it with waist-deep water.

Today, many people would be crossing our river, and I was so glad it was dry. It was in August 1926 that the first Christians were baptized at Ruruma. And so, our entire area Tanganyika church, which numbered then about 17,000 members, had been invited to come and celebrate with us. We expected several thousand would attend the three-day meeting. We had invited the entire missionary family to come for at least one of the days.

"Mel, come quickly," I shouted. I had just spied the first group of guests. "Look, there's a bus crossing our river." I was really excited as I called my husband to the window. I had never imagined a bus could come to our Ruruma Mission Station. After all, the road wasn't much more than a cow-trail, and there was no bridge across our block-wide sand river.

We watched as people continued to stream across that river. During the day, five trucks crossed the river, bringing people from the more distant stations. But most of the guests came by foot, the women gracefully carrying their loads on their heads and babies on their backs. Finally, I saw a Jeep coming up the road from the river, and ran to welcome the first of the missionary family.

It was up to fellow missionaries, Inez Olson, Eileen and me, to host the missionaries. We had planned our menus carefully, since our nearest grocery store was 60 miles away. We started out with eleven at our supper table on Thursday evening; the climax came Sunday, when we were 65 for both dinner and supper.

Sunday was a wonderful day of celebration. A pioneer missionary to the area, Pastor Lud Melander, spoke of how the work had started there 30 years before, and shared much about the obstacles that had been overcome, and the joy in serving.

Then our chief evangelist, Yakobo Ntundu, got up to speak. I can still hear his voice echo over and over again to that mammoth crowd outdoors: *Neema! Neema! Neema, tu!* (By grace! By grace! Only by grace!) It was exciting to direct our church choir of 50 voices at that morning service.

After dinner we had a Communion service—outside again, of course. The 136 girls that I had been teaching at the Girls' Middle School had been asked to sing for this large celebration. As they sang *Haya Tumshukuruni* (Let Us Thank Him) in Swahili, I'm sure all of us were thanking God for His wonderful grace which had enabled people to believe in Jesus and to establish a church. We followed with "Lift Thine Eyes" in English, an acknowledgment that it was God who had been at work these 30 years.

Neema, Neema, Tu! Truly, it was "By grace, by grace alone" that this had come to pass.

Dorothy E. Hanson Lofgren *is married to Pastor Melvin I. Lofgren. They have four children: Dr. John P. Lofgren; Dr. David J. Lofgren; Pastor Ruth Lofgren Rosell, and Pastor Timothy M. Lofgren; they have 17 grandchildren.*

Dorothy and Mel served on the Augustana Lutheran Mission field in central Tanganyika from 1949 to 1961—at Ruruma, 1950 to 1959; at Isanzu, 1960 to 1961.

Dorothy worked with the African women, teaching sewing, cooking, child-care and housewifery as well as Bible Studies.

She also established Sunday Schools, translating materials into Swahili, and training teachers.

She taught music at Ruruma Girls' Middle School.

She served for a time as treasurer of the Mission.

From 1961 to 1976, Dorothy taught Christian Education at the Mwika Bible School on the slopes of Mt. Kilimanjaro in northern Tanzania.

The years 1977 to 1989 were spent in Southeast Asia—in Malaysia for eight years and in Singapore for four years. Here she prepared a course for training Sunday School teachers, wrote courses for Vacation Bible School, and conducted seminars for teachers. She also taught evening classes at Trinity Theological College in Singapore.

In 1989, Dorothy and her husband returned to America and now reside in Bella Vista, Arkansas.

A SAFARI OF MIRACLES
Adeline Lundquist Hult

John stopped the Jeep on the escarpment road in the Southern Highlands of Tanganyika. We walked to the edge and looked over. It was scary! At the bottom of a steep embankment, several hundred feet below, we saw the rusted wrecks of a bus and truck.

John commented, "If God hadn't sent His guardian angels to watch over us, we'd be down there."

With a trusting face and calm voice, Elly, just turned seven, replied, "Oh, well! Then we would have been up in heaven with God!"

As we returned to the Jeep, I pondered the inconsistencies of how we live our faith. We teach our children to love Jesus and trust Him, but then we show them our fear of death.

Fifteen months earlier John and I, with our three children, Margaret, Eleanor and Danny, had arrived in central Tanganyika. We'd lived at both the Wembere and the Isanzu Mission Stations for our three months of language training. In September we moved to Iambi, our first home in Africa. John was the doctor at the mission hospital. Margaret, almost eight, went to Kiomboi for boarding school; Elly, six, started home-school; and Dan, four, wore his jeans out sliding on the big rock with the bell-tower in our yard. Everyone was excited in December when baby Martha was born. We'd made many adjustments, learning how to cope in a different culture and how to work and live in this new environment.

Not only had I learned to barter at the back door for eggs, milk, and vegetables, but also to handle these purchases to feed my family safely. All our drinking water was boiled on our wood range. The milk was first run through an old-fashioned farm cream separator. Our children liked to watch the house-helpers "grind" the milk. Then the milk and cream were pasteurized on the stove. A new experience for me was to boil the butter after it was churned. This produced ghee, a clarified fat that could be stored without refrigeration. John provided our meat supply with the game he shot. What we didn't use immediately, I canned, for the freezer compartment in our kerosene refrigerator was very small.

Water was hand-pumped from a cistern into a tank in the attic, so we had running water when the cistern wasn't dry. Our gas-driven washing machine was a luxury, but it was hard to start. My helper, Danielsoni, smiled as he asked, "Mama, may I use your shoe?" Putting it on his right foot he could push harder on the starter and would persist until he heard the putt-putt of the motor.

I soon realized that a home in Africa was to be shared. Before we had even finished unpacking, we hosted the advisor for all leprosy work in the British Commonwealth and the American Leprosy Society. His family accompanied him as well! A short time later the director of our national church body's youth department and his wife were our guests. While entertaining the Provincial Commissioner of Central Tanganyika, I had no meat on hand except ground zebra which I made into a macaroni casserole. He obviously enjoyed it for he asked for two extra helpings. I never told him what he was eating!

Our home was always open for missionaries coming through who needed a place to sleep. Della Brown, a missionary teacher, lived in our attic bedroom for several weeks and was subjected to strange night noises. Her nocturnal visitors were a family of owls who had nested in the wall near her bed.

We enjoyed having our African friends visit and hold Bible studies or meetings in our home. I was honored when one of our nurses, Kristalumba, asked me to create her wedding dress.

There were sad times, also, when we lost dear friends, such as Martini who died of polio, and one of our nurses who died in childbirth. That first year was full of learning experiences.

By August, 1958, we needed a vacation. John made arrangements to visit Makete Leprosarium in southern Tanganyika to observe their system of treatment, in order to help plan the program for the new leprosarium being built near Iambi.

The logistics of a family trip were challenging. Iambi had only one vehicle. If we took it on safari, our nurse would have no transportation. Since Kiomboi station had two vehicles, it was decided we should use one of them. We appreciated this, but there was one drawback. John was not familiar with this Jeep and its particular quirks. It was a right-hand-drive truck, with a wooden frame and roof built over the bed. The sides and end were enclosed with heavy wire mesh. A seat behind the cab held two passengers.

Missionary friends loaned us their tent for our trip. I had never camped before coming to Africa, so we took a trial run to Lake Basuto some thirty miles from Iambi. We heard the hippos bellowing in the water and grazing during the night. That was a fun introduction to camping, but most important to me: I learned what items were essential and which we could do without.

For our safari we loaded the truck with one-burner primus stoves, *debes* (five-gallon kerosene tins) for boiling water and for stove shields, tent, cots, sleeping bags, blankets, safari crib, tub for boiling diapers, medicines, clothes, pots, pans, and food for two weeks. Jerry cans of extra gas and a second spare tire were also stashed on board. We figured out how we could all sit in the cab if necessary, but usually two of the children would take turns sitting in the back.

Starting off on a Saturday morning, we drove fifty miles to Singida. We filled the Jeep with gas and eagerly set forth. About twenty miles out, the generator malfunctioned. We returned to Singida where Ali Singh, our garage mechanic, installed a rebuilt generator and sent us on our way again. That night we slept at Itigi in a government rest house with rustic accommodations.

We set out early the next morning on the unpaved road to Mbeya. It was three hundred miles on a little-traveled road; we met only four vehicles all day! Much of the landscape was thick thorn-bush country with occasional clearings of small villages. As we continued south, the countryside became more mountainous and green. The hills were covered with coffee trees and tea plantations.

After filling our gas tank from the jerry cans, we worried when we didn't find a petrol station. We stopped at a Catholic Mission where they supplied us with enough to get us to our destination.

Thirty miles from Mbeya we started the ascent up the rugged terrain on the edge of the Rift Valley. At the summit, the mountains drop off sharply to the valley below. The dirt road down the escarpment was narrow, with sharp hairpin curves. The vistas were gorgeous, but we hardly dared look at them while descending the steep grade with no shoulders or protective barriers. Then, without warning, our brakes failed. John was aghast! We were picking up speed rapidly when he spotted a service road leading uphill to the right. He skillfully steered onto it and we coasted to a stop without mishap. We offered a sigh of thanksgiving.

What were we to do? Somehow we had to descend over a thousand feet to the city of Mbeya in the valley ten miles below us. John thought if he put the Jeep into the lowest tractor gear, we could creep down safely. I was fearful, but could offer no other solution. It was dusk, and the only alternative was to spend the freezing cold night in the truck high in the mountains. With darkness approaching we didn't want the children in back, so we all squeezed into the cab.

Inching along, we made some progress. Suddenly the truck slipped out of gear! John desperately tried to engage the gears without success. As we began to pick up speed, he turned sharply toward a bank on the right to stop us. It did, but he wasn't able to turn sharp enough so we hit at an angle. The right front wheel crawled up the bank. Slowly, slowly we felt ourselves rolling over onto the left side. Dan, Martha and I were on the bottom of the pile. John, on top, managed to open his door upward and climb out. Standing on the side of the car, he lifted Margaret and Elly out and helped them to the ground. Next he rescued Dan who had been seated on a *debe* in front of me. Finally, I handed Martha up to him, and then I crawled out. We had been packed in so snugly that none of us had even a bump or a scratch!

By this time it was dark. Fires were visible in a village in the valley below, but it was difficult to judge how far away it might be. John walked up the road to set two *debe*s on the curve to serve as reflectors if a car should happen along. With the pale light of a hurricane lantern we removed our tangled mass of loads from the truck. The Jeep had suffered little damage and most of our supplies were intact except for a few broken eggs. The children, who hadn't let out a scream, cry or whine, climbed with me into the back of the truck, sitting on the metal mesh side. With blankets around us we cuddled together to keep warm. John walked toward the village to get help.

A few minutes later we heard cars approaching. John, about a quarter of a mile away, also heard them and hurried back. Several men in a buffalo-hunting party were returning to Mbeya later than they had expected.

"You're lucky not to be stranded here! Usually no one comes down this road after dark, especially on a Sunday night!"

Their head lamps had shone on our *debe*s so they knew something was wrong. Without that warning they might not have been able to avert another accident. After helping us reload our gear into the truck, they crammed all six of us and some of our luggage into their two Land Rovers for the ride to Mbeya. On the way, we learned that we'd been found by the right people. One was a Sikh police officer who told John to file a report at his office in the morning. Another was the European owner of the only garage in Mbeya, who promised he'd fetch John early the next day to retrieve the Jeep. How thankful we were when they deposited us at the hotel where we had reservations.

We'd planned to spend only one night, but it took three days to fix our brakes. Living in the hotel was a treat. The children took separate baths in full tubs of water, something they never did at home with the scarcity of water at Iambi. Roaming about a city of 5000 was exciting after living in a rural area for a year.

We proceeded to the leprosarium at Makete, where we were hosted by a Danish nurse. The children fondly called her Aunty Rigmor. The British doctor's family included children of similar ages so playmates and toys made the time go quickly. Our new friends shared in Elly's birthday party. John gained valuable information about the running of a leprosarium. That weekend we drove south to Lake Nyasa to camp on the beach which was a delightful interlude.

On our return, we spent two days at a rustic fishing camp in the Livingstone Mountains. Our shelter was a thatch-roofed rondavel with a near-by primitive kitchen. John caught four beautiful trout in the Kiwira River. When he started to clean them, the African cook at the camp took the basket of fish from him. Later, he returned the fish fried just right for our lunch. They were delicious. For once John didn't have to clean his own fish, but I wasn't so lucky. Martha needed fresh diapers badly. I scrubbed dozens of them by hand and laid them out on the grass to dry.

Because our generator was malfunctioning again, we checked in at the hotel in Mbeya once more. Half an hour after our arrival, a barefoot messenger knocked on our door saying an American couple were eager to see us. Col. "Doc" and Mildred Meisch from San Antonio, Texas, on a hunting safari, had stopped in Mbeya for just one night. As they checked in, they saw our names on the register just ahead of theirs. John had visited them years before when he was in the army. They were friends of his aunt, who had kept them posted on us, but they didn't know in what part of Africa we lived. Such a delightful surprise!

This was my last opportunity for Christmas shopping so Mildred accompanied me to buy gifts for the children. She was intrigued buying Christmas toys in August, and I enjoyed her company.

The car was repaired by 3:00 p.m. Saturday so we started on the long ride back to central Tanganyika. We doubted we'd find a rest-house, but planned to camp along the road to break up that three-hundred mile drive, all rough corrugation or foot-deep sand.

Driving up the escarpment out of Mbeya, we remembered our exciting trip almost two weeks before. We checked all the curves—there was only one with an exit road in the whole thirty miles! Approaching the spot where we rolled over, we stopped to see it in the daylight. About fifty yards from the site, the road had no banks on either side! We saw the rusted vehicles far below us in the chasm and realized what a close call we had had.

At Chunya, forty miles north of Mbeya, we looked up Don and Mimi Mustard. Don had recently married Mimi Bicchieri, the daughter of an Italian mining family from Kirondatal, a few miles from Kiomboi. Always hospitable, they persuaded us to spend the night since it was already late.

We left early the next morning, driving five hours without even a proper rest stop. This was tsetse fly country. Every time we stopped the car, they swarmed about us. After hitting an especially hard bump, we heard strange noises. We were dismayed to find an engine mount had broken. We slowly drove on because there was no way to fix it at that spot. By noon we were out of tsetse country and we located a railway service area where John tied up the engine with a tow cable. His temporary tie-job held for the next two hundred and fifty miles, but we didn't dare go more than twenty miles an hour. Since we were far behind schedule, we opted to drive as far as we could.

At 11:30 p.m. we wearily pulled off on the shoulder of the road. After removing our loads, we used the truck as a shelter. We didn't bother to change clothes, just crawled into our sleeping bags as we were. The kids slept soundly, but with Martha zipped also into my narrow sleeping bag, I was not very comfortable.

After a makeshift breakfast, my family presented me with a gift, a pair of gold earrings. The date was Monday, August 25th, my birthday.

An hour later we arrived at Lud and Esther Melanders' mission station. We were dirty, wearing the same clothes we had donned Saturday morning, with Mom wearing fancy earrings! In their bathroom, a *debe* of murky brown water for flushing stood near the stool. A note above it read: "Please help us save water. We are sorry it is dirty. The elephants arrived at the watering hole before we did!"

After scrubbing ourselves and putting on clean clothes, we felt 100% better. Esther served us delicious coffee and goodies before we continued on our way. Stopping at the roadside for the last meal of our safari, we made sandwiches from whatever food we had left.

But something was definitely in the air. The children could hardly contain themselves. Because the wind was blowing hard, they led me around to an open door on the leeward side of the Jeep. On the front seat was a birthday cake with lighted candles! John had bought a tinned fruit cake into which the children had inserted candles in flower holders. I can't remember any cake that meant more to me. Thus ended an eventful safari!

Do you believe in miracles?
Our brakes gave out on the only curve where there was a side road.
We lost control of the car where there was a bank on one side.
Rescue cars arrived when they should have passed long before.
We knew without a doubt that the Lord kept us safe on that safari!

Adeline Lundquist Hult *was a missionary teacher in British North Borneo (now Sabah, Malaysia) for four years before marrying John Hult in 1956. They served in Tanganyika one term from May, 1957 to December, 1960. John was a doctor at Iambi Hospital where they lived the first year. They moved to Kiomboi in October, 1958.*

After returning from Africa, they lived in Aurora, CO, for twenty-nine years. Adeline did volunteer work while John served as a physician for the Denver Neighborhood Health Program, working among those who could not afford regular health care.

The Hults have five children: Margaret Ruud, of Port Angeles, WA; Eleanor Scott, Girdwood, AK; Daniel Hult (deceased); Martha Norman, Corvallis, OR; and Timothy Hult, Denver, CO.

After retirement they moved to Corvallis, OR, which is nearer the geographical center of their ten grandchildren.

WHAT HAPPENS WHEN GUIDES GET LOST?

Lois Bernhardson

"Is there anybody here who could help us?"

It was early afternoon at the Iambi Leprosarium. Looking up from my desk in the nurses' office, I saw two Barabaig men carrying spears, brown blankets knotted over their left shoulders. "My wife has been in labor for two days," the spokesman explained. "Our midwives have not been able to help her. Could you come to our home and help her before it's too late?" There was concern in his voice.

Dr. Stan Moris, the doctor in charge, appeared at the door. Hearing the conversation, he asked, "Where is your home? How can we get there?"

"*Si mbali*" (not far). The men pointed eastward and responded in chorus.

Dr. Stan and I quickly assembled the needed equipment and set off in the hospital's four-wheel drive Land Rover with the two Barabaig men as our guides. This was cross country driving — the area had no roads; the Barabaig needed none. They were, after all, headed home, and knew the landmarks of home as seen from any direction. They would spot a rock formation and shout, "Go left!" Or, seeing an animal track, "Turn right!" Trusting our navigators who had roamed the area all their lives, Dr. Stan obediently followed their directions.

Sure enough, after about two hours we came upon a clearing with a few low earthen homes surrounded by a fence of thorn branches to protect cattle from marauding predators. The grandmother met us at the door with the good news: "About an hour ago a normal baby girl was born!"

Dr. Stan and I followed the grandmother into the windowless home to greet the mother and new baby. After our eyes had adjusted to the darkness — the only light was from a fire in the middle of the room — Dr. Stan examined the mother and child and found all was well. We were free to return to the leprosarium. Outside the house, family members thanked us profusely for coming. "*Asante sana!*" (Thank you very much!) With that, the father presented us with a gift: a big red rooster, legs tied together with a string.

With our same trusty guides as navigators, we started back to the leprosarium, following the same "left, right" procedure as before but the route seemed different. This did not seem strange; with no roads, there could be many routes to Iambi from Barabaigland. Conversation, however, between our guides was becoming more animated. Since we did not know their language, we could only interpret the tone of voice. Then the one who spoke a bit of Swahili called out, *"Simama, Bwana!"* (Please stop, sir!)

"Do you suppose they can't see any familiar landmarks?" Dr. Stan asked with some anxiety. It was getting late, and darkness falls quickly once the sun has set.

One of them climbed on top of the Land Rover to check out our location. He again gave directions which we followed, but after about a half-hour, another animated exchange broke out between the two men. One of them sounded quite agitated.

"It's about dark. What do we do now?" There was no answer, but I don't think I had really expected one. Now both men climbed on top of the Land Rover and looked in all directions.

When they finally got down, they said, "We aren't sure where we are. We can't see any familiar landmarks."

The sun had set; it would soon be dark and we could not continue. We knew we were out in bush country with no houses nearby, and the only living things were the wild animals: lions, wildebeest, hyenas, etc. We had no water or food—except, of course, the rooster, but decided against that. We had no choice but to stay right there in the Land Rover until it got light enough to find our way home.

I had the front seat for my "bed" for the night, with the rooster at my feet on the floor beside me. The three men were in the back of the vehicle which was like a pickup box—just a metal floor with metal sides. I doubt we slept much, but it wasn't many hours before we were abruptly awakened, not by the roar of wild animals, but by the exuberant crowing of the red rooster at my feet.

As soon as it got light, our guides climbed on top of the Land Rover once more and saw some familiar landmarks. We were only about two miles from home!

Our co-workers were very thankful to see us home safe and to hear that all was well with the mother and baby. They had entrusted all of us to God's care, knowing that with Him *"The night is as bright as the day, for darkness is as light to you."* Psalm 139:12

I don't remember seeing either of our two guides again, but we were thankful they had come to the mission, and that we were available when they needed help. Perhaps this experience paved the way for their being open to the Gospel when hearing it again.

WHAT IS MY MOST IMPORTANT POSSESSION?

"Where did I get all this stuff—and why do I save it?" From time to time I ask myself these questions! We all seem to accumulate so many things and sometimes wonder what is useful and/or needful; what will just add to our needless pile of "stuff." I considered the question: "What is my most important possession?"

One day when the doctor and I were at a dispensary, a young man came to be examined. He showed us several pale patches of skin on his left arm. "How long have you had these on your arm?" the doctor asked.

"*Sijui*" (I don't know) he replied. He did know something about leprosy, was suspicious of these patches, but had tried to cover them up. He had said nothing to anyone about them. He knew that others who had leprosy had been ostracized by their families. However, when he began to lose sensation in his fingers and toes, he became worried. He found an excuse to be close to the local dispensary the day he heard that the mission doctor was coming.

After a physical examination, the doctor said: "Yes, you have leprosy and I would advise you to come to the leprosarium for treatment."

"But where will I stay and what about my wife?" he asked.

"We have small houses where you and your family can live and you can have a small plot of ground where you can grow some maize (corn) and other things for food," replied the doctor.

"What about our son who is in school?" he questioned.

"He can come along; we have a primary school for the children right at the leprosarium."

"What about my medications?"

"You will get your leprosy medications twice a week. Also, because you have decreased feeling of pain in your fingers and toes, you will learn how to prevent deformities and complications."

The next week Yakobo, with his wife and son, came to the leprosarium and settled in one of the houses. He came faithfully for his medications and heard the Christian message in his own language twice weekly. His wife helped at home with the field work; Danieli started school. He was soon studying with the fifth graders, playing soccer and other games with the children.

Each Sunday the family attended worship services at the station chapel with the other leprosy patients and missionaries. One Sunday was a special day for the children; two of the older boys received Bibles in the Swahili language to help them prepare for confirmation classes. As I came out of the chapel that morning, I saw these two boys sitting in the shade of a small tree eagerly paging through their Bibles. "See my book — a Bible all my own!" Danieli exclaimed. The word "book" was singular — it was not only a Bible — it was the first and only book either of these boys had ever had! The Book was now their most important possession and they guarded it well.

After several months for some and years for others, the day came when the patients would be discharged from the leprosarium. This would be a *Sikukuu* (day of celebration) for everyone at the leprosarium. When Yakobo's lab test became negative, the family gathered their household goods such as rope beds and farming tools and loaded them on a lorry (truck) for their journey home. Several others who left that same day had all their possessions tied up in a *shuka* (a cloth 1½ yards long by 1 yard wide) or placed them in a reed basket. We watched them leave on their homeward journey with a basket on the head or the *shuka* tied to a stick over their shoulder.

No matter how much or how little they had when they left, they made sure that their *cheti* (discharge card) was in a safe place. This was their certificate, signed by the doctor, saying that they could return home without any fear of transmitting the disease to anyone else. It was their certificate to freedom and the start of a new life and they guarded it well!

The medications had brought healing to their bodies; it was our prayer that the Word of God, which they had heard and seen in action, would have entered their hearts. Then they would also have the *cheti* of a new life of freedom in Christ their Savior.

In spite of all the "stuff" we accumulate in our lives, our most important possession is always the assurance of our new life in Christ, which brings peace, joy, and hope each new day.

Lois Bernhardson's *early years were lived on a farm in Comstock, MN, a fact that served her well, especially during her missionary years. After high school she graduated from Bethesda Lutheran Hospital School of Nursing, Minneapolis, MN.*

Combining part-time private duty with her studies, Lois attended the Lutheran Bible Institute in Minneapolis for two years, then answered the call of the Augustana Lutheran Church to go to Tanganyika as a missionary nurse.

Her first work in Tanganyika was on the former German Mission fields in the northern area of the country. These were the so-called "orphaned" fields; with no resident doctor, the responsibility for diagnosis and treatment fell on the nurse.

In 1959 her request to work at a leprosarium was granted and in preparation for assignment to Iambi Leprosarium, she enrolled in a 12-month Medical Assistant's Laboratory Course at the University of Minnesota. At Iambi she set up a small laboratory and trained Tanzanians to do basic laboratory procedures. She also taught, supervised and served in varied nursing capacities.

Some of those capacities didn't call for a nurses' cap. For instance, sometimes things needed repair—like with a screw driver; sometimes the leprosarium farm staff needed a driver for the tractor. And of course, very often the dispensary nurse needed to drive through bush country in a four-wheel-drive vehicle to travel to her dispensaries. Lois was grateful for her farm origin.

After resigning from the Mission Board in 1965, she spent 22 years teaching in schools of nursing in the Twin Cities area. She has continued to study to increase her skills and keep up on changes in her field. She has also found joy and satisfaction in doing volunteer work at hospitals, Christian service organizations and especially at her church as a Stephen Minister.

SINGING THROUGH TEARS

Ruth Holmer Friberg

It was early afternoon. I was in the process of writing prescriptions for the outpatients at Kiomboi Hospital. They were lined up on the backless benches with their *cheti* (note) from the laboratory showing the results of the tests taken earlier in the day. The noise and bustle of the morning had passed and all was quiet and orderly. To write prescriptions was not my usual assignment but Dr. J. B. Friberg was away and it had fallen to my lot, with most of it being very routine.

Suddenly feet came running from the O.B. ward. *"Bibi! Bibi! Njoo upesi, Mwelu anakufa!"* (Miss! Miss! Come quickly, Mwelu is dying!)

I dropped everything and ran down the sloped open passage that led to the delivery room. Mwelu, who had just delivered a beautiful healthy baby, was lying limp and unconscious. Her pulse was unsteady and hardly palpable. I left the assistants to rub her arm and hand and dashed to the office to get a cardiac stimulant.

After the injection, while I was kneeling by her low iron delivery bed, Mwelu rallied. She began to point to the ceiling with her right hand and her left arm and hand were groping for her husband's hand. Her husband, Petro Msengi, one of our most faithful and capable older dressers (a man trained to dress wounds and do other medical work), had slipped into the delivery room and was standing just behind me. Mwelu called out and talked excitedly in the Lyamba language which I did not understand (I was still struggling with Swahili, not having been long in Tanganyika).

This is what I was later told she was saying: "My husband, my husband, give me your hand. I see Jesus standing up there calling me.

"My husband, please give me your hand. I must go to Jesus. *Mulamu!* (goodbye!)"

As I knelt there she went limp again. After trying unsuccessfully to revive her and getting no vital signs, I put aside the stethoscope and looked up at her husband behind me.

"Petro, she's gone!" I said.

Petro stared at me for a moment or two and then startled all of us by breaking into a hymn. It was sung in Lyamba but I knew it well:

Jesus, keep me near the cross,
There a precious fountain,
Free to all, a healing stream,
Flows from Calvary's mountain.

   In the cross, in the cross,
   Be my glory ever,
   Till my raptured soul shall find
   Rest beyond the river.

Petro went on to sing the second verse and the third and fourth.

Near the cross I'll watch and wait,
Hoping, trusting ever,
Till I reach the golden strand
Just beyond the river.

His strong voice quieted and he covered his face and wept silently.

Meanwhile word had gotten out to the other hospital workers. Petro and Mwelu were first generation Christians. The brother ran over to the O.B. ward and began to shake himself, wailing the horrible death wail that can be heard for such a great distance. It was the shriek of despair of those who do not know where their loved one has gone—those who have not the knowledge of Jesus' salvation.

I looked again at Petro. He was left with a tiny baby as well as other children and his burden of grief. But he could sing, knowing where his beloved Mwelu had gone; she was with Jesus, her Lord and Saviour.

Never before had I been given such an example of the difference that Christ makes in the lives of people: certain hope versus blind despair.

Since that time I have often seen that peace and hope gleam at funerals, wakes and services where Christians gather, albeit with tears in their eyes. They sing to the Lord at the most difficult time of their lives—facing the tragedy of death and yet knowing the comfort of Jesus. Their loved ones are home with the Lord, no longer troubled by the pains of this world. With Petro I still sing "Jesus, keep me near the cross."

CAUSE FOR THANKSGIVNG

"Habari, Mwalimu Teofilo?" (What's the news, Teacher Teofilo?), I greeted my patient. "How are you?"

"Oh, Mama! I hurt all over. I am so weak and so tired!"

Truly, *Mwalimu* Teofilo was the picture of misery. Every movement was painful. He was emaciated, only a shadow of the man we knew as a very fine teacher at the Teacher Training School at Kinampanda, second to Mr. Clague-Smith, the headmaster. He had been brought over to Kiomboi Hospital a very sick man. As I remember it, he had blackwater fever which is so often fatal.

We had set up a small private room at the end of the mens' ward which bordered on the courtyard inside the hospital. He had been with us for several days but his emaciated body looked as if he had come from a concentration camp. He had become my special project. I gave him his baths in bed and rubbed his back and oiled his body to prevent bed sores and relax his muscles. I also supplied his food, as the hospital didn't provide food. His dear old father, Hiyob, was with him much of the time.

"Oh, Bibi (Miss), I just want to die!" he complained.

"Teofilo," came a sharp reprimand from his father. "Teofilo, you mustn't complain. That's a sin and you must be thankful for all the Lord has done for you."

I smiled at these two Moravian Christians. But there was a deep concern for Teofilo. Once again I was without the doctor on the station. I was a very green, inexperienced nurse. I had seen little of death in my nursing career, but to my eyes Teofilo looked like a dying man.

"I'll be going now," I told them. "I'll send down your supper and then come down to see how you are." I saw to it that he had water to drink and that the dresser on duty would hear him if he called.

The bicycle seemed unusually heavy as I pedaled up the hill to the nurses' house. I felt, to put it mildly, way down. As I walked into the living room I looked up to the heaven hidden by the ceiling, clenched my hands together and cried out in desperation.

"Lord," I prayed, "You can't let Teofilo die while the doctor is away. He's needed at Kinampanda. You can't let him die."

How good God is. *Mwalimu* Teofilo Kisanji did live to return to his teaching and later went on to theological school, becoming bishop of the Moravian Church of Tanganyika. I have a picture of him taken on the steps of Augustana School (for missionary children) sitting between Esther Feuter, a Moravian missionary kid, and my daughter Margaret on one of his visits to the Lyamba district.

Ten or more years had passed since his illness and my emotional crisis. He lived to serve his country, his church, and his Lord for many years. We later met several times, always as dear friends with the memory of a battle won in the Lord's name.

Ruth Holmer Friberg *was born in India to missionary parents and attended boarding school through sixth grade. Her aim from childhood was to return to India as a nurse "to care for babies." As her parents were unable to return to India, she attended high school and two years of college in DuBois, PA.*

She graduated from the Johns Hopkins School of Nursing and became an RN in 1942. In 1943, while serving as college nurse, she completed the requirements for a B.S. at Augustana College, Rock Island, IL.

Commissioned as a missionary nurse by the Augustana Lutheran Church in 1944, Ruth was requested to go to Tanganyika instead of India because of the severe personnel shortages, a side-effect of World War II. German missionaries were interned by the British administration.

Travel was also complicated by the war. It took five to six months for her and her nine travel companions to reach the field.

Ruth served at Kiomboi Hospital for two years, then married Daniel Friberg, fellow missionary and first principal of the theological seminary of the Lutheran Church in East Africa. Ruth continued to serve in a medical capacity wherever the family was stationed.

The Fribergs raised six children: Joseph, Margaret, Mary, David (Pete), Steven and John, all of whom now serve in various capacities in the church at large. Ruth and Dan make their home in Minneapolis, MN. She enjoys gardening, bird-watching, stargazing, stamps, reading, piano, entertaining and traveling.

FROM BURDEN TO BLESSINGS—
FROM PROBLEMS TO PEACE
Effie Youngblom

We had waited for six weeks in New York City for a neutral nation's ship that would take us across the Atlantic. It was still wartime. Finally, passage was found on the Portuguese freighter, Tarpon, leaving from Philadelphia in mid-September 1944. My newly- ordained pastor husband, Howard, and I were eager and enthusiastic in spite of the wartime atmosphere. We felt God's hand as we affirmed often together, *"The Lord is my Shepherd."*

We were eight passengers, three young missionary women bound for the Sudan, three businessmen, and ourselves. The accommodations were good and the food appealing. None of us was overly disturbed by seasickness. We could truly say, *"I shall not want."* But there were constant reminders that our country was still at war. One evening we were summoned on deck to see the shadow of a military transport moving a half-mile away. Then, after two and a half weeks, our brightly-lighted ship reached Lisbon, Portugal.

There a longer wait was in store, but we were not alone. Two other missionary couples and three singles lodged at the same hotel, also awaiting transportation and also puzzling about the best uses of the bidet! Some weeks later the singles were able to continue their trip. The rest of us waited seven weeks. But our anticipation remained keen and at last a Portuguese passenger ship set out with 100 or more missionaries going to Africa.

Howard and I were favored by a neat, bright corner cabin and enjoyed all the amenities provided: the Captain's dinner, games, concerts, band music, relaxing in deck chairs, seeing whales and porpoises, being initiated for passing over the equator.

The route was roundabout. At Christmas we were in Capetown, South Africa, for a two-day stop. Howard and Pastor Rolander (always called "Occie"), planned a Christmas service for all the passengers. Occie directed the singing of carols; Howard gave the Christmas message.

Our destination was still many miles away. Beira, Mozambique, in Portuguese East Africa, was our next stop and our next opportunity to learn patience. Here we waited for four weeks.

I asked Howard, "Do you suppose there is anything I can do to aid our getting to Tanganyika?" I'm not sure it helped, but I found work as a secretary in a shipping office for a week, thinking it might influence our getting passage. *"He leads me in right paths for his name's sake."*

It was January 1945 when we finally disembarked from another crowded Portuguese passenger ship on the shores of East Africa at Mombasa, Kenya. Early we were learning the truth of the Swahili proverb, *"Haba na haba hujaza kibaba"* (Little by little the bucket is filled). An American naval ship brought us finally to Dar es Salaam, Tanganyika.

The last major part of the journey was the train ride upcountry. The trains traveled twice a week. They were not bullet trains, but after our weeks of waiting in other ports, they seemed almost like speed personified. As we gained altitude from the hot and humid coast, we were happy to feel the cooler, airy climate of the Central Plateau at Singida.

Only one stage of the journey remained. A fully-packed truck took us the 45 miles over the very bumpy road to Kiomboi Mission Station where we were to have language study. It had been six months since we had left our homes in the USA's midwest, a long honeymoon journey indeed!

We were eager to learn and to experience "Africa." We went sight-seeing: an eight-mile walk to Ruruma Mission Station for a visit; an excursion to see ancient rock paintings; attending a night-time funeral dance; observing an African primary school where I was given the only available chair.

We earnestly studied the language, interspersing study sessions with occasional walks to the *shamba* (garden) to pick a papaya, a mango, a lemon, or an orange. I worked in enough time to sew up mosquito nets for our beds.

Our optimism did not waver; we were happy to be finally at our real destination. Worship services at the Kiomboi church were inspiring. The benches were filled, with other worshipers listening at the open windows. Everyone sang enthusiastically the responses to the song leader's verses. We began to distinguish readily between the Lyamba and Swahili languages as they were used. Though we had not yet been given our place and work assignment, we felt we were making good progress at adjustment. We were at peace and felt God's leading.

It was in April that the first of our "darkest valleys" began. I was diagnosed with rheumatic fever and transferred to the missionary nurses' house for six weeks. There four nurses alternately cooled my brow and doled out pills and made me comfortable. I was grateful.

One evening Nurse Ruth placed the pills in my hand. I asked, "Is this for all of us?"

"All of you? Who…?"

"There are angels beside me," I replied. Truly, *"Thou art with me."*

The crisis passed and was seemingly only a hurdle before September came with the word we had been waiting for. Howard was assigned as Headmaster of the Kinampanda Teachers' Training Center. A van loaded with our trunk, book boxes and all our luggage was to take us the 25 miles to our new home. We were joyfully looking forward to a new experience, the beginning of "real service."

As we traveled, this state of reverie was suddenly broken when fire broke out in the van's engine. Two African helpers pushed the car to a nearby *boma* (home enclosure) for safekeeping. It was dusk and we lit our lantern. Mishaki, one of the helpers, assured us that he could lead us to the Kinampanda Station. We walked and we talked and we walked. After calling *"Hodi!"* (Hello!) at several scattered homes, our guide needed further directions. We reached Kinampanda at one o'clock that night.

Orientation to life at Kinampanda was an international education. We met the Director of the Mission, Dr. George N. Anderson, an American. We met the headmaster of the school whom Howard was to replace, Sidney Clague-Smith and his family, soon to return to their home in England. We were housed briefly with Herbert and Greta Uhlin from Sweden.

The children of these families delighted us with their linguistic abilities, alternately speaking English, Swahili or Swedish as they instinctively seemed to know the appropriate language of their playmates or listeners.

Howard spent long days at the school. We became acquainted with *elevenses* (tea breaks), and *lorries* (trucks) bringing supplies from Singida. We were settled in and life was assuming a fairly normal pattern.

In the middle of November, Howard left me at Iambi Station while he attended the annual synod convention at Singida. But then, unexpectedly, I had a miscarriage and we lost Mary Alice. When Howard returned with Pastor Martin Olson, a funeral service was held. Mary Alice was buried in the Iambi Cemetery.

Because of the medical complications, I spent several weeks in the nurses' home at Iambi. Again there was a compassionate doctor and a nurse who cared for me. By now we were saying, *"We are afflicted in every way, but not crushed; perplexed, but not driven to despair; …struck down, but not destroyed…."*

Disaster struck again when a high fever continued despite the high doses of Atabrine (used to treat malaria). We sent a "runner" with a message to the doctor at Kiomboi. A van was sent to bring me to that hospital station and to the nurses' home once more. Nurses, both missionary and African, kept vigil over me for six months to combat rheumatic fever. A new medicine, penicillin, had just been introduced. I was very sick, but never fearful. I felt the truth of the psalm once again, *"Even though I walk through the darkest valley, I fear no evil; for you are with me; your rod and your staff—they comfort me."*

Dr. Bertil Friberg, nurse Ruth Holmer and African nurse Maria were truly attending angels as they ministered to my needs. Elaine Palmquist came from Ushora Station to relieve Ruth. Pastor- Evangelist, Simeon Petro, prayed at my bedside; Pastor Herbert Magney in the later months read to me. Howard biked from Kinampanda when he could get away for a few days.

"I had a scary experience," he announced when he came one day.

"Tell me about it," I replied.

He gave a big sigh and began his story. "After classes on Friday I decided to go hunting. I saw a zebra and began to follow it. I lost sight of it many times. After a while I realized that I was going down the escarpment and it was getting dark."

"Oh, night comes so quickly. There is just no twilight. What did you do?" I asked.

"I found a dry creek bed and followed it upward. I looked for landmarks, but nothing seemed familiar. I then heard the roar of a lion. Quickly I climbed the tallest tree around. I recognized nothing but the horizon.

"I stayed in the tree, contemplating my situation. The tune, 'Home on the Range' rang in my head and I began to sing lustily for a long time. I stopped when a tiny light shone far off."

"Who...who...?" I gasped.

"Immediately I climbed down to wait. There came the training school students marching with a gun-bearer beside Mission Director, George N. Anderson. He stepped up to me and said, 'Dr. Livingstone, I presume?' Was I ever glad to see him and the students!" *"Though I walk through the darkest valley..."*

In spite of Howard's entertaining stories, time seemed endless as I waited to return to our own house. Morning glories blooming in the bedroom window cheered me each morning; I wanted to plant them in Kinampanda.

But reality needed to be faced. I had spent more time in bed during our brief sojourn in Africa than I had done anything else. Mission personnel had served me to the utmost in my many emergencies. They had left their own duties to treat me. My greatest fear was that their care and concern for me was keeping them from their primary task of ministering to the medical needs of the Lyamba people. I felt I had become a burden to everyone!

We knew it was best for us to return to the States. In August of 1946, two years from the start of our journey, and after barely one and a half years in Tanganyika, Howard and I boarded an American military ship at Dar es

Salaam. A missionary nurse retiring after 30 years from the Pare northeast region traveled with us as my nurse to dispel any objections from the American crew.

"Goodbye, Africa," I whispered as we left.

"We'll be back," Howard replied.

"No, I won't be able to return," I sighed.

For fifteen years Howard yearned to return to Africa. But each of my physical exams proved that a problem existed. Finally, the Mission Board did not encourage us to apply again. Howard set his goals on American pastoral work. My health gradually improved while I lived in a rural area.

Why did these illnesses happen after our long period of anticipation and travel? Was I only a burden? A failure? I must leave in God's hands the answers to these questions. But this I know, I have been gloriously blessed by the lives of those who ministered to me. Just knowing these angels of God is a joy that continues to this day. My prayer for them as for us is that *"surely goodness and mercy shall follow us all the days of our lives, and we shall dwell in the house of the Lord our whole lives long."*

A burden? It seemed so to me. But blessed, *Yes!* Problems? Of course. But the *Peace* that endures is bigger than the problems ever were.

Effie H. Youngblom was born in Marquette, Michigan. She is a graduate of Northern Michigan University and holds a B.S. degree. She took additional studies at the University of South Dakota and Southwest University of Missouri.

Effie taught in elementary and middle schools in Michigan, Nebraska and Missouri.

She is married to Pastor Howard Youngblom. After their short time in Tanganyika, 1945-1946, together they served Lutheran parishes in South Dakota, Nebraska, Texas, Missouri and Kansas.

The Youngbloms had two children, Janice Lubeck and John (deceased).

The writer and her husband reside in Lindsborg, Kansas.

REVISITING AFRICA

Elenor Danielson Dowie

FOLLOWING A DREAM ACROSS UNFRIENDLY SEAS

My dream began when I was a child in our Junior Missionary Society. My home church, First Lutheran in St. Paul, Minnesota, was where we kids met, intent upon serving the Lord. It was then that I promised to prepare my life to become a missionary. I faithfully read reports from Lutheran missionaries in China and Africa.

"Someday, Elenor, we will go to those enchanted places, meet the people and tell them about Jesus!" Just a childlike dream at first, but with God great dreams can come true. That first dream came shortly after the end of World War I. As readers will see, it came true during World War II.

So my dream started in St. Paul and became a reality in Kiomboi, our mission station in East Africa. Come to think of it, my childhood home bears the name of another missionary who served the Lord so long ago. His sea travels were largely confined to the Mediterranean world. My journey took me across great oceans where enemy ships and guns were designed to destroy. St. Paul also experienced the danger of the sea. Two thousand years later, missionaries aboard the Zamzam would have their brush with death. But I must get on with my story.

So in imagination, let's gather a few Africa missionaries to talk about the things we liked most in Africa. It is a bitterly cold January day, so I have built a fire in our family room fireplace. We are cozy and warm as we sit in a circle to exchange memories.

"Well, Elenor," Ruth asks, "What did you like about Africa?"

"Of course I liked the people who were as helpful to us as we tried to be to them. For me their language was so much fun to learn. I hope we talk Swahili in heaven. I'm sure we will because God knows every language.

"I recall how the women never carried belongings in their hands, always on their heads. Even a spool of thread went on the head. A ketchup bottle filled with oil could easily be carried that way. They used the oil to rub their black skin until it shone in the sunlight. Their bodies were straight and tall. Excellent posture allowed them to perform such balancing acts."

Ruth: "I remember seeing women with huge loads of firewood on their heads. They made little donuts out of grass to protect their scalps. Some firewood is from trees with thorns two or more inches long."

Elenor: "Do you remember those long thorns, Edna?"

Edna: "Do I remember! We made our Christmas trees from those thorn trees. We did have some wonderful Christmases, didn't we?"

Elenor: "While I put another log on the fire, Edna can tell us more about our Christmas."

Edna: "I remember going down to the river in Ruruma to cut the tree. When we came back our African friends were watching us from the kitchen and were amused. 'These crazy *Wazungu*; they are bringing a tree into the house!' They always called white people '*Wazungu*,' a word really meaning Europeans. Anyway, we made simple decorations out of paper and tin cans. Since there were no stores to shop for gifts, we had to rely on our handicrafts for our presents."

Elenor continuing to reminisce: "My first Christmas was in Ruruma. Early in the morning our African friends came jogging down the narrow winding paths, singing antiphonal songs, the leader singing a line and the others responding. While waiting for the church bell to be rung, they slept on the church benches. The bell would awaken all of us to the joy of Christmas morning. The church was full to overflowing. Pastor V. Eugene Johnson told again the story of Jesus' birth. The old familiar Christmas carols had been translated into Lyamba, the tribal language. How they could sing! After the service we gathered outside to exchange Christmas greetings and handshakes.

"But that same day had its unhappy moments. An abused woman was brought to our door for help. I applied antiseptic to her nasty head wounds and to the compound fracture of her arm. I can still picture the jagged bone showing through the torn flesh. Later we took her to Kiomboi where Dr. Bertil Friberg treated her at the hospital. Then he joined us for a traditional Christmas dinner which was prepared by his wife, Eileen, a gourmet cook. Later we read the Christmas story and exchanged gifts."

From the land of fantasy back to the real world. Today is a lovely spring day, so different from that bitter January day when in imagination I gathered my missionary friends around our fireplace. They have retreated into memory where I will always cherish them. The ashes lie cold on the grate.

It is now June 1, an anniversary. Exactly 53 years ago today we arrived in Singida.

The time for leaving America was very uncertain. We were in the midst of World War II and were told to be ready at a moment's notice. I received my call while I was camp nurse at Mt. Carmel, the summer camp of the Lutheran Bible Institute, at Alexandria, MN. Our passage was on a Portuguese ship. Unlike nations at war whose ships were blacked out, our ship could sail with bright lights since Portugal was a neutral country. We were nine adults in our party and two boys. We had passage only as far as Lisbon.

The American ambassador in Lisbon thought we were crazy, headed for East Africa with passage only to Portugal. Pastor Martin Olson and his wife, Dr. Georgia, were arranging the trip for us. Many other missionaries on their way to the Congo were already stranded in Lisbon. What a welcome they gave us! While Marty and Georgia were negotiating further passage, we had almost two weeks to enjoy the sites of Lisbon and its environs. Little ladies stood in the streets selling flowers. We went to a bank to learn about Portuguese money.

Trivial incidents added a human touch to our great adventure. Ebba had purchased an alarm clock and had asked the clerk to wrap it securely. Ebba did not know that the alarm had been set. As we were walking along the street, the alarm began to ring. Unable to get to the clock, we had to laugh as the alarm kept ringing. While eating at a sidewalk cafe, little children would circle our table, crying out, *"Bakshish, bakshish."* We found a few coins for their outstretched hands.

Meanwhile, Marty found a Portuguese ship going as far as Beira, Mozambique, on the Indian Ocean. I wondered what would happen to my luggage. In Philadelphia the custom inspectors had been so rough, tearing apart all my things which I had packed so carefully. They had even checked my picture frames for potential secret messages. No trouble in Lisbon, however.

Our new ship headed south along the western coast of Africa. Mrs. Edythe Johnson introduced us to Swahili.

Whenever we came to Portuguese territory, we could go ashore. Esther would say, "Now our feet at last are on African soil." Esther, Velura and others in our group had been on the ill-fated Zamzam. Consequently they had not reached Africa after their ship had been torpedoed by a German U-boat.

We stopped at the Canary Islands where the women from shore brought their beautiful handmade wares out to our boat. They laid their craftwork on the deck, hoping we would buy.

Reaching the mouth of the Congo River, many of our friends whom we had met in Lisbon, bade us goodbye. A river boat would take them to their mission stations. We continued on to Capetown.

Now the ocean became very rough with waves dashing up over the deck. The sea was very unfriendly. Recalling their experience on the Zamzam, Esther and Velura clung to each other. The rest of us were not too comfortable either.

When we reached Capetown, we were not permitted to leave the ship. We sailed around the Cape into the Indian Ocean. There we ran into a bad storm; the ship lost power in one of its engines, and went around and around in a circle. The captain ordered the ship back to Capetown for repairs. While in the storm, our porthole had blown open, letting in sea water. The crew came in to tidy up our cabin.

At last our ship docked in the harbor of Beira, Mozambique, where all our luggage was unloaded. The food in the hotel was wonderful; we ate as though we had never seen food before! In fact, I had two desserts. However, our meal was spoiled by a terrible example of racism. When a black waiter dropped a tray of food, the *Mzungu* (white boss) slapped him. We were all so angry that we wanted to go up and slap the *Mzungu*!

The next day Marty sought out the US ambassador. Again we were chided: "What is wrong with you missionary folks, trying to travel in war time? It's been months since a ship has come this way going to Dar es Salaam!"

Expecting a long stay, we took our bicycles out of storage, and rode down to the beach every day. Velura called our attention to the white sand. There were several wrecked ships on the beach. It was a fun and learning experience to explore them. So the Indian Ocean had its sea disasters. We heard that a few days earlier a swimmer had lost both arms to a shark; we didn't dare go swimming.

But soon our carefree days were over. A Norwegian freighter came into port. It had just enough room to accommodate the eleven of us missionaries. Was this God's guidance that we should board a ship under the flag of a nation at war? Apparently so. The captain invited us to eat at his table, relating stories of ships which had been sunk by the Germans. In our cabins we found rubber body suits with instructions how to use them should we encounter an emergency. At night the captain paced the deck, looking in every direction while his ship zigzagged to avoid German U-boats. When we arrived in Dar es Salaam, the captain said, "You can thank God that we have made it!"

Small boats came out to meet our ship. We and our belongings were loaded into them. One of the boats was overloaded and about to sink. Marty stepped over into another boat to avoid disaster.

The next day we left Dar es Salaam by rail for Singida. People came out from everywhere to greet the train as it went by. We arrived in Singida on June 1, 1944, three months after leaving America.

African Christians and our own missionaries were on hand to meet us. *"Jambo!"* (Hello!) *"Habari gani?"* (How are you?). At last God had brought us safely to East Africa.

One of my first impressions in Tanganyika was the beautiful rose garden Ruth maintained at Kiomboi. Water being scarce much of the year, our bath water drained out to her garden and kept it lovely.

Much of my time was spent visiting "bush schools." With an African guide, I would walk ten to twelve miles each day. Since Kiomboi had no resident pastor, Evangelist Simeon Petro was our leader in the Kiomboi church. Frequently I helped him by translating English into Swahili. In turn Simeon taught me some Lyamba, the tribal language.

One of my best memories is my work with young African girls. We had a Sears catalog and I could order cloth for their sewing class. I ordered many beautiful colors of fabric. So I was ready for the girls when they came. I hear them singing now as they were singing outside our house: *"Hodi, hodi hodi!"* In America we have doorbells to ring. The girls sat on the floor to sew. I brought out the new cloth, a yard of this and a yard of that. The girls held the pieces at arm's length, admiring the colors and giggling as they selected a piece. Then they happily sewed away at their head scarves. The next Sunday they came to church with their new headwear from Sears, Roebuck and Co.

Once Simeon asked me whether any Africans would ever go to America to study. "No," I said, "I don't think so."

I was planning to return to Kiomboi after my furlough in America. I carefully packed away everything to be there when I would return. But God had other plans for my life, and I have never returned to Kiomboi. Simeon, however, despite my doubts, did come to America and studied in Minneapolis.

We met together at a party in my home in Rock Island. Here we were, in America, having fun speaking Swahili so many years later. So far and yet so near to Kiomboi.

It is now well over fifty years since our little group of missionaries arrived at Kiomboi station. Some of us were young and inexperienced, eager for the great venture ahead. To write about Africa is like revisiting it. How blessed I am that God opened the doors for me to dwell for a while with Africa's people and in their land.

When Simeon came to America he helped to restore those memories. *"Bibi* (Miss) Danielsoni," he said, "think of the progress we have made as Christians, thanks to all of you missionaries! You brought us the gospel. On Saturdays you helped us prepare our sermons for Sunday's worship. You taught our young girls to sew with needle and thread, and now I am taking a sewing machine back to my wife!"

"Well," I replied, "you and your people gave us so much in return. God's work is like that, love one another. Acts of kindness toward one another are the building blocks of friendship. The girls in my sewing circle planned a farewell party when I was about to leave. Together they put into song the story of how I had come to Africa and how we had become friends. One girl led the song with voice and drum while the others responded with chant."

With the prayers and support of church members in America for our work in Tanganyika, we were able to cross cultural barriers. We found the words of St. Paul so close to our own lives: Faith, Hope, and Love.

Elenor Danielson Dowie's *life began in St. Paul, MN; upon finishing secondary education she attended and graduated from the two-year course at the Lutheran Bible Institute in Minneapolis, MN. After one year of preparation at the Immanuel Deaconess Institute and three years in the Immanuel School of Nursing in Omaha, NE, she was ready to sit for the Nebraska State Boards in Nursing and gained her R.N.*

Commissioned by the Augustana Lutheran Church for service in Tanganyika, Elenor served from 1944 through 1948 at Kiomboi in a variety of ways: parish work, teaching, translation, and bookkeeping.

In 1949 while on furlough, she married Dr. Iverne Dowie. This changed plans to return to Tanganyika. In various midwestern locations where her husband's teaching career has led them, she has given meaningful service, including at the Immanuel Convalescent Home in Omaha. By taking a course in Medical Record Administration and passing the National Record Exams she became certified as a Registered Records Administrator.

Elenor and Iverne have one daughter, Ruth, and three grandsons. They make their home in Rock Island, IL.

AMY'S HAT

Amy Larson Woyke

"Where did you get that hat?" A blunt question like this was not character-istic of Mabel Larson, a somewhat reserved, very correct missionary teacher in Arusha, Tanganyika. She probably didn't know whether to laugh or cry at the sight of her guest, a new missionary, wearing a high-crowned, wide-brimmed navy blue felt hat.

I had purchased it the day before during a hot shopping foray in Moshi, 50 miles east. A well-meaning older missionary had picked it out to protect me from the tropical sun. I thought I had acquired the ultimate in tropical fashion. I privately thought it was outlandish but wanted to conform to what was appropriate.

My stay in Arusha was a breather before the sixth and last leg of a weari-some, almost month-long journey from Minneapolis via three cross country rail trips, two ocean voyages, and coming next, an all-day bus trip. Fortu-nately, I knew nothing about buses except Greyhound, so no worries marred the evening in Arusha with Mabel, Della Brown and Lois Fisher, two other missionary teachers, who arrived from Singida later that very day.

When they came I was introduced as the "new kid on the block." During the course of the evening Mabel said, "Amy, show them your hat."

As I complied, Della and Lois took one look at me, immediately collapsed in uncontrollable laughter and gasped, "We don't wear hats like that. Where on earth did you get it?"

The hat was placed in my luggage for the long bus ride the next day to Singida. I was too embarrassed to wear it. It was a miserable ride, sitting in the lumpy front seat of the bus with the hot tropical sun beating down on my bare head and a face prone to sunburn. What an initiation to Africa and travel!

When I arrived in Singida, of course one of the first questions was "Don't you have anything for your head?" Another hilarious session occurred when the hat was modeled. My next purchase was a "stylish" helmet. You'd better believe that the hat incident followed me my entire four-year term.

Incidentally, Dean "Pete," a missionary pastor, thought he had the perfect solution for its use: To STRAIN PETROL (gasoline)!

The ultimate question remains: What happened to Amy's hat? *"Sijui!"* (I don't know!)

Amy Larson Woyke *served as a registered nurse at Iambi Mission Hospital from 1955 to 1959. She was born in Worthington, MN and baptized in First Lutheran Church.*

As a "preacher's kid," she spent her growing years in Minnesota, Canada and Nebraska. Amy graduated in nursing from Immanuel Hospital in Omaha, NE in 1950 and from the Lutheran Bible Institute, Minneapolis, Missions course in 1955.

She was a member of Worthington (MN) Municipal Hospital nursing staff 1950-1954, after which she went to Tanganyika. First Lutheran Church (the church where she was baptized) sponsored her while she was in Tanganyika.

Following her return to the United States, she continued nursing for sixteen years at Lutheran Deaconess Hospital and seventeen years at the Augustana Home, both in Minneapolis, MN.

She was married to Carl Woyke in 1973, and retired from nursing in 1993. They reside in Minneapolis, MN.

GOD, YOU DO PLAN WELL!

Ruth Hedlund Peterson

You never know what might happen on April Fool's Day! For Les, studying at Augustana Seminary, Rock Island, Illinois, and Ruth, Assistant Librarian at Augustana College nearby, April 1, 1946, was a red letter day! That's when we first met.

On one of our first dates, when Les said, "I want to go to Africa as a missionary when I finish seminary," that set my mind full of presumptuous questions. "What *might* that mean for me? Hadn't I always, from the time I was small, eagerly read every missionary story I could find in our small church library? Why, oh why, didn't I follow my early desire to be a nurse? Why did I get sidetracked into a librarian's degree? What good would that be for me in Africa? Would my college majors in history and literature perhaps help me in teaching there?"

Recently I had asked the Lord for new avenues of service for Him. Was this possibly His answer? Indeed, the Lord was to show me. Within the year we were married and on our way to Tanganyika—to spend 25 years serving His church there. To my surprise I found that my early training served me in good stead in various ways throughout our five terms; I had no problem finding ways to serve in teaching, sewing classes, and even library work!

Early in our first term there was a voice at the door, *"Hodi, hodi?"* (May I come in?) One of our eighteen bush school teacher-evangelists was there. He said, "Mama, those pictures you gave us help us to learn the Bible story, and the children love to color them and put them up at home. They have no other pictures on their walls. *Asante sana* (thank you very much). May we have more pictures?" He was referring to the sheets I had mimeographed for a month of Sunday School lessons. I had included a simple Bible verse pertaining to each of the drawings. I gave each evangelist a few color crayons that had been sent in Lutheran World Relief "school kits" from our U.S. congregations. We really appreciated those kits.

Many years later I was reminded of this early heartwarming experience with the Sunday School teachers. Della Brown, in charge of the Sunday School work throughout our synod, came to me with a request for help. "Ruth, hundreds of Bible story pictures, mounted on colored construction paper, have been arriving at the Singida office from U.S. congregations. I wish we could get them out to the evangelist/teachers in the bush schools all over the synod. Each one could have a file of pictures chronologically arranged to follow the church year. Pictures are a tremendous teaching aid, and our teachers have little access to them."

Della then added, "This way they could use them year after year. It's so good to have the home churches sending all these pictures, and we should put them to the best possible use. Would you have the time to help us sort, number, and file them?" So began days of cataloging. I was glad to help and enjoyed the work and fellowship with Della.

An early opportunity for me to work with African Christian girls came when our dear *ayah* (nanny), Salome, said to me one day, "Mama, some of us girls would like to sew kerchiefs for our heads. If you could get us some of that plain material and some colored thread, we would like to make our own designs and embroider them." How glad I was to help this dear girl who gave so much of her time, love, and care for our young daughters.

Salome's friends were so eager to sew that we invested in a bolt of *"americano"* (unbleached muslin), which was reasonably priced at the Indian *dukas* (shops) in nearby Singida, and also balls of brightly colored thread which the girls loved. Soon our weekly sewing class included several mothers also. Later they even sewed bras and panties. When the colored feed sacks arrived in mission boxes from our U.S. congregations, the class was happy to sew skirts and blouses too.

All the time spent with their *ayahs* helped our children to learn Swahili and even the tribal language. Many times they picked up words faster than we ever imagined. One Sunday morning in church I suddenly heard, *"Mwelu, mwelu, mwelu,"* (Holy, Holy, Holy) sung in a small, clear voice! I looked up. There was Luella (aged three) standing in front of the altar, hymnbook in hand, beginning the liturgy for her Dad! She had slipped away from Rachel and me as we sat in the front row waiting for the service to begin. Les brought her back to me as soon as possible. My face was red!

Before long we were able to have a sewing class also at the Mkalama Leprosarium not far from our Isanzu station. Les served as missionary pastor there as well as at the station. We were happy to have a missionary nurse assigned to service at the leprosarium and at our station dispensary. "Auntie Helen" became an important part of our village family.

The leprosarium grew fast. The patients needed help with food as well as medical care. With government permission for weekly hunting, Les brought them meat weekly. A little rest house was built near the grounds of the leprosarium where the nurse could stay and could thus spend more time with the 500-some patients.

There I could take our little girls with their *ayahs* while I had a sewing class with the women patients. I marveled at the way they were determined to sew even with severely crippled hands. What a blessing I received from this experience!

I wrote once for the American Leprosy Missions of this experience of teaching these determined women with deformed, suffering bodies. When I had started the sewing group, I thought that many of them would come just out of curiosity. Now I ask forgiveness for that skepticism. They truly showed me that with determination they could literally "sew without fingers."

Some of those who came the first day holding up their stubs of hands did say, "Mama, look at me, how can I sew?" But within a few weeks they were finishing the hem of a yard square head cloth.

I especially remember Elizabeti. Her name had been crossed off the first time when she said, "Mama, I can't." But she came again, a hopeful look on her face, saying, "Mama, I want to try." Her hands were twisted humps, her fingers short little stubs, probably without any feeling after leprosy had done its work. But she pushed that needle with her knotted hand or else pulled it with her teeth. The stitches, so laboriously completed, were much neater than those of some of her more fortunate companions. And they were beautiful to my eyes, as was the expression on her face at every tiny word of encouragement.

Far from looking for pity, this group had a spirit of friendly rivalry, chatting easily together, laughing and teasing over clumsiness. There were earnest, patient attempts to rise above self-pity. As their teacher, I always felt a tremendous uplift just being with them, and at the same time, was truly humbled in seeing their joy in their hope of an eternal life in Christ.

Later at our Mgori station, I again had sewing classes with the women. One day I heard, "Mama, look, I'm helping the ladies to sew." There was Luella (aged five) perched atop my tall kitchen stool with the sewing class women lined up waiting for her help. I had been called into the house for a bit, so she was ready to fill in! The confidence she showed was typical. She had so much interest and determination to sew that she'd even tried, on her own, to use my machine and had put the needle through her finger.

More teaching came for me with home classes of kindergarten and first grade for our children in preparation for their schooling at Augustana School at Kiomboi, about 75 miles away. Luella, at age 7, was the first to go, and the confidence she had shown with the sewing stood her in good stead. Because she so confidently left for school, it made it easier for us to say goodbye and also helped to know she was there for our younger ones when they went. It was hard to see each of them in turn go off for three-month terms away from us, but we were very thankful for Augustana School, the fine teachers and houseparents, and the kindness of mission families living at Kiomboi.

And here it was that the library training I had received earlier was put to work. Because the school was new, the library was just being established. There were close to 1000 books just received from the U.S., and help was needed to get the library organized.

On a few occasions I was asked by teachers at Kinampanda Teachers' Training School to help in an advisory capacity with the library there. I became increasingly grateful for librarian training and said often, "God plans all things well."

For almost seven years our place of service was at Ihanja Bible School. Being there meant that we lived near other missionary families. We shared much good fellowship, and as faculty wives, we shared in cooking, sewing, and homemaking classes for the students. There were many lesson notes and worksheets to type and mimeograph. The library needed to be set up, and those books cataloged as well. One crippled student liked the library work and was very good at it. He continued to assist even after we had left. It was good to know that the library could be a real help for the Bible School students.

Our first year at the Bible School was quite a change for us, being in a school schedule with classes to prepare. I could see Les was really pressured. A bit later he said, "I just have too many hats. I am the principal besides teaching classes, the vice-pastor of the congregation here at the station, and the treasurer of the mission garage in Singida where the mission cars are serviced. I don't see how I can do justice to any of it."

I wondered how I could be of some help. A light bulb went on in my head. Maybe that history degree could even be of use here. ("God, you *do* know how to plan, don't you?") I asked Les, "Do you think I could manage to teach one of your classes? I always have liked history. Could I take your Church History class?"

I knew I might have a hard time teaching in Swahili. I had mainly used simple household Swahili around the home and in teaching the women. Les felt we should give it a try. So I taught that class and later one on the *Life of Martin Luther*. It was a challenge teaching 30 eighth graders, and I probably made many mistakes; but the students were patient and helpful, and I also learned much right along with them.

Our farewell from the congregation where Les was pastor at the time meant a great deal to us. That was Ngimu Lutheran Church. The people of Ngimu became some of our closest friends. When we left the Ngimu Valley in 1962, they gave us a very long, heartfelt farewell.

We will never forget Mama Sarah, who spoke for the women. She stood right in front of our family—all seven of us lined up in the front row—looked straight at us, and said: "You Wazungu (Whites/Europeans) could have brought us cattle, and cattle are our wealth, our bank. But the cattle would have died from different diseases or been killed by animals, and they would all be gone. You could have brought us clothes—bright red, yellow, blue, and green clothes. We like them very much and always need them. But we would have worn them out, and they would be all gone. You could have brought us money, and we need more and more of it. But we would have spent it all, and it would all be gone. But you brought us the church of Jesus Christ, and no one can take it or Him from us."

In a few sentences, Mama Sarah had summed up our real purpose for being in Tanzania. What a blessed close to our 25 years in East Africa!

Ruth Hedlund Peterson *was born and raised on a Wisconsin farm. Ruth attended Luther College, Decorah, IA, earning a B.A. She also attended the University of Michigan, Ann Arbor, MI, for her B.A.L.S.*

Ruth is married to Pastor Leslie C. Peterson. They have five children; Luella Weir, Rachel Jones, Marilyn Friberg, Roberta Bainbridge and Paul Peterson.

Their missionary service extended from 1947 to 1972, serving at: Isanzu Lutheran Church, 4 years; Mgori Lutheran Church, 8 years; Wembere Lutheran Church (with safaris to the Watindiga), 1 year; Ihanja Lutheran Bible School, 6½ years; and Kiomboi Lutheran Bible School, ½ year.

The writer and her husband reside in Menomonie, Wisconsin.

THE END OF THE WORLD IS HOME

Lois Fisher Okerstrom

"Singida? That's rather like the end of the world there, isn't it?"

Such was the comment made by a colonial government Englishman sailing with us on the S.S. Mantola, a combination freighter-passenger ship bound for Dar es Salaam, Tanganyika. We were a group of thirteen missionaries, some returning to Tanganyika for second and third terms, others of us brand new.

Seeing we were traveling together, the tall, bearded gentleman garbed in white tropical shorts and knee-length stockings was curious as to our destination. One of the veteran missionaries had casually answered him, "Singida."

But I was a new fresh-out-of-the-States missionary, single, and the youngest of the group, and those few words of the stranger's description of our destination drove more than a bit of apprehension into my mind. Although I had heard missionaries speak and had read of our church's work in Africa, I actually knew very little other than that God had said in big, bold black letters, "I want *you* in Africa."

The oppressive heat through the Red Sea and the bleakness of the surrounding desert landscape was strange and frightening enough. What *would* it be like at our destination? Just where *were* we going? How was it that someone who seemed to know the country well could describe it as "the end of the world?"

Days later, as we traveled by train upcountry and then by bus, eyes were wide to look for this "end of the road" place. The surroundings did look strange and different, but I could readily see houses and people. I felt we were not quite at the end of the world, and could even see that the road stretched beyond Singida.

But it was dark when I arrived the following day forty miles further at Iambi Mission Station, where I was to have language study. No street lights or other lights were to be seen. Even roads were difficult to identify as "roads." Maybe this was the "end of the world".

Before going to bed, my language study hosts at Iambi tried briefly to orient me to my surroundings and prepare me for the next day. They said that the area was well populated. I looked forward to seeing for myself the next morning.

That morning's impressions remain vivid and intense in memory. The sights, the sounds, the smells all poke their heads prominently through the windows of my life even after forty-five years. They crowd my mind as if I saw them all *this* morning.

I saw only a few people walking. I could see *no* houses. How can it be well populated? I learned. The low brown sun-dried brick houses blended into the same-colored soil.

I was told I should come up to the hospital after I had finished breakfast. "The hospital is crowded," Nurse Alice had said. "All beds are taken. But you must come up and see the new kitchen."

I followed her suggestion, but before finding her, I had walked into a ward. The beds were almost all empty!

Puzzled, I asked her, "Where are the patients?"

"Oh, they are walking around outside."

That answer brought only more confusion. The only response I could muster was "I see," though obviously I did not.

But Alice continued eagerly, "Let me show you the new kitchen."

"Kitchen?" Though I had never before actually seen a hospital kitchen, this tiny brown building with a few pots snuggled onto sets of three molded stones somehow did not fit my mental image of a hospital kitchen.

I decided this was, perhaps, after all, "the end of the world," and I queried God, "What am *I* doing here?"

But the One who had months before made it very clear that this *was exactly* where I was supposed to be seemed to answer, "You do not need to know that yet; but I know and I am with you." And I was learning the ways of the village quickly that morning.

As the days went on, the "end of the world" perspective disappeared. The *sights* gradually became familiar and loved: the soft colors of dawn over Mt. Hanang; wide, blue skies appliquéd with fluffy clouds; the brilliance of sunset between the twin palms at Ihanja; friendly African smiles at almost every turn; the intricately-woven nests of the yellow weaver bird dangling from pervasive acacia thorn and candelabra trees; bright bougainvillea and sweet frangipani bushes; sprightly periwinkles persisting in bloom during the long dry season.

There were the fires of the stubble of the old harvest in the valley as the people prepared their fields for cultivation; women sitting on warm afternoons braiding one another's hair or deftly weaving a colorful basket;

shepherd boys standing on one bare foot with the other propped against the opposite leg.

The *sounds* became like the voices of cherished friends: women splitting the air with their joy as they trilled their excitement at hearing beautiful choir numbers in church; choruses of birds singing in early morning; the greetings of friends walking along the pathways; the welcome hiss of the Primus kerosene stove after three unsuccessful attempts to get it lit; the *ngoma* (drums) and *filimbi* (fifes) of the middle school marching band.

The *smells* and *tastes* were new and enticing: of freshly-made butter in the churn; bread baking in the wood-burning stove; the first rain as it settled the dust on the road; the unique delectable tastes of guava and mango; the sweetness of Indian *chai* (tea) with milk and cardamom; the spiciness of curries.

But all these sights, sounds, smells and tastes pale in significance when compared with the supreme unadorned joy of getting to know *people* of strong faith.

Let me tell you first, with awe, about Mama Salome. My visit to her has shone in my heart through all the years since then, a memory which has stuck to the "ribs of my soul."

I had heard of this Turu woman who was born with deformed legs and feet. She lived not far from Kijota Mission Station in the village of Mutinko. I had sought for an opportunity to visit her when serving as parish teacher at Kijota. This came from the African pastor who invited me to accompany him down the dusty road those few miles. We walked and talked and as we arrived near Salome's house, the local evangelist met us.

Salome's was a typical Turu house of the time, low with flat roof, made of mud plastered into wood poles. The kraal was enclosed by the thick sticky minyara hedge. Chickens and a few cattle were inside the kraal; the rest were obviously at pasture. The smell of manure and clabbered milk was pungent.

A low three-legged stool was brought for me to sit on. Salome sat on the ground dressed in a tattered cloth, browned by the dirt on which she sat. It was the dry season and the earth was hard-packed by the hoofs of the cattle which were herded into the kraal each evening.

But the *smile*! The smile of Salome was broad and sweet, radiating joy and a welcome to melt any heart. We exchanged the usual greetings, and as we did so, I noted the orderly pile of firewood cut in similar lengths. The *panga*, the machete-type knife commonly used for cutting firewood, was nearby.

As I commented on the neatness of the pile, I wondered silently if she could possibly have cut the wood herself. Salome explained. "I cannot cultivate the millet and corn as other women do; I cannot go out to the forest and chop down the wood. But I can sit here and cut it into firewood for cooking."

I was ever so impressed with her ability to compensate for her handicap and even more by her cheerfulness. But something else caught my eye. To the side of the larger pile, I spied another cluster of wood. It looked some-how different, just wood, but by itself, special.

I asked Salome, "What is this pile?"

"Oh, that is my tithe."

"Your *tithe?*"

"Yes," she replied. "I set aside one stick in ten for the use of the evangel-ist. He comes here regularly to read God's Word to me and to pray with me. This wood is my thanksgiving to God for his teaching me."

As Salome then received from the pastor the communion bread and wine, her joy in Christ's presence was so very real and ardent that I could only bow my head in humility and thankfulness. This act of devoted stewardship must surely delight the heart of God and make the angels in heaven sing aloud in jubilation. Though handicapped in body, Mama Salome was clearly not handicapped in spirit.

Another stalwart person of faith who remains strong in memory, I met some years later. When working in adult literacy among the Turu people, I was asked to accompany an exchange evangelism team to the Isuna area. This was true hinterland. My task was not that of preaching or teaching, but to be driver of the four-wheel drive Land Rover for the team.

But a preacher was there. Firm faith, zeal, dedication combined with tal-ent—these are the attributes which come into sharp focus as I remember the young Turu evangelist who shared the preaching task with the African pastor.

Petro had only had two grades of education in a small bush school, those simple "institutions of learning" which the mission established very early in its history to teach the basic three R's, plus the fourth R, Religion, Christi-anity.

But Petro's mind was keen, his enthusiasm for learning eager, his zeal to preach the gospel unrivaled. He knew his Bible well. I asked him how it was that he came to Christian faith.

Petro quickly replied, "I heard people singing in the bush chapel and went in. The words were of the hymn, *'When He Comes with Clouds Descending.'* I somehow believed this Man was and is God and that He would come again, and I wondered, 'What will He think of me when He comes?'"

Young Petro became an evangelist in this distant outpost in Turuland.

As we traveled that week we came to villages almost untouched by the Christian message. Delivered with passion and love, Petro's sermons at each place were alive with God's Spirit. It was as if there were flames of fire on his tongue as he spoke of God's supreme love for His created people, and His desire to draw them to Himself. Petro seemed literally aglow as he preached.

Reaching the last village at the end of the week *and* perhaps of the road, we found the people waiting quietly, many of the men leaning on their walking sticks, the women sitting on the ground clad in their *kaniki* cloths (black cotton).

But, following the preaching, and in contrast to the previous places we had visited, there was no response now. The people sat mute and motionless. There was not hostility, there was not affirmation. Everything seemed very gray as if thick fog had descended out of the wind-washed azure blue skies.

Later in the car as we left that small community, I asked Petro, "Why was there no response to your message? It was so clear and beautiful, filled with God's great love for these people."

Petro looked at me as if I were quite ignorant, but still with his radiant smile and sunny faith. He was not discouraged. "Oh, don't you know?" he answered. "These people have lived in darkness without Christ for a long, long time. It takes more than one sermon to bring Light."

And so I continued to learn, from the people in a remote village. Seeds are planted, but God's Spirit sometimes works very slowly.

God's beautiful and unique people come in all colors. I must introduce you to one more. Her name was Vivian Gulleen, but everyone called her "Bing." She was a long-term missionary teacher who readily responded to any call the mission or church gave her. Bing was outspoken, big of voice, big of heart. Africans understood and loved her.

Bing was among the five of us, all teachers, who often traveled together for our annual vacations. As we traveled, we memorized Bible verses in Swahili, and sang hymns, in both Swahili and English. The first song of each morning was *"Again Thy Glorious Sun Doth Rise,"* but woe to you if you began to sing it before the sun had actually risen. Bing would immediately object, "No, no, no, it isn't time yet."

One vacation was to be spent on the shores of Lake Nyasa in southern Tanzania. Because we were to "camp" in an old, long-unused German mission house, we had to bring many things with us: bedding, pots and pans, food items. There was no direct road to this house, so we left our Jeep on one side of the lake, and hired men in long dugout canoes to bring us to the other side. All went well until we were ready to disembark.

Suddenly a whole group of women rushed into the water, grabbed our loads and without a word started off with the loads on their heads. "What is happening? Where are they going with our things?"

But a friendly African man with clerical collar was also there on the shore. "It is all right; they are your Christian friends. They have simply come to help with your loads."

We relaxed, but then we saw the women running very fast. Now what? The "what" was a swarm of bees, and the women were trying to outrun them.

Later, getting settled in the vacant house, we introduced ourselves to the pastor and had a brief, but pleasant visit. He returned the next day to see how we were getting on and if we needed anything. We asked him if he remembered our names.

With a shy smile, he said, "No, but the people here have already given you special names."

Curious and surprised, we asked, "What are they?"

Softly and quite sheepishly he answered, *"Bibi Kelele na Wenzake"*—("Miss Noise and Her Companions.")

The people had quickly learned to know Bing, and her wonderful, booming, loving voice. It did not take her many days to turn the vacation time into something more than rest and relaxation. She kept saying, "We must do something for the women of the village." So it was that with the help of the pastor, the women gathered together and Miss Noise's voice was used to lead a dynamic Bible study, to pray together with them, and then to teach a cooking class, making a simple nutritious custard for their children.

You were wrong, Mr. Stranger on the ship. Singida is *not* the end of the world; even the distant outposts in Turuland are not the end. They are places with God's people, people whom He loves and who love and worship Him.

The end of the world can never be the place where *God* wants you to be. Instead that place becomes *Home.*

Lois Fisher Okerstrom *was born and raised in Topeka, Kansas. She is a graduate of Bethany College, Lindsborg, KS, with a B.A. degree in English Literature. She took additional studies at Scarritt College in Nashville, TN and Pacific Lutheran Theological Seminary in Berkeley, CA.*

Lois taught week-day religious education in the state of Virginia and then served as Director of Christian Education and Youth in a church in Berkeley, CA.

In 1952 she was commissioned as an educational missionary to Tanganyika where she first served as parish teacher, then taught at the school for missionaries' children, and later directed the Turu Adult Literacy Program.

Following three years in Ethiopia at Radio Voice of the Gospel under the Lutheran World Federation, she returned to Tanzania where she was Director of the Student Wives' Study Program at Makumira Lutheran Theological College.

After her return to the U.S. in 1970, Lois married Roy Okerstrom of Berkeley, CA. They live in El Cerrito near San Francisco where Lois is involved in church women's leadership roles and group hiking activities. Lois says, "I count God's call to serve in Africa as one of the greatest joys and privileges of my life. The central Tanzania plateau truly did become 'home.' Tanzania's people, its language, and its culture will always have a very big place in my heart."

MALARIA, TERMITES AND MIRACLES

Elaine Peterson

"Call Elder, I think I'm going to die."

"You've probably got malaria. Take some chloroquine."

"I did, but I can't keep it down."

"Just try again."

This was the major conversation my husband, Dean, and I had that first night upcountry in Tanganyika at Ihanja Mission Station, 500 miles inland from the coast at Dar es Salaam.

Here we were invited to study Swahili as guests of Elder and Renee Jackson, and we were experiencing our first bout of malaria. It was the fall of 1952 and we had traveled six weeks by car, train, and boat from my husband's little country church in South Dakota where we had been commissioned as missionaries. It was very significant for me to be commissioned with my husband, as it was only recently that wives had been recognized in this special service. Every step of the way brought us closer to the place we each felt God had been calling us for a number of years.

The malaria, we thought, was contracted two weeks earlier on shipboard while we were sitting in the Mombasa harbor, Kenya. Dean (often called "Pete") had no qualms about calling our host in the middle of the night; they had grown up together in South Dakota as cousins.

Now it was the heart of the dry season, so everything looked hopelessly dead that first morning upcountry. The Tanganyikan "dresser" (medical worker) from the dispensary came to check on us and to take a blood slide. In the few Swahili words we had learned on ship we asked, "*Jina lako nani?*" (What is your name?)

He replied, "*Naonekia*" (meaning in Lyamba, I have seen the light).

This man who knew very little English, but was to tutor us in Swahili, helped to lift our spirits that first morning with both his smile and his medical treatment.

We were among the first missionaries to have a month of Swahili study jointly with missionaries from various countries and churches working in different areas of Tanganyika. It meant traveling by train several hundred miles from Itigi to Mwanza, bringing along our army cots, bedding and mosquito nets, a bucket in which to wash clothes and to bathe, a Tilly pressure lamp and also eating utensils for ourselves and our 22-month-old son, David. No disposable diapers!

There were several hard weeks of study, and we had made good progress, though there was yet much we didn't know about Swahili. But the time had passed quickly and we were on our way home from the language school.

"What do we do now? It's getting too dark to see and there is no African moon tonight."

This was the question fellow language student Lois (Fisher) put to us as we traveled the 60 miles from Itigi train station back to Singida. Darkness comes fast in equatorial bush country, and we were a long way from our destination. Pete was driving the Bedford station wagon which had been left for us at Itigi with a note warning us that the lights were not working. He was trying carefully to avoid the pot holes and sandy bumps prevalent along the road.

"Well, we do have that Tilly pressure lamp you bought!" I replied.

"Brilliant idea," Lois offered. "But I don't think that will show up much from inside the car."

"No problem," quickly answered Pete. "I'll sit outside on the fender and hold it while you drive."

All went well, until coming into a sandy dip and seeing at the same time a herd of donkeys on the road, Lois slammed on the brakes. As Pete was jolted off the fender, he continued holding the lantern running down the road. I ventured that this was probably the strangest sight these donkeys had ever experienced in the African night!

One of the reasons that we were running late that evening, besides the train schedule, was because we had stopped to see the progress at the new mission station being built at Isuna just off the main road.

Happily on our way again, Freda Oman, one of our group said, "Oh, I left my jacket back on the cistern." Pete reluctantly turned around and when almost back to the station Freda says, "Oh, here it is, I was sitting on it."

"Freda, you try my patience!"

"Well, patience is a Christian virtue!"

And so another part of orientation is learned—living together as a missionary family.

The big old stone house at Iambi that was to be our first real home after seven months of living out of suitcases was a real challenge as it had sat empty for two years. Termites had riddled the mud plastered walls and some of the wood ceilings. This took weeks to repair but it was home at last. Termites continued to be a nuisance as they would often tunnel their way up through the cracks in the cement floors into cupboards and even our piano. One day we came home to find they had made their dirt mound between the wall and the head board of our bed.

There were other challenges: cooking on a woodstove; buying milk by cupfuls from various neighbors; separating, boiling it and making butter and ghee from the cream; conserving water that was collected in a cistern during the rainy season and hand-pumped into a tank in the attic each day; washing only once a week with our Maytag wringer washing machine that was run by a gasoline motor. Water for washing clothes was heated in three five-gallon tin containers called *debes* over an open fireplace outdoors the morning of washday. Our clothes (no *drip-drys*!) were ironed with the sad-irons that my mother and grandmother had used.

Then there was canning and preserving food for the dry season, butchering game meat to put in our kerosene fridge, and buying basic supplies once a month or so in Singida 50 to 70 miles away depending on the weather.

The church elders at Iambi chose three people, Amosi, Danielsoni and Wanswekula, who became faithful helpers for the many and varied tasks of running a household and raising three small children in the bush for the next four and a half years.

Each day brought unexpected events; life was never boring. One evening before dusk a non-Christian lady was carried to the Iambi Mission Hospital on a makeshift stretcher. She had suffered severe pain for five days and no doubt was hemorrhaging internally. She was diagnosed as having a tubal pregnancy. The hospital doctor, Dr. Stanley Moris, called together some of his staff for an emergency operation: Daudi Filipo, a Lyamba trained medical assistant; missionary nurse Ann Saf; and a Lyamba nurse, Kristiana.

"The hospital generator isn't working, so someone is needed to hold the big flashlight overhead."

"I have never witnessed an operation before but I will do it," I volunteered. As I stood on the stool looking down at the bloodiest situation imaginable and witnessed black and white hands working together in harmony to save a life, all my fears vanished. Days later that lady walked out of the hospital healed and I was permitted to be a part of that miracle!

"Christ is risen. Hallelujah!" It was Easter morning at Iambi, and as was the custom, the Christians gathered at the graveyard for an early morning sunrise service. Because of our three small children I was unable to attend.

However, I stood listening on our big screened veranda that stretched along one side of our house. There had been a death of a non-Christian a few days before so the traditional death dance was also in full sway at the home not far away where this person was buried. From that direction I heard the mournful wailing of the bereaved as they shuffled to the beat of the drums. I heard the professional *mbutu* horn players, people who were hired to play on the traditional horns made from the horn of the kudu, one of Tanganyika's most beautiful antelopes. In the opposite direction the voices in the cemetery were raised in joyful and victorious singing, "Christ is risen. Hallelujah!" What a contrast—from darkness to light, despair to hope!

That was the reason I was there as a woman and part of the old Augustana Lutheran Mission field. The love of the missionary family and of those early African Christians in Lyambaland was a great orientation for the next thirty-some years when God's call lead me to other places in Tanzania.

Elaine Peterson *is married to Pastor Dean Peterson. They have four children, David, now in Arusha, Tanzania; Rebecca Peterson-Davis, Bonners Ferry, ID; Thad, Arusha, Tanzania; and Michael, also in Arusha, Tanzania.*

Dean and Elaine served the Iambi parish, Central Synod, Oct. 1952 to April, 1957. From July to Dec., 1958, they were involved in language/literature at Kinampanda, Central Synod.

From 1959 to 1972 they were on the faculty of Makumira Theological College near Arusha. From 1973 to 1988 they were stationed at Oldonyo Sambu, Arusha Diocese and engaged in Theological Education by Extension (TEE), as well as the Parish and Conference Center.

WIYUKA ! (HE AROSE!)

Alpha Jaques

In the pre-dawn darkness, I faintly heard singing in the direction of Iambi Church. It was my first Easter in Tanganyika and I was planning to attend the sunrise service. The singers, assembling at the church, carried either flashlights or lanterns to light their way. The cemetery was located nearly a mile away on a rise overlooking the beautiful Ndulumo River valley.

We marched together in procession, singing resurrection songs which speak of hope and the promise of eternal life in Christ. As the darkness brightened into dawn, as it does so rapidly near the equator, we gathered at the newest grave and sang,

"Lo in the grave He lay, Jesus my Savior,…

Up from the grave He arose, with a mighty triumph…"

Joyous proclamation of the power of the resurrection sounded in the cemetery that morning! This most beautiful Easter anthem will always bring back poignant memories of my first Easter in Tanganyika.

But as we were singing, we began hearing death wails and the penetrating boom-boom-boom of the *mbutu* horn from the other side of the valley. These were unmistakable signs that death had visited a family living in darkness without Christ.

Those of us gathered in the Christian cemetery that memorable morning were powerfully reminded that the task of sharing the good news of Christ's victory over sin and death is an urgent imperative for the Church and every Christian.

This experience of mingled joy and despair at the cemetery was repeated again the following two Easter mornings. It was as though the Lord was making sure we had heard His call to be His witnesses.

THE SURVIVOR

"You are needed in the Admitting Room!" The urgency in the voice of the hospital worker made me hurry. I wondered what I would encounter when I opened the door.

Seated on the bench was a Barabaig man; next to him cowered a little boy about age seven, judging by the age-characteristic gap in his front teeth, apparent because most of his upper lip was missing. Where were his eyes? His nose? They were covered with a mass of crusts, dried milk and dirt. "What happened to this child?" I gasped in horror.

"We have only begun to get some details," replied Isaac Mkumbo, Iambi Hospital's Medical Assistant. He and the laundryman, Asheri, were in the process of securing a history of the injury. Asheri had grown up near the Barabaig people and spoke a related language. He had long since become the hospital's official translator for any Barabaig patients.

He went on to explain, "The boy and his grandmother had been sleeping outside of the thorn bush compound when a hyena came by and took a bite from his face." The thickness of the crust made it obvious that this was not a recent injury.

"When did this happen?" I asked, still trying to comprehend.

"About two weeks ago," replied Isaac. When I asked the father why they had waited so long before bringing him, he told me they live about thirty miles from here and didn't think he would live anyway. But when he began begging for food they decided to bring him to Iambi Hospital. This was a surprising decision, since the Barabaig people cannot accept the weak and defective in their society. Any such are taken out to the wilderness and left to whatever fate may befall them.

Patiently, gently and painstakingly, Isaac and two nurses began teasing away the hardened mask. Once removed, they found the nose missing, the left eye severely damaged and the right eye swollen shut, in addition to obvious signs of infection. Because we had no resident physician at Iambi at that time, he was sent to Kiomboi Hospital for evaluation.

We learned a short time later that once the swelling had diminished, the right eye was found to be intact and functional, but the other one needed to be removed to protect the sight of the intact eye.

Within two weeks of this incident, both Isaac and I left the country. He was scheduled to participate in a two-year medical upgrading course in Germany. I was due for a year of furlough.

Some months after my return, I received an update on the boy from the missionary physician and the nurse who had attended him at Kiomboi. Once the infection had been cleared, they could make arrangements to send him to Nairobi for plastic surgery.

But the family refused and took him home. Later, when the nurses heard that he had died, they assumed that he had not been taken home but that the family had abandoned him in the wilderness.

Isaac completed his two-year course in Germany and continued his training in Dar es Salaam to become a fully-qualified physician. After his third year of study I saw him in Singida. He asked me if I remembered the little Barabaig boy. "Yes," I replied. "I heard that he had died."

"Not so!" said Isaac with great warmth in his voice. "You know how the Barabaig reject anyone defective or disfigured. Well, they took him from the hospital but left him in the bush. Amazingly, someone found him and brought him to Haydom Hospital."

I could hardly believe Isaac's report. That child was *meant* to live! He had survived the attack by the hyena, the infection that followed, and the terrifying stay in the bush!

Isaac continued his story; "I had occasion to see patients in the Salvation Army's Children's Home in Dar es Salaam, and was astonished to see this very boy there. Then I learned he had been taken from Haydom to the Children's Home so he could have the needed plastic surgery.

"When I saw him, he was a bright, healthy ten-year-old. But when I mentioned his scars, his smile changed to a stony stare. Though his face had healed, it was evident that his emotional wounds were still raw and painful," Isaac told me.

We stood silent for a time, remembering the strange turns in his story; coming from a culture where Jesus was unknown, rescued twice from certain death, each time brought to a hospital where he encountered Christian compassion, then placed in a Christian children's home. How did all this fit into God's plan for him? What might be the rest of the story?

Evangelical outreach to this tribal group was only beginning at the time this boy was injured. Now there is a growing vital church in that area. Tribal customs change slowly, but we trust that now there is increasing recognition that every person has worth and is, in fact, precious in God's sight. Some thirty years have passed since this boy first encountered Christian compassion. We do not know the continuation of his story. We can only pray he met the Great Physician who alone could heal his wounded spirit.

HOW TO LEARN IN A HURRY

An ocean voyage—what a delightful prospect! My mind conjured up images of relaxed days on deck, playing shuffleboard or simply resting in a deck chair, feeling the gentle rocking of the ship.

So much for images! My time on board was put to more utilitarian purposes. My traveling companions were Rev. Ludwig Melander and his wife Esther. On a similar voyage ten years earlier, she had had regular language classes with a senior missionary. Thus convinced of their value, she became my kind but firm taskmaster. While crossing the Atlantic Ocean, I became acquainted with Swahili greetings and responses. Since I had not studied a foreign language in high school, this was all new territory for me.

While in London I had a respite from language study, but when we were once again enroute, we had barely entered the Bay of Biscay when the daily discipline of memorizing vocabulary began. There seemed to be no other way to assimilate numerous nouns, gain fluency in dealing with multiple noun classes, plurals, adjectives and the most frequently used verbs. Steere's *Swahili Grammar* dominated the next month, with the Mediterranean Sea, Suez Canal, Red Sea and Indian Ocean as backdrops to my study of words! Words! Words!

A stormy stretch on the Indian Ocean reminded us to count our blessings. Prior to that time, we had had ideal sea travel. We were grateful to disembark at Dar es Salaam (which means peaceful harbor).

"Slow" and "slower" characterized the subsequent rail and bus trip to central Tanganyika. As we were nearing Singida, I saw a spectacular sunrise which seemed to welcome me to my new home. However, I had only the weekend free with my language study hostess at Wilwana before beginning three months of intensive all-day study. This time my mentor was Martin, a Tanganyikan.

I had been assigned to Iambi hospital, so after completing three months of language study, I moved to Iambi where I was to continue language learning with special emphasis on the terminology needed for medical work. Thus the focus was not exclusively language learning, but language and orientation. My language teacher, Wazaeli, was an excellent teacher, committed to helping me learn the language well. Each time he came for class, he had a long page of study questions, typewritten and single spaced.

But where I *really* had to put my learning to use was at the hospital. For the first time in over four years, Iambi was to have a resident physician and surgeon. In preparation for her arrival, Ann Saf, the nurse in charge, was primarily occupied in preparing surgery supplies. Only one of the hospital staff, Onesiforo, the Rural Medical Assistant, could speak English and he was in charge of in-patients. My assignment, then, was to the out-patient department where I would see selected patients with one or two nurses' aides helping me. None of the nurses' aides had more than four years of primary education using Swahili. Their Swahili was not much more advanced than mine. I had a challenge before me!

First of all, I was not well-versed in tropical diseases: they aren't too common in Minnesota! Then the vast majority of the people did not speak Swahili. Therefore, my questions had to be translated into Lyamba and the answers into Swahili. It was a time-consuming and a most frustrating exercise.

Did I make mistakes? I'm sure I did. Very likely, mistakes were made that caused a great deal of hilarity in the aides' residence afterwards. But the very frustration I experienced in my morning's work was a powerful motivator for study in the afternoon.

Bit by bit those vocabulary lists I had so laboriously memorized on shipboard became part of my working vocabulary. The greetings and those painfully phrased questions became more comfortable to use. My hours, weeks and months of study were paying off.

On a bus enroute to Tanzania, many years later, I used Swahili in speaking to the other passengers on that long, weary trip. During the many hours of waiting at the border, when rain delayed customs clearance, a curious passenger asked me, "How is it you speak such good Tanzania Swahili but you're coming from Kenya?" I answered with a bit of amusement, "Well, many years before you were born, I lived in Tanzania and learned Swahili there."

Yes, what I had to learn in a hurry years before, was still opening doors to witness for Christ.

Alpha Jaques *lived her early years in Aitkin County in Minnesota. After finishing high school and brief employment in a home for the aged, she completed a three-year course at the Swedish Hospital School of Nursing in Minneapolis, MN. After graduation as an R.N., she combined attendance at the Lutheran Bible Institute with part-time work in various nursing positions.*

Alpha was commissioned by the Augustana Lutheran Church in 1954 for service in Tanganyika and went to the field in May of that year. Her assignment after language study was to Iambi Hospital where she served for two four-year terms.

During her second furlough, she took a parish workers' course and in 1964 she began work as a parish worker, first at Kijota and later at Kinampanda. In 1975 she joined the World Mission Prayer League and pioneered new medical work with the Samburu people in a remote area of Kenya.

Since returning to the U.S.A., Alpha has served in both parish and nursing positions. She now lives in Litchfield, MN, and is involved in volunteer work at Zion Lutheran Church and in the community. She spends one day a month at Global Health Ministries in Fridley and enjoys gardening.

TESTED

Marilyn Buchanan

Jenny was so surprised she dropped her fork and it clattered noisily to the floor.

"Really? You were a *missionary* in *Africa?*" Recovering the fork, she accepted a clean one from the waiter.

"Yes, Dean and I accepted a call to Tanganyika in late 1957."

Jenny and I were meeting over lunch to discuss a project we were working on together at church. Although we had known each other about a year, she had not been aware that Dean and I had been missionaries in Africa, until the subject of "missions" had come up today.

"I didn't know your husband was a pastor."

"He isn't. We were *lay* missionaries."

"I suppose this was something you had always wanted to do?" Jenny queried, still incredulous.

"No, it certainly wasn't!" I replied. My mind flashed back to that day in January, 1957, at the San Francisco airport—the stony, grim faces of Dean's parents, my mother's tears as she clung to me so tightly that I had to pry her fingers loose from my arm so that we could board our flight for New York, the first leg of our journey.

"No, I didn't even know then that lay people could be missionaries. In my mind, it was pastors and other trained church workers who were missionary workers in foreign countries. And, as you supposed, I thought it was something they had always wanted to do. I had attended Sunday School at Bethany Lutheran Church in Berkeley, California, since I was small. Later I was baptized and confirmed there. Dean and I were married in that same church."

"My parents were not church members. Dean became a member of Bethany through adult instruction. He too had attended Sunday Schools, but his parents were not church members either. The Lord blessed us with two sons, and they, too, were baptized at Bethany. We were very active in our church. Dean served on the council, I taught Sunday School, and we were counselors to the youth group."

"Sounds like it was a great church," Jenny commented, "but how did you get to *Africa*?"

"I'm coming to that. The *call*, when it came, was a *big surprise*!

"Our former parish worker at Bethany, Lois Fisher Okerstrom, had left the parish to become a missionary in Tanganyika. I was really awed that she could make such a decision! We had kept up a correspondence with Lois in Africa. One day in 1957 a letter came to Dean and me from Lois in which she said, at the end, that pastors sent out to preach the Word were frustrated by having to spend far too much time trying to keep the financial books on the field, constantly reporting to the Treasurer of the Board of World Missions in Minneapolis, for which they had not been trained. Also they spent a lot of time under their cars, trying to keep them running. She said they 'badly needed a field treasurer. How about the Buchanans? Ha, ha!' "

"Did she really mean it as a joke?" Jenny asked.

"Well, it certainly seemed ridiculous at the time. My husband is a CPA, and, at that time, was just getting his own practice started. We had just bought our first home and were still getting things fixed up. It was a very inopportune time to receive a call! The Lord thought differently, for that is when it came. Dean read Lois' letter. I read it later. In about a week, I said to Dean, "What did you think about Lois' letter—wanting us to go to *Africa*?"

"Interesting," he said. "I've been thinking about what she said."

"After we had indicated to each other that we had *not* just taken it as a joke, we began to discuss the possibility seriously. The Spirit had *already* begun His work in us! Dean wrote for more information. I wrote Lois several more letters inquiring how children fared out there."

"Oh, I can see how concerned you would be about *that*!" Jenny exclaimed. She still had children in junior high school.

"Even if we ourselves were willing to go to Africa, was it fair or prudent to take the children out there? What if they got sick and died? We were very torn by this. And, if we did decide to go, what about Dean's CPA practice? What of the home we had not even been in a year?"

Jenny shook her head. "Sounds like an impossibility!"

"Besides this, *time* was of the essence (they wanted somebody out there 'yesterday!') Dean's letters were all answered positively, and an interview was set up. I received assurance that there was a fine school for missionaries' children at Kiomboi, and that one of our mission hospitals was located at that same station. Now we began to talk and consider in earnest."

"Sounds like you had a lot to think about!" Jenny interjected."

"What came next was the most trying, emotionally exhausting time of my life! We were told that if we accepted, Maywood School of Missions (which all other missionaries attended before going out) would be waived, and we were wanted out there immediately. Dean had a *business* to sell! We had a *home* to sell! We had a car to sell. We had to buy enough things to last for *four years*, including clothes in different sizes for the children. We had to search for things like flat irons and steel drums to pack everything in!"

"Oh, my word!" Jenny exclaimed, as she tried to envision getting all those things together for her own brood.

"As it turned out, the above problems were not nearly as traumatic and soul-wrenching as those we encountered when we told our parents what we were contemplating. Were we 'crazy giving up everything we had been working for?' Were we going to take 'those two darling boys out to such a dangerous place—our only grandchildren?' They questioned our motives. They pleaded and wheedled. They even got to the children, telling them that they didn't want to go to such a place."

"Oh, how awful for you!" Jenny empathized.

"I cannot fully explain how torn and heartsick we were. Then the Holy Spirit began to minister to us (certainly to *me*!). This was mostly by Bible verses which kept popping into my head, verses I didn't even know I knew by heart. Verses about going to a land where He leads, and *"Know that I am with you and will keep you wherever you go, and will bring you back to this land; for I will not leave you until I have done what I have promised you"* (Gen. 28: 15). *"Whoever loves father or mother more than me is not worthy of me; and whoever loves son or daughter more than me is not worthy of me"* (Mt. 10: 37)

"I know that is true," Jenny said, "but *what* a choice!"

"I *knew* we were being *tested*," I continued. "We prayed a great deal. About this time the Dean Petersons were home on furlough from Tanganyika, and we visited them in Minneapolis. They had just recovered from the Asian flu that was rampant that year. Their suggestions about what to bring, if we decided to go, were most helpful. However, they evidently were not quite over the flu, because Dean and I both got it and were very sick. Now we were physically sick *and* sick at heart. It was then that the Spirit came up with the 'clincher': *"Satan has demanded to sift all of you like wheat, but I have prayed for you that your own faith may not fail..."* (Lk.22:31-32).

"So you accepted?" Jenny surmised.

"Yes! We passed physical and psychological tests in Minneapolis. We had numerous shots and vaccinations. Dean's business sold! We kept praying, 'Lord, you know we need a buyer for the house, if You want us to do this.' He kept testing our faith to the very end. We finally found a buyer and signed-off on the house *the day before we left*! The car we left with Dean's father, who sold it for us.

"At the airport I had to keep prying my weeping mother's fingers from my arm so we could leave. So, you see, our going out to Africa was a different calling from most of our other missionary colleagues, some of whom were second generation missionaries, some had other members of their families in mission work, or at least most had the backing and support of parents. We were, however, given much support by our home church, where we had our commissioning."

"I don't see how you survived all that!" Jenny sighed.

"Once under way, we felt *peace!*"

"As I think back on that difficult, soul-searching time, Jenny, besides the pain, I remember vividly the ministering and *closeness* of the Holy Spirit. My fervent prayer was 'Lord, four of us are going out, please, let four of us return!'"

"Were you ever ill?" Jenny asked.

"Oh, yes! However, the Lord was with us through good times and bad. He *never* failed us!"

"Tell me about your trip out to Africa," my friend asked, as the waiter took away our salads and we waited for dessert.

"There *were* problems. Of course, we had to secure visas, get yellow fever shots and several other injections. When we reached Europe there were language difficulties, and the Orient Express train definitely did not live up to its reputation, it was extremely filthy. We were not told there was no dining car. Once again doubts crept in, as we watched our children go without food or *drink* for over a day.

"Things were better at first when we boarded our ship in Italy bound for East Africa, until both Dean and Danny became sick with high fevers. Danny had seven antibiotic injections, which didn't seem to help much. Again doubts assailed us. What had we done?

"Everything was very strange to us once we landed in Mombasa, Kenya—the language, the customs, the costumes, the smells. But the Lord provided help in the form of a British District Commissioner who had been on board ship with us. Then again in Moshi, at the foot of Mt. Kilimanjaro, missionaries Don and Ruth Trued were there to meet us and to answer our many questions.

"The ride, however, over African roads in a Jeep was a jolting experience! African roads are sometimes described as 'two bicycle paths running parallel.' They were thick mud called *mbuga* at that time of year."

"I shall never forget arriving at Kinampanda, bone-weary and feeling like we had come half way around the world, which, of course, we had! The Lord had prepared our way well, as a wonderful family, the Vernon Swensons, had volunteered to be our language hosts. There was an empty house on the station, and beds had been set up there for us. All our meals were taken with the Swensons. Pastor Vernon Swenson not only led us in devotions, but also taught us much about Africa, the work, and the teacher's training school there at Kinampanda.

"We made numerous safaris to our other mission stations to get acquainted and get Dean ready for his work. Dear Doris Swenson washed all our clothes, as well as theirs, in her gasoline-powered washing machine, with wringer, for the three months of language study!"

"Really?" Jenny asked, incredulously. "They did *all that?*"

"I helped with hanging the clothes out and bringing them in, when we weren't having a lesson. I shall never forget the selflessness and kindness of these good people! I still remember Doris sighing, and saying of our clothes, *'My, they're so new!'* (I think they must have been about at the end of their four-year term)."

"Our language lessons and teaching Mark first grade kept me busy everyday. Children entered boarding school at second grade. They were taught first grade at home; later this was changed, and even first graders boarded. This change came just when our second son, Danny, was ready for first grade. He was the youngest child in Augustana School! At that time there were about 90 children at school."

"I'm sure it was hard to let him go!" Jenny sympathized.

"It was difficult for all the families to have to send their children off to boarding school. However, the fact that it was a Christian school, with loving Christian houseparents (Fred and Martha Malloy at that time), made it somewhat easier. The Minnesota curriculum was used, and children were usually ahead, or where they should be, when they returned to the U.S. They attended school for three months, then had a month at home with us."

"Oh, I'll bet you were glad to have them home."

"Yes," I laughed, "but I did get called 'Aunty Martha' a lot! Of course when they went back to school, Aunty Martha was called 'Mom' for a while.

"Teaching Mark, studying Swahili, and various safaris kept us really busy during language study time. My biggest problem was that the change in altitude made me so sleepy, it was hard to study, especially in the evening."

"After language study, we moved to Ihanja station to another home whose occupants were home on furlough. Since Dean was the first field mission treasurer, there was no treasurer's house. We were to move again, after about a year, to the town of Singida (another empty house!). Finally, a new treasurer's house was built at Kititimu, a station just two miles from Singida. We resided there until our return to the U.S."

"My, you certainly moved a lot!"

"After language study, Dean's Swahili vocabulary increased in accounting and church-related words, while my vocabulary added words needed to run the home and cook."

"Yes, I can see how you each needed a different vocabulary," Jenny agreed.

"I was busy setting up our home and learning how to work with our house-help, a near-essential in a land where all water had to be pumped by hand from a cistern into an attic holding-tank, then boiled for all drinking and tooth-brushing. Milk had to be separated and then boiled, eggs tested when bought at the door, all bread home-baked, wood chopped, bath water heated on the wood stove, and even meat cut-up from whole animals after a hunt!

"Dean took over the accounting and budget responsibilities for the schools and hospitals operated by the Augustana Lutheran Mission. He opened the first Christian bookstore in Singida with the help of Lois Fisher and Marian Halvorson, our literature/literacy workers. The bookstore was a real witness to the community."

"I can see how it would be. Were you involved with the bookstore?"

"Only in lending moral support. I think I was still looking for my niche. I was pregnant with our third child, Jane, then; and all the moving and new house-help had kept me more than busy.

"Through the bookstore, Dean was able to purchase textbooks directly from the UK for the schools at wholesale prices, saving the mission a good deal of money. The profits were used to fund adult literacy programs. Then he started a mission garage next to the ALM offices in Singida. Pastors and other missionaries no longer needed to spend days or a week in Arusha waiting for their Jeeps to be repaired. He was able to secure parts more rapidly. The mission fleet of vehicles was switched to Land Rovers. Parts for them were obtained more easily. Those who were there to preach, teach, do itinerate evangelism, work in the hospitals, etc. were able to get on with their work."

"One day, while still living at Ihanja, I was to learn how frustrating it could be to try to be charitable in Africa. I was putting the wash out on the clothes line, when a small Turu boy came to the back door, stark naked, and his nose running all down his face. He was coughing. The wind was blowing and it was the colder time of the year. 'This child is going to get pneumonia, if he doesn't already have it!' I thought. I told him to wait, and went inside and found a warm knit shirt that belonged to my son, and put it on him. He went away happy.

"I wish the story ended here. However, the next day the same child was back again, naked, asking for a *shati* (shirt), and I had many people show up at my door asking for clothing! I learned that the child's father had taken the boy's shirt and sold it for *pombe* (beer)!'"

"Not much different than here these days!" Jenny said sadly.

"Yes, except here there are agencies to help those with true needs," I countered.

"In January, 1959, our first and only daughter, Jane Louise, was born in Nairobi, Kenya—my third Cesarean section. A new baby and five-year-old Dan kept me busy during the rest of our time at Ihanja station. When we moved to the town of Singida, it was a very busy time too, with many guests. The mission house there was jokingly referred to as 'the Singida Hotel'. There were no hotels at that time, and missionaries stuck in town for one reason or another, were always welcome. I remember that on our tenth wedding anniversary we had at least a dozen people sleeping in our living room and on the *baraza* (porch)!"

Jenny laughed. "Well, that was different!"

"Our final move was to the new treasurer's house at Kititimu, a new mission station. After the work of getting settled there, and training a new cook, I found a way I could make a contribution."

"Oh, tell me about that," Jenny asked.

"Some wives were nurses and helped at the dispensaries and baby clinics. Pastors' wives helped with parish work and women's groups. I had no training in those things. However, in 1961 Pastor Bob Ward, a former U.S. Navy radio operator, returned to the field with thirteen GE 100-Watt VHF reconditioned radio transmitter/receivers for twelve mission stations and one mobile unit for his vehicle. Pastor Ward did itinerate evangelism. He was also our only radio repairman!

"These radios were like a 'party-line,' and there needed to be a central operator to call all stations at the designated broadcast times, and find out who had messages for whom. Then the central operator acted as a 'traffic coordinator,' using Navy radio jargon to give each station their opportunity to transmit (e.g., 'ALM-6, king to ALM-4'). I agreed to be the central operator."

"Oh, so you were a 'ham'!" Jenny teased.

"Well, not really, as you will see.

"Soon I watched as a 60-foot antenna (three 20-ft. sections) was raised outside our Kititimu home, with a great deal of struggle and manpower. There were two sets of guide wires and two securing feet in blocks of concrete. Antennae had to be erected at each station.

"The radios were to be operated by generators. Up until that time, only a few stations had power generators and electric light at night. Everyone else used kerosene lamps. Now almost every station had a generator, petrol or diesel operated. One station used a car battery for power. These had to be turned on for radio broadcasting at 7:00 a.m., 7:00 p.m., and noontime for the hospital and anyone wishing to contact the doctors.

"These radios helped dispel feelings of isolation, particularly at more remote stations. As a mother, I know it eased our minds to know that if our children were ill with malaria or other sickness, we would be able to speak with the doctor at the next broadcast."

"Oh, I can see what a God-send that must have been," Jenny exclaimed.

"Often people could arrange meetings by knowing when someone would be going into town. Important messages could be relayed, for we had no telephones, except in Singida."

"Once, at Ihanja, the dresser from the dispensary came running up to our door, shouting *Hodi! Hodi!* (May I come in?). There was a man in the dispensary who had been bitten by a cobra when he reached into a hole. Not only had he been bitten, but he had stayed there and killed the snake! Then he had jumped on his bicycle and pedaled hard to the dispensary, pumping the venom all through him!"

"Oh, my word!" Jenny gasped. "What did you do?"

"Dean jumped in the Jeep and they went to the dispensary and he and the dresser loaded the man into the back of the Jeep and they raced for the hospital. They had only gone about ten miles when the dresser rapped on the window behind Dean and shouted, *Amekufa!* (he is dead!).

"Besides really important messages, we sometimes had one like a missionary wife wanting to 'remind Hal to get potatoes, I forgot it on the list!' Trips into the town to the *duka (shop)* were infrequent, and people at more remote stations had to stock-up for quite a while."

"Well, I can see that forgetting the potatoes really took on more significance!" Jenny chuckled, as we picked up our check.

As we headed for my car, I continued, "The radios had a range of 'line of sight'—50-60 miles. The radio sets continued in operation from 1961 to 1977. I was central operator from 1961 to May of 1962, when we returned to the U.S."

As we got into the car Jenny asked, "Were you ever sorry about your decision to go to Africa?"

"Oh, no! In fact, I ended up with the feeling that we received even more than we gave!"

"But, what about your parents? Did they ever forgive you?"

"Well, after we reached Africa, I wrote them faithfully every week. For a long time my mother did not answer. Finally, after I wrote that I was pregnant again, she began to write once in a while. Dean's parents did write, and send us things. I guess you could say they forgave us, although I doubt they ever understood that we were truly called to go. In fact, it seems that God wasn't through with us yet. After our return, He led us into Christian higher education. Dean accepted the position of Financial Vice-President at Pacific Lutheran University, Tacoma, Washington. After twelve years there, he accepted the challenge of the same position at California Lutheran University, Thousand Oaks. When he retired from CLU, after 15 years there, he became a consultant to small private colleges, mostly church-related, nation-wide."

We had reached Jenny's home. "Well, this has been a very interesting day," Jenny said as she got out. "I've certainly learned a lot more about you."

"Well, as you can see, Jenny, the Lord has richly blessed us since we gave Him our 'Yes!' Remember, not only four of us returned safely—but all five of us! The Lord is good, *great is His faithfulness!*"

Marilyn Buchanan *was born and raised in Berkeley, California, attended Berkeley High School and the University of California, Berkeley. At the University, she met Dean Buchanan, who had just returned from service in the Merchant Marines (1947). They were married in September of 1949 and had two children, Mark (1951) and Daniel (1953).*

During high school and college she worked as a telephone operator, and later as a bank teller. After the birth of their children, she remained a homemaker.

In 1958 she became a lay-missionary with her husband, Dean, to Tanganyika. A third child, Jane Louise (1959), was born in Nairobi, Kenya. The family returned to U.S. in May of 1962.

The author's husband subsequently became Financial Vice-President at Pacific Lutheran University (12 years), and at California Lutheran University (15 years). After raising her family, the author took additional courses and became a hospital ward secretary (part-time) for 13 years. She and her husband are now retired in Santa Maria, California.

THE CHALLENGE:

USING WHAT THEY HAVE

Lore Heidel

It was near midnight, in a business meeting of our annual missionary conference. Fighting sleep, I was startled by the sound of my name and was instantly brought to full attention: "Lore, would you consider becoming the therapist at Iambi Leprosarium?"

Would I consider it? I was a registered occupational therapist currently serving as a housemother at our Augustana School for missionaries' children.

Would I consider being the therapist at our newest development—the Iambi Leprosarium? Approximately 400 patients would be brought to Iambi for treatment, many needing my help. Would I consider getting involved in that enormously important work? Oh, yes; yes, I would consider it—of course I would. *You bet I would!*

We had been hearing for some time of the desperate need for a facility that could offer intensive treatment and rehabilitative services to leprosy patients. Their needs were great and the idea of being on the ground floor of a bold venture such as this intrigued me.

Besides, I was excited about getting back into my own profession. The plan called for the development of a five-person team: physician, lay manager, nurse, lab technician and a therapist who would have to function as both a physical and occupational therapist. The facility would not be ready for occupancy for nearly a year; the staff could move in as soon as accommodations were completed. There was much to be accomplished during those months of preparation.

Thoughts tumbled around in my mind; how would I start? I had not a single piece of equipment, I'm not a physical therapist and on top of that I knew little about leprosy. Am I afraid of the disease? I asked myself this question.

Actually, I was, but I felt if the rest of the team were ready to commit themselves to this ministry, why would I not be willing? If God needs us there, He will look after us. Of course, we would take the necessary precautions.

I began thinking rationally at that point. I could make some equipment such as weaving looms with the help of our Indian carpenter. I could learn from books about the treatments used in physical therapy. Also from textbooks, I could learn about the disease of leprosy and its management.

It was an exciting day when Veda Hult, the nurse, and I moved into our temporary quarters. The formerly empty site was taking shape with buildings being erected and agricultural projects started. Some of the patients had been transferred from the two older leprosy colonies. Now my work could begin.

Under a large fig tree I set up my open air "treatment room" with a table and two benches. The leafy branches protected us from the burning sun. We started oil massage and specific exercises for those crippled hands. The results over time were amazing to me.

In my study of the insidious nature of this disease, it became clear to me just how critical prevention of deformity is in the management of leprosy. Frequently the hands and feet lose sensation. Pain, which is really a friend to us, is not present to alert these people to the danger from burns and injury from sharp objects such as the ever-present thorns and rocks. If the injury is not cared for promptly, ulceration may occur. Unprotected bones soften and eventually absorb. *Prevention* is *the* key.

As I studied, it became increasingly clear that there are specific ways to prevent injury: *If* they had shoes, they would not have so many cuts on their feet. *If* they had crutches, they could avoid putting weight on ulcerated feet. *If* they would learn to use hot pads, they would not burn their hands. Shoes. Crutches. Hot pads. Fine in theory, but the patients needed to learn to use them. Educated vigilance prevents deformity.

Among the new arrivals were two men with skills that fit in with my program of prevention. I saw a patient wearing sandals crafted from car tires. "Where did you get these?" I asked him with great curiosity.

Nonchalantly he replied, "Oh, I make them!" He became the shoemaker for the other patients. We scrounged around for old tires, used the inner tubes for the straps, then started mass production of sandals. Most patients had come to us without protective footwear.

I also noticed a man who was carving wooden spoons. I thought, "Maybe he can be our crutch maker!" I told him of our need and gave him a pattern. I asked him, "Would you be able to make us some?" There were trees out in the bush that would be suitable for crutch making. We needed many of them.

From mission boxes, stored for some time waiting for the building to open, I found supplies useful for both physical and occupational therapy. With fabric on hand, hot pads were made to protect insensitive hands from being burned handling hot earthen cooking vessels.

Meanwhile erection of the needed buildings was proceeding; in due course we learned that the Rehabilitation building was next on the list. So I eagerly watched the walls going up, and could hardly wait to move into it.

When the day had come that my helpers and I could move into our new building, we had already accomplished a great deal. Patients were scheduled for treatment sessions; therapy assistants were trained and ready to start work.

The building plan made it convenient for supervision of the assistants. There were three rooms: occupational therapy, physical therapy, and an office/storage room in between. We installed five large weaving looms. I had been given 1 000 pounds of yarn, so that allowed us to begin right away teaching the craft of weaving. An old hand-crank Singer sewing machine was viewed with great interest by the patients since none of them had ever operated one; they had only seen them at the shops.

We kept everyone busy who wanted work or wished to learn a new trade. The therapy rooms became filled with patients from morning until evening; they were eager to learn to sew, crochet, embroider, paint, cut and weave. Everyone wanted *kazi* (work). In fact they called me *Bibi Kazi! (Miss Work)*.

Work did wonders for our patients, both in skill development, rehabilitation of their stiffened joints and giving them a new sense of self-esteem.

LIVES TRANSFORMED

"Teach me to sew," Daudi begged. I had been handing out craft materials to some of the patients in the men's ward. Teach Daudi Kingu to sew? Would he be able? How could I teach *him* to sew? He had lost all his fingers to injuries and ulcerations. As I examined what remained of his hand, I found he had only a small cleft between his palm and the stump of his thumb.

But he was so desperate that I thought I needed to give him a chance. I nailed some burlap from a sugar sack onto an old picture frame and demonstrated some simple stitches to bring the needle up and down, using a large blunt needle and some brightly colored yarn.

Never have I seen anyone more excited than this little old disabled man to tackle the craft of embroidery. I had drawn some lines on the burlap with a felt tip marker which he was to follow with stitches. He pushed the needle down with his palm and pulled it up with his teeth. He effectively used what he had!

After some practice, Daudi became our most popular picture maker. I drew the picture on the burlap and he would cover the entire piece of burlap with colorful stitches. He made one picture after another; each one sold for two shillings. The money would be shared; with some of the proceeds, more yarn would be purchased, and Daudi now had an offering to bring to church. He happily said, "Now I can thank my Lord."

Then there was Mikaeli, an amputee, crippled and multi-handicapped; he was the recipient of our first and only wheelchair. He was extremely grateful for it and became one of the most steady attendants in my occupational therapy unit. He learned to operate one of the big weaving looms and never seemed to tire.

He became an eager student at our literacy classes; once he learned to read, he regularly attended our Monday morning Swahili Bible classes. He had received a Bible as a reward for graduating from his literacy course. Mikaeli became more and more excited about God's Word as he was now reading it for himself. His cup was running over with the blessings of the Lord.

He shared the Good News all around the hospital ward as he went from bedside to bedside reading the Scriptures to others that he himself had just learned to read. Mikaeli became an extraordinary blessing to many.

Clemens was a troublemaker; he had open sores on both hands and feet. He was restless and would not stay in bed so he could be treated and healed. His crippled hands were useless. He was a man with a bad temper, depressed and withdrawn.

He started to show a bit of interest in the hand-crank sewing machine and learned to use it; then he became fascinated with his new work. He started to use crutches and could get around with safety, not harming himself.

Because of his faithful use of crutches, the open sores on his feet started to heal. Then he learned to operate a treadle sewing machine. Soon all the hospital sheets were sewn by Clemens.

His hands, through daily massage and exercise, were loosening up. He was now able to use a pair of scissors and soon was doing more complex sewing tasks such as uniforms etc. He became my first helper in the occupational therapy department.

Yes, and he became a new man! With his self-esteem built up, he saw possibilities for himself as a working man. He also learned to read and write. The most wonderful part of his whole transformation was that he became a

Christian! He had reason to give thanks to God. This man, who was once known as a troublemaker, became a peacemaker.

There were many special people at the leprosarium and each had his own story. There was an awakening among those who came to work and it soon proved to be that work was a much needed therapy for leprosy patients.

I treasure those memories. Some of the greatest blessings I have received were those of witnessing how the Lord had changed the lives of some individuals and that I could have a part in that transformation.

Lore M. Heidel *grew up in Leipzig, Germany. She is a 1956 graduate from the London School of Occupational Therapy. She was commissioned by the Augustana Lutheran Church as a missionary in 1956 to serve in Tanganyika as a housemother for the missionaries' children at Augustana School, Kiomboi.*

In 1959 she was assigned as Physical and Occupational Therapist at Iambi Leprosarium. In 1967 she started a rehabilitation unit at another Tanzania leprosarium and continued there until 1970.

Since her return to the United States, she has served in a variety of settings in Minnesota with patients having a wide range of disabilities. Each individual presented a unique challenge to assist her/him to return to an optimum level of functioning. In retirement Lore lives in Benson, MN.

PORTRAYERS OF THE PARABLES OF JESUS

Freda Gentz

Something about many African people that I shall never forget is the way their daily lives portray many of the parables which Jesus told.

My remembrance of one early morning took place at the beginning of the growing season. New grass was popping up along the footpath to the clinic, and in the air was the fragrance of freshly-spaded ground.

A young African farmer was working in his field nearby. He wore a black wrap-around cloth and carried a bag of grain over one shoulder. He smiled when he saw me, and greeted me with the usual greeting, *"Habari za asubuhi?"* (What is the morning news?)

I answered, *"Habari ni nzuri!"* (The news is good!) Then he reached into his shoulder bag, brought forth a handful of millet seeds and scattered them on his newly-tilled field.

Well! What an amazing scene I was looking at! That young African man was, *in person*, the sower who went forth to sow the seeds. As I watched him, I heard in my mind as an echo the words of Jesus telling me the parable of the sower. *"A sower went out to sow, and some seeds fell on the path, and the birds came and ate them up. Other seeds fell on rocky ground, where they did not have much soil, and they sprang up quickly, since they had no depth of soil. But when the sun rose, they were scorched; and since they had no root, they withered away. Other seeds fell among the thorns, and the thorns grew up and choked them. Other seeds grew on good soil and brought forth grain, some a hundredfold, some sixty, some thirty."* (Matthew 13: 3-8).

It was very exciting to see that parable portrayed, right before my eyes, in the way that Jesus told it!

The shepherd parables (Luke 15:1-6) were also portrayed among African shepherds. A footpath had been trodden past my front door where every morning friends and neighbors walked past on their various errands. One early morning my neighbor came by, carrying a sheep across his shoulders. He met some of his friends and while greeting one another, they talked loudly and excitedly. His friends asked him, "Where did you find your sheep?" Then a lot of loud discussion broke out among them, because he told them how he had discovered his sheep hiding among bushes for fear of a lion or a leopard. Then his friends commented, "You were very brave to go out in the wilderness in that dangerous time of the night!"

Dangers were ever present for the African shepherds. Another neighbor of mine experienced danger and tragedy also. He came to report that during the night a leopard had leaped over the corral that surrounded his house, and had stolen a lamb and escaped with it! To hear him tell about it was like listening to the words of another parable that Jesus told: *"Very truly, I tell you, anyone who does not enter the sheepfold by the gate but climbs in by another way is a thief and a bandit. I am the gate… Whoever enters by me will be saved, and will come in and go out and find pasture. The thief comes only to steal and kill and destroy. I came that they may have life, and have it abundantly."* (John 10:1 & 7-10).

During the harvest season one can see a picture-parable while viewing an expansive beautiful valley where there were many African homes and millet fields. At harvest time each African family picked the millet tops by hand and piled them on their threshing floors near their home. The next procedure was to beat the millet tops with long whips, to loosen the grain from the husks. Then the grain was lifted up overhead in winnowing baskets, and poured out slowly, so that the kernels of grain fell into another basket while the chaff was blown off by the wind. The chaff fell into a pile on the ground. Then in the evening, when the wind had died down, the whole valley was dotted with small fires that had been lighted by each householder in order to burn up the chaff.

To me, this was an illustration of the teachings of John the Baptist who said, *"His winnowing fork is in his hand, and he will clear his threshing floor and will gather his wheat into the granary; but the chaff he will burn with unquenchable fire."* (Matthew 3:12) This is an illustration of Judgment Day.

However, we have no reason to fear the Day of Judgment, because Jesus has said, *"Whoever hears my words and believes in Him who sent me, has eternal life, and does not come into judgment, but has already passed out of death into life (eternal)."* (John 5:24).

Having seen these parables, portrayed by the Africans, has given me more understanding than if I had not seen them so vividly in action. These mental snapshots often come to my remembrance, especially when I read them in the Gospels. Tanzania, as well as other Eastern world nations, is a place where the Bible comes alive.

WHO IS THE GREATEST?

Many are the sacred memories I have of African families gathered together in their homes. Love and honor are two intangible gifts bestowed upon their elderly, and also upon little children. The parents and other older members of each extended family put effort into including and teaching the younger children about their own value within their family. They are given little household tasks; they are taught hospitality towards visitors. The little children were usually praised for their obedience to their parents and elders.

There was always time for the parents to spend with their children. For example, one day while visiting in homes, I came upon the scene of a father teaching his year-old daughter to walk. They were out in the shady yard of their home. The father stood a short distance away from his little daughter to encourage her to walk over to him. He stretched out his hands to her and said, *"Njoo, Mukombe!"* (which means, "Come, old lady!"— a term of honor and endearment in the Lyamba language.)

So I asked him, "Why do you call your little daughter *Mukombe?* She is still a baby, only a year old, and not even able to walk yet."

Then he replied, "We call her *Mukombe* to honor her! You see, she has recently come from the other world of God, and we old people are soon to go there." (Those words became more emphatic when expressed in the African language, and in that father's tone of voice.) This was a completely new insight to me: the honoring of a small child because she had so recently come from God's presence in heaven.

That African father expressed his faith in God with thoughts similar to those of King David, in Psalm 139:13-18:

"For it was you who formed my inward parts; you knit me together in my mother's womb. I praise you, for I am fearfully and wonderfully made. Wonderful are your works; that I know very well. My frame was not hidden from you, when I was being made in secret, intricately woven in the depths of the earth. Your eyes beheld my unformed substance. In your book were written all the days that were ordained for me, when none of them as yet existed. How weighty to me are your thoughts, O God! How vast is the sum of them. I try to count them — they are more than the sand!"

The little daughter took a few unsteady steps toward *Baba* (father)—she appeared happy and was encouraged to walk, and when she was near enough, she threw herself into her father's arms. He held her close and praised her. Then he put her down again for another little lesson in walking.

In reference to this word-picture of an African father and his little child, two other Bible references come to mind:

Luke 18:15-17 *"People were bringing even infants to him that he might touch them, and when the disciples saw it, they sternly ordered them not to do it. But Jesus called for them and said, 'Let the little children come to me, and do not stop them; for it is to such as these that the Kingdom of God belongs. Truly I tell you, whoever does not receive the Kingdom of God as a little child will never enter it!' "*

Matthew 18:1-5 *"At that time the disciples came to Jesus and asked, 'Who is the greatest in the Kingdom of Heaven?' He called a child, whom he put among them, and said, 'Truly I tell you, unless you change and become like children, you will never enter the kingdom of heaven. Whoever becomes humble like this child is the greatest in the kingdom of heaven. Whoever welcomes one such child in my name welcomes me.' "*

Freda Omen Gentz *was born and brought up in Cambridge, MN. She is a graduate of the Lutheran Bible Institute, Minneapolis, MN, and the Bethesda Lutheran Hospital School of Nursing and became an RN in 1950.*

In 1952 she was commissioned by the Augustana Lutheran Church as a missionary nurse to serve in Tanganyika. She lived at Ushora and Ihanja, supervising dispensaries. Later she served on the staff at Kiomboi Mission Hospital., until 1961.

Freda states, "I enjoyed African families very much, their hospitality and their expressions of God's love."

Upon her return to USA, she studied at the University of Minnesota, and in 1966 Freda married Edgar Gentz. They have had a continuing ministry to chemically addicted persons; for four years they operated a home for chemically addicted women. Freda continued using her nursing skills in a nursing home and volunteered for twelve years with the Contact Twin Cities Helpline.

A MOONLIGHT ENCOUNTER

Martha Fosse

"Hodi!" (a verbal substitute for a knock) *"Hodi!* Wake up! You are needed in the delivery room!" Enveloped in deep sleep, I barely heard the insistent call at my bedroom window. *"Hodi! Hodi!"* Suddenly I became alert. It was the granny midwives trying to get my attention!

Reluctantly leaving my warm bed, I went to the open window. The faithful midwives stood with their little lantern in the bright moonlight. I asked, "What is the news?" The more experienced of the two explained the problem.

"I'll be right down," I replied. It was 2 a.m. Maybe if it didn't take too long, I could get in a few more hours of sleep. I dressed rapidly and went out to the porch carrying my flashlight. I stopped suddenly. On the front walk, silhouetted in the moonlight, was a large animal! He stood there on the front walk as though waiting for me. By the shape of his muzzle and characteristic sloping back, there was no doubt in my mind that my visitor was a hyena.

I prayed, "Lord, You are the one who called me here. You know I am needed down at the hospital. Bring me there safely." I went to find my pressure lantern, lighted it and pumped it up to its brightest intensity. Thus armed by both prayer and my lantern's light, I again approached the front porch.

The hyena was still there. Was he really waiting? However, when he saw the brilliant light, he seemed to melt into the shadows on the other side of the road. I was on my way, surrounded by the heavenly host!

Aside from encounters of the four-footed variety, those night-time summons were memorable for other reasons. The moonlight cast fantastic shadows on the familiar landscape; aluminum rooftops gleamed in the silvery light. Judging by the insistent beat of the drums, people in the nearby village must have been awake too. Occasional shouts and bursts of laughter drifted my way on the east wind. That free illumination always calls for celebration. Far in the distance could be heard the unmistakable roar of a lion or the eerie laughter of hyenas.

Those solitary walks became times of worship, as I would recall the Psalms:

"When I look at your heavens, the work of your fingers,
*the moon and the stars that you have established; ... "*Psalm 8:3
"The heavens are telling the glory of God;
*and the firmament proclaims his handiwork."*Psalm 19:1

No street lights or neon signs dim the breath-taking Milky Way; it is broader and brighter in the southern hemisphere than in the north. Many more stars of the first magnitude are found there. Near the equator, the stars seem less remote. The Southern Cross constellation could be located easily and reminded me of Christ's salvation for all people.

The silence of the sleeping hospital that night was shattered by the high-pitched wail of a newborn safely delivered. It was a welcome sound. Shortly after, I picked up my trusty lantern and trudged wearily up the long hill. It had been an eventful night. My bed would feel good. Later, as I was almost asleep, I gratefully remembered the Lord's promise in Psalm 91, *"No harm will befall you."*

SEED TIME AT KIOMBOI HOSPITAL

"I have been thinking about the phonograph records in our language that the evangelist uses at the hospital" said Israeli, our house helper. "I'd like my neighbors to hear them. I wonder if the evangelist would let me borrow them sometime because my friends have been asking questions."

I replied, "That's what they are for, to introduce people to the Gospel. "Let's ask him tomorrow." Israeli was referring to the Gospel Recordings records that present the Gospel message in nearly 5,000 indigenous languages of the world. At that time, in the mid-50's, only 78 RPM records were available, but today cassette tapes with hand-wind tape recorders can be used in areas where there is no electricity and batteries are too expensive.

On a Sunday afternoon, with the old spring-wind record player and a half dozen Lyamba records, Israeli, his wife Ulumbi and I started out for his village. He was excited at the opportunity to share the Gospel in this novel way with his neighbors. It was about a five-mile journey to his home, down winding pathways.

Upon arrival I was astonished to find a large group of people waiting for us. How could forty people fit into their little house? But Israeli followed the old adage, "Where there is heart room, there is house room." It was wall-to-wall people in that two-room house that afternoon. With awe I realized that for many of these people, it was their first hearing of the Good News. They listened attentively, then expressed appreciation for the recordings. Thinking back to Jesus' parable, there were represented in those neighbors the various soils: rocky soil, soil choked with thorns and the good soil. Because of Israeli's initiative, it became seed time in his village that memorable afternoon.

Another opportunity to sow seeds occurred later that week. A Barabaig woman had been admitted and had surgery. Her accompanying husband seemed rather uncomfortable in this alien environment, far from his cattle herds. This grave man would pace back and forth along the covered walkways at Kiomboi Hospital looking bored and dejected. It wasn't possible to engage him in conversation as he didn't speak Swahili, the lingua franca of East Africa; nor could we speak his language.

But we did have a means of reaching him with the Good News. Gospel Recordings technicians, in the early 50's, had made recordings in the Barabaig language also. As I brought out the hospital's phonograph, he watched me with increasing curiosity. The record recounted the parable of the Good Shepherd and begins with the frantic bleating of a sheep.

I now had his full attention. Where was the sheep? He looked in every direction but, oddly enough, the sound seemed to be coming from that box! When he heard someone speaking in his own language, inside that same box, his normally impassive face broke out into a wide grin. He listened intently, then rushed to the bedside of his wife to tell her of his remarkable experience.

In time, she recovered and they returned home. We trust this couple was reached again with the Gospel when the church was established in their vicinity.

In the next bed was Saada, an elderly women. She had been admitted with an enlarged abdomen and persistent nausea. She too had surgery. When Dr. Moris operated on her, he found that she had extensive, inoperable cancer. Neither chemotherapy nor radiation was accessible to her in that era.

Some of the nursing students took her on as a special prayer project and gently introduced her to the Great Physician. I will never forget that red letter day when Wankembeta, a second year student, come rushing up to me breathlessly announcing, "Saada had become a Christian!"

Saada slowly began to gain strength for her homeward journey. But one day she began vomiting and was in agonizing abdominal distress. Dr. Moris suspected a bowel obstruction, so it was back to surgery for her.

To his astonishment, when he opened the abdominal cavity he found only adhesions. All the masses had completely disappeared! The Great Physician had inexplicably healed both body and soul. The seed had found good soil indeed; it was a day of great rejoicing at Kiomboi Hospital.

Martha Fosse *was born and raised in Minneapolis, MN. She took pre-nursing courses at Augsburg College. At Swedish Hospital School of Nursing she completed a three-year diploma course and passed the requirements for R.N. She is a graduate of the University of Minnesota's School of Public Health with a B.S.*

After working as a public health nurse in Rochester, MN, she took the two-year missions course at Lutheran Bible Institute, Minneapolis, MN.

Martha was commissioned as a missionary nurse by the Augustana Lutheran Church for service in Tanganyika. From 1953 to 1958 she was a staff supervisor at Kiomboi Hospital and assisted in teaching at the nursing school.

Upon return to the U.S.A., she completed a Master's program in education at Peabody College in Nashville, TN. She taught nursing in Minneapolis for many years and later was a patient educator in a church-based clinic.

Martha now works as a volunteer at Global Health Ministries, an agency that supplies Lutheran health care facilities in developing countries with donated supplies and equipment.

Martha makes her home in Richfield, MN.

Although she spent relatively few years in Tanganyika, that unforgettable experience has enriched her teaching, profoundly altered her values, provided her with a large extended family and deepened her spiritual life.

OLD LETTERS COME TO LIFE

June Singley Nyblade

Today I opened the box of letters I had written to Mom and Dad from Tanganyika. The yellow-edged air forms were filled with tiny writing. With a whiff of dust, an array of memories wafted out surrounding me with nostalgia. How much I had forgotten. What silly mistakes we made; what responsibilities were ours; what skills we learned; how much we accomplished. How clever we were; how foolish, how courageous! But were we ever afraid?

April 6, 1955

Ihanja Mission Station will be our first place to live. High on a windy, barren hill the immediate area surrounding it is flat. We can see forests in the distance and across the valley on the horizon are the great granite outcroppings around the village of Puma. There are a few hospital buildings, a church, and two other missionary homes a short distance from us on this station.

The little foliage about the house was planted by Renee and Elder Jackson whom we are visiting today. They will be going to Karatu, a station in the northern area. This burnt-brick house, topped with a corrugated metal roof, has so much space we will rattle around in it until we buy some furnishings. One of the first things I must do is make curtains for these big windows. I like the continual wind gusting around this hilltop, but it shakes the doors and windows, making mournful sounds through the night.

August 20, 1955

Orville had to be away several nights again this week. As our worker, Rebeka, left this afternoon she hesitated and said, "Mama, aren't you afraid to stay here alone?" I suppose she was hinting about staying with me, but it never occurred to me to ask someone to stay. In my naivete, I had never thought about it and told her that if I were inclined to be fearful, I would have stayed in America. Of course, Dotty Anderson is in a house just a short way off, so I am not completely alone on the station.

November 3, 1955

I finally got around to sewing curtains. My priorities got shuffled. Coping with a wood-burning stove, pasteurizing milk, finding time to study Swahili, playing with Becky who is now walking, all of these became more important than covering our windows. The first few nights, as I lay listening to the wind and the hyenas howling around the house, I realized that no one would be walking about, peering in our windows. But now we will be entertaining the whole mission for their business meeting and it would be nice to have the curtains up.

June 6, 1956

Walter received presents today on the event of his baptism. Patrick's wife (Patrick works for us) sent six eggs, a papaya, a head of cabbage and two pounds of green beans. Pastor Clemens Kingu, who baptized Walter, sent him a huge wild duck.

Pastor Clemens has from time to time sent us a leg of impala, or wild pig. Acts of kindness like these, and when the choir came to serenade me after Walter's birth, are very touching, making us feel accepted within the community.

December 28, 1957

Early Christmas morning, we gathered with the Christians of our Ihanja parish to sing praises to the Christ Child. Two hundred people came this year, the most we have had in the three years we've been here. I shivered walking through the pre-dawn mist, with the other shadowy forms silhouetted by the light of swinging lanterns, as we made our way along the path toward the dark church. One by one we shuffled in and huddled closely on the cold benches while our lanterns were taken forward to light the lectern and pulpit.

When the altar candles were lit, the people began to sing the old familiar carols, softly at first but then with gusto. The pale grey light of dawn outlined the glassless windows. Slowly the warmth of the tropical sun flooded in. A stray dog wandered up and down the aisle hunting for his master; babies cried and were comforted; a pressure lamp hissed; but the glorious message of Christmas rang out above all those distractions and captured my heart and mind.

April 25, 1958

This has been a trying week for us. When Orville went to Singida to collect two women guests from the States, he discovered their arrival would be delayed two days. Returning to Singida on Tuesday to meet the women, he expected to be back here for supper. Edythe Kjellin, the nurse who supervises the dispensary on our station, came on Tuesday morning. As she passed Singida on her way, she heard that when not finding the guests in Singida, Orv and Vern Swenson had started out to hunt for them, fearing that their transport might have broken down. I did not worry that first night.

All day Wednesday, I went about my work, wondering and waiting and preparing another meal for our expected guests. Supper time came. I was glad to have Edy to keep me company. By bedtime, anxiety had gotten the best of me. My good hearing can detect the rumble of a vehicle from far down in the valley, but there was no sound of the Jeep. All sorts of dire imaginings rolled in my head as I tossed and turned that night.

Thursday morning, a messenger stopped by to tell us that Orville and Vernon had gone about 150 miles to Babati where they learned that a broken axle on Hal Faust's car had kept him from escorting the guests to Singida. He had put the women on a bus and they had passed Orv and Vern on the way. Edy and I both breathed a sigh of relief and a prayer of thanks that they were safe.

People writing from home ask, "Aren't you afraid out there?" That Wednesday night I was, and I imagine Doris Swenson and Louise Faust must have been also, as we worried and wondered what had happened to our husbands.

August 17, 1960, Kiomboi
Andrew Arnold Nyblade was born last night at 10:20, just before the generator went off. Someone rushed out to start it again, so Dr. John Hult and nurses Lois Austin and Freda Oman could finish attending Andrew and me. That probably sounds scary to you at home, but I was happy to come back here to Tanganyika to our mission hospital to have this baby.

The "sick-bay" attached to the nurses' home has two hospital rooms, a nurse's station and a well-equipped delivery room. Meals are served from the nurses' kitchen. One couldn't ask for more personal and devoted care in which to deliver a baby.

Bev Henry and her baby, Joyce, born August 9th, are still here although they have moved to another missionary home to make room for us. Shirley Augustine is also here with her premature baby, Cindy Lou. Since the baby is gaining nicely, they turned off the incubator today.

December 9, 1961, Kititimu
Today is Independence Day for Tanganyika. I have a banner proclaiming *Uhuru na Amani* (Freedom and Peace) stretched across our back porch. Everyone walks by here on the way to town. Lois Swanson, our neighbor, says of Independence Day, "We missed the U.S.A. one in '76 but we're here for this one in '61." I made green *Uhuru* shirts for the boys to wear to the celebration, as the national colors are green and black.

At the lowering of the British Union Jack and the raising of the Tanganyika flag, there were both tears of sadness and shouts of joy. The celebrations will continue for several days with sports events, speeches, and parades.

We are thankful that it was an orderly and peaceful transition. These past few months many of the Indian community left the country, fearing political turmoil. Our missionary community had made arrangements for someone to man the inter-station radios, just in case, but most everyone felt the emphasis of *Uhuru na Amani* would carry the day. And it did. Any worries or fears that lurked in the back of our minds evaporated as life goes on.

March 11, 1963, Mgori

Saturday when I was teaching one of the school girls how to scrub floors, I was called to the office door. As I opened it, a young primary school teacher came staggering down the path, gasping for breath, and collapsed on the door step. He had been stung just a few minutes before by a wasp and was having a violent allergic reaction.

Orville had gone to Arusha but fortunately had arranged for another car to be left with me in case I would need it. Kalebi, the man who cuts wood for us, helped me get the teacher into the Land Rover. He was shaking so much that Kalebi had to hold on to him while I drove. We were half a mile up the escarpment when I noticed the gas gauge was on empty. Back to the house we went for petrol.

By this time the teacher was writhing with pain. While Kalebi pumped gas, I ran to get the antihistamine syrup I use for the children when they get asthma. After three spoonfuls of that the teacher quieted somewhat.

Off we went again, with what seemed to me a snail's pace as the escarpment of the rift is very steep. It is sixteen miles to Singida from Mgori, but we made it and rushed the teacher into the hospital waiting room. Before they could even get ready to treat him, he went limp. I hollered for the doctor to hurry! A nurse rushed in with a shot of adrenaline. The teacher revived a little, but he began to have terrific pains in his head and chest. Kalebi and I could hardly hold him on the table.

The nurse ran for another injection which seemed to work, although he went through ten more minutes of agony. I can still hear him crying, over and over, *"Mungu, unihurumie!"* (God, have mercy on me!). He was given a sedative and in fifteen minutes quieted and had a good heart beat. By then I felt as if *I* needed a shot of adrenalin. Kalebi and I stayed until noon to be sure the teacher was recovering and then we hurried home, as I had left all the children, just shouting over my shoulder to our cook, "Take care of them till I get back."

March 24, 1963, Mgori

I'm sort of sick to my stomach tonight because I just wrecked our new three-kilowatt generator! Orv and the mechanics had just finished installing it Friday. Since Orv is going to Arusha tomorrow, he had given me a lesson last night on how to start the machine. It needs to be cranked.

This evening we drove two cars back from Singida so I'd have one here while Orv is gone. Since I got home first, I started the generator and forgot to pull the crank handle off the shaft. As soon as it started spinning, I realized my mistake. It was going at a terrific speed and I didn't dare try to get past it to reach the turnoff switch. I just took the children and got as far away from it as I could and waited for Orv.

With the weight of the handle spinning at that speed the vibration got louder and louder. There was a wrenching noise. The lights began to flicker, sparks flew and I was afraid the whole thing would blow up. The lights went out, but still the motor went on.

Finally Orv drove up and assured me that it wouldn't explode since the fuel was diesel, so we went to see what had happened. The motor and generator had been stripped loose from the cement base and had fallen against the brick wall. All the nuts and bolts were lying on one side and the handle was over in a corner. If it had to happen, I'm glad it happened tonight while Orv is here. I don't think I'll ever start the generator again even if it can be repaired.

October 14, 1963 Mgori

"What right do you missionaries have to try to change native people's beliefs? What they believe works for them." A nurse, caring for me when I had hepatitis while in the United States, spoke to me that way. I wish she could have been here this week. We have just hosted our Southeastern District meeting of the Women of the Lutheran Church in the Singida Region. Ninety women came for four days to study and fellowship around the theme, "Jesus Christ Is the Light of the World."

Mgori Mission Station is two-thirds of the way down the forested, eastern slope of the Rift Valley. The women walked here, women of all ages, many carrying babies on their backs. One group of nineteen came almost twenty miles, leading a blind woman.

Every Saturday for the last month our local women walked into the forest on the escarpment to cut firewood for this meeting. I drove the truck up to meet them and haul the loads back. The missionary mechanic shot a waterbuck for us, which the women preserved by cutting the meat in thin strips and rubbing them with salt. We hung the strips in my attic to dry, since this area has leopards and the meat wouldn't be safe hung in the trees.

My food committee piled into the truck one day for a trip to Singida to buy the rice, beans, oil, salt, and sugar we'd need. The women bought maize locally and arranged for grinding it for our basic meal. Onions, tea, and roasted peanuts rounded out our menu. The only water at our station is the few inches left in our cistern, so barrels of water were hauled the sixteen miles from Singida.

Since many of the women are beginning readers, they spent much time practicing the Bible verses they would read for devotions.

They practiced and discussed how they would demonstrate one of the women's secret tribal rites of passage. It was not certain until the last day if the women would do this, until one old woman said, "Not everyone has to do this. Only those who feel freed from the practice and are not afraid." That did it. Everyone agreed.

Many have criticized Christian missions because traditional customs, steeped in secrecy and fear, were forbidden for believers.

As the women planned the conference around the theme, Christ Is the Light of the World, they wanted to demonstrate how that Light and Christ's call to love and service had supplanted the secrecy and fear of the traditional ceremony performed around a young mother after the birth of her first child.

This ceremony is an initiation into a woman's place in society: behavior during childbirth, bearing children for her husband's clan, and labor in the fields raising food for the family. Fear is instilled by the presence of "the lion" and the *murimu* (a bead-covered gourd), with the threat of death to any who reveal the secrets, and to any man or uninitiated young woman who would see them.

Because this practice has been a central event in the lives of Turu women, the women wanted to substitute a Christian ritual which would be dramatic and inspirational. It was decided that this showing would be after the closing worship on Sunday. A candlelight service of blessing was chosen, not just for new mothers, but for any woman who had had a baby that year.

The week went well. Cooking was the biggest problem as we had underestimated the amount of water and had to make extra trips to town. Our teaching sessions were well received. It was my first time to hear our Tanzanian women teach and they were excellent. The program included topics about being a joy for our elders, about birth, the dangers of female circumcision, child care and youth, play, cooking, stewardship and Christian marriage.

At the close of the first day, after the women had considered the subjects of birth, infancy, early childhood and youth, we held our candlelight worship service. Each woman with her infant on her back came forward to the altar to receive her candle. The pastor took the flame from the altar, lit each mother's candle, whereupon she held it high, a symbol of the light of the gospel she would pass on to her children. The words of the benediction mingled with the aroma of the flickering candles in the solemn silence of the church as we ended our first day.

In Tanzania, work is often accompanied by singing, not only to enhance the rhythm of the task, but to express one's feelings. One of the local teachers, gifted in choir directing, taught the women new songs, adding inspiration at the close of each day and preparing a credible choir for our Sunday closing worship.

When the worship was over and the speeches of thanks given, the women announced the demonstration of the "lion" and *murimu*. The initiate is instilled with fear by being told she is going to be taken to a lion. The "lion" is an earthenware pot, covered with a wet goat skin, held taut by two women. Three other women stand over it, holding arrow shafts, which they rub and rotate against the skin while others drip water on the shafts. The water, bouncing off the vibrating skin, sounds just like a lion's roar.

The women had trouble getting the lion to roar, so for a few minutes there was pandemonium as all the old women pushed forward to offer advice while the men and children stood on the benches to see better. When the lion's roar echoed around the church, the women began to chant and the mother of the initiate came in on her knees, leading her kneeling, blindfolded daughter by a rope. The young woman who played the part of the daughter was a real actress, depicting the frightened initiate as wailing, straining on the rope and finally fainting. When the blindfold was removed so she could see the lion, two women began fighting over the goat skin like hyenas. They were on hands and knees, growling and grabbing the skin back and forth with their teeth.

When this acting was over, the young mother was made to sit on the ground. The elder women brought a set of bells which they rang all around her while chanting and dancing. She had to spit on these bells. A hoe was presented to her, a symbol of her work in producing food. Last of all, a bead-covered gourd, the *murimu*, was brought to her so she could pledge allegiance to it, believing it assured her the blessing of fertility.

When the ceremony was over and everyone quieted down, several women spoke about how learning of God's love through Jesus Christ had brought release from the fear and futility of this practice. Particularly moving was the thanksgiving of a young teenage girl, that this fear was now removed from her life.

That week I grew closer in understanding my Turu women friends. Their faith and courage in the face of a legacy of fear, superstition and physical hardships will always be an inspiration to me.

June Singley Nyblade, *born June 26, 1927, was educated at Wilkinsburg High School, PA, 1941-45; Allegheny College, 1945-47; University of Michigan, 1947-49; and earned a B.S. Degree in Dental Hygiene. She was employed first in Plymouth, MI, public schools 1949-51; then Davenport, Iowa and San Diego, CA, in private practices, 1951-54.*

Married in 1951 to Rev. Orville Wesley Nyblade, they had six children, five of whom were born in Tanzania. Daughter Becky died in 1997.

June and Orv served as missionaries in Tanganyika /Tanzania from 1955-1991. June worked in public health and advocacy work for women and children, establishing an "Under 5's Clinic" and a house building program.

AN ASTONISHING CELEBRATION

Carol Anderson

It was a new experience for this Norwegian-American, but it promised to be a beautiful one—a sunrise Easter celebration.

The path to the church at Nkungi was barely visible under the faint glow of the pre-dawn sky. I looked for other walking figures, but could see no one.

Reasons came to mind: "These dear people may not have a timepiece—Some may have to walk many miles to reach the church—One can't discredit them for not being punctual—They deserve high praise for conquering the many obstacles which could prevent them from coming at all—Surely they will be there according to Tanzania time."

The church was still dark when I arrived. No sound came from the dark interior of the church. I thought no one was there. Groping my way to a bench, I managed not to trample on the few persons I began to see nearby.

As I waited quietly in the absolute silence, my eyes gradually accommodated to the dimness. What a thrilling, joyful astonishment to discover that the church was full of people! Our risen Lord was loved so much by so many that none took a chance on missing this significant festival. The act of worship had already been taking place for many minutes, for an hour or more for some, yes, even on the journey to the church.

I was glad when they said to me, "Let us go to the house of the Lord."
Psalm 122:1.

Carol Anderson *was born in Sinyang, Honan, China, to missionary parents. She attended the American School for Missionaries' Children, on Kikungshan, through grade seven. Continuing her education in the United States, she graduated from Murray High School, St. Paul, MN. A five-year college/ nursing course was started at Concordia College, Moorhead, ND; continued at Fairview Hospital, Minneapolis, MN, and fi-*

nally was completed at the University of Minnesota where she received her B.S. in Public Health Nursing.

After varied nursing experiences in the U.S.A., including seven years as a visiting nurse with the Family Nursing Service in St. Paul, MN, she was commissioned by the Lutheran Church in America, to serve in Tanganyika, E. Africa.

From 1967 to 1976 she carried various responsibilities in hospital and community settings. An important part of her work was supervision of maternal and child health clinics promoting health education. The goal set for her by Pastor Musa, President of the Lutheran Central Synod, was "to assist the local people to carry on without foreign personnel." This goal had previously been Edythe Kjellin's assignment until her retirement. Carol responded to her commission with an accolade: "What an enormous challenge to try to fill the unfillable shoes of Edythe Kjellin!"

Of the variety of rewarding experiences since her return to USA, a most notable service has been, in her words, "With help, caring for Mother Adelia in her home until her death after 104 years of abundant living." At present, Carol says she is "temporarily retired and relocating to Eagan, MN."

TAKE THE CHURCH TO THE PEOPLE

Ruth Trued

GETTING ACQUAINTED

For two days the train chugged along at fifteen miles an hour from Dar es Salaam to the small town of Itigi, allowing us to absorb the feel of Africa. Leaning out the window of the slow-moving train, I could smell the land, hear the sounds, and watch the sights. We were coming very close to our destination.

Don, my husband, and I had answered the call from the Board of Foreign Missions to serve in Tanganyika (later Tanzania), East Africa. Of the 120 tribes in Tanganyika, we knew that we would be working among the Lyamba, Turu or Barabaig people. Now it was slow-down time. Time to think about the people we would learn to know during the next several years.

Sometimes the train stopped near small villages of mud houses and thatched roofs. Men, women and children dressed in plain or brightly colored cloths loosely draped around their bodies walked up and down the train selling vegetables, bananas, papaya and mangoes. Their handcrafted grass baskets and mats, and polished ebony wood carvings sold quickly.

"Jambo!" (Hello!), called a small child dressed only in his birthday suit as he led a blind man by the hand toward our first-class coach. It was not easy to look at the old man with disfigured eyes, stooped shoulders and tattered clothing. The two of them were begging for a shilling. My heart felt sorrow as I gave them a coin and wondered if many blind people lived where we were going. Little did I know that in a few months one would be my best helper.

Stepping off the train with the Beyerhelm family at Itigi, we were met by a strong blast of hot wind and a dark-skinned Indian who claimed he was sent to meet us. Skeptical at first, but seeing there was no alternative, we loaded our bags and luggage in the taxi. It became obvious that there was no room for us to sit! So, after tying suitcases on top of the car, with bags bulging out the sides, we breathed a silent prayer for protection as we crowded together for the 70-mile trip to the village of Singida. "Crowded" took on new meaning when three more people appeared with their loads, squeezing in where there was no more room to squeeze! Later, we learned that the Asian Indians were the main merchants of the area and controlled most of the transportation.

One numb leg and arm at a time, we emerged from the taxi at the mission station in Singida, thanked the driver for a safe trip and eagerly unloaded our belongings. There we learned that Don and I would study Swahili in the home of Pastor Ruben and Helen Pedersen at Kinampanda, the Teacher Training Center for African students.

Entering Kinampanda, or any other mission station, is not like entering a town. Rather, it can be described as following a road in a pasture with small trees and shrubs, then suddenly coming upon a clearing with a sign designating the place. It was just getting dark when we arrived at the Pedersen home. Several Africans and about six missionary families were waiting for us. When the children called us "Auntie Ruth" and "Uncle Don," we knew we were in a warm place among friends.

Awakened by the smell of hot coffee and rolls, we were royally welcomed by Rube and Helen. They started our first Sunday in Africa by presenting us with *Membo ma Kiklisito (Songs of Christ)*. At church that day we could understand one word, "Amen." For three months, the Pedersens adopted us as part of their family. They graciously opened the way for our orientation into an unfamiliar culture, and led us to the people through the common language of the country, Swahili. They taught us how to live and sing "On The Sunny Side!"

As president of the Lutheran Church of Central Tanganyika, and acting Headmaster of the Teacher Training Center, Rube was a *fundi* (expert) in many things. One of his talents was directing a mixed chorus of approximately 100 voices at the school. "Ruth," he said, "Don and I need to repair a vehicle and fix a tire. Would you please teach my choir this week?"

No problem, I thought. "Sure, Rube, I would enjoy that. Where is the music?" He handed me a melody and said I could easily arrange it into four parts. There was no need to give everyone a copy because no one could read notes. I sang bass, and they sang bass. All parts were learned by rote and I was truly amazed!

Helen was a nurse and accustomed to emergencies. One Sunday after church a young boy came whimpering to the house with a three-inch thorn jammed into the top of his foot. He had been playing barefooted soccer with his friends when the accident happened. Skillfully, Helen removed the thorn, cleaned and treated the foot, and sent him on his way. On another Sunday I would treat Helen, but not as skillfully.

That Sunday, in a remote village at the foot of the escarpment (a long, steep, cliff-like ridge separating the plateau from the valley), the Pedersens and we were scheduled to lead a communion and baptismal service in a new congregation. It was the dry season, very warm, with no movement of air. At the top of the cliff, we stopped the Jeep, looked down the rutted, treacherous road, and decided to walk the rest of the way.

Carrying a bucket of water for the baptisms, a bucket of boiled drinking water and the wine for communion, the four of us carefully descended the rocky slope. The crowd was assembled under a tree where a crude altar had been fashioned from tree limbs.

About half way through the three-hour service, Helen fainted and fell into my lap. No one seemed to notice. My heart nearly stopped.

"Helen, are you all right?" No response. Should I interrupt Rube while he was preaching? My eye spotted the bucket of water—the baptismal water—and I hesitated, but only for a moment! I eased her body to the ground, hopped over the altar rail, grabbed the bucket of water, and splashed some on her face. No one will ever know how tremendously relieved I felt to see her eyes open. The service was only slightly delayed.

One week Helen was called to assist in the care of a newborn baby. Rube was away at a meeting. Don and I were left to survive on our own. Wintyapa, the cook, could not understand my faltering Swahili, and I definitely couldn't understand hers. Even a form of sign language was not adequate. So, I let her take a vacation. This was not a good idea but it did become a beneficial learning experience.

I decided to cook a fresh roast for dinner. Earlier, Don and Rube had gone hunting to bring home meat for the school and mission station. All they could find was a buffalo—a very old buffalo. After two hours of cooking, the meat was still tough as an old shoe and could not be sliced, so I gave it to the worker who chopped firewood for us—he would know what to do with it!

Fortunately, Doris Swenson, Pastor Vernon's wife, invited us for supper. "Doris," I asked, "what is your secret for cooking wild meat?"

"Oh," she responded, "you need to simmer the meat all day or cook it in a pressure cooker to make it moist and tender, and to kill worms found in the meat!" I wondered if we would survive the week!

It was time to bake bread. Opening a bag of flour, I discovered it was crawling with worms and promptly threw it out. The next bag of flour could have walked off the shelf, and the closest grocery store was in

Singida, many miles away. We wouldn't be going there for a month or two. Either I would never eat bread again, or I would adjust.

When Helen came home, the first question I asked was, "Do we use flour with bugs in it?"

She answered, "Does the flour have bugs in it?"

"Yes," I replied emphatically.

"Well then," Helen said, "we use flour with bugs in it!"

Our three months were finished! Don and I had become acquainted with the people, their land and language. Students from the Teacher Training Center had helped us pronounce the words and learn their meaning, and we were ready to pass the required government written and oral exams. The Missionary Conference would soon make the decision to place us among the Lyamba people at Kiomboi where there was a hospital, a training center for nurses, primary and middle schools, and a school for the children of missionaries. There were approximately twenty outdistricts, each with small churches made of mud, corn husks, pounded dirt and tree limbs, with rows of logs to sit on. This would be our community and home for a while.

LET'S HAVE MUSIC

"Uncle Ray (principal of the boarding school), is it four-thirty yet?" asked an eager piano student as she studied the list of practice periods on the wall. I listened from the music room to others as they checked their time, and hoped the enthusiasm of this first week at school would continue through the term.

The Augustana School, first grade through eighth, was located at Kiomboi. They needed a music teacher and I was delighted to be of service. Forty children, (twenty beginners) wanted piano lessons, and there were only five pianos on which to practice. A strict schedule of 30 minutes per child per day was a good start.

"Let's have a band!" I suggested to the upper grades.

"We can't have a band without instruments," they said. Some of the parents heard about the idea and before long you could hear a lot of blowing and bowing coming from the school. One lone violinist put up a good fight for orchestral rights as he joined his clarinet, trombone, baritone and trumpet friends. Someone gave us an African drum hewn from a log, stretched with zebra skin. A few bells and a piano completed the percussion section. Simple arrangements from my own music and student compositions provided enough music to help us make a joyful sound.

We sang in the classroom, learned a bit of theory, and listened to stories about great composers. Keeping time with the rhythm band instruments was fun in the lower grades, and so was learning to play the pretty red, green and black tonettes. Sometimes, student nurses from the hospital would come to listen.

"Auntie Ruth," said a fourth grade student, "we work so hard to keep time and play the melodies correctly, how do the African children learn music?"

Good question, I thought. They don't read notes and count as we do, yet they can make clever tunes on tin flutes and beat complicated rhythms on handmade drums. Barefooted and wearing uniforms, the children march, sing and play in their school competitions. One day, I heard a boy playing beautiful melodies on a handmade marimba. He and his father had built the instrument by using different-sized gourds from their *shamba* (garden).

Highlights of the year came when parents arrived from long distances to take their children home for vacation. After many hours of practice, we enjoyed singing in groups, striking up the band, and playing piano selections for the proud families and guests. Three months of school followed by a month home with family was the regular routine.

REMOTE PLACES

"Take the Church to the people," Don commented, as we planned a week-long safari. The trip would take us from our Wembere home in the valley, up the steep escarpment, through Kiomboi, down a deeply rutted and rocky part of the escarpment to Tulya. Following cow paths, traveled only by the local herdsmen, we would drive through dense thorn bushes and rough fields to the remote area of Kidaru.

First, there were food and sleeping preparations to make. I filled a basket with roast impala sandwiches, bananas, papaya, and fresh vegetables from our garden, together with a few potatoes, onions and tins of food. We remembered the boiled drinking water! Don packed the small kerosene stove, matches, methylated spirits, and candles for the evening. Also, mosquito nets, cots, and fly spray.

"We have a very sick leprosy patient," said Nurse Lindy as we were ready to leave at 6:00 a.m. "He needs to be carried on a stretcher, and he must go to the hospital today!"

Standing near the Jeep, ten people hoped to catch a ride up the escarpment to Kiomboi. This time there was no room for them. We took the sick man, three members of his family, and their supplies of water and grain. Families always fed and cared for their own who were in the hospital.

After leaving the family at the Kiomboi Hospital, we ate lunch under a huge tree. Last Sunday under this same tree there was a festive three-hour service. Don helped the African pastor baptize 99 children and commune 3,000 adults. I played the old pump organ and everyone sang as women added high trills to the glorious sound.

Back on the road again, we tried to reach Tulya before nightfall. The dirt road was rough and rocky with many holes. Suddenly we hit a bump, the engine fan made an awful clatter, and Don slammed on the brakes. The motor mount had broken, and the frame mounting cracked in two! The jolt finished what had been started sometime ago. By using a tire iron and a chain, Don fixed it temporarily.

The sun was low in the sky, and we were afraid to descend this part of the mile-long escarpment in the dark. Backing off the road into a secluded area, we prepared to spend the night in the back of the partly-enclosed Jeep. While I fixed supper, Don set up the cot with a mosquito net, and put food supplies in the cab away from ants or animals. By 7:00 p.m. darkness had covered this quiet spot away from all civilization. It had been a long day and we were ready for a good night's sleep. However, on this very night the rain descended in torrents! Cold and damp, we were held captive in cramped quarters until mid-morning when the rain quit as quickly as it had started.

"*Bwana* (Sir), are you all right?" called Evangelist Petro from a short distance away. "A man walking by your vehicle last night reported to the village that you might be having trouble." After the rain, Petro and two other Christians had climbed the escarpment to see if we needed help. Their gesture of kind friendship and concern was heart-warming, and we invited them to join us for a cup of coffee. The decision to retrace our steps to Kiomboi was a wise one. There we secured a more dependable vehicle for the rest of the trip.

At the foot of the green-covered escarpment, between two trees overlooking a beautiful lake, sat a *kabanda kadogo* (little hut). Built with Don's own two hands, it measured 8 x 14 feet. Our very own home! It had two small windows which often framed curious faces catching a glimpse of the strange white people. Nearby, under a large baobab tree, private from only one side, was a wash stand and barrel of water for bathing. Farther away, hidden among the bushes and downwind from the hut, was a six-foot hole called "*choo*," rhymes with "go." Or, in plain English, an open-air toilet under the sky. From this humble home at Tulya, we saw clusters of mud houses and heard voices talking, laughing and scolding.

Few people here had heard the Good News, and our mission was to "take the Church to them." So, armed with a phonograph and recordings in the tribal tongue containing the message of Jesus and His resurrection, we found a shady tree under which to sit. Joining us were Evangelist Petro and half a dozen other Christians who had come to give their testimony. Don and I played our trombone and baritone instruments until a crowd was gathered. Intently, old men and women, young folks and children listened to the music and recordings. The Chief of the tribe had heard our message in another village, and had followed us here. He wanted to listen again. "I want to become a Christian," he said. "If the voice in that box says so, then the story must be true!"

We needed to repair the primary school and the teacher's house at Kidaru. Since there were no skilled workmen in the remote area of Kidaru, Tulya's Evangelist Petro selected three of his best workmen to go with us. We also took several bags of cement and other equipment for the building project.

It was very hot and dry. Slowly, we fought our way up and down deep ruts into soft fields, and through dense thorn shrubs and trees. Over a hill, we came close to a water hole where the stench in the heat of the day was suffocating. Here we saw a herdsman and his cattle both drinking and bathing in the same green, stagnant water.

Checking our watches and speedometer, we had gone five miles in 45 minutes. Something was wrong. We must have missed the baobab tree that would indicate Cow Path Left instead of Cow Path Right! Men and women hoeing in their fields and small naked children following the Jeep were pleased to show us the way.

Approaching Kidaru, there was a sharp corner and narrow descent with huge rocks on one side, and a six-foot drop to the river on the other. Putting the Jeep in tractor gear, we inched down toward the river. There were no bridges. We didn't know exactly where to cross, but the Africans knew. Stepping into the water, they tested soft places, and guided us safely to the other side.

At the primary school, teacher Yeremia joined Don and his crew to haul rock and sand from the river for the cement job. I set up cots in the school office and fixed lunch. From the back of the Jeep we cooked meals on our Primus pressure stove.

Juliana, the teacher's wife, was so glad to see us. She welcomed us by sweeping the floor, covering the small table with a clean cloth, and placing a tin can of pretty pink flowers on top. The room had one window, a desk, a couple dozen rakes and hoes, and several bags of corn. The supply of corn was later ground and made into mush for feeding the school children. Lizards scampered up the wall. We kept our nets tucked in tight that night!

Just before dark, Don took Yeremia, the workmen and a local guide hunting, hoping to provide meat for the evening meal. They came back with a zebra, as well as the favorite of most missionaries, an impala. We butchered the animals quickly and distributed the meat to those who went hunting with Don, before the laughing hyenas came to claim their share.

Birds hilarious with the joy of a new day and the persistent gnawing of rats in the far corner of the room brought a restless night to a halt. Juliana and I visited with each other as she watched me take down the net and cots. "Juliana," I asked casually, "do you see many snakes around here?" The thought had haunted me several times during the night.

"Oh, yes," she responded, "we killed one yesterday longer than Bwana Truedi is tall, and the children have already buried it. It was hiding behind the bags of corn in this room!"

I was not amused, but laughed and said, "I'll believe that when I see it." A few minutes later, and to my great astonishment, two boys came dragging the black cobra by the tail and dropped it at my feet. It measured eight feet without the head, which had been cut off by the medicine man!

Needless to say, I was happy when the work was finished and we could go back to our home in Wembere.

CHRISTMAS AT IHANJA

Our toddler son, Steve, made us a proud threesome as we clung to our seats on the bus and bounced down the dusty road toward our new home where Don would be teaching at the Ihanja Bible School among the Turu Tribe. The ride was frightful. With a heavy load of people and cargo, the bus driver knew little fear as he seemed to thrill at the sight of narrow escapes, swerving at folks walking along the graveled road, speeding down steep hills, around sharp corners and in loose sand. Helplessly, we prayed earnestly for a safe trip. Steve wasn't afraid! He watched the ostrich with its long, graceful, silk-stocking-like legs, giraffe, impala, zebra and wildebeest as they formed a unique reception along the way.

Ihanja Mission Station was a friendly place to live. One day a man came to our house looking for a job. Although congenitally blind, he traveled by foot and knew the countryside well. Raheli, the girl who helped us cook, clean, and also watch Steve, told us that the man did not have a Christian name, he spoke only in his tribal tongue, but she had heard that he was a good worker. During the rainy season, we collected rain in a huge underground cistern and expected it to last through the dry season. I needed someone to hand pump the water from the cistern to a tank in the attic and this blind man was eager to do the job. On time every morning, he would sing softly while he worked, and never quit before hearing the sound of "full."

Then, one day he didn't come to work, nor the next. The African neighbors told me he had gotten sick and died. Why was it so easy for people to die in this country? I would never know if this trusted, dependable blind person knew about the love of Jesus.

"Don, it's almost Christmas and we don't have a tree," I remarked.

"There are no evergreen trees in this part of the country," he responded.

Raheli thought that a hike in the *pori* (woods) could help us find something nice. So, after supper in the cool of the evening, the four of us went to find a Christmas tree.

"Look what I found," called Steve. "This bush is pretty!" Yes, it was naturally decorated with balls the size of black walnuts. This had to be the perfect one. We chopped it down, put it in a bucket of wet sand, and set it in the living room for all to see. That night, a funny thing happened. While we were sleeping, the plant became warm and all the little black balls opened. In the morning the entire house was crawling with ants!

With the two other missionary families on the station, we planned a Christmas Eve party and invited a few Tanzanian friends. We thought it would be fun to initiate the idea of a gift exchange with a limit of approximately two shillings, 28 cents in American money. After an evening of singing, telling stories, and refreshments, we saved the gift exchange until last. Some folks received eggs, others a bag of peanuts. I received a live chicken! No one suspected that four chickens were wrapped in newspapers, quietly waiting their turn at the party!

On Christmas Day the service lasted the usual nearly three hours. This was a special service when all the outdistricts would come to worship in the main church at Ihanja. There was singing, many greetings, including one from the Chief of the tribe, family baptisms and communion. The Swahili sermon was translated into the Turu tribal tongue. Folks walked barefooted for miles to participate in this festive celebration. Halfway through the service, one woman with her baby tied on her back got up, shook hands with her friends, and left for the eight-mile trek home.

"Asante sana!" (thank you very much!), the Sunday School children said as we handed them a ball of brown sugar—their favorite treat! They were pleased with colored Bible pictures sent to them from Sunday School children in the States. After the service the children followed the African pastor's blind son to his home where their mothers had prepared a meal of corn and beans. A trench with hot firewood made a good stove for the *madebe* (five-gallon metal containers) filled with simmering food. Everyone sat in a circle on the ground and politely waited. When the food was ready, it was served on woven grass plates or metal lids. Using their fingers as utensils, the children happily feasted on corn and beans. We did not realize that this would be our last Christmas in Africa.

"Kwa heri," cried Raheli, as we shook hands and said good-bye. "I know we'll see you in heaven," she smiled as we waved and left Ihanja, and Africa.

During seven years of work in Tanzania, the African soul had touched our lives. Every missionary man, woman and child had become our family. It would be that way forever.

━━━

Ruth Trued *has a Bachelor of Music degree from Bethany College, Lindsborg, KS, and has taught vocal and instrumental music in the public schools of Kansas, Illinois, New Jersey, and Augustana School at Kiomboi, Tanzania, East Africa.*

She was a Realtor Associate in Ridgewood, NJ, and has held leadership positions in church women's organizations.

Ruth and her husband Don reside in Lindsborg, Kansas. They have two adult children, Steve and Kathy.

LEARNING THE 4 R'S
IN TURU "BUSH" SCHOOLS
Della Brown

"I think the best way for you to get acquainted in this new job is to visit some of our twenty-eight bush schools, as well as the six government registered primary schools." It sounded a bit daunting — thirty-four places to oversee! But I had expected challenge; why else was I needed?

The speaker was Pastor Clemens Kingu, the very fine Tanzanian pastor of Ihanja parish where I had been stationed after three months of language study. "We don't expect you to go by yourself," he continued, "so I've assigned one of the church elders to help you find the way."

Our plan was to leave at 6:00 a.m. in order to reach the school by 8:00. When we arrived, I was shocked to note there were no desks. However, vertical poles driven into the ground at regular intervals supported horizontal poles that served as improvised benches for the twenty to twenty-five pupils.

At that time, in the early 1950's, there were too few registered schools for all the children eager to learn. So "bush schools" were opened to teach reading, writing, arithmetic, agriculture and Christianity.

The teacher at this school, Paulo *Nasongelya* (I give thanks) was a remarkable young man. He had had only six years of primary education. He noticed I was carrying a big chart with many Bible pictures, so I was invited to have the first hour.

I recall that I first showed the picture of Jesus carrying a lamb in His arms and shared the story of Jesus hunting for the lost sheep. I had their undivided attention as they learned part of the 23rd Psalm, *"The Lord is my shepherd; I shall not want."*

Then the children went outside for their arithmetic, reading and writing lessons. In those "bush schools," unlike the registered schools, they had no notebooks, pencils, chalk or slates. But each child had a short stick to scratch out problems in the sand! The teacher wrote words and sentences on his large slate for the reading lesson. Each pupil scratched the words in the sand.

During the noon hour Paulo took the class to the school garden for their agricultural lesson — planting millet and corn. During their recess, Paulo invited me to his home to rest and have lunch.

His wife had a good fire going outside, and she brought a stool for me to sit on. Paulo took a cob of corn and put it into the hot ashes. I can see him yet as he blew off the ashes and gave the roasted cob to me. The kernels were really dry and hard, but I chewed and chewed until I finished the cob. But when he came with a second cob, my jaws were so tired, I thanked him and said I couldn't eat any more.

The afternoon classes started with marching to the rhythm of the drums, followed by a singing period. Then came the drills and review of the morning classes; the children then were dismissed so they could start on the long walk to their homes.

It was now about four o'clock and my guide and I started our eight-mile walk home. This first visit to a "bush school" was typical of many subsequent visits to other classes.

When Christmas came that year, the students from all twenty-eight bush schools and six registered schools were on the program at church—singing, clapping and drumming from 9:00 a.m. until 3:00 p.m.!

After most of them had gone home, Pastor Clemens told me about the Muslim father who came to his home and asked, "Tell me, please, what is this message that makes people so happy and sing with such joy?" Little wonder that God used the "bush schools" in the entire community, so the church grew with God-given grace.

NAGUNWA: "I'VE BEEN REDEEMED"

From my office vantage point, watching the Iambi villagers go by on my front path, I noticed one person in particular, an elderly man I knew as *Nagunwa* (I've been redeemed). Every Saturday he walked to the church carrying a broom across his shoulders.

One Saturday as he came from the church, I stepped out and invited him to come in. As we sat down together, I asked him, "Brother, I'd like to hear about what drew you to become a Christian."

I'll never forget the expression on his uplifted face as he started to sing, "What a Friend we have in Jesus" (in the local language—Lyamba). The glow on his face is still visible in my memory.

Then he started to share how the message of Jesus was such good news that he had traveled from one village to another in that entire valley, to share his faith.

Later, others told me that each month Nagunwa had walked hundreds of miles during all the years from his baptism until now in his "preaching-sharing mission." I soon learned that it was witnesses like Nagunwa who brought hundreds of people to experience "being redeemed" as they themselves had been.

Della Brown *spent her childhood and youth in Hallock, MN. She graduated from the Lutheran Bible Institute in Minneapolis, MN.*

In 1952 she was commissioned by the Augustana Lutheran Church for service in Tanganyika as a parish educationist. Her first parish responsibility at Ihanja Mission Station was to train village teachers for the 28 bush schools and to organize Sunday Schools. She had much to do in preparing lessons for all the Sunday Schools and to give training to all the Sunday School teachers who had been recruited in the villages.

After several years the church leaders asked her to move to the Bible School at Ihanja. She taught at the Bible School both at Ihanja and later at Kiomboi for 13 years until her retirement in 1977. After retirement she served as a volunteer parish worker in the congregation of which she was a member in Portland, Oregon. She now resides in Tacoma, WA.

GOD'S SPECIAL PROTECTION
Eileen Nelson Jacobson

PROTECTED IN LONDON

"Ma'am, are you all right?" asked the surprised school girl as she caught up with me at the foot of the long stairs where I had just slammed into the wall.

I was still standing up—much to my amazement—in my three-inch high, narrow heels! I had just flown down the long flight of steps, having caught my heel on one of the upper steps. My camera bag was still on my shoulder! The palms of both hands were pressed flat against the wall at shoulder height; I hadn't even bruised a finger! To this day I cannot explain such an amazing feat except to say that there must have been an unseen angel lifting me up!

The child who had accompanied me was showing me the way out of a primary school in London. I had gone there to observe classes during my layover in England enroute to Tanganyika; my teaching position was waiting for me at the Kinampanda Teachers' College. Since I would be working with Tanganyikan student teachers in a school system that was inspected periodically by British educators, I thought it would be helpful to make a visit to such a school as this.

Later as I reflected upon my aborted fall, I thought of how I could have been lying in a London hospital with broken bones, not knowing a single person in that big city. My loved ones back home would have been in a state of high anxiety. Needless to say, I was filled with gratitude to God who had watched over me. He had spared me much anguish! Psalm 91:11-12 became very meaningful to me: *"For he will command his angels concerning you to guard you in all your ways. On their hands they will lift you up, so that you will not dash your foot against a stone."*

This wasn't the only time that I experienced God's special protection. There were many times. Let me tell you of the night that I came very close to meeting danger on my path!

DANGERS IN THE DARK

"Always take a light with you when you're walking outside at night" was advice that I had taken seriously. However, this particular evening I had not planned to stay on at the school office after dark. I didn't even have a flashlight with me.

I was ready to go to my house, about a block from the classrooms at the Kinampanda Teachers' College. "Will you check my lesson plan?" asked one of the students. He was scheduled to teach at a nearby primary school the next day. Before he could do that, he had to have his lesson plan approved. Another student asked to get his plan checked, and several more did likewise. By the time I was free to leave, it was dark—but not too dark to find my way.

As I walked, I prayed that I would not step on any poisonous snakes. That was my main concern. In those days, the 1960's, wild animals weren't usually seen on the school campus or near our missionary houses. However, at times in the evenings, I could hear lions in the distance, down in the valley.

My walk home was uneventful. The next morning when I came to school, I heard the students say. "Did you know that two big female lions were seen over at the Middle School last evening?" That school was just across the road from ours!

"What time were they there?" I hastened to ask.

"About eight o'clock."

"Oh, no! That was the time when I was walking home!" I exclaimed. "What would I have done if I had seen them? I think my heart would have stopped!"

To think of meeting those lions is something I do not care to ponder even now—some thirty years later! Do I believe in God's protection? Oh, yes, I do!

EGGS IN A SUITCASE—A BOLD STEP OF FAITH

"A gift for you," she said as she handed me the chicken eggs out of her suitcase.

"Have these been boiled?" I asked. Learning that they had not, I was amazed that the shells were not cracked after a long, bumpy bus ride of several hundred miles. "How did you dare to carry them in your suitcase?" I inquired after hearing that her husband's good suit, which he was to wear for graduation the next day, was also packed in that suitcase!

Her answer, simply stated, amazed me! "I prayed that God would keep the eggs from breaking." What child-like faith and trust!

That was my introduction to Mrs. Kessy, the attractive wife of one of our Chagga students at Kinampanda Teachers' College. David Kessy had been a student in our boarding school for two years, and now he had successfully completed the requirements for graduation. Recently he had approached one of the other faculty members, Ida Marie Jacobson, and myself regarding an important matter. "This place has meant so much to me," he said. "I'd like to have my baby baptized here the weekend of my graduation. You've been my teachers, and I've been thinking how meaningful it would be if both of you could be sponsors at my daughter's baptism." Of course, we were very honored!

Little Joyce Mary was about nine months old, and her seven-year-old sister came along also. It was no simple feat for Mrs. Kessy to have made this journey to an unknown place; it was a real step of faith. She had never before been this far away from home. Coming to Kinampanda with two young children meant a very long day of tiring, stressful travel. Besides, she was to be a guest in the home of people whom she had never met. However, she had surely heard from her husband about Ida Marie and me. We were most impressed with this gracious woman and certainly blessed by her visit.

David Kessy was one of the mature students at our college, which was designed to accept only male students. Most of them were in their late teens or early twenties, but David had been out of school a number of years. He was very grateful for the opportunity to become a primary school teacher. Asking us to be baptismal sponsors was just one of the ways that he showed his appreciation for our efforts. The bond between black and white had been strengthened!

Eileen Nelson Jacobson *was brought up in Alexandria, MN. She attended the Lutheran Bible Institute, Minneapolis, MN, and holds a B.S. degree from St. Cloud State Teachers' College, St. Cloud, MN., She taught in elementary schools for three years prior to her service in Tanganyika.*

She was commissioned in 1955 by the Augustana Lutheran Church as a missionary teacher in Tanganyika.

She served as a teacher at the Ruruma Girls' School and Kinampanda Teachers' College until 1968 and at Augustana School for the final six months of her term. She returned to the U.S. in 1969.

In 1975 she was married to Charles D. Jacobson of Long Prairie, MN. They now reside in Alexandria, MN.

DID THEY MISS ANYTHING ?

Martha Malloy

Did they miss anything? Did American kids growing up in Tanzania lose out on important aspects of American culture because they were not attending school in the U.S.?

I'm not sure I can answer that question. What I do know is that there were exciting and unique events in their school lives which could not have been duplicated Stateside. It was my privilege as housemother at an American school in Africa, named "Augustana School," to witness these events. I was known by the children as "Auntie Martha." My husband, Fred, called "Uncle Fred" by the pupils, was involved in these events as well as being occupied with many other tasks.

Olympics Sports Day was one such event. It always evoked great enthusiasm. There was true excitement in the air for several weeks; this was going to be a big weekend. Parents and preschool siblings would be coming for the festivities.

The whole school was divided into four teams: Lions, Leopards, Giraffes and Elephants, each with a captain and loyal participants, each wanting to run up points for his or her team throughout the busy day.

The events started at 9 a.m. and progressed with growing excitement throughout the morning and after lunch. College kids home from the U.S. for a visit assisted; they scheduled and supervised all the events at various times and places: running, high jump, broad jump, basketball dunk, sit-ups, push-ups, gunny sack race. Everyone could participate in each event as he or she chose. The final event was the big basketball game that included both boys and girls.

The attire of the day was jeans and white T-shirts which had the animal emblem of the respective team as well as a head-band and arm-band with the same symbol. The big kids had designed the animals, but all participants colored their own gear, working on it two weeks ahead of time. Bamboo spears with cardboard shields attached were poked into the ground in a special design at the edge of the school yard. These would be picked up later when the children paraded around the station and gathered finally at a huge bonfire.

There was a picnic lunch, then the children had time with their families before the activities started again at two o'clock. The sports finished at 5 p.m. and the awards were given. Winners were presented with Augustana School "A's" made by the older boys and girls of "Tommy" (Thompson's gazelle) skin mounted on red felt.

After supper with the guests in the dining room, the kids joined ranks and had a parade around the mission station. There were drummers and fun songs. As they went by the hospital they got big applause. The children wound around the huge bonfire, had their devotions and sang some more.

It was always a festive, long day and the little ones were oh, so tired when I got them into the shower room, and ready for bed.

Since the parents were able to come so seldom, we packed a lot into this weekend. Sunday morning after Sunday School and worship services, we had a special dinner. Uncle Fred then led the school choir, garbed in their white robes, in singing to all the guests.

The choir later received an invitation to travel to the northern area of Tanzania to present some concerts. Fred asked our son, Dan, attending college in the States, to send us some new music. Fred had observed that one student, Sherman, had been working with some of the kids on their choir parts. Since Fred couldn't spend a lot of time teaching the kids, he asked Sherman to do that "officially." Each morning after breakfast until school time, Sherman gathered the kids around the piano and drilled them rigorously until all three parts knew their notes well. When the choir got together to practice, Uncle Fred was so pleased as the choir zipped through their new songs. Soon they were ready for their big concert tour.

They sang for the seminary students at the theological college at Makumira; they sang in the big Moshi Lutheran Cathedral where many of the parents who taught up on Mt. Kilimanjaro at the Bible School and the Girls' Secondary School could come and hear them; they sang in the town of Arusha. Everyone was thrilled with the trip and felt we had great concerts.

Our Halloween parties proved to intrigue and interest everyone, Americans, Europeans and Africans alike. Our African friends needed explanations to understand the costumes; some mothers had gone "all-out" with elaborate and beautiful costumes. There were ostriches and elephants, ballet-dancers, pirates, bathing beauties, astronauts, nurses and doctors. I went as the "Old Woman in the Shoe"—who had so many children she didn't know what to do. Of course we had judges and prize winners following the bobbing for apples, a cake walk, a ghost house, a fish pond for prizes. It was so much fun to hear our African workers' reactions; they were game to do it all.

What else was unique about life for these American kids at Augustana School in central Tanzania? On their home stations, all our children had seen a lot of house building by the Tanzanians. The older boys asked permission to do some construction of their own. They said they had the perfect spot. They knew the protocol of not disturbing a local footpath (which crossed our school grounds in many places) or not going close to a grave (the church's graveyard was just behind the school).

The location of the mud brick pit was chosen and the younger boys were enlisted to carry water to mix with chopped-up straw and grass to add to the mud mixture. This was packed into brick molds which they had borrowed from their Tanzanian friends. The consistency of the mix had to be just right when they put it into the molds. They laid the bricks out in long rows to dry in the sun. The hardest part was to have patience for the sun to do its work so the real construction of the house could begin.

The plans had all been laid out before they started. They had built-ins: table, benches, wall shelves, cupboards, stairs to balconies for bedrooms and shelves for clothes' storage. All the boys were so excited about this project. They rushed to the dorm each day after classes and changed their clothes quickly so they could continue their "work." They loved it!

When the girls saw what was going on they volunteered to make curtains, tablecloths, pillows and covered cushions. They wanted to be involved also!

The balcony and roof were made of eucalyptus branches. We wondered if they would be safe enough. Uncle Fred checked the barkstrip connections and found them sturdy.

Friends were invited in for tea. They invited African kids and also missionaries who lived on the station. The girls baked cookies in the evening for Saturday afternoon tea parties. Everyone had a turn at being invited.

The rainy season took its toll on the house during vacation month, so when the new term began the big boys had a lot of repairs to make. They then plastered both outside and inside with a good coat of mud.

So many other activities and happenings come to mind when I think of Augustana School. "Let's go for a hike" was a cry that rang through one dorm room, then another, then a third. It wasn't often that all the kids, all ages, insisted on going in the same direction—to the "Jungle Jim" tree! This huge baobab tree with its aerial roots was a favorite spot, with branches to walk on as well as to hold on to. Some wanted to stay up there forever! It was only the whiff of the barbecue grill set up nearby and my ringing of the bell that brought them down!

Outside of the school shower house, the contour of the sand bank was just perfect for miniature roadways and escarpments. This was the favorite spot for the little boys to play with their Dinky cars. You could always find a few boys out there, sometimes the big and middle boys also. They brought water to make proper landscapes and new roadways. They also furnished the sound effects of their vehicles!

Uncle Fred was "forever" taking pictures and setting up occasions for photography. Then he and many of the older kids developed them in the darkroom. Fred took pictures of each grade for the school newspaper, *The Kiomboi Bugle,* and for many of the events. Some of the kids became so proficient they continued with developing when they left Augustana School. One of our boys did all the photography and developing for the year book at Rift Valley Academy (high school in Kenya) the year he graduated.

Mid-term weekend breaks when the children were hosted at other mission stations; adventurous two-day trips to and from school in the middle of the rainy season when bridgeless rivers had to be forded; all of these happenings have their own stories to tell. One girl wrote her weekend hosts about an outing when Uncle Fred went into the bush to hunt and returned to the picnic spot with a wart hog: "Wasn't it fun gutting the pig!"

When friends in the States learned about the job and its myriad responsibilities that Fred and I had in Tanzania, they have questioned me, "How in the world did you get a job like that?"

I told them, "We answered an ad!"

My sister, who lived in Vancouver, had sent us a Canadian Lutheran Quarterly to read. She did so because it contained an article she had written about her church's completed building project. But in this publication my husband discovered an interesting item:

> *Wanted: Contractor with diversified experience to teach African Nationals the Building Trades. Matron to run a boarding school for Missionaries' children.*

We talked it over, called the listed agency, and had an appointment to meet with them on the day before Thanksgiving in 1957. The following April found our family, all six of us, in a DC6 on our way to Africa.

We were sent to Augustana School so the missionaries would not have to spend time home-schooling their children, but could devote more of their time working among the African people. The children were in our care when they were not in the classroom. The four teachers took turns having study hall after supper after which we had them for story time and devotions.

We had a staff of fifteen; they were loyal workers and there was little turnover. Our housekeeper was Creole French from the Seychelles Islands. Local African girls sorted and mended labeled clothes. The staff worked with bottled gas for cooking, electric washing machines, charcoal irons, refrigerators run by kerosene. We had electricity when the generator was on from 6 to 10 p.m., and at other times if surgery was going on at the hospital.

Our students were predominantly American, although we had a few Norwegian, Swedish, German, Tanzanian and British among them, a good mix. Most came from missionary families, a few from U.S. government employ.

We were at Augustana School for two four-year terms, surely among the most rewarding and interesting years of our lives. And we have cause to believe that for the children at this special school, they were happy years also. If they missed out on certain aspects of school life in the United States, there was much to make up for it!

Martha Hedman Malloy's *roots are in White Bear Lake, Minnesota, where she presently lives in retirement.*

She and her husband, Fred, are the parents of Dan, Helen (Sis), Mike and Steve. Following their eight years at Augustana School, Martha and Fred worked the next eleven years in Ethiopia, Fred in construction and Martha in community development. Together they organized a cotton industry of spinning, weaving and embroidering traditional Ethiopian garments.

They returned to Minnesota in 1977 where Martha worked as a purchasing agent for USDA, Agricultural Research Service, and the University of Minnesota. Fred passed away in 1990.

GROWING THROUGH GRIEF

Lora Anderson

The wound of sorrow was ever present those days and weeks and months, ready to be re-opened. I began working at the library at Tumaini Secondary School in Kinampanda, Tanzania. I would gradually forget my own problems during a morning of work, only to find the weight of sorrow hitting me like a stone as I turned onto the path that led home.

Our return to Tanzania two months earlier after a year-and-a-half in the United States had been a tiring but triumphant journey. Gene, my husband, carried one-year-old Zachary on his back and I carried five-months-old Lincoln on my back. We had aluminum framed backpacks in which the boys could sit high up to enjoy the view.

Missionaries Herb and Bonnie Monson, resident nearby in Arusha, met us at the new Kilimanjaro airport at the end of our twenty-six hour flight from Minneapolis via New York and Nairobi. We stayed with them a few days before we headed back to the bush country and Kinampanda, a 250-mile trip. They shared our joy and pleasure in our new family.

When we arrived, tired and dusty, Mary and Wellington Eddy greeted us with open arms. We would be eating at their house until we got settled. One of the new staff houses was supposed to be finished for our arrival. It was not ready so we slept in the vacant parsonage until we could move into the new house.

The water system in the parsonage was plugged so we had to transport our water supply from an outside faucet. It was a difficult time.

After we moved into the new house both Zachary and Lincoln became ill with diarrhea. For two weeks our days were spent changing diapers, comforting and feeding babies and worrying. Our nights were spent washing dozens of diapers and several changes of bed linens.

We made several trips to the local dispensary with the babies and finally, to Kiomboi Hospital. Dr. Frank Jones and his wife, Elise, welcomed us to their home where we stayed several days while both boys were treated for malaria. Lincoln was given fluids intravenously for dehydration.

When it seemed that both boys were getting better, we returned to Kinampanda. Two days later, Lincoln became very dehydrated again so a nurse gave him fluids intravenously. He was so hoarse we could scarcely hear him cry.

After a 24-hour period when Lincoln seemed to be improving, he started vomiting so I took him back to the hospital at Kiomboi. Because there were no lab facilities to determine the exact cause of Lincoln's illness, Dr. Jones suggested that he should be taken to the Kilimanjaro Medical Center near Moshi, 250 miles away.

Gene and I had decided it would be best if Zachary stayed home since he was yet convalescing. Because of work, Gene remained there with Zachary. We arranged for Elder and Renee Jackson to take Lincoln and me to Moshi.

There was a mechanical problem on Elder's Land Rover and we had to wait all morning in Singida for repairs. Lincoln had severe diarrhea and had not eaten for two days. I was feeding an electrolyte solution to him by spoon.

The trip to Arusha took seven hours. Renee helped me with Lincoln, feeding the fluid to him every 15-20 minutes and changing his diaper.

When we arrived in Arusha at sundown, we drove immediately to the Herb Monson house. I jumped out to call ahead and be sure the doctor would be at the hospital in Moshi. When I returned from my call, Edy Kjellin, a nurse who was staying with Monsons, said that my baby was dying. Herb went in his car to get an Asian doctor friend of theirs who lived nearby. We all rushed to the hospital but we were too late. Our precious little Lincoln was gone.

I returned to Monson's house, lost with no little boy to hold. I clutched the pillow on which his sick little body had lain all day.

Herb returned to the hospital and brought the lifeless body of our son back to the house where Edy Kjellin prepared it for burial the next day at Kinampanda. Herb arranged for a plane to fly several of us back. I was physically and emotionally exhausted and couldn't face that long journey by road.

Herb left at midnight to drive to Kinampanda to tell my dear Gene the sad news since there were no phones. He also took a small wooden box with a cross decorating the top. Through that sleepless night, what glorious comfort the Holy Spirit gave me as I greeted friends who had come to share my sorrow.

The next morning we placed Lincoln's body in a small container to carry with us on the plane. A large bouquet of flowers was gathered from the garden. Louise Olson, Bonnie Monson, Elder and Renee Jackson, and Edy Kjellin supported me in my grief as we flew from Arusha to the airstrip at Kiomboi.

Gene was waiting at the airstrip and I sobbed as I ran for the comfort of his arms. Dr. Frank Jones was there, crying with me as I told him what had happened.

We drove the twenty miles to Kinampanda. I ran into our house and snatched Zachary into my arms, thankful that I had one little boy left to hold.

After an hour passed, the grave was dug and the service planned. Gene and I went for one last look at the earthly remains of our son before the coffin was closed. Mary Eddy had placed red moss roses around his little face. We walked behind the coffin as friends took turns carrying it to the church. Our Heavenly Father gave us His strength that day as we sat through the funeral service with rays of sunlight streaming down on the coffin. My Lord lifted my voice to sing "Children of the Heavenly Father" with the others as the small wooden coffin was lowered into the grave. All took turns filling in the dirt on top of it. I laid the lovely bunch of flowers from Bonnie's garden over the raw mound of earth just before we turned to walk home.

It was difficult to separate from that small part of ourselves lying in a grave under a large African thorn tree. He had been here on earth for only five-and-one-half months. So many dreams were built on him. If we did not have faith that Lincoln Eugene Anderson lives because Jesus Christ, Son of God, died for him that he might have eternal life, our sorrow would have been unbearable.

Weeks later, even with the sure belief that Lincoln lives with our Lord, I still succumbed to guilt feelings about his death. I think it is natural for any parent to feel this about the death of a child for whom they are responsible.

Through prayer and talking with Gene, I finally gave my burden of guilt over to the Lord. He forgives. All I needed to do was ask His forgiveness for any wrong thing I had done or anything I had not done that may have caused my baby to lose his life.

It was healing to have Zachary and Gene to care for and to love me. It was important to me to have a daily routine to grasp hold of.

Day by day reminders of my loss I learned to handle well; meeting sympathetic people, attending church or visiting Lincoln's grave.

Unexpected events, though, could still unsettle me. Mary and I went on a shopping trip to Singida. We visited a friend of hers who had a baby girl. I asked how old the baby was and when she replied, "Five-and-one-half months," I fell apart. I ran out to the car, leaving Mary to explain.

After the school term began, an opportunity came for us to move into one of the older staff houses.

With this move, I was at last able to look upon the sorrowful events that had taken place as part of the past and make a small step toward the future.

THE ANDERSON INN

Iambi Leprosarium served as a place of hope for those who had leprosy. For those in whom the disease was detected early, there was a chance of full arrest. For those in whom the disease was more advanced, there was treatment and training. For those who were lame or disfigured, there was hope in reconstructive surgery and therapy following it.

The leprosarium served a wide area of the Central Synod of the Evangelical Lutheran Church of Tanzania. In 1966-69 when Gene and I lived and worked there, it was supported through the Lutheran Church in America and American Leprosy Missions. At that time, about five hundred people with leprosy lived on the five-thousand acres set aside for the leprosarium. One hundred of these people were hospitalized and given total care. The others lived in self-constructed houses and raised their own food crops. They would walk to the hospital for bi-weekly treatment, DDS, given in pill form to arrest the disease.

Iambi Leprosarium was a town in itself. There was an airstrip for small planes to land, several hospital wards in separate buildings, a mill to grind corn into flour, a church that drew people from a wide area around, a primary school since there were many children with leprosy, and houses for patients and staff.

The staff members at the leprosarium were provided with housing since it was a place at the end of the road. Gene and I were given a four-bedroom house in which to live. It was a lot of space for the our small family but we soon discovered that many visitors would come. A trip to isolated Iambi Leprosarium usually involved an overnight stay. We became the hosts of the Anderson Inn, gladly providing hospitality to all. Government officials, medical personnel, church dignitaries, missionaries from other fields of work and tourists were all welcomed. Gene's parents visited us for three months and friends from America made visits as well.

There were many large windows in our house. My treadle sewing machine was placed in front of one of these windows. As I sewed, many times I was greeted with the sight of Barabaig men, seeing their mirror image reflected on the window, jumping up and down, sending their brown blankets flying. The Barabaig are a semi-nomadic cattle-herding tribe who follow traditional ways. Groups of them crossed the leprosarium in their quest for grass and water for their cattle.

Furniture was provided for our house. We added a couch to two wooden-frame lounge chairs already provided for the living room. Our dining room table was a sturdy wood one and had ten chairs. There were beds provided in all four bedrooms.

My kitchen was equipped with a woodstove and a bottled propane gas stove. Our refrigerator ran on kerosene. Cold water in the kitchen and bath was piped into the house from a community water tank. Water was pumped up daily from a reservoir to fill this tank.

A propane flash-flame heater in the bathroom provided hot water for baths, always welcomed by our guests after a long, hot, dusty safari.

To stay healthy we boiled and filtered all our drinking water. Food preparation was time-consuming. I baked bread, cookies, pie, or cake daily. Our garden, the local people and a market in Singida were the sources of our fresh foods.

Clothes washing was done in a wringer washer. I hung them on a line outside where they dried quickly in the wind. Ironing was done using flat irons heated on the stove.

Electricity was a treasured commodity. A diesel power plant served the entire leprosarium producing electricity for three hours each evening. I used my electric meat grinder, food blender and milk pasteurizer during this time. Gene started the generator each morning for power for the inter-station radio which was our daily contact with others serving the church in the Central Synod. One morning a week we let the generator run longer so I could plug in my washing machine.

The local cows were "fresh" a few months each year and we were able to purchase milk from neighbors who had cattle. The remainder of the year we used powdered milk. We raised chickens for eggs and cooking. Locally-butchered cattle and hunted wild game were our main sources of meat. The beef was very tough so we usually ground it into hamburger for spaghetti sauce, meatloaf, etc. Antelope and gazelle meat was more tender. We could have steaks and roasts after a successful hunting trip. We shared much of the meat with our neighbors.

Flour, macaroni, rice, sugar, salt and other staples were purchased on weekly trips to Singida, a two-hour trip by Land Rover. A store called the Central Provision Mart catered to European tastes. Many canned, packaged and bottled foods could be purchased there, as well as butter, cheese and bacon.

Perpetwa Manaseh came to us looking for a job as a house helper. She learned her tasks quickly and soon took the burden of dishwashing, house-cleaning, and washing and ironing clothes from me. She worked six hours a day, five days a week and more when we had guests and needed her help. I enjoyed baking and cooking so I continued those tasks although Perpetwa was eager to learn those, too, and assisted often.

My teaching ability was soon put to use. I started an English class for hospital patients and a crafts class in the occupational therapy department of the hospital. I also helped women in the community learn knitting, sewing and baking.

We had a black Labrador dog, Shiku. She could roam freely during the day but had to be locked in at night. Dogs are a favorite food for leopards and there were many leopards in the area. The night watchman would often report seeing one as he made his round. Hyenas are also nocturnal and we often heard their whooping sounds as they vocalized.

All the non-medical areas of the work at Iambi Leprosarium fell under Gene's management: the three-hundred acre farm, maintenance and repair of buildings and record keeping for all the finances. His office was in our home so I could keep track of what he was doing or where he was going.

Gene usually made a weekly trip to Singida to get our mail and supplies. One or more of the staff would accompany him. These trips brought reminders through letters and magazines of a different life so distant from ours.

When a knock came at our door, we never knew what to expect. It could be someone seeking help with medical, farming or family problems. It could be patients or staff needing a favor. At various times the knock meant a trip to the police to take in illegal beer brewers, someone stealing corn or cattle, a man who beat his wife, or a patient who had stabbed his housemate.

Strange insects, reptiles and mammals made life interesting. Once as I was serving a meal for guests, a bat swooped down from the attic. Dinner was delayed as the women, myself included, ran for another room while the men found a broom and captured the bat. On another occasion a large rat and I tried to occupy the bathroom at the same time. The rat won but was caught in a baited trap later that night.

Skinks and lizards roamed the house, eating insects. I didn't mind them. Beetles, moths and spiders were abundant during the rainy season inside the house and out. Two silver-dollar-sized black beetles lived in the house. We named them Mary and Joseph. Although I always shook out my shoes before putting them on, I didn't find scorpions very often. Scorpion stings can be painful. We always warned our guests.

Since I wasn't well-versed about species of snakes, I treated all of them as dangerous. I carried a stick to scare snakes away when we walked through grass. An eight-foot python was killed near the dam reservoir. A large puff adder was found near the hospital. One of the nurses was hit in the eye by a spitting cobra. Her glasses protected her eyes from serious injury.

Visitors to the Iambi Leprosarium were always amazed that most of the people there did not show outward signs of leprosy. If the disease was detected early, it was treated with DDS, a drug used with great success that arrests the disease.

We were often asked if we were worried about "catching" leprosy as we worked with patients. The bacillus that causes Hansen's disease (leprosy) is a slow growing organism. It is one of the least contagious of all infectious diseases. It is transmitted by direct contact over a period of time. Sound measures of cleanliness suffice. Each time we worked with patients, we wore clean uniforms and washed our hands thoroughly with soap and water.

Dr. Herbert Plock was the doctor-in-charge at the leprosarium. He and his wife, Elli, had come in June of 1966 after serving in India for 14 years. Dr. Plock, a surgeon, had become interested in leprosy and studied surgical techniques. He concentrated on repair of hands and feet of people crippled by the nerve damage that leprosy can cause in advanced stages.

Lore Heidel and Marjolijn Schuyff were the two therapists at Iambi Leprosarium. They worked with patients to retrain hand and leg muscles to function again. Simple exercises and massage were part of the physical therapy.

There was also a large occupational therapy department with weaving, basket-making, embroidering, sewing and other crafts to occupy minds and fingers. Many materials that were used, such as yarn and cloth, were gifts from Christians in Europe and America. I often helped with patients who were learning sewing in the occupational therapy department. We had only one pair of scissors so I usually cut out the blouse or child's dress or shirt for them. They would then sew it together with hand stitches. One woman had only a thumb remaining on one hand. She held her needle in a crease where her fingers had been and used her thumb to hold the cloth. Most of the patients succeeded in finishing some article in which they took tremendous pride.

Bernadine Oberg, a nurse from Wisconsin whom we had met during orientation at Concordia Seminary and who attended language school in Nairobi with us, was nurse-in-charge at Iambi Leprosarium. She and I worked together sorting the supplies that were donated by church women's groups in Europe and America.

One afternoon Bernadine and I had a harrowing and hilarious time together helping women patients choose a dress. We had the dresses sorted by size and laid out on a table in a small room. We let several women at a time into the room to select a garment. Others, afraid they would be forgotten, were beating on the door. The women pulled the dresses over their heads without undoing buttons or zippers. If the dress went on, that was the one they wanted. Several women got stuck in dresses that were too small and we had to extricate them.

A young Tanzanian couple, Hosea and Anna Namilikwa, was indispensable to the leprosarium. Hosea was a medical assistant. His three years of training was more technical than that of a nurse but less than a doctor would receive. Hosea also had an additional six months specialty training in leprosy work in India. He could carry out most of the routine hospital work to allow Dr. Plock to devote much of his time to surgery. Anna Namilikwa was a nurse on the staff at Iambi Leprosarium.

Some of the many guests we hosted at the Anderson Inn arrived by small plane, landing on the airstrip. We would be informed on the inter-station radio of a plane flying in that day. The airstrip would be mowed and cleared of termite mounds in preparation.

On one occasion, Dr. Wheat, the government leprologist, came in one plane from Dar es Salaam, and the Flying Doctor Service brought an eye specialist from Nairobi on the same day. The people, who always flocked to the airstrip when a plane was due, were amazed that there could be *two* such "birds that carry people."

Besides the staff people mentioned, there were many others who helped to make Iambi Leprosarium a place of hope. Simeon was the driver and mechanic who kept the Land Rover and farm machinery in repair. Nalingigwa was the evangelist for the Christian congregation. As a patient whose leprosy was arrested, he related very well to the problems of the people there. At the hospital there were three additional nurses, three orderlies and several aides. Two laundry helpers and four janitors kept everything clean. Two cooks prepared the meals for the hospitalized patients.

It was my privilege to witness happiness on the face of one man who had lived at Iambi Leprosarium for twelve years and now was able to return home after surgery and therapy. His family welcomed him with joy. Homecomings were the goal of the work at Iambi Leprosarium.

Lora Anderson *is married to Eugene Anderson, educator. They have two sons, Zachary and Dietrich. Lora and Eugene lived in Tanzania 1966-70 and 1972-73, at Iambi Leprosarium at Nkungi, and Tumaini Secondary School at Kinampanda, both in the Central Synod of the Lutheran Church in Tanzania.*

Lora graduated from St. Peter High School, MN. After two years at Gustavus Adolphus College she transferred to the University of Minnesota where she graduated cum laude in 1960 with a degree in Home Economics Education. She taught home economics classes at Clara City, Hutchinson, and Owatonna high schools, all in MN.

While in Tanzania, she volunteered as an English as a Second Language teacher. She also volunteered in the occupational therapy department at the leprosarium and as a domestic science teacher and in the school library.

Lora is currently self-employed. Her eighteen-year-old business is designing and sewing wedding dresses. Singing in church choir and making doll dresses are further interests. She taught Sunday School for 25 years and has served on community and church boards.

THE HEALING TOUCH OF JESUS

Jessie Aldrich

So many friends got up early that September morning in 1949 to see us off on the train. They were all giving us good-byes as we would not see them for four and a half years until our furlough was due. They were singing hymns as we pulled out of the depot. They promised to remember our work in their prayers. We were deeply moved.

We were four nurses, all new to international travel: Pauline Swanson, Lois Bernhardson, Alice Turnbladh and myself. In five days we would reach Dar es Salaam, stopping at New York, Paris, Cairo, Khartoum and Nairobi en route.

We switched from air travel to slow moving train in Dar es Salaam for the final 500 miles upcountry to Itigi. At Dar es Salaam, the capital of Tanganyika and a modern port, we went through customs. We were confronted with a new civilization, a new way of culture, living and thinking. We were avid travelers and awake at daybreak, observing that the country around Dar es Salaam was flat. As we traveled inland, the elevation changed; we saw hills and valleys, streams of water and rivers, foliage and trees. Here we viewed the beauty of God's creation and praised God for his mercy in bringing us safely on our way.

Tanganyika's industries were agriculture and mining of minerals. The farmers harvest maize, wheat, garden vegetables—potatoes, corn, peas, beans, tomatoes and peanuts. They also grow coffee and fruits—grapefruit, lemons, oranges and bananas. The farmers raise cows, goats, and sheep that they graze and sell for profit.

Farming is sometimes done communally. In lieu of tractors, perhaps as many as a dozen people hoe together, preparing the ground for planting.

The countryside was dotted with wild animals: impala, elephant, buffalo, zebra, lion, and wildebeest. The foliage was unfamiliar also: thorn trees, baobab, tall grasses and hibiscus shrubs.

Near our destination, we noted that the homes were made of sun-dried mud bricks with thatched roofs. Their food, we learned later, is primarily *ugali* (a thick porridge made of millet or corn flour) which they roll into a ball and dip into whatever sauce has been prepared—quite often a spinach-like vegetable called *mchicha*. The cooking pot usually is placed over the fire balanced on three stones—an economical hearth.

We were met the next morning at Itigi by one of our missionary physicians. He gave us a quick tour of Singida, the government headquarters for that area and our main shopping center. We could buy most of our supplies there.

We continued our journey to Kiomboi that was 50 miles away. We had lunch at Kiomboi Mission Station, where there was a large church, school, and hospital. The annual missionary conference was soon to be held there. Meanwhile it was exciting to meet some of our new colleagues and the nationals who worked on the station. We also learned a little about local customs. We were told that the people who are animists believed they could go to the hills, forests, or mountains and find God.

At the conference, we received our language study and work assignments. I was placed at Wembere, a station nine miles distant and 1000 feet lower than Kiomboi with a backdrop of a beautiful waterfall.

After three months of full-time language study, we began our work assignments half-time for an additional three months. Language study consisted of private work memorizing long lists of Swahili nouns and verbs, and engaging in conversation with national workers on the station. Sometimes we were assigned to a teacher from the primary school who sat with us in the afternoons and read stories and conversed with us about daily happenings.

As Wembere Dispensary nurse, I also had responsibility for the patients at Tintigulu Leprosy Colony and a small dispensary at Ntwike. These were ten and fifteen miles from Wembere. In preparation for our work assignment, at Kiomboi we received orientation in tropical disease diagnosis and treatment from nurse Margaret Peterson. We studied about leprosy, bubonic plague, poliomyelitis, hookworm, malaria, relapsing fever, and conditions such as elephantiasis and snake bites.

We learned about the management of epidemics such as bubonic plague for which the area was quarantined, all homes visited and sprayed with DDT to kill the fleas which carry the bacillus pasteurella pestis. In addition, rat poison was distributed to cut down on the rat population since rats are host for the fleas.

To determine how effective that strategy was, the people brought tails of rats they had destroyed to government representatives in the area for a small bounty. Quarantine was also done in epidemics of poliomyelitis.

Prayer was essential for dealing with our daily problems in both hospitals and dispensaries. This daily routine was begun by the staff: a period of Bible reading, singing, discussion and prayer; after inpatient rounds were completed, outpatient devotions were held. For many, this was their first exposure to the Gospel. There was no lack of opportunity for evangelism.

Laboratory tests such as blood slides and stool samples were done as needed for both inpatients and outpatients. Occasionally it became necessary to transfer patients to Kiomboi Hospital for medical evaluation by missionary physicians. We also visited areas around Wembere and had health teaching days. We would gather under a large shady tree and teach the people the causes of illnesses and how to prevent them by using good health habits.

Some miracles occurred during our ministry in the dispensary and hospitals. One female patient had developed an infection in her leg and contracted tetanus. She was not able to walk, and her jaw was clamped shut so that she could not eat. Her relatives took her home during the night; we informed the government officer that we had sent to Kiomboi hospital for medicine that would heal her and that we wanted her brought back for treatment. She returned and received the tetanus antitoxin and recovered from her illness. One morning when we were making rounds, this woman was walking around the courtyard and was able to eat. The people who saw her were amazed to see this great healing. We all thanked God for her recovery.

Another incident concerned a baby who had severe malnutrition and was having difficulty breathing. We took this baby into our dispensary and fed him with an eye dropper. After extended treatment, he got well and was able to go home after three months. In his home area, we had a praise service because God had healed him. Many people came to the service and thanked God for the boy's healing. It was a great meeting; everyone was rejoicing as this child was now a healthy boy.

The last incident concerns a young man who brought his little boy with a fever of 103 degrees. He had pneumonia and was admitted to the dispensary. I asked the father if he could stay in the dispensary for further treatment. He answered, "We are not able to stay."

I asked "Do you know our God in heaven and Jesus Christ who died for our sins?"

He asked, "Who is Jesus Christ? I've never heard of him." I put my hands out to hold the baby and told the father who Jesus was. He answered, "We will stay."

I also told him, "We have an evangelist in the dispensary. He will talk with you so you can learn more about Christ." He couldn't wait until he saw the evangelist. Several days later the baby recovered and returned home.

MAY 1952

After I had worked at Wembere two and a half years, I was transferred to Iambi Hospital. During a time when both the missionary pastor and the physician were on furlough, Alice and I worked mornings in the hospital, and in the afternoon Alice did some pastoral duties. She was nicknamed Pastor Alice and I was nicknamed *Bibi* (lady) Doctor. Alice and I had a good time working together and trying to keep up with all the station responsibilities. We had some patients with difficult medical problems and complicated deliveries and needed to take them to Singida to the government hospital where we found help from a doctor.

I thank God for my parents, the Church, pastors, teachers, and friends who made it possible for me to have the privilege of sharing Christ and giving medical help during my experience in Tanganyika. This experience has opened the door for me to share my witness for Christ wherever I am. It was and still is a rewarding experience.

Jessie B. Aldrich *was born in Orient, SD, but she lived in several communities in both North and South Dakota since her parents, a doctor-nurse team, founded rural hospitals. Her father, a physician and surgeon, with his specialties of setting fractures and delivering babies, practiced frontier medicine, traveling in winter often by horse-drawn sled. At times their home was used as a hospital. All of this was good preparation for Jessie's work in Tanganyika.*

Jessie attended the Lutheran Bible Institute in Minneapolis, MN, and is a graduate of the Bethesda Lutheran Hospital School of Nursing and became registered as an RN in Minnesota. She was encouraged constantly by the ministry of the World Mission Prayer League in Minneapolis.

In 1949, the Board of World Missions of the Augustana Lutheran Church commissioned Jessie as a missionary nurse. She served in Tanganyika until 1954, stationed at Wembere Mission Station, supervising dispensaries at Wembere, Ntwike and the Tintigulu Leprosy Colony. Her last assignment before furlough was at Iambi Mission Hospital.

Unable to return to Tanzania after furlough, Jessie continued serving in various nursing capacities in Minneapolis and Boca Raton, Florida, until her retirement. She now lives in Huron, SD. She states, "Through the years I have continued my mission of witnessing for Jesus Christ, with many opportunities for sharing the Good News."

NURTURING MISSIONARY KIDS AT AUGUSTANA SCHOOL

Anne Hall

"Whee! I can read!" shouted a little first grader after completing his reading readiness program and receiving a book. He took the book to his dormitory room and read to his houseparents, his sisters, to the staff and his friends. Now a physician back in Tanzania, his jovial farewell, "Oh, Mrs. Hall, thank you for teaching me to read" was a heart-warmer. Nothing makes a teacher feel more fulfilled than to have her children enjoy learning.

My being in Africa was a direct outgrowth of time I spent as a volunteer parish worker in Washington, D.C. It was there my friends nicknamed me "Sunshine." One day the pastor called me into his office and said, "Sunshine, I have just returned from the Mission Board meeting. I'd like to ask you to pray about going to East Africa. I heard about an urgent need for a teacher there." He went on telling me about the school for children of our missionaries in Tanganyika.

I was a bit taken back and argued, "There's plenty of work right here. I think Washington, D.C. should be our mission field!"

But I did not prevail. Despite my initial protests, I was commissioned on my 41st birthday, July 9, 1961. Soon after, I set off with my two children, fifteen-year-old Michael and seven-year-old Gretchen, headed for Tanganyika, East Africa, called to teach at Augustana School at Kiomboi in the Central Province.

Fellow missionaries met us at the air terminal in Nairobi and took us by car, with get-acquainted stops enroute to Kiomboi. As we traveled through the game preserves, which seemed to us like an unfenced zoo, Gretchen exclaimed, "Oh, Mom! Look at all those animals! Elephants, lions, zebras! May I get out of the van and go play with them?"

"No, Doll!" with tearful laughter and big hugs. "I'm afraid you'd be their dinner if you tried that. You have to stay here with us—all safe and sound!"

Gretchen is still a lover of animals though. She has worked for many years as an assistant in a veterinary clinic.

How does one distill the wonder of five years of living with a group of children growing up together? The family love, so poignantly evident when parents visited the school during the term. Their group singing prompted a Tanzanian friend to say, "They look and sound like angels." It was a joy to see them achieve academically. Best of all was their stalwart faith, one evidence of which I saw during a year of drought. "Auntie Anne, the rainy season should have started long ago. Today in prayers we prayed for rain. The boys even put out our rain barrels to catch water for us." And that night the rains did come. *"If we have faith, as a grain of mustard seed..."* Just a coincidence?

"Oh, Anne, I've seen many Christmas programs in my lifetime, but none like this one! It was as though these children really felt and lived their parts!" exclaimed one of the parents coming up after the pageant with tears in her eyes and a big hug for me. Recently one of my former MK (missionary kid) students, who was introducing me to her husband, declared, "She made Bible study come alive for us! It was *fun* studying God's Word!"

Since there was no *baba* (father) in our family, the *bibis* (single women) decided that we belonged to them. The Kiomboi *bibis* invited our family to join them on a safari during vacation time. We headed south. However, when we came to the South Africa border, passport check became more than a routine. The official informed me, "Mama, your family cannot cross over because according to our standards you are colored, your son is black, and your daughter is white. We don't mix races down here." My family regretfully turned back.

But we did not escape racism, even living in East Africa. When it was time for Michael to go to high school, he applied at Kijabe, Kenya, as all our MK's (Missionary Kids) did. Getting into the right secondary school posed problems. His mission family refused to give up until he was accepted and became the "darling of the crowd" at Rift Valley Academy. The administration at RVA went to the Father about taking my child into their school. They were led to take him and never regretted it.

Memories of discrimination back in the U.S.A. led me to pray for healing unity in God's body. May His light and love chase away all racist attitudes soon and very soon. May members of our now scattered village let their lights of divine love chase away all darkness of segregation.

We entered into the life of the Kiomboi congregation and shared in the joys and sorrows of the members. I remember a night when the father of one of our pupils stood at our door, "Oh, Mama, please pray for our baby," he pleaded. "We had to rush her to the hospital; the doctor said she might not live through the night." With a note of desperation in his voice, he again implored, "Please, pray, pray, Mama." My housemate and I promised to lift up that baby to Jesus. We prayed with the distraught father and afterwards he returned to the hospital.

At 3 a.m. another knock on the door awakened us and two happy parents shouted with joy. "Mama, God heard our prayers! Our baby has regained consciousness, her fever has subsided and she's going to be all right!" Hugs and prayers of thanksgiving abounded. Such was life in our village. These experiences armed us for the valleys. God kept us all under the shelter of His wings.

EPILOGUE

Lift high the cross, The cross of Christ proclaim
*Till all the world adore His sacred name.**

Whenever I sing that majestic hymn, I have a mental picture of the beloved cross that graced the church at Kiomboi. "Is the same church still there?" I recently asked a Tanzanian friend who had visited Kiomboi while on a vacation back to his homeland.

"Oh, yes, Mama Hall, and that big cross, that some of your American friends made possible for us to erect, is still there too!" he replied with a note of joy. "Do you still have the smaller replica which was made for you to remember us by?"

"I certainly do! It hangs on the wall near my apartment entry for everyone to see and reverently admire," I assured him.

His companion added, holding her Bible, "And God now is speaking to my people in the language of our area, too."

To God be the glory for translators, pastors, medical teams and all other laborers in His body throughout the world. May God continue to guide, provide, and use us to His honor and glory wherever and however He may choose.

Anne Hall *was born and grew up in Washington, D.C. She had post-secondary education in the District of Columbia Teachers' College, from which she holds a B.A., also in Biblical Seminary in New York and at Howard University in D.C.*

---

* George W. Kitchin and Michael R. Newbolt, *Lift High the Cross* (Carol Stream, Ill.: Hope Publishing, 1974). Used by permission.

She has taught in public and private schools in the District of Columbia, has served as Parish Worker at Augustana Lutheran Church in D.C. and as Youth Director on the Lower East Side of Manhattan, while pursuing an MA at Biblical Seminary.

In 1961 she joined the staff at Augustana School for missionaries' children at Kiomboi and served there as teacher and part of the time as head mistress, until 1965.

From 1966 to 1974 she taught in the public schools in the Minneapolis, MN area. Health problems forced her into early retirement. But the time has not been wasted. She says, "God has graciously permitted me to intercede for hundreds of people ..." and, expressing her love for children, she adds, "I still have children of every race and nationality call me Grandma!"

THE WOMAN FROM USUKUMA
Elna Mae Lindahl

"Who will tell me more about Jesus?" The speaker came from, and would return to, an area where no Christian witness had yet penetrated. Her words have haunted me ever since I heard them; as a result, this has to be my most memorable experience from my years at Wembere Mission Station in Tanzania.

Her name was Kili. She was tall, distinctive, and a member of the Sukuma tribe which lived out on the plains beyond our mission work at Wembere. The area was known as Usukuma. Time after time, members of her tribe came to us for medical treatment. They walked long distances, often more than a day's walk from their homes. As a rule they were examined, treated and spent the night before returning home the next day. Occasionally they needed more treatment and stayed several days.

Each morning at our hospitals and dispensaries a time was set aside for singing of hymns and reading Scripture, which was interpreted by the evangelist in charge. This time was called *sala*. It was attended by all the outpatients as well as the inpatients at the facility. Following *sala*, the evangelist mingled among the patients to answer any questions they might have.

One day Kili presented herself for treatment. She seemed to be a more self-assured and confident woman than most in her tribe, but she was in obvious distress. After examining her I explained, "Kili, I believe you need to go to Kiomboi Hospital to be seen by the doctor. It appears to me that you may need to have surgery."

This was not what she expected and she was obviously distressed that she could not be treated and return home. "Mama, I can't go to Kiomboi for treatment. I have no family member to care for me in the hospital."

Kili agreed to remain at Wembere Dispensary, and sent word home to her family. Some days later her relative came prepared to stay with her at Kiomboi Hospital.

So at last, the day had come when I could drive Kili to the hospital where she was examined by Dr. Stanley Moris, who confirmed that she did indeed need surgery. Following surgery, she remained at Kiomboi for some time before her return to Wembere.

When Kili returned to us she greeted us with a request to stay at the dispensary until she felt ready to make the long walk home. We welcomed her with open arms. Each day she participated with the other patients in the morning *sala*, at which time the evangelist shared the story of Jesus and His love for all people. She became a familiar presence at the dispensary.

Then the day came when she felt ready to walk back home. I was working in the office when she came to say goodbye.

"Mama, it is time to leave you. I came as a stranger and you took me in. Now we have become friends and I am well. Every day as I sat under the tree here and at Kiomboi Hospital I have heard about this man Jesus who lived many years ago. He was a very loving person, the Son of God. I know now that He even loves me." I assured her that Jesus did truly love her and that she was a child of God.

She continued, "Now I am well and today I will go home and I will tell my people about Jesus who loves them too. I can't read that book that tells about Him, so who will tell me more about Jesus?"

What frustration I felt as she stood there before me that morning! I could picture her return home with her new-found faith and no one in her whole area to nurture her and help her grow except God Himself. I committed her to our Father who is able to do exceedingly abundantly above all that we ask or think.

NOTE: A few years later, the Central Diocese of the Lutheran Church did reach out in witness and service to the Sukuma people.

Elna Mae Lindahl *was born and grew up in Osage City, KS. She is a graduate of Trinity Lutheran Hospital School of Nursing, Kansas City, MO., and is an R.N. She holds a B.S. degree from University of Omaha, Omaha, NE.*

She was commissioned in 1951 by the Augustana Lutheran Church as a missionary nurse for service in Tanganyika. Before leaving for Tanganyika, she spent some time at the national leprosarium in Carville, LA. She supervised dispensaries at Wembere, Ntwike and Tintigulu Leprosy Colony until 1961.

After returning to the United States, she attended the School of Anesthesia at St. Mary's Medical Center, Duluth, MN., and is certified as a Registered Nurse Anesthetist. She served in that capacity until her retirement in 1984. She now resides in Fayetteville, AR., and enjoys, among other things, oil painting, wood carving and travel.

HIGH GRASS IN THE WIND
Elli Plock

LIFE AT IAMBI LEPROSARIUM

For fourteen years I was a missionary doctor's wife in the East African land of Tanzania. Iambi Leprosarium was the name of the hospital in which we worked. Only people who had leprosy were admitted during the first years. In the latter years the name changed to Iambi Hospital and patients with other diseases were also treated.

I want to tell you something about the surroundings, the landscape, so that you can imagine what my home was like for those years.

The colors of the land were dry and burned, like the colors of pottery. But when the rains started, everything turned green and the grass of the savannah grew tall. The houses of the doctors, Tanzanian or German, stood on a plateau. From there I could see far over the country. Acacia trees and thorn bushes grew on the slopes. The hospital was situated somewhat lower. On the other side was a lake, from which drinking water was pumped to a tank on a building and from there ran through pipes into the different houses. But in the rainy season, when the water in the lake was stirred up, the water in the bathroom was dark brown like cocoa.

The hospital also had a big farm and started a scheme of cattle rearing. So patients always had good food. In 1966 there was still a big forest in the near distance and at night leopards came to visit the chicken house and tried, while jumping on the tin roof, to break into the building. But the forest was also a good place for hunting zebras or gazelles to get meat for a change in diet. Near the lake the hospital owned a banana plantation and other fruit trees grew nearby.

On the plateau we had a mango orchard on the edge of which grew high mulberry trees. From the berries I made good-tasting jam. When I had time, I lopped the trees myself. In the distance small hills could be seen rising towards the sky. Against the blue sky the bare rocks looked beautiful.

Our city was Singida, fifty miles away, where we got our mail and provisions. To go there we had to cross streams and drive over sandy roads, which were only two tracks in the sand. If you got off the track, the car would swim. But woe! If a car came toward you, which seldom happened, a perfect maneuver was necessary to be able to pass that car. On the left and on the right was high elephant grass or forest.

As requested by the Tanzania government, my husband also visited seventy dispensaries three times a year as the doctor for tuberculosis and leprosy for the entire region. On these longer trips we drove through many forest areas. An African forest is a mysterious region. It is like riding into the depths of an old tapestry, darkened with age, but marvelously rich in green shades. Once, as we turned a corner in the forest, we suddenly saw a group of giraffes. We stopped the car and the giraffes, four big ones and two small ones, real baby giraffes, stood quite still and turned their long necks into our direction—tapestry animals.

Near the hospital was a small shop where I could buy sugar, oil, also spoons and other items needed in the household. For other foodstuffs we did not need to go to Singida. We grew many things ourselves. In the garden behind our house we planted vegetables like sweet peppers, beans and cabbage, and on small fields a kind of lentil and long rows of mustard plants. We used the pungent powder or paste, prepared from the mustard seeds, for rice and curry meals. Milk was brought by the little son of a farmer, who lived about 2½ miles away. In order to get two cups of milk during the dry season, we had to buy 7½ liters every day during the rainy season when he had plenty of milk. I made butter and cheese and the most wonderful curds you can imagine.

I had a house helper who assisted me with the work in the house. In the garden I had the help of Naligwa Kiula, a man of such small stature that he could have been of the pygmy tribe. When he wanted to marry, he told me, he asked the missionary lady for whom he worked at that time for her advice, but she did not agree with his first two choices. Only the third one was right. "You marry that girl and you will get many children."

So he did, and they had seven children, all of small size as was his wife. Naligwa was a special person, being quite a philosopher. When he sat down for lunch at noontime, we would talk about life and death. I learned about beliefs, legends and customs, which were handed down from generation to generation.

More and more people settled near the hospital, mostly former patients, who were healed but still had to take their medicine regularly for years, perhaps for their entire lives. When so many people settled there, they needed much wood to build their houses and for cooking purposes. The landscape grew lighter and lighter. The wild animals withdrew to more distant places.

I visited a former patient, who lived alone at the end of the slope. It was a picture like in paradise as I passed high trees and stood suddenly in front of his small hut. Two chairs stood in front of the hut and I was invited to sit down. I noticed a small ladder leading into the house to an upper room. On this ladder, climbing up and down, were pigeons, perhaps ten of them. Beside the chair a dog was lying and in the middle of the courtyard a small black bird, not disturbed by the cat who was sleeping in the shade near the house. What an experience! I thought of big cities and their noises and loud activities and compared those with this picture of beauty and silence and warmth, in spite of the poverty of the host.

I was always fascinated by the fact that the patients who lived around the hospital, even some who were blind, were mostly happy and serene. Perhaps it was a feeling of security, being sure that in case of mishap or pain, the doctor was there to help them. Another cause for being satisfied with life was to be surrounded by people with the same disability. There was no disadvantage or exclusion from society or discrimination against them by other people for fear of infection.

The best thing of all was that we had a workshop in a new building with a trained shoemaker. The most modern machines we could afford were bought because of the help of Mr. Andrew Keiding of Milwaukee, Wisconsin. He was a man of an exceptional great heart. He had already given us assistance in India, when we worked in the hospital which bears his name: Andrew Keiding Hospital. He died in the year 1986 at the age of 98 years.

Another interesting area near the hospital was the airstrip, on which small aircraft landed. These planes had brought the Flying Doctors from Moshi Hospital before we came to Iambi. These surgeons operated on difficult cases of crippled legs or feet. But since they did not have much time and seeing the very bad deformities and disabilities of the limbs, they very often amputated the leg or the foot. Then a prosthesis was made. But it did not last long, because walking on the rough, sandy ground would destroy or break the prosthesis very quickly. After a short time, when patients saw that Dr. Plock did not amputate any limbs at all, they gained confidence in him and came even from far away, asking for an operation for themselves.

Now I will lead you from the outskirts into the hospital. I will tell you about the work I did during these fourteen years. I had not studied medicine, but going out to India, our first place of work, I was trained as an assistant for operations, in case my help was needed. I got special permission to practice in a big hospital.

We arrived in Tanzania in 1966. Six months before we came, my doctor husband, Herbert, studied the special leprosy operations in the Karigiri Leprosy Sanitarium in South India. I had seen leprosy patients before in the streets of cities, but never such a big group of patients with severely damaged extremities or big nodules on their faces and horribly smelling ulcers, waiting for the visit of the doctor. It gave me a shock. But when I saw the lady doctor, kindly, with a smiling face, take each of those smelling legs into her hands and examine them or test the bad eyes of others, I understood real Christian love and I promised myself to act in the same way.

In Iambi we did not have much time for language study. Surgeries started shortly after our arrival. Herbert was the first surgeon in Iambi Leprosarium. He had one aim: people should come early, after they discovered the first spot on their skin—and they all knew exactly how that looked—so that they could be healed before there was real damage done.

I distributed pamphlets with information and instructions on how to take precautions in daily life, all illustrated with pictures easy to understand. Of course, there were many who already had damaged legs or hands or eyes. These crippled extremities could be operated on and the progression of the disease could be stopped with the new medicines. Operations were mostly done in the morning, so I could write statistics of our trial of clofazimine in the afternoon. This was a new medication we were testing.

"Habari za asubuhi, wazee?" (How are you all this morning?)
"Nzuri, daktari!" (We are all well, thank you, doctor!)
A picture comes into my mind. The radio in the men's ward is playing a popular hit. The doctor, entering the ward for his daily visit, dances a few steps to the music. Great laughter in the large room! Even years later, the story of this happening was told among the men.

Coming into the ward later in the morning, the doctor saw Mikaeli crawling on the floor. One leg had been amputated before we came to Iambi and he had no fingers at all. He was such a poor individual! Because he had no fingers, he could not hold crutches and he could not walk without them. He was completely dependent on others, even having to be fed.

The doctor chose this man for his first operation. I assisted him. On both hands he made a deep cut between thumb and forefinger, pulled and stitched a cutaneous flap across the cuts. After healing, this man had new thumbs, could hold crutches and move about. He also could hold a spoon and eat alone. He became a happy man, traveling by bus to see his son and relatives. It was a relatively small operation, but it helped the patient considerably. He had been miserable, being dependent on his copatients and hospital staff for everything, and now he was a free man.

I also worked in the physiotherapy department when there was a need. Many leprosy patients have a drop-foot or a drop-hand. If that was not operated on, they would get ulcers on the underside of the toes, because they do not feel pain and will walk into glass splinters or step onto a nail. Then infection sets in and destroys the tissues and bones.

There was Nikodemo, an older man with very large feet and a drop-foot, left and right. It was difficult for him to walk. Before and after the operation he had to learn in physiotherapy how to use the leg muscles in a different way. The tendon is pulled through tibia and fibula and sewed under the front part of the foot. After he had learned to use the leg muscles correctly, the tendon pulled up the foot and he could walk normally. After returning to his home, nobody could see that he had had leprosy.

The doctor always did re-constructive plastic surgery; he did not amputate a single leg or arm. The operations often looked terribly dangerous to me, while assisting. Sometimes the bone of the lower leg had to be sawed through, the foot brought or turned into the right position and blood vessels, tendons and muscles sutured, and at last the skin of the wound stitched. Then the patient got a plaster of Paris dressing and the healing could begin.

Don't think the doctor had all the modern instruments at his disposal! We went to Singida and searched in the different shops for hammer, saw or chisel. Then he worked on them until the instruments served the purpose for which he wanted them. After sterilization they were the finest-looking surgical instruments anywhere!

A curious event happened one morning. While I was at the hospital waiting for the operation to begin, a group of people arrived, four of them carrying a man on a wooden bed. The whole body of the man was full of blood. Especially the head showed an ugly picture. There was an open cut over the whole cheek to the ear. The teeth showed through the cut. I told the doctor of the new arrival. He ordered that the man be washed, and the head shaved and to bring him into the operating room. This was not a leprosy patient. What had happened?

The wife of this man had a lover. The husband returned too early from his trip and surprised both of them in his hut. Then the wife asked the lover to hold the husband, while she struck him several times with a heavy machete in the face and skull. After the doctor cleaned and stitched all the wounds, the man had an excellent appearance. Husband and wife resumed life together—and they lived happily thereafter for many years!

I reminisce: It is 8 o'clock in the evening. I am alone in the house. I feel lonely. The doctor is on safari to some of the dispensaries in the region. The sitting room windows have no curtains. It is dark outside. As I watch the stars, I suddenly see that a big grass fire is starting down at the foot of the slope. It is summer season and the dry grass is tall. At this time the Barabaig people, who live among the Lyamba people near our home, start such fires every year. When the dry grass is burned, the new green grass, the fodder for their cows, will come out sooner.

The fire, spread as far as I can see, slowly crawls up the hill towards the plateau, on which stand the houses of doctors and nurses. The verandah of our house has wooden poles. But there is a gap of about one meter between grass and verandah. On the broad side of the house is the garden, only soil and green plants. In front of the fire all kinds of small animals flee in the direction of our houses, mice and snakes and wild birds. Together with my neighbors I work hard near the houses to beat out the flames with green-leafed twigs, and we succeed in killing all the flames.

It was general opinion that a member of a nomadic tribe could not get leprosy, but that was not the case according to my experience. We had several Barabaig people as patients. They are in some way related to the Maasai, another nomadic tribe.

One day I was invited to the wedding of a Barabaig girl. It was very interesting to watch the ceremonies. When I arrived, only elderly women stood in a large circle. One of them, the mother of the bride, held in one hand a kind of shield and in the other one a stick, with which she was striking the shield to give a kind of rhythm. And in accordance with this rhythm all the rest of the women were jumping high. I was invited into the circle and did my best to jump as high as I could.

Suddenly the bride appeared, her whole body smeared with cow dung, hair and face painted red. A thin rope was put around her neck and she was pulled by her mother on this rope around the kraal. The bride was weeping bitterly to show that she was very sorry to leave her parents. The bride-groom was not seen. I was told he was sitting somewhere together with his friends, drinking beer.

I had a good relation to the Barabaig. The men are tall, lean, good look-ing; the girls are beautiful. Their huts are tiny and low, just a place to sleep in. And the cockroaches are big, about six centimeters long, who crawl at night over their bodies. I had the *dawa* (medicine) for these disgusting, trou-blesome insects.

Shortly before my last Christmas in Tanzania I received again, as in previ-ous years, a certain sum so that I could give a gift to the last remaining *askaris* (soldiers) who were still living in our area, who had been soldiers in the German army in *Deutsch-Ost-Afrika* (German East Africa). This money came from the German Consulate in order to show respect to these old men.

When I came out of the house I was moved to tears, when they stood, one by one, at attention and called out the words their officers had commanded in German: *"Stillgestanden! Links, rechts!"* (Stand still! Left, right!) Left, right! Old men, backs bent. They were very happy to receive this gift.

The patients in the Iambi Leprosarium made my life happy. I am so glad I could work with them. There was always a breath of goodness and kindness around them. When I think of them, the beginning of a song comes to my mind: "Above the clouds, freedom will be boundless."
Some of them were very humorous and all of them were on friendly terms with time; and the plan of beguiling or killing did not come into their minds. I learned a lot from them.

I do not know to whom I am indebted for this poem, which explains my feelings:
> *Heavenly Father, in our journey through life*
> *Teach us to look back with gratitude*
> *   and count our blessings;*
> *To look around with compassion*
> *   and serve those in need;*
> *To look forward with confidence*
> *   and trust you for all that's to come;*
> *In the faith of Jesus Christ our Lord.*

Elli Plock *is the widow of Dr. med. Herbert Plock, M.D., M.S./Germany. Their children are Dr. med. Uta Gregor, nee Plock, specialist in psychoanalysis; and Dr. med. Ernst-Gernhard Plock, specialist in plastic and traumatic surgery, head surgeon.*

Elli Plock served as a missionary with her husband in Tanzania from 1966 to 1980, living at Iambi Leprosarium.

The Plock's children grew up in India and were educated at the American boarding school in Kodaikanal. Later they studied in Germany.

Elli lives in Wolfsburg-Neindorf, Germany.

IN THE HANDS OF AN AWESOME GOD

Beverly Henry Wessman

"Beverly, today you are acting on the written promise you made to God when you were nine years old! As instructor of religious education of 5th graders at a public school, I read your underlined statement: *'I'm going to be a foreign missionary.'*

"You became a special child to me when your mother passed away a few months prior to your writing this, and I believe your widowed father, like Hannah, dedicated you, his child, to the Lord." These were Miss Rosene's greetings at the Sunday morning worship farewelling my husband, Rev. David Henry, and me the day we embarked on our six-week honeymoon trip, on our way to serve in Tanganyika.

At college, as a Church Organist/Parish Work major, I met then-seminarian David. Two years later he applied for overseas ministry in Tanganyika upon ordination. The Mission Board stated that he met all requirements except one; only *married* men were sent.

Consequently, the first weekend of June, 1952 we married; the following weekend he was ordained and I attained the legal age of twenty-one. The next weekend we were commissioned to Tanganyika and I became "a foreign missionary," hired by my husband to be his church organist/parish worker without a resume, paid in advance by large amounts of love, understanding, and spiritual guidance, with immeasurable increases through his two terms of serving Sepuka Mission Station.

We were the youngest of the missionary family of the 100-plus Augustana Lutheran missionaries in Tanganyika. When we first met Pastor Hal Faust in Africa, David took Hal's welcome-to-Tanganyika greeting of "You really robbed the cradle, didn't you!" with a big smile, turned to me with a hug and replied, "God dropped this baby in my arms."

As African girls marry very young, they did not view me as a youngster. From day one, I prayed God would use my young spirit, my awareness of David's confidence in me, and the newly found reinforcement of a genuine supportive missionary family to keep me alert to the challenge before me. My priority was to be the best wife I could possibly be—after all, *having a wife* was a determining factor of acceptance by the mission board for shepherding an African flock! *"Being that wife* is awesome! *But God, You* are an awesome God! Keep me spellbound in your hands."

Upon arrival at our own village, Sepuka, entering the parsonage by the back door, I stared at three stacks of mud bricks on planks atop wooden horses alongside my kitchen wall. The inside mud brick wall was up about seven feet, a tall lean barefoot bricklayer was layering bricks atop that wall to reach the ceiling as another young loin-clothed lad handed him more bricks. The house was completed with 18-inch-thick stone outside walls, eight rooms inside, all with whitewashed walls and cement floors—except for the kitchen! These partial brick walls would be mud plastered and whitewashed.

The missionary family who had housed us during language study had sent some staple foods with us, some fresh green beans from their garden, and canning jars. So on my first day in my first parsonage I canned a few pints of beans on a *Primus* (a Swedish single-burner pressure-kerosene stove), amidst Tanganyikan workmen singing their rhythmic work songs in their tribal tongue as they built the wall.

Our barrels had arrived, so we found the initial necessities for food preparation, cleanliness, and bedding. Basic furniture, provided by the mission, was all in place in the other rooms. On a prior visit to Sepuka, Dave had interviewed candidates for household help and hired Martini (named after Martin Luther) and Clemensi.

We were blessed with one marvelous asset no other mission had, and that was a spring-fed cistern! All other cisterns went dry in a long dry season, being dependent on the rains. But not ours. Clemensi dutifully hand-pumped fresh water from the cistern to a large tank in the attic holding a two-day supply. He also cut and gathered firewood for our cooking stove, filled ten-quart kettles with water and boiled it for drinking, filled the stove reservoir with water for washing dishes, and kept the stove fire burning.

Within a few days the whitewashed kitchen was adorned with basins on 6'x3' wooden tables (having no sink). Fastened to the table were the milk separator for preparing our milk and cream, and a Montgomery Ward churn for making butter. We had enough milk supply within a few weeks to make ghee (cooking fat) for ourselves and other missionaries who had difficulty getting milk.

Every day boiling the butter fat in a huge kettle, I poured the finished product, eventually filling a five-gallon tin to the top. Fond of the whey, Martini took it home to share with his family. I, a new bride, now ran "The Henry Co-op at Sepuka Village" as ghee-renderer, bookkeeper, and salesman.

Co-dependency between missionaries made us family! A 'runner' walked cross-country many miles to bring us a beef quarter periodically from another mission where the Christians butchered beef under missionary supervision. Hunting time was limited so wild meat supply was not constant. Our local Christians sold us eggs and chickens and Dave would occasionally hunt guinea fowl or quail.

Martini, our cook, prepared fowl with minimal instruction, but David, raised on a farm, quickly taught me butchering to work with Martini. When a *swala* (impala, like a deer), *pofu* (eland, a large antelope), or *ngiri* (wild boar) was unloaded from our vehicle, out came the cleaver, sharp knives, quart jars, big frying pans and pressure cooker. Soon several quarts of delicious canned meat lined the pantry shelf, after first filling the small top freezer unit of our kerosene-run refrigerator. May I add, an eland steak puts American T-bones to shame!

Our government district offices and shops were located in Singida, seventeen miles away. The road leading there was a deeply rutted gumbo mud track often impassable during the rains, appearing to be a series of lakes during the rainy season. It was known to be the worst road of the whole district. Our four-wheel drive vehicle often got stuck. Our African passengers, anxious to shop in town, were quick to help get us out.

I learned early to keep an inventory of food supplies to last four weeks during the rainy season. We kept the barrels we had shipped from America in the attic for storing our 50-lb. bags of staples like flour and sugar.

One morning I left for school to teach the girls' sewing class, leaving Martini recipes for chocolate cake and vanilla ice cream. That evening when I didn't see the desserts, I asked Martini where each was and he replied, "Where you designated them to be, *'tanuruni'* (in the oven) and *'barafuni'* (in the freezer), Mama."

My thought of the cake having been in the oven all day set my mind awhirl. When I found my cake batter frozen solid in the freezer and the ice cream floating in the warm oven, sudden realization hit! I had interchanged the two words for oven and freezer. We all burst out laughing at my language goof and praised Martini for explicitly following my recipe.

One day I asked Martini what his family would consider a treat. I wanted to prepare a picnic for them Sunday after church. He immediately replied, *"Tafadhali* (please), macaroni *na jibini* (and cheese)." The picnic basket was all packed with the piping hot dish packed last. We piled in the truck and headed for the *pori* (wooded area) about fifteen minutes away, to a favorite spot of ours at the base of a large rock pile where baboons reside.

We were welcomed by baboon chatter and aerobics above us as we spread our meal on the plastic tablecloth. I lifted the last fruit bowl and thermos of drink from the picnic basket, I looked up at Dave with a blank expression and exclaimed, "Oh, no! I didn't pack *any* silverware." Quick as a dart, Martini was up with his pocketknife cutting tree limbs into forks for all. We cupped the macaroni onto our plates as the baboons' chatter grew incessantly louder.

Before having a family of our own, I traveled to the Kiomboi School for missionary children to teach piano. Marie Matsen, our closest missionary neighbor, was also asked to teach. So we traveled together several months, once or twice a month depending on the weather, to add music appreciation to the curriculum for the talented children of our missionary family.

Our carpenter, *Tomaso*, (Thomas) became a very close friend to David through his work. I bonded quickly with his family since their first-born son, Joni, and our first-born, Elizabeth, were born the same day. We often celebrated their birthdays together. I sewed clothes for both as birthday gifts, and we took pictures of our two celebrities. On their third birthday, we served a big kettle of popcorn, birthday cake, and kool-aid to about a dozen of Joni and Beth's friends on the bed of our pickup truck. A second kettle of popcorn had to be popped! The guests delighted in presenting gifts of eggs, peanuts, or a homemade toy car or doll fashioned out of sugarcane or corn husks.

One boy who delivered much of our daily milk supply presented Beth with a *debe* (five-gallon tin) full of peanuts. We have a snapshot of them sitting on the path with her feeding him some we had roasted. After being roasted and shelled, most peanuts found their way to our meat grinder which had a special attachment to finely grind them into creamy rich peanut butter, needing only a little salt added. Peanut butter/banana became a favorite sandwich.

When one of our evangelists lost his wife in childbirth, *Bibi* (Grandma) came to the dispensary to care for the newborn. I was called upon to make formula, show *Bibi* the procedure, and see the baby dismissed a few days later with the satisfaction of formula availability. As it turned out, I was called upon many times after that to tend to her and other babies' medical needs. Dr. Spock's book became my constant companion.

Our own daughter Elizabeth required medical attention numerous times in her early years. Consequently, through mutual concern for our children's welfare, I gained greater insight into the hearts of the African moms. How loving and caring they are! They are good moms, but needed guidance and lessons in nutrition and health care to battle the diseases and adverse conditions causing high infant mortality.

"Children are God's gift loaned to us for their earthly stay until they are returned to their Creator." This truth became a reality early in our second term when we had three daughters, Elizabeth, Miriam and Kathryn. One Sunday when David was holding a church service 50 miles away, since the resident missionary was on furlough, our Elizabeth took ill with what appeared to be a seizure.

Our African medical assistant sent for an Indian merchant three miles away to drive us to the Singida Government Hospital. There we were taken right into the home of Mr. and Mrs. Thwaite, an English couple, who located Dr. Markham. The Indian drove on to notify David to come in the morning so we could take Beth to our mission hospital at Kiomboi. Dr. Markham gave her medication to slow her heartbeat, but soon realized there was little hope. At midnight she took her last breath. Mr. Thwaite and Dr. Markham drove to break the news to David who came immediately.

Four days earlier, we had taken the wife of our evangelist, Yonatani, to this same hospital where she and their only child died. Now we were, like Yonatani, looking to God for His comfort and strength to uphold us in our grief. But we realized David and I still had each other and two precious daughters.

Via runner, news spread to the missionary family at distant mission stations. The next day, many of them gathered together with the children at the school where I had taught piano, for the funeral service at Kiomboi. There we were upheld by a host of African parishioners of our congregation of Sepuka and Kiomboi as well. Underneath were God's everlasting arms.

Pastor Melvin Lofgren and his wife Dorothy, who as parish worker at my home church during my youth had been my mentor on missions, took us home with them for a few days to share in our grief.

Missionary family ties are very strong, and a blessed supplement for would-be-loneliness for immediate family from whom we were distanced by two oceans. Co-missionaries became our children's Aunt Dorothy, Uncle Mel, and Grandpa Lud, etc. Lud Melander, a veteran missionary to Tanzania, often entertained all the missionary children with his violin, hugs, and narratives on many occasions. *"Blest be the tie that binds our hearts in Christian love."*

"SOS—Doug, come over immediately to the missionary hospital delivery room!" Another missionary wife, Shirley Augustine, had delivered prematurely a baby girl a week ago. Because of her previous miscarriages and knowledge of the Rh factor, Shirley's husband, Doug, had built up his blood during her pregnancy, planning to be prepared for a total blood change if needed. But now he was at the hospital, ready to take his wife and daughter home. In a flash, he ran to the delivery room to find Dr. John Hult requesting his blood for *me!* Our daughter, Joyce, had just been born, but I lay hemorrhaging in shock.

As I was receiving the blood transfusion, I sensed a tingling in my body. I opened my eyes to see my husband's and Dr. John's hands folded over me, praying. I heard them thanking God for sending Doug to Kiomboi and giving me the gift of life-saving blood at the precise hour of need. What a day of rejoicing, as David and I now once again had three daughters. *"The Lord gave, and the Lord has taken away; blessed be the name of the Lord."* (Job 21). Joyce Meribeth's birth announcement had this scripture quote with the added words: "The Lord giveth again!"

How I envied other missionaries with nursing background. But with their input, and monthly visits of a missionary nurse supervising our dispensary, I acquired knowledge and confidence to start classes on health care for the African women. The classes included Bible Study, and health education or sewing instruction.

I remember being discouraged after my first few sewing classes at how slowly the women were stitching their garments. The wife of our primary school teacher offered to help me, and she exclaimed, "Oh, Mama! *They* are not all *left*-handed like you. Have them put their needles in their other hand." I had to learn to sew right-handed myself to fully comprehend the handicap!

Teaching Bible was difficult at first, requiring study and preparation in English, presenting it in Swahili (the lingua franca used for communication among different tribal groups) with an educated woman further translating into their tribal tongue, Turu. As my own daughters often attended the classes with their *ayah* (baby sitter), the women delighted in chatting with them. How quickly they, though small, grasped even the tribal tongue, growing up with it! I had to study and listen carefully to converse in Swahili, never acquiring much ease with the Turu language.

Classes required supplies, most of which came from our American supporters. I wrote letters weekly to either request or thank churches for used clothing, bandages, cotton squares for ulcer and burn victims; flannel blankets and kimonos for the babies born in the maternity ward; school and sewing supplies including feed sacks from midwest farm parishes. One feed sack sufficed for a school girl's blouse.

Correspondence was almost a daily task, one of the most important mediums of witnessing what global mission is! It also was therapy for me as I met with my supportive prayer partners back home through the writing. David did some correspondence, but I—his parish worker (right?)—faithfully wrote our parents weekly, and touched base often with our sponsoring congregation, Irving Park Lutheran Church of Chicago, as well as many individuals and rural parishes in the midwest.

During our second term a rural Congregational Church in Janesville, Wisconsin shipped a heavy country school bell for our new church, replacing the tire rim and metal pipe hanging from a tree. Now from atop a tall wooden tower pealed a rich, far-reaching toll calling Christians to worship. Only through letters could we begin to give that country church in Wisconsin a sense of our African congregation's gratitude and song in their hearts, *"We are One in the Spirit, We are One in the Lord!"* Letters linked us with congregations, giving us the opportunity to share the story of the Gospel's power working in Africa in response to their prayers and gifts.

Our school's marching band asked me to sew a flag and banners to be worn across their shoulders. They proudly displayed them at a soccer game with radiant smiles, which gave me insight into a new sewing project.

At an Indian store I purchased several yards of white drill material, cut out an altar cloth, and embroidered the words *"Mweru, Mweru, Mweru"* (Turu for "Holy, Holy, Holy") in large green italic letters across the front, thus providing our mud brick altar with a meaningful cloth.

Our little thatch-roofed mud brick church had received a cross, flower vases, and communion vessels from another Tanganyika congregation, and from Irving Park Church a pump organ that I played each Sunday. I adopted the African mamas' method of fastening a sleeping baby with a wrap-around-cloth papoose-style on my back, and pumped and played the organ as my baby slumbered peacefully.

Clemens Sima, a youngster in our parish who worked for the mission to support his widowed mother and pay his older brother's school fees, came to David one day with the good news that his brother had completed teachers' training. Now Clemens desired to further his own education. Having witnessed his faithfulness in handling family affairs and living a sincere Christian life, we chose to finance his schooling.

How rewarding a few years later to witness his graduation from Kiomboi Nursing School! Clemens became an itinerant nurse to several dispensaries, and later served at the leprosarium. He and his wife Marian, also a nurse, raised a family of seven children, the first born named David after my husband, the second Joyce after our daughter. We proudly claimed Clemens as our Africa son, continuing to uphold him in prayer through the years after our last visit with him in 1959.

We were blessed in 1963 with the birth of our own son Daniel, born in America. Our family then faced a major shift in our lives when David, beloved husband and father, was tragically killed in an automobile accident. I regret that after my husband's death in 1965, I lost contact with Clemens but kept praying our lives would cross paths again.

Thirty years later Lois Swanson, nearing completion of her missionary service in Singida, came to the realization that a couple who had moved to Singida to retire and operate a health clinic in their home—yes, they indeed were my son, Clemens, and Marian. Lois placed a letter of mine in their hands, and it inaugurated a long-yearned-for reunion. Our meeting at the throne of grace had never been broken, but now we could meet again also in correspondence.

Thanks be to God for directing my life to serve in the awesome role of missionary wife, placing Clemens in our lives to carry on the ministry of nursing to his own people, and continuing to use both of us in our retirement years.

Two years ago I retired from the Administrative Assistant position of my home church to marry Gene Wessman, who was a childhood Sunday School classmate. He proposed to me with a prerequisite to marriage: "If you marry me, you do not marry me singly. I do care for another woman, you know."

My thought was, "Who's that?"

"You will be marrying me as joint caregiver to my 92-year-old mother."

I accepted this joyous proposal! God never intended for us to retire from Christian service, so the present years of retirement are simply extensions in new directions of my original calling to serve our Awesome God.

Beverly J. Henry Wessman *was born and raised in Rockford, Illinois. Upon completion of two years at Augustana College and one year at Lutheran Bible Institute, she married Pastor David N. Henry in 1952.*

Together they served in Tanganyika, E. Africa, at Sepuka Mission Station from 1952-1962. Their five children are Elizabeth (1953), Miriam (1955), Kathryn (1957), Joyce (1960), and Daniel (1963). Elizabeth died in 1958 in Tanganyika, and Pastor David was tragically killed in an automobile accident in the United States in 1965. There are seven grandchildren.

In 1994 the author married Gene Wessman, and thus gained two stepdaughters, Shellie and Trudee. Gene is a retired machine tool assembler. Bev and Gene now live in Rockford, Illinois.

DOES GOD ANSWER PRAYER?

Ruth V. Halvorson

Why? Why did she have to die? She was too young, only seventeen. Now such a beautiful baby girl is left without her mother. Who will care for her?

Didn't God hear our prayers as we stood beside her bed with our hands placed on her head, pleading with Him to have mercy on her and heal her to His glory? We even rebuked the enemy in Jesus' name. We truly wanted it to be done for His glory. We tried to claim healing for her by faith, but it was hard to pray.

She never even knew we had prayed. There was no sign of improvement. The incoherent mumbling and terrible restlessness continued until soon she became too weak even to be restless; then she quietly slipped away from us. The bottle of her husband's blood that might have saved her life was half-full when the words came from the doctor. "It's too late—she's gone!" But she couldn't be gone! Yes, it was true. As I myself listened through the stethoscope, the heart was silent.

"Why?" The unspoken question filled my thoughts as the tears filled my eyes. We had fought desperately for her life all afternoon. Everything possible medically had been done; we tried to commit her to the Lord and claim his promise, *"If you ask anything of the Father in My Name, He will give it to you."*

Was our faith so weak that we couldn't believe that God could reverse the severe symptoms of relapsing fever and anemia? True, she had had a severe hemorrhage three days ago when she delivered her first baby at home. But didn't God cause the medicines to be discovered as tools for us to use?

Then came the question, "Is it really God's will to heal the sick now in our day?" If it is not His will, then we who try so desperately to bring healing through all types of medicine and care are working against His will in doing this; I do not believe this is true. Again, the question—"Why wasn't she healed?"

The enemy continued flooding my mind with doubts until I came to the place where I almost felt that it doesn't help to pray.

But—there was another voice to listen to. Through the confusion, the grief, the doubts and questions came the voice of peace, in thoughts that found these words:

> "Trust in me, my child. Your prayers are heard and answered. My ways are not your ways, neither are your ways my ways. This young woman, for whom you have prayed, is my child and I have called her to myself because of my love. Her baby is also my child and will be cared for. You do not know the life of sorrow and hardship from which I have taken her. So trust in me and do not doubt. Continue to bring the sick to me in prayer and when it is the best way, you will see physical healing too. My way is perfect, so trust and rejoice in me."

Oh, the peace that flooded my heart as the inner assurance from the Holy Spirit came that showed me again that His promises are true and that the Lord is absolutely trustworthy.

The next day I learned about Pili's life-story. Only about one year earlier this young girl had given her life to Jesus Christ. She had been brought up in a strict Muslim home. It was through her sister, the lovely Christian wife of one of our male staff nurses, that she was converted. They were true sisters, with the same mother and father. *Pili* (pronounced Peelee) made her decision to follow the Lord after having lived with Miriam and Clemens for quite some time. There she heard the Word and saw a faith that was real.

The day she was baptized and confirmed in the church at Kiomboi, her witness to her faith in Christ brought much rejoicing to the Christians here, especially to her sister Miriam. Up until this time she was the only Christian in her family. Pili's name was changed that day to Kristina.

A short time after this, Miriam and Kristina's mother died at Kiomboi Hospital. Soon this young Christian girl was forced to return to her Muslim father. A marriage was arranged to a man much older than Kristina, who already had four wives. Kristina ran away to try to escape this match, but her father found her and forced her into the marriage.

Yesterday, Kristina was admitted to the hospital as "Pili Salimu." She had not been permitted to use her Christian name. There had been no prenatal care. Who knows what she had suffered at the hands of the other four wives or others in the extended family?

The large bruise on her abdomen showed the marks of forced attempts using heavy pressure to aid in the expulsion of the four-pound-five-ounce baby girl. Amazingly enough, she was doing well in our nursery.

No, we do not know from what kind of a life this seventeen- year-old girl had been spared. But we know that God hears our prayers, for He did have mercy on her. He took her to be with Himself. Her sister took the pre-term infant when she was discharged.

We do not always ask aright, but the Holy Spirit interprets our prayers according to the will of God; His way is perfect. We rejoice now that Kristina went to be with Jesus. Though our prayers were not answered in the way we expected, we know God's perfect will has been done. His promises are true and we will continue to pray for His healing and transforming grace in our own lives and in the lives of others.

We still have much to learn.

"MR. BEEP"

The sun had not been up very long, but already there were two to three hundred people in line to receive care at the outpatient department of Kiomboi Hospital. In the distance I heard, "Beep...beep...be...be...beep." Soon I saw a small fragile looking man coming down the path toward the hospital. He carried a long stick bent at the end, which he pushed along the path before him. He continued the constant "beep...beep...beep" as he found his way toward the long line of waiting patients.

I watched as he came to the line, expecting him to stop at the end and wait his turn like everyone else. But to my surprise, as he came near, the people began to step aside one by one and allow him to pass. Without comment from anyone, except for an occasional greeting, he beeped his way to the very front of the line.

I thought, "How nice of everyone to be so kind to blind 'Mr. Beep.'" I went into the hospital and forgot about him, as my day became very busy.

When I left to go home for lunch, I was surprised to see "Mr. Beep" sitting near the hospital. At closer range I could see that his ragged clothes were not much more than seams hanging on his thin frame. I greeted him, asked his name and then asked, "Did you get the help you needed this morning?"

"Yes, a little," and he showed me the white tablets tucked into a small envelope. It looked like the standard treatment for malaria. Since he obviously needed something more substantial to cover his thin body, I suggested he please wait while I went up to the attic to find some used clothes for him to wear. He smiled and said, "Yes, I'll wait."

I found a rather large pair of white surgical scrub pants with no tie at the waist, and a fairly good white shirt. Giving them to him I apologized: I knew the pants would be far too large, and I had nothing to give him to tie them on. He smiled and his face lit up as I told him what I was giving him. "No problem—I'll find something to keep them on."

I asked, "Do you come to church?"

"No," he replied. "Not yet."

Then I continued, "Now that you have some clean clothes for your body, wouldn't you like to come to church and hear how Jesus Christ can make you clean and new on the inside?"

"Yes," he said, "that would probably be a good idea. I will come next Sunday."

Every Sunday, from that day on, I saw "Mr. Beep" sitting with his white shirt tucked into the scrub pants, gathered by a rope at his waist. He always sat near the front on the men's side of the church. I wish I knew when "Mr. Beep" actually became a Christian, but I believe we shall meet again when we'll all be free of our handicaps!

Ruth Halvorson *was born in Duluth, MN. She is an R.N., a graduate of the School of Nursing at St. Luke's Hospital, Duluth, MN.*

After some years of employment as a registered nurse in the U.S.A., she was commissioned by the Lutheran Church in America to serve as a nurse-midwife in Tanzania after completing a preparatory course in Edinburgh, Scotland.

She served as Maternity Supervisor and Nurse-Midwife Tutor at Kiomboi Lutheran Hospital, Tanzania, from 1964 to 1974. After her return to the U.S.A., she was in private practice at Ruth's Maternity/GYN Clinic, Mount Vernon, WA, until her retirement in 1997. She lives in Mt. Vernon, WA.

HE LEADETH ME

Doris M. Swenson

This is my story. Yet not only mine, but of the lives of many who have been intertwined with my life, especially the women of Africa in Lyamba-Turuland in Tanzania. It is the story of how God has led our family throughout the years, particularly while living in the Singida area of the Augustana Lutheran Mission. Truly, *"He Leadeth Me"* (also a personal and family favorite song). But, how did God lead?

Let me tell you.

As a teenager in western Kansas, I didn't hear many missionaries speak, but I did share in programs led by capable women of the Women's Missionary Society of Sharon Lutheran Church. It was an intergenerational group that met monthly, driving to a town home or 15-20 miles to a ranch, for a planned potluck after the morning worship. We studied *The Mission Tidings* magazine and answered questions about missionaries—those on the Augustana mission fields.

One missionary, Edna Miller, did visit the western Kansas churches, and stayed in the parsonage with us. How I looked up to her! At that time I actually thought of missionaries as the most perfect of God's creatures, willing to serve and sacrifice in far-away places. From her I received the name of a pen-pal, a student at Ruruma Girls' School. Years later I met that person in our home at Kinampanda!

At Camp Wa-Shun-Ga, near Junction City, Kansas, I was challenged by Pastor Nelson, missionary to China, "If the Lord has never told you *not* to go, how do you know that you shouldn't?" I never forgot that!

During Bible School days in Minneapolis, Minnesota, I came to chapel, searching to find God's will for my life. Those who spoke of great need overseas, especially Africa, touched my heart. Another person at the Lutheran Bible Institute at that time was Vernon Swenson, and as we dated and talked, he asked me if I'd be willing to go to Africa if we became engaged. Not too amazed that we both felt that call, of course I answered "yes." And ever after we were convinced that, if the Lord called us, we would go and He would lead us.

After Vernon's graduation from Bethany College, Lindsborg, Kansas, and completing seminary with summer appointments between, we studied at the Kennedy School of Missions, Hartford, Connecticut. We also read Hjalmar Swanson's book, *Touring Tanganyika*, over and over.

And so it was that, with our passports and other documents in order and our barrels packed, we embarked on the first part of the voyage to Africa. Never will I forget the train pulling out from the Sharon Springs, Kansas railway station that October morning and my father and brothers standing among the faithful flock from Sharon Lutheran Church. It was goodbye for a long time. The impressive commissioning service had been held at Salemsborg Lutheran Church, Smolan, Kansas, Vernon's home church, and good-byes said to Vernon's family soon after.

Our ship docked in Dar es Salaam harbor a week early, and, being anxious to get upcountry, we sent a telegram to our mission's president in Singida. He never received the message. Consequently, we and the Bob Ward family arrived in Singida by bus with no one there to meet us! Finding a Jeep near a shop in Singida, Vernon and Bob inquired of the English-speaking owner whether that was a Mission Jeep and if perhaps they could use it to take the Wards to Mgori, their language study place.

That left the children and me alone in the Singida *Hoteli!* I was sure that Vernon would not be back that night. Had I not read that safaris always took longer than intended? The beds and mosquito nets were clean. The bacon and eggs and toast with tea were tasty. And Vernon did come back that night.

Finding a lorry (truck) the next morning, we were on our way to Ruruma, our language study place. What a surprise to meet a mission teacher seated beside us! He pleasantly introduced himself and sang a favorite Swahili song, *Mungu Ni Pendo* (God Is Love). This has been taught to many at furlough times. Stopping at Kinampanda at the Renner residence, we were invited to stay until our Ruruma hosts would be back from vacation. What a hospitable home we found with this experienced missionary family.

Within a few days we were brought to Ruruma Station, our home for three months. Bright curtains had been hung at the windows, which made the dark cement floor and once white-washed walls less visible. We had a good kerosene pressure lamp as well as a lantern. There was no generator for electricity nor a car.

Shortly after arriving at Ruruma, Vernon left to attend a Pastors' Conference at Ushora. Those evenings after the evening meal at the house of our co-workers, Vivian and Inez, the children and I walked home, about two blocks—David in the buggy, Daniel by my side, and I with the glowing lantern in my hand. I was sure there were leopards lurking behind the trees or along the riverbank as the African darkness descended upon us.

At home the children were tucked into their beds and I too lay down to rest. As I went through the events of each day, anxious for Vernon to come home, sleep eluded my weary body and mind.

There were those strange, new sounds in the darkness of the night. The peculiar, penetrating, haunting sounds of the drums beat in rhythm with my heart, and the bellowing sound of the *mbutu* (long, horn-like instruments) spread out like tentacles into the darkness as I lay there on my bed, sleep still evading me. It was another death dance and would keep on until near dawn. "Lord, I know you have brought us here to serve you and to bring the message of your love to this place. Help me, Lord." How often I have prayed that simple prayer, "Help me, Lord!"

In the morning the light truly "dispelled the darkness," but the sounds of the drums are never to be forgotten. The cemetery was near our house and I watched when the Christians carried their loved ones on upside-down beds from the nearby church for burial, singing songs of hope as they literally marched to the graveyard to the beat of the songs. What contrast when non-Christian relatives came by and threw their bodies upon the grave, then ran away from it all, wailing in utter hopelessness! But for these too, we had come.

"Are all the mosquito nets down and tucked in?" I asked. "It's 5 o'clock." One of the most harmful insects in all of Africa, one of the smallest in size, yet one of the most feared, was the anopheles mosquito, which carried the dreaded malaria parasite. Malaria was one of the worst enemies as far as sickness was concerned. We did all we could to prevent that bite for ourselves and our children, but David and I soon became ill. "I can't walk any farther," I said one day as I lay myself down under the old fig tree in the noon-day heat. Seeing our predicament from their screened-in porch, Inez called to us, "Just wait a little while."

I was helped to our house and a runner (messenger) was sent to Kiomboi to ask the doctor to come. He and the missionary pastor came that night, but had to leave the car on the other side of the wide sandy river and walk across. *"Hodi!* May we come in?"

"Karibu!" (Welcome!), Vernon answered as he opened the door. "Thanks so much for coming." In the lantern glow they appeared like 'angels of mercy' giving encouragement and hope to our family, along with good medicine for David and myself. I was impressed! And, oh so thankful!

"We must have a car," Viv Gulleen wrote to those in charge at Kiomboi. A car we got, but without brakes! So, our first trip to Singida included getting the car repaired. Precariously driving across rivers without bridges and stopping on an ash heap instead of smashing into a "road-closed" barrier, we got to within a mile from Singida and had a flat. Unfolding the buggy and putting the children into it, Viv, Inez and I walked to town. All of us later had our basket meal at a table behind the repair shop, explored Singida and were back at Ruruma after dark, in a car *with* brakes!

After language study, Kinampanda became our home for four and one-half years. We settled temporarily into the large stone and mud house overlooking the beautiful valley between the escarpment and Mt. Hanang. How I longed to travel down into that valley as others were doing! We unpacked the few but useful items brought from the States and made the place as homey as possible. There were curtains to make, an old couch to cover, and some painting to do.

During those days of orientation while Vernon was getting ready to take over the principalship of the Teachers' Training Center, I was mostly caring for the children and teaching Daniel the Calvert Kindergarten Course. Getting to know missionaries and Africans and having overnight guests was a pleasure.

In our second house, the new principal's home on the ridge of the *pori* (forest), we managed the station post office and for a time the dividing of fresh produce that came from Arusha. There were guests and visitors, including British officials who came to inspect the school. How one of them liked waffles! So did others. We would set up two Primus stoves by the table, using the old black waffle irons from the States. Seasonally, onions, tomatoes, peanuts and bananas were bought at the door; and mangoes, guava and papaya came from the valley. We'd save eggs for the children during the nearly egg-less times and our "sweets" were cinnamon rolls made out of bread dough, "Crazy Chocolate Cake" mixed in the pan and date bars. We made lots out of birthdays, especially the children's, with all the missionaries, like extended family, getting together for a party. Angel food cake mixes were saved for those times.

There was no way a missionary wife could divorce herself from her husband's work. During my lifetime I have continuously learned two very important life perspectives—flexibility and being prepared. There were the quick safaris that needed food and boiled water to take along, whether it was Vernon taking a sick person to Kiomboi or people stuck in mud ruts and needing food and shelter for the night. There was often the changing of schedules or meeting times.

Most of my work outside of family and home was with the African women, usually assisted by a teacher's wife. Always there was Bible Study, then perhaps baking bread in a versatile *debe* (five-gallon tin) improvised oven, or cooking guava sauce, a good food for small children. In fact, that, together with mashed bananas, was one of the first foods given to our children, along with Heinz baby foods. The women were fascinated and their husbands glowed as the wives learned to turn shirt collars and mend socks.

There were animals—lions, rhinos, leopards, giraffes, hyenas in the *pori* surrounding much of the station. The most beautiful animal, I thought, was the graceful giraffe. The one I least liked was the hyena and more so after one looked me right in the face through the living room window. I'm sure he was laughing at me!

"You are needed at Iambi and the leprosarium," was the core of a letter Vernon showed me one June day. Very soon we moved so that he could lay water pipes from the river to the hospital and manage the farm which produced food for those ill in the leprosarium hospital.

Moving from Ruruma, where we had been placed for our second term, took us down the rugged escarpment road to the valley below. There grew the papaya, mango and fig trees. The terrain before us was of incredible beauty, spotted with thorn trees and an occasional baobab tree like a sentinel guarding the landscape.

It was decided that our main home would be at Iambi and that we would commute the six miles to the leprosarium. Our two daughters, Sharon and Rebekah, and I joined Vernon often at the leprosarium, "camping" in the vacant missionary home there.

There was the narrow, sometimes turbulent, river to cross. Dr. Stan Moris, a veteran missionary doctor, carrying mail and medicine, at times crossed upsteam on a huge tree limb that extended across the river. I regret that I never saw that crossing place, as of course we never crossed there with the children.

There were fun times, especially when Daniel and David came home from school—having picnics, making mulberry pies, eating corn on the cob, climbing rocks, going in a boat on the little lake, and Christmas time when there were parties for the African workers and their families and at other missionaries' homes.

We often worshipped at the leprosarium church. Sometimes Vernon preached and had baptisms, bringing the baptismal water to those who could not come forward. The healthy would sit on one side, the sick on the other. After memorizing the most Bible verses, Isaki and Eliasi received awards of new Swahili Bibles. I'll never forget their young faces, scarred, yet beaming, as they sat on the step below the altar in front of the congregation. Neither will I forget how we greeted one another by holding up our open-palmed hands.

But more vivid to me than anything else was observing the patients as they walked from their little nearby farms to the clinic to receive their medicine spooned out by a nurse. Others, worse off, received good care for their ravaged bodies and bandaged limbs in the hospital. That left an unforgettable impression on me! It was as if they were coming to the Lord Jesus himself. They knew how to say thanks and many praised God. The staff there, both African and missionary, rated high on my list of caregivers!

Our move to Kititimu Mission Station, near Singida town, came about when Vernon was again asked to fill a real need, this time that of bookstore manager and later as Treasurer of the Church and Mission. Both of these offices were in Singida, a small town like a county seat, the hub of the mission field.

At that time I had a vision of our going out to the villages with a mobile book unit as an extension of the bookstore, but that never materialized. What did materialize for me was working with the women of the *Mungu Maji* (God's Water) Lutheran Church. Here too we had Bible Study and prayer. There were cooking and baking lessons. Some learned to make communion bread. Here too was a faithful helper, Rebeka.

At that time we met in the little well-built mud and wattle church. Fastened above the entryway was a distinctive cross. A leak could appear in the roof during the rainy season and then the women would say, "Mama, you have the Bible. We'll hold the umbrella over you." And so they did. Those beautiful women!

Near the church there was a government center and school. When some of the Muslim women, no doubt wives of government leaders, came over to join us, some of the men became concerned and sent representatives over to see what was going on in that little church. After Rebeka and I explained what we were doing they seemed satisfied and said, "If the women like it, let them come." Did the women clap? I think so, at least in their hearts. So did I.

Anna was one of the group at *Mungu Maji*, dressed simply in a black *shuka* (cloth), but a gem of a woman who radiated joy and friendship. She was my friend. I was hers. We conversed very little verbally, she speaking Turu and I Swahili. But why did we need to? Her husband, a faithful station worker at Kititimu, whom I came to know while overseeing the outside workers for a time, became a Christian, and not long afterwards so did Anna. Once, when Anna became quite ill, she walked as far as our home on her trek to the Singida Government Hospital. I had her lie down on our couch to rest and she was forever grateful when I took her the rest of the way in the car.

Near the time of our leaving Tanzania for furlough, we were seeking guidance about our return. In a weakened condition after a hepatitis bout, I was at a communion service in Singida town. Walking by me when going to the altar, Anna squeezed my hand. I was in tears and her supporting presence was comforting.

At one end of the spectrum of God's leading my life stood the women of Sharon Lutheran Church. At the other end were those Lyamba and Turu women. I stand in the middle, thanking God for the privilege of sharing with both, all of us recipients of God's grace and mercy. Truly, *"He Leadeth Me."*

Doris M. Swenson, *born in Chappell, Nebraska, in 1924, spent her childhood years in Nebraska and South Dakota, and high school years in Sharon Springs, Kansas.*

Post high school education included studies at Bethany College, Lindsborg, KS; the Lutheran Bible Institute, Minneapolis, MN; and the Kennedy School of Missions, Hartford, CN.

Doris is married to Pastor Vernon G. Swenson. Their children are Daniel, David, Sharon Barber and Rebekah Peterson. Doris and Vernon served as missionaries in the Singida area of Tanzania from 1954 to 1966.

GOING ALONE ?

Helen L. Johnson

A soft *"Hodi"* (a 'knock' by voice) outside our bedroom window awakened me and I sat up startled. It was bright daylight already, although I knew it hadn't been for very long. Almost on the equator, Tanzania experiences twelve hours of light and twelve hours of darkness the year around with hardly any dusk or dawn.

Raheli, the young girl who worked in our home, would be coming any minute, but apparently the caller at my window hadn't found her in the kitchen as yet.

"Jambo!" (Hello!), I returned her greeting. "What brings you so early this fine morning?"

Marta, one of the midwives from the medical clinic, stood at the window dressed in her white uniform. She explained, "A healthy baby girl was born just an hour ago, but the afterbirth will not come. Could you take this new mother to Kiomboi?"

The hospital station was some 28 miles away, and there the doctor would be able to deliver the placenta.

I respected the judgment of Marta and Elizabeti, the two midwives at the clinic, knowing they would have tried every means available to us at Kinampanda to deliver that afterbirth. So I replied, "Of course, I will come *sasa hivi* (immediately)."

Raheli soon arrived and I gave her instructions for the day. I had no worries leaving our two children in her care. They loved it when I went to our well-baby clinic once a week and Raheli fixed the noon meal and had complete charge of the children.

Fortunately the Jeep was all gassed and I drove down to the Teacher Training School to tell Leigh, my husband who was the headmaster, about my sudden safari plans. But then I had a definite feeling, a premonition that said, "Maybe you shouldn't go alone."

I ended my hurried explanation to Leigh, "Do you suppose one of your students could go with me?"

And so it was that Lameki and I started out. We picked up the family, new baby and their loads. The men transported the new mother on a litter made of two poles with cloth suspended between them, and they all got into the back of the covered Jeep.

This was not the first time I had made such a journey and I never ceased to be amazed at the quiet dignity and stamina of the African women riding over that bumpy road in their condition.

After we delivered our patient safely to Kiomboi Hospital, Lameki told me, "I was very happy to be chosen to accompany you on this safari."

"Why?" I asked.

He replied, "I have ordered a bow and some arrows which are being made for me by an evangelist who lives in a village right near the road." Since it was the dry season, making passage easier, we would be taking this high road home to Kinampanda from Kiomboi.

We had lunch with missionary friends at the hospital station and then started home. About half way, as we were riding along singing Swahili songs, there was suddenly a terrific jolt! The left front axle had buried itself in the soft sandy road and the wheel of the Jeep went rolling on ahead of us coming to rest in the ditch. Total shock!

But quickly Lameki said, "I will run on to the evangelist's house and borrow his bicycle. Then I will return to the hospital station and get help." By the time he had returned from the evangelist's house, I had written a note to our Kiomboi friends telling them of our plight.

The first bicycle Lameki borrowed gave out a few miles down the road, but he was able to borrow another from someone living nearby. In Africa, it is the custom always to help someone who has *matata* (trouble) on safari.

Meanwhile, back at the Jeep, I was alone with my thoughts. I remembered the three lonely sheep we had passed and then around the next corner the pack of African wild dogs hot on their trail. I thought about the darkness coming quickly at 6 p.m. and began to pray for Lameki's safety—and mine, too. I didn't quite know what to expect sitting there on that lonely road in a strange neighborhood.

With joy and relief I heard the approach of a Land Rover (4-wheel drive vehicle) just before 6 o'clock. Our Kiomboi friends had come to rescue us. The bicycles were returned, the bow and arrows picked up, and we arrived home safely just in time for the 7 p.m. inter-station radio messages. The operator from Kiomboi informed us that our patient had been delivered safely of her afterbirth.

"But, what if Lameki had not gone along?" I asked myself. "Thank you, Lord, for the still small voice that said, 'Maybe you should not go alone!' "

Helen L. Johnson *was born near Wapello, Iowa, in 1927. She is a retired school nurse, presently living and doing volunteer work at the Christian Renewal Center, Silverton, OR.*

Helen and her husband, Pastor Leighland E. Johnson, who passed away in 1997, were on the mission field in central Tanzania from 1958-1962. Leigh was Headmaster at the Kinampanda Teacher Training Center and Helen volunteered as a nurse at the dispensary where she held weekly obstetrics clinics.

Helen has two children and six grandchildren.

THE ESSENTIAL INGREDIENT

Lola Erlandson

THROUGH THE RIVERS

"Do you think we can walk that far?" My two friends and I were discussing our trip from Kiomboi where we lived to Wembere, another station nine miles away. Finally we decided; with enough determination, it could be accomplished. We could have driven a car, but where was the adventure in that? We would walk, but before the day was over we almost got more than we bargained for!

One of our Tanzanian friends, Wankembeta, was going along to lead the way. We were going not by road but cross country. We were looking for adventure—remember? It is very easy to get lost on African trails, but with Wankembeta leading the way we knew getting lost wouldn't be one of our problems since Wembere was her parental home. We'd have other excitement before the day was over!

The long awaited Saturday finally dawned; it wasn't clear and sunny, but dismal and cloudy with a gentle rain falling. Refusing to be discouraged, we donned raincoats, rain hats and heavy-soled walking shoes.

We were finally on our way—carrying our lunch and especially boiled drinking water, a must-have for any trip, however short. We were sure we'd make the trip in four hours. Little did we know then what would happen later! Trips in Africa are never predictable.

The Tanzanians we met on the way must have thought we were a little out of our heads. One old man just shook his head when we told him where we were going. He knew it wasn't necessary for us to walk, and to tell him we wanted to walk just for the fun of it, would be more than he could comprehend.

It was still raining as we came to our first obstacle—a river. In fact, we'd have three rivers to cross before we arrived at our destination. Most rivers in Tanzania have no bridges. During the dry season the river bed is dry and no bridge is needed, but during the rainy season the water runs with such force that most of the bridges would wash out. This river was quite wide but not much water in it yet. We could easily wade across—shoes and all!

By the time we reached our second obstacle the rain had stopped. Yes, it was another river we had to cross, only this river had more water that was rushing and rolling along. We knew the current was much too swift to wade through. What should we do? We looked at one another, each silently thinking the same thought. "We should have stayed home. It's foolish to be out on a day like this!"

As we voiced our thoughts, we wondered if we should turn back. Our spirits weren't so high now. We knew that if this river is high, the one we had just crossed would be high also. We were stuck between two rivers! However, we knew enough about these rivers to realize that if we waited long enough the water would go down and we could cross. Our Tanzanian friend went for help while we tried to dry off. We were not to be daunted and have our day ruined completely. We would sit on a rock, eat our lunch and sing songs!

An hour went by and still the water was too deep and dangerous to cross. At least the sun was shining and my friend, Pauline, would have a chance to really dry out. She discovered her new raincoat was not all the salesman had said it was. It was not rainproof!

Another hour went by and the river was still raging! We had drawn a crowd of Tanzanian herdsmen eager to help us. One of the men had a plan and our hopes were beginning to rise again. This was the course of action we would take: the men would drive their herds of cattle through the river to weaken the current and we would follow through right behind them. We had no time to be fearful. We had waited two hours and our patience was wearing thin. Here was our chance! We each took the arm of a Tanzanian herdsman and they took us safely across. As I clung tightly to the arm of my rescuer he must have sensed I was afraid. (I was!) He kept saying in Swahili, *"Usiogope! Enda pole pole."* (Don't be afraid! Go slowly.)

Without these able-bodied helpers, we would never have made it across. We were soaked to our waists but what a relief to be on the other side. These men were our "knights in shining armor," rescuing women in distress. We thanked them over and over and although they were proud to be able to help us, I'm sure they thought we were a little crazy. We were most likely the talk of the village that night. Our second obstacle was overcome. We wondered how many more we'd have before the day was over.

Instead of crossing the third river, we discovered we could go around it by walking three extra miles. The hot African sun was beating down on us now and we needed our helmets. It is never a good idea to be out in the tropical sun without protection. Our folded up raincoats became our head gear. Somehow we got them to stay on our heads. What a strange sight we must have been, trudging along. Our spirit of adventure was wearing thin; we were sunburned, our legs ached, our clothes and shoes were still wet. We were glad to be on the last lap of our journey. After descending a thousand-foot escarpment, we could see our friend's house and we knew nothing could stop us now!

We had some good laughs when we thought back on our trip, yet were so thankful for the men who helped us across the river. And even in our foolishness, God's protection was over us. He was there to watch over us.

Oh, by the way, we didn't walk back. We went by car. We'd had enough adventure to last for some time.

NEVER AGAIN A WHITE BLOUSE

To travel by bus in Tanzania is an experience. I had no idea just how interesting, until I traveled from Singida to Arusha.

I remember the bus well. It was old—so old I thought it should be in a museum. As I climbed aboard, I was sure it would die before we reached our destination. However, I was determined to go even though the motor coughed and sputtered as we chugged out of Singida.

It was my first trip by bus in this new land. I was still very much a stranger. As I looked around me, I found I was the only white person. There was no one to talk to as I did not know the language. The driver and his helper were both Tanzanians and I could tell as he drove up the road he was a good driver; he knew how to avoid most of the ruts in the road. If I didn't learn anything else on that trip, I learned never to wear a white blouse. Every time we hit a rut, the dust would come flying in the windows and through the cracks in the door settling on my once-white blouse and clean hair. We were traveling in the dry season.

The bus was nearly full. In one corner sat two Indian gentlemen; in another row were Arab men in dingy white gowns, turbans wrapped loosely around their heads, and then Africans, mostly men. One especially attracted my attention. He was dressed as an American cowboy: ten-gallon hat, jeans, a loud red shirt with a kerchief around his neck. The only thing missing were the cowboy boots. To top it all off, he was carrying a guitar.

"Do you know how to play that guitar?" I wanted to ask, but I did not know his language. There were perhaps three or four different tribal groups on the bus and if they didn't know Swahili, they were perhaps feeling as left out as I was.

All along the way we stopped to let people on the bus. At one stop, two very attractive young women boarded, wearing dresses made of animal skins with fancy beadwork woven intricately on their dresses. On their arms and legs and around their necks they wore foot after foot of copper wire. This is worn day and night, and as I learned later, the wire must be cut to get it off.

We had now reached a beautiful plains area where wildlife was abundant and no hunting allowed. How fascinating it was to see giraffe, zebra, wildebeest and many species of antelope! They had no fear of buses or cars, as they were living on one of the game preserves and had never heard the sound of a gun. I never tired of seeing these magnificent creatures which were free to roam in their own surroundings.

Looking at all the animals, I forgot about the decrepit bus which was sputtering again. Then with a coughing gasp, it stopped. After much discussion which I couldn't understand, the driver and his helper did something to the motor to get it going again. But before we could start out, they took a big bucket to the nearest water hole. The radiator must have sprung a leak. From then on we stopped at every water hole. I now felt we were really going in on a "wing and a prayer."

"How much longer is this trip going to last?" I was complaining to myself. I was tired of bumping and bouncing over the rough roads. How could anyone get as dirty as I was in just one day of travel? The fine red dust was ground into my hair, my clothes and my face. I was really ready for that good warm bath at the end of my journey.

In the midst of my silent complaining, I looked out the window and saw the most magnificent sight. It was breath-taking! I was looking at the snow-clad peak of Mt. Kilimanjaro. The setting sun was shining on the snow giving it a golden hue. To think that a mountain rising up only three degrees from the equator could wear a cap of snow the year round!

While looking at this majestic mountain, I lost all track of time and before I knew it we were pulling into Arusha. Immediately on arriving, I learned this bus had taken its last trip and a new bus would go out the next day. I had traveled one day too early, yet I wouldn't have missed this ride for anything.

THE ESSENTIAL INGREDIENT

Prayer was the key that kept Augustana School going. I know it for a certainty. These children were entrusted to us by their parents who lived in many different areas of Tanzania. Because it was a boarding school, the children were with the teachers and houseparents more than they were with their own parents. We were assured many times that we were all in their prayers. It was an awesome responsibility, so we definitely needed to ask for the Lord's guidance and protection. With 50 to 60 energetic children attending school—normal children who loved to go on hikes, climb trees, build forts in the back yard or play soccer, there were bound to be some mishaps. We did have doctors and nurses living on the same station, for which we were very thankful. Even so prayer was very important to all of us. Several incidents come to mind.

"Auntie Martha, come quick! Knut has been hurt bad!" One of the boys came running into the dorm. It was after school and as Auntie Martha and I ran outside, we both breathed a silent prayer, fearing the worst.

"We were building this tunnel and Knut's head just got in the way of our hoe! We didn't mean to do it." The other boys were feeling very sorry. The hoe had really come down right on top of his head and he had a deep gash down to his skull with blood running all over. We breathed another silent prayer as we rushed him down to the hospital. The doctor gave us some assurance as he said, "Head wounds are always bloody. He'll be all right after I get him stitched up. Be sure to keep him quiet for awhile as he may have had a slight concussion."

That was our hardest job. Knut wanted to go back out and dig more tunnels. His parents lived in northern Tanzania and we had no way of contacting them quickly if something serious would have happened. I'm very sure they had prayed for him that day and God had answered their prayers. His head healed rather quickly.

"Are you going to the Blue Hills this morning?" It was Saturday and I had walked over to school just as a group of older boys and girls were all set for their hike. They loved to take trips to various areas and they had given names to all the special places they claimed as their haunts. They were never bored nor lacked for fun things to do on Saturdays. This morning was different, however.

A little later we heard this cry, "John's in big trouble! While we were exploring a cave, we ran into a nest of bees and the bees are all over him." He was absolutely covered with bees and having been stung so many times, he was becoming physically ill. I don't remember how we removed all the bees, but he had over a hundred stings on his body. Those bees were angry! The doctor gave him some medicine and told him to rest.

Later this came out: "You boys go back to school and we'll stay here and pray." The girls decided that would be their plan as they were not near the cave where the bees were. I truly believe God honored their prayers as John did not suffer any ill effects from all the stings—just a lot of discomfort at first.

One more incident comes to my mind as I think of the importance of prayer. In my fourth grade social studies class we were discussing Russia. I was telling them, "The leader of Russia is Nikita Kruschev and he belongs to the Communist Party. He doesn't believe in God. He's not a Christian."

"Not a Christian?" piped up one of the girls. "Then why aren't we praying for him?"

We did pray for him many times. Only God knows how our prayers were answered.

Lola Erwin Erlandson *grew up in Concord, NE, is a graduate of Wayne State University and taught in Nebraska elementary schools for a number of years.*

In 1953 she was commissioned as an elementary level teacher by the Augustana Lutheran Church and placed at Augustana School for missionaries' children at Kiomboi in central Tanganyika. She served there until 1968.

After returning to U.S.A., Lola taught in various schools in Nebraska while living with her mother in Concord.

In 1978 she married Warren (Bud) Erlandson and learned about life on the farm near Wakefield NE.

In 1986 they moved in to town and developed new hobbies. Lola enjoys quilting; he does wood carving. They treasure time in Chicago with their daughter, son-in-law and first grandchild, Anastina. "What a joy she is!" says Lola.

ARRIVAL

Arlone Weston

I remember being extremely tired and thinking I only had to stay one year if I didn't like it. I was feeling "mushy" mentally and physically after two days of air travel. The smell from crates of young chickens in the back of the plane on this last leg of the journey from Nairobi to Arusha didn't help. Oh well, I had my return ticket so I could leave if I wanted. Then the plane was landing. Being last off, these thoughts went through my mind, plus the fear that today there would be no one to meet me. As I slowly made my way in the direction of the terminal building, a man and three boys came walking toward me. The man introduced himself as Orville Nyblade and the three boys as his sons Walter, Russell and Andy.

Tired as I was, my eyes popped open on the ride to Makumira Theological Seminary where I was to spend the night. I remember the three distinct sections we passed through to town: the mud and stick homes of the outlying African section; the concrete block *dukas* (stores) of "India town" filled with people in colorful saris and turbans; and then the downtown business area with its blue clock tower. Too soon we were turning in to Makumira.

Now my memory gets hazy. I know I drank at least a gallon of homemade lemonade. I know I was introduced to what seemed like 100 people who, of course, wanted to meet and greet the new teacher for their children's school. That meeting and greeting was almost enough to make me turn around, as I have never felt comfortable meeting new people.

Finally, everyone had left and June Nyblade and I were just sitting and talking at the dining room table. Much to my surprise I found out that my mother's family and June's had attended the same church in Pittsburgh, and she probably had gone to high school with some of my mother's cousins. I think that is when I started to relax and feel that all of this might work out after all.

It was hard to sleep that night. I was too tired, too excited, and a bushbaby was too near with its cries.

The next morning came quickly. Still tired, I retraced the journey of the previous day back to the airport. Orv explained that the school kids would travel by bus to Kiomboi (where the school for missionary children was), but I was going to fly via Missionary Aviation Fellowship (MAF). That was mighty kind of the school board to arrange, as it was an all day body-shaking trip by bus. When I saw the four-seat Cessna I thought, "No problem, I've been up in these before."

After getting all strapped in, the pilot said, "Let's pray."

"Eek, what for? Can't this guy fly?" I said to myself. "Was there something wrong with the plane?"

It was already too late to change plans as we had taxied to the end of the runway.

"Amen," said the pilot. And with that pronouncement off we went.

He didn't say another word until after an hour or so when he casually mentioned that we were flying over the Lyamba escarpment. During all this time I was eagerly looking out the window searching for anything exciting, but all I ever saw was a landscape dotted with trees. No towns, no animals, just trees and miles and miles of brown earth. It reminded me of what much of California looks like away from the cities.

Soon after crossing the plateau the pilot pointed out the school and immediately went into what seemed to me to be a perfect dive-bombing run on the compound. I saw people waving; I started to look for the airport. The pilot headed off into nowhere. A bit anxiously I now looked all around and saw absolutely nothing that remotely resembled an airport. Then we went into a wide turn and started going down. All I could see was grass. I had no real time to get very scared because bing, bam, boom we were down and coasting to a stop just as nice and easy as could be.

Out we hopped into the middle of nothing. A boy herding goats at the edge of the grass airfield stood nearby watching us. Looking all around, I tried to take everything in at once—the blue of the sky, the wide openness of the land, and the stillness. After spotting the windsock I figured we were in the right place. Of course I had no idea where that was. Timidly, I asked the pilot if I was supposed to walk somewhere. He was busy unloading school supplies from the plane.

"Oh no. Someone from the school will pick you up shortly," he replied.

"Aha, that's why we buzzed the school," I thought.

Soon a VW Kombi (the camper VW) came barreling up. Neal Stixrud, pipe in mouth, stepped out and asked if I was Arlone Morrison. After I said yes, he opened the side door of the Kombi and started loading the school supplies and my stuff while managing to avoid hitting two lively little girls, his daughter, Lindsay, and the houseparent's daughter, Heather.

In no time the VW was loaded and we were off. To this day I'm not sure I said good-bye, much less thank you to the pilot. The dirt road to the compound had too many bumps and ruts to count. Partway through the ride Neal remembered to introduce himself as principal of the school plus 7th and 8th grade teacher, and to identify the girls. The town of Kiomboi took three blinks of the eye to pass through and dust followed everywhere. Everything seemed to be a different shade of brown and yellow. Everything was covered with dust—plants, buildings, people, animals.

Finally we were pulling up in front of the Stixrud house. Annette Stixrud came out to greet me, shushing Neal as he asked if I wanted to talk about the school. When she said I looked as if I could use a cup of tea and invited me in, I knew I would survive.

Epilogue:
Much later, in spite of all my doubts, fears and apprehension, I realized that God was behind this venture and had wanted me to be right where I was at Augustana School, Kiomboi, Tanzania.

***

Arlone Weston *was born and raised in southern California. In 1967 she graduated from the University of California at Santa Barbara with a degree in history, and completed her post-graduate teaching credential in 1969. She was a teacher in Tanzania, at Augustana School for missionary children [1969 to 1971], and International School Moshi [1973 to 1975].*

IS GOD A PERSONAL GUIDE?

Mary E. Eddy

The whole community was appalled and I was devastated. Why did my husband, Laverne Shuey, a 37-year-old farmer, die so unexpectedly? Laverne had consulted our doctor early that day and found out he had a swollen epiglottis, which the doctor said indicated a heart condition. He died about five o'clock that afternoon.

I said, "God, you permitted this for a reason. I don't want to stand in the way of that reason." A friend, our mail carrier, shared the following verse which gave me special comfort: *"Father, I desire that those also, whom you have given me, may be with me where I am, to see my glory…"* (John 17:24). Laverne was in the presence of Jesus, beholding His glory. I couldn't wish him back here.

Proverbs 3:5-6 became my anchor: *"Trust in the Lord with all your heart, and do not rely on your own insight. In all your ways acknowledge him, and he will make straight your paths."* I could not lean on my own understanding but only trust in Him to guide me. He did.

I returned to college to earn my bachelor's degree in elementary education. Upon completion I joined the staff in the Department of Parish Education of the Augustana Synod headquarters in Minneapolis, Minnesota.

One day a secretary from another department shared her exciting news of friends home on furlough from the mission field. She added, "They were past forty when they went out the first time!" That statement seemed to be all I heard. It kept echoing and re-echoing in my mind for days.

I finally asked, "God, are you speaking to me? I know I can go next door to the mission office and talk to the director but—that would be *my* doing. I want to be sure it is *You*, Lord, who is disturbing my otherwise peaceful mind. So therefore, like Gideon, I'm going to put out the fleece! If I could meet Dr. Burke outside or anywhere away from his office, I'd say, 'If I weren't past forty, I would apply to go to the mission field as a teacher.'" Dr. Burke was the assistant mission director.

The next morning, as I drove to work, I experienced a peaceful, quiet spirit, rejoicing in the Lord. I happened to be the first arrival on our parking lot. A car drove up beside me. Who was it? Dr. Burke! I screamed silently, "God, do you answer that fast?"

Well, we greeted one another with a "Good Morning," and stubborn me, I started walking toward the building without saying my "planned speech." Then I felt as if something hit me and I heard, "What did you pray for?"

I wheeled around, returned to Dr. Burke and blurted out my "planned speech." He was pleased, but directed me to see Dr. Hammerberg, the mission director, who dealt with personnel. In parting, he advised, "Go before Friday." I complied!

When I followed this admonition and walked into Dr. Hammerberg's office, he had on his desk a letter from the Central Synod, Tanganyika, requesting a teacher for Ruruma Girls' School. I had walked right into my future life!

After that, regardless of what obstacles or discouragements I met, including major surgery, I knew, I knew, I knew I was going. The weeks of preparation went quickly and I was commissioned as a missionary to Tanganyika in June, 1959 at Oak Park Lutheran, rural Clearbrook, Minnesota.

Isn't God marvelous? What a Guide!

THE UNINVITED GUEST

Before dawn, while sitting at my desk in my new home in Tanganyika, correcting my students' exercise books by the light of a kerosene lamp, I happened to glance into the next room, my bedroom. Horrors! What did I see but a young cobra slithering out from under my bed! The shiny concrete floor was too slippery for the snake to exit quickly. Good thing! I had time to run outside and grab two large stones which I very carefully set on each end of the snake. I then dashed into the kitchen to get the *panga* (resembling a machete) and chopped the helpless snake into several pieces! My big question was: From where did it come? Are there more of them in my house?

A couple of evenings later, with a flashlight in my hand, I started up our open stairway. Halfway up the stairs, a similar cobra met me with its flat head raised up about a foot!

Again, into the kitchen I dashed for the trusty *panga*. When I returned, this very accommodating snake had stuck its head at least six inches away from the staircase. Swish! Down came the *panga*. The snake pulled itself onto the stairway, but it had met its doom. Are there more in my house? Where?

A few nights later, after returning from taking a patient to the hospital, I checked to see if all the doors were closed. *"Kumbe!"* (expression of amazement) The door between my office and the front porch was open and a cobra was slithering into my office! Again, I ran for the *panga*. When I returned, the snake was squeezing its way behind the door frame where some of the dried plaster holding the stones together had fallen out. This poor snake, also, was no match for the *panga!*

This was the last one. But from where and how had they come into the house? I recalled that the kitchen helpers had previously killed a big cobra in the wood box. Possibly that had been a female and was the source of these three smaller cobras. This large house was made of stone and plaster. Sometimes the dry plaster would fall out and we would repair it with mud and brush on matching paint. It had seemed as good as new.

My life was certainly filled with variety and adventure!

BRAND NEW LIFE

It rained and rained and rained some more. Two women with their babies on their backs appeared at my school office door. "May we and our children come to sleep at your house tonight? Our houses have fallen in!"

Of course I said, "Yes." I lived alone in this large house.

About 8:00 p.m., they arrived with their children and grandmother. "The men can sleep with the cows," they said. After supper they had the chance for a nice tub bath. Then in a bedroom with a full-sized bed and two mattresses on the floor, they were all tucked in for a good night's sleep.

Later that evening, while I was working on my next day's school preparation, I heard a *Hodi* at the door (visitors call *Hodi, Hodi!*, instead of knocking). There was a group of people accompanying a pregnant woman who needed to go to the hospital nine miles away. I sent for Samweli, our school helper, to drive them as I had guests sleeping in my home.

About a quarter of a mile from the house they encountered the unbridged river. Unfortunately they got stuck during the crossing. I ran down to help. With ropes tied to the front of the Land Rover, and men pulling and pushing, we got across. Fortunately, there was no need to awaken the sleeping schoolgirls in a dormitory to help. That occasionally happened.

Samweli asked me to drive to the hospital. Upon return, approaching the river, I tried to straddle the deep ruts but we got stuck again. We decided to leave the Land Rover until morning because it had rained further up the river and it was now full of water. Occasionally, the "wall" of water coming down would be so strong it would force everything downstream, be it cars or cows! But fortunately, this time it wasn't that forceful. The men said,

"We'll hook arms and drag our feet on the bottom of the river; we'll get across okay."

Arriving at my house, I asked, "Do you want to come in for tea?" Foolish question! Of course they did. So at 3:00 a.m. those four or five men and I had tea!

My guests had slept soundly, unaware of any of the night's activities!

Isn't a variety of circumstances the spice of life?

AN UNEXPECTED OPPORTUNITY

I was home on furlough when I received a phone call from the president of Central Synod asking if I would consider being the English teacher in a newly-opened secondary school. I returned to Bemidji State University to earn enough additional credits to get a secondary school English certificate.

One day I received a letter from a friend in Tanzania stating, "There is a British bachelor at the Tumaini Secondary School who is just right for you." Well, I had other thoughts. I wrote back to her: "If he is old enough to be interested in me and still a bachelor, there must be something wrong with him." I have had to eat those words! I arrived at that school in July 1970 and the following June, Wellington Eddy and I were married! We felt very well-matched, God's gift to us.

My life was greatly enriched through Wellington. Then God saw fit to take him *Home,* in August, 1974. He was a victim of cancer.

God does not expect us to understand but to trust and obey.

ARE EVIL SPIRITS REAL?

On the Tumaini school campus one day I met Edward, a most humble and intelligent student. He wanted to chat. He asked me, "Do you know that evil spirits are real? If a person has something against someone else's parents, that person could put a curse on their child and he would suffer its consequences the rest of his life. But you people don't believe this. You just call it superstition."

I answered, "Don't say I don't believe; Jesus dealt with many evil spirits." I had no idea that he himself was that child.

Edward came from a Muslim family. His father had died when he was a baby. Later his mother married a Roman Catholic. Her father then became so angry with her that he put a curse on her child, Edward.

Having recently returned from our short furlough to England, USA and Norway, Wellington and I showed slides to our students at church one

Sunday evening. Shortly after returning to our home, a couple of students came and asked us to come to the dormitories. They added, "Edward has that crazy illness." Of course we went, not knowing what to expect. On the way the boys kept saying, *"Ni shetani tu!"* (It is Satan! It is Satan!)

We found Edward lying on a mattress outside his dormitory. Several boys were holding down his arms and legs. Edward fought and raved, "Let me go. Let me go. She is calling me. I'm going to die. I'm going to die. Felix, she wants you, too!" I knelt and put my hand on his head and spoke to him. But he raved on and on.

The Muslim boys kept saying, "It is Satan."

I asked the boys (about 50 of them or so), "Do you believe that Jesus is stronger than Satan? If you do, let's kneel!" They all went down like one man. I commanded that evil spirit, in the name of Jesus, to come out of Edward. He raved on. A vision of Jesus on the cross came before me and I thanked and praised God for the shed blood of Jesus and for defeating Satan by His blood.

Edward calmed down. Looking at me, he asked, "Mrs. Eddy, why are you here? Where am I? What's going on?" A shout from the boys: *"Amepona!"* (He is healed!)

I noticed that he limped when he went into the dormitory.

The next morning I went to see him and before I left him I prayed for the release of the pain in his leg.

Is Satan alive and active today? Most certainly!

IS THERE HOPE?

The night of the Senior Secondary School graduation, Edward had another visit by an evil spirit. The following morning he came to my office to relate the confrontation to me. Then he said, "I was told that I will never be really free until I get married, and have a son. Then the curse will go into my son."

I exclaimed, "Oh, Edward, that's a lie! There is victory in Christ!" I invited him and his friend Danieli to come to my house daily for Bible reading and prayer. I loaned Edward a book which I thought would be helpful to him.

When he returned it, he said, "I can relate to every one of the victims mentioned. I know exactly how they felt."

I said firmly, "Let's follow the suggestions given in the book as to what the one with the evil spirit should do."

Edward confessed Jesus as his Saviour. Then he asked God to forgive his mother for taking him to witch doctors. She didn't know that witchcraft was an abomination to the Lord. As he was praying, he suddenly stopped, grabbed his chest, and cried out, "It's gone, it's gone! I'm so light! I'm free! It's gone!" How we praised God and rejoiced!

I asked him afterwards, "What is gone?" He answered, "The vice-like grip in my chest."

He was released! Free!

Remembering that he had previously told me that he *never* went out alone in the dark as he was always afraid he would kill himself, I challenged him to go out that evening alone after dark, knowing he had Jesus with him. The following morning he came early and said, "I have walked all over in the dark. I am free!" Then he stopped, turned to me and said, "*Now I know* why I had to come to this school!" The evil spirit was gone! He was free!

What a good and gracious God we have! Praise Him!

Mary Eddy *was born and educated in Clearbrook, MN. She attended a one-year normal teaching course in Bagley, MN, and taught rural schools until attending and graduating from the Lutheran Bible Institute.*

During World War II she married Laverne Shuey and went with him to Tacoma, WA, where she taught elementary school.

In 1954, Laverne died of heart failure. Mary then earned her B.S. in Elementary Education at Bemidji State College, Bemidji MN. After this she served for three years in the Department of Education at Augustana Lutheran Church headquarters, Minneapolis, MN.

In 1959, Mary was commissioned as a missionary teacher to Tanganyika where she taught in the Ruruma Girls' School. During her home leave she earned her Secondary School English teaching certificate at Bemidji State University.

Upon her return to Tanzania, she taught at Tumaini Secondary School at Kinampanda and it was there that she met and married Wellington Eddy, a co-teacher in the school.

Wellington died of cancer in 1974. The following year Mary was asked to be on the staff of the newly opened Ihanja Technical Secondary School. She taught there until her retirement in 1979. She now makes her home in Clearbrook, MN.

A MOUNTAIN TOP EXPERIENCE—

LITERALLY

Veda Hult Magnuson

Bone weary, stretched out on the scree before beginning the final ascent of Kilimanjaro, I turned to look toward the east. The sun, like an enormous orange ball breaking through the clouds, gave us new hope that we could reach the summit. I lay there soaking up the peace; all was so quiet, so still, so beautiful in this vast cathedral of our Creator God.

A co-worker, Elna Mae Lindahl (better known as Lindy), and I had planned for months to climb Kilimanjaro, the highest mountain of Africa. Now, on the fourth day of our climb, we were nearing the ice-rimmed summit.

Ahead was the steepest and most dangerous part of the entire climb. The unsure footing on the loose scree, the scarcity of oxygen causing my headache and shortness of breath made me wonder, "Was Musa right when he assured me, 'You will reach the summit'?" For sure my brain wasn't working normally! I had tried to mentally repeat the Lord's Prayer and couldn't get beyond "Our Father, who art in heaven." I tried again and could get no further. I did feel close to heaven at that moment. (Some would say I was almost four miles closer! Kilimanjaro is 19,340 feet above sea level.)

Kilimanjaro is one of the world's natural wonders: Within three days your feet will carry you from the tropics to the arctic, from banana trees to a glacier, summer to winter. All of Africa's climate zones—desert, savannah, rain forest are found on this solitary mountain, rising snow-capped from the equatorial plains on the Kenya-Tanzania border.

Lindy and I began our 60-mile round trip safari by foot at Marangu. Preparations for this trek included arranging for others to cover our nursing assignments in Lyambaland. Then we needed to borrow warm clothes, mittens, wool socks and hiking boots—no small feat when living in the tropics!

We were fortunate to have Musa, a calm, intelligent, patient and experienced mountain climber as our guide. We passed by his *shamba* (field) the first morning; his earnings from guide work helped pay the school fees for his son.

"*Jambo!*" (Hi!) the interested locals greeted us heartily as we met them on the wide path. We marveled at the bright blue sky, the vibrant green of coffee bushes and banana plants, coming as we did, from the arid Central Plateau. Invigorated, we quickened our pace.

"*Pole pole,*" (Slowly slowly) Musa cautioned us: "Not so fast!" Our bodies needed to adjust to the changing altitude.

We thoroughly enjoyed the walk through the dense rain forest; even during the heat of midday, the sunlight rarely broke through the canopy of vine-covered, mossy, tall trees. No mattresses greeted our weary bodies at Bismarck Hut that night. Our sleeping bags were placed directly on the bare boards of the bunk beds. But our sleep was not hindered in the least.

Breakfast the next morning proved to be the only meal I remembered of the whole trip. After enjoying our bananas and oatmeal, fried liver and tomatoes, Musa brought the final course: a platter of eggs and bacon. He knew this was the time to store up energy for the coming days when most climbers lose interest. His objective was to get his charges to the top.

Leaving the rain forest that morning, our first glimpse of Kilimanjaro's snow crowned peak was awe-inspiring. I no longer wondered why some Africans likened it to the "Throne of God!"

Above the timberline, the narrow trail wound through the moorlands' knee-deep grass, slick from last night's rain. My walking stick saved me from slipping as we trudged single file, *pole pole,* slow and steady, up and always up. It was sunny up here, but looking down at the dark rain clouds, I wondered whether the 24 giraffe we had seen en route to Moshi the other day were getting wet.

Vegetation kept changing with the altitude and diminished rainfall; the colors became increasingly muted: from green moss and gray lichen to the greenish grass and lavender heather. Soon the grotesque giant groundsels, some 100 years old, dotted the landscape. Towering taller than men, they stood like sentinels observing our trek.

The rooftop of Peter's Hut was a welcome sight at the end of our ten-mile hike. It had taken us all day to reach this objective.

Looking down through the clear atmosphere that evening, we could see the twinkling lights of Moshi. Also, somewhere down on the eastern slopes, was Machame. Many years ago my parents and three older brothers and sister had lived there. As a child growing up in Missouri, I would study the old black and white photo of the mountain and wonder, "Would I, could I some day see it in person?"

As we left Peter's Hut the next morning, the landscape became more barren. Our need to rest frequently reminded us that the oxygen level was steadily diminishing.

We ate a dry sandwich lunch among the boulders at the base of rugged Mawenzi, the lesser of Kilimanjaro's twin peaks—Kibo and Mawenzi. Although 2,000 feet lower than Kibo, it is known as a dangerous, difficult climb.

We headed west through a bleak, lifeless desert toward Kibo Hut far in the distance but looking deceptively close. We watched clouds come and go, and passed right through them as we made the gradual climb crossing the Saddle. Musa no longer needed to caution us to go *pole pole;* our legs and lungs reminded us. Upon reaching Kibo Hut very weary, we were more than ready to crawl into our sleeping bags at 5 p.m.

Musa gave the wake-up call at 1 a.m. After forcing down some dry bread and tea, we left our tin hut and stepped out into the total darkness of an equatorial night. Musa's bobbing lantern led us on our way.

Before us was a mere two miles to the summit, but it was a steep climb of about 3000 feet. Furthermore, the scree, or loose volcanic gravel, made the climb increasingly difficult. At first, we paced our rest stops every 50 steps; as the hours crawled by, we reduced our goal: 45, 40, 35—down to 5 before we reached the summit.

Halfway up, we took a short rest in a cave. Although I was wearing several layers of clothing, I literally shook from the cold. My left foot felt like it was freezing even though I was wearing three pairs of socks.

A crescent moon now appeared to augment Musa's lantern light. My mountain stick became like a supporting friend in the loose scree. The ascent was so steep, the oxygen so scarce that I would literally fall down—not horizontally, but onto the 45-degree slope of the mountain—for the welcome rest every fifth step.

I lay there, trying to get my breath, trying to get the strength and courage to keep climbing. I marveled at Musa's patience and at the ease with which he climbed. But for his encouragement, I would never have come this far.

Then came the grandeur of that never-to-be-forgotten sunrise. Were we actually looking down on Mawenzi, which only yesterday had seemed so high? But this musing was a luxury I could not long indulge. Up and onward!

Then we actually did reach Gilman's Point! We were on the edge of Kibo's crater. Exhausted, I could only lie down and sleep, my head protected from the snow-covered rock by a wool scarf folded to make a pillow. A helmet protected my head from the penetrating rays of the blinding sun above. Lindy wrote both our names in the register of climbers who had reached the "Roof of Africa," Africa's highest mountain peak.

I thought of our veteran missionary and pioneer explorer, Dr. Richard Reusch, a friend of my father's, who had made this climb over 40 times (!) searching for answers to questions about the crater that had long puzzled geographers.

Now we had a new challenge—changing gears for going down rather than up. Our descent, slipping, sliding and skiing down the scree alarmed Musa. "*Pole pole*," he warned. It would be all too easy to lose one's footing and roll beyond control, to the right or left off the marked route, into danger—even tragedy. Lives have been lost on this mountain.

A brief stop at Kibo Hut allowed us to catch our breath during a short rest and to sip some sweet tea for energy. Then we were off, across the Saddle past Mawenzi and down to Peter's Hut.

The descent made me aware of a set of muscles I had not thought of on the way up. Oh my aching legs—braking instead of climbing! Exhausted, I had one objective: *Sleep!* We had been hard at work since 1 a.m.; now it was late afternoon.

On awakening the next morning, we saw straw flower crowns adorning our helmets, telling the world that we had reached the summit.

On the final day, coming the rest of the way down the mountain, our senses were numb; we scarcely noticed the panoramic views that had so fascinated us on the way up. Musa's admonition, *pole pole*, now became an empathetic "*Pole!*" (in this case it meant, "Sorry! I'm sorry your feet and legs are hurting so much.")

On the wide road, nearing the Marangu Hotel, our "*Jambo!*"'s to passersby were considerably subdued. At the hotel, we found the large jar of dill pickles Lindy had purchased before the climb; she had bought them to bring back to Wembere for a special treat. After a long drink of water, we decided to sample just one of the pickles. Soon we were quarreling over the last one!

After a good sleep, Lindy and I discovered we were ready to return to the everyday experiences and challenges of our life and work at Kiomboi Hospital, Wembere and Tintigulu Dispensaries. It was as if in this mountaintop experience, God had let us catch a glimpse of his glory, his plan and purpose for our lives.

Refreshed and renewed, we went on our way rejoicing.

Veda Hult Magnuson: *For Veda, Springfield, MO, was the home community to which the family gravitated when they could be together. As the daughter and sister of missionaries, such occasions were particularly precious because they could not be taken for granted.*

Her post-secondary education began at a junior college, Luther, in Wahoo, NE; she then enrolled in the School of Nursing at Immanuel Hospital, Omaha, NE. After graduation, Veda completed the Missions course at the Lutheran Bible Institute in Minneapolis, MN, combining her studies with nursing. At Augustana College in Rock Island, IL, she earned a B.S. degree.

She was commissioned for service in Tanganyika in 1953 and served until 1962. She served in a supervisory role at Kiomboi and Iambi Hospitals, in the Wembere, Tintigulu and Ushora Dispensaries, and lastly in the newly opened Iambi Leprosarium.

Her role changed when she married the Rev. Norman Magnuson in 1965 and assumed new responsibilities in the home and the parish.

A MARATHON OF MISHAPS

Inez Olson

"Fire! Fire!" The trip's belated start in the dusk was shattered by the alarmed shout from a passenger in the back of the bus. Sparks from the exhaust were flying up into the deepening dusk.

The driver, unimpressed, hollered back, "If there's a fire it has to be in the front, not the back."

Fellow missionary Della Brown and I, traveling from Mbeya to Singida in Tanzania, settled down for a twenty-four-hour trip that turned out to be a two-day marathon of mishaps. We were scheduled to arrive in Itigi, a transfer point, at 6 a.m., but we were delayed by our four-hour late start and some unscheduled mishaps.

At midnight we were awakened by a lot of excited chattering and laughter. The bus had struck and killed an antelope. What does one do with a dead antelope—all that meat for free? Leave it lying there? How can anyone think so foolishly? You butcher it, of course! The driver threw the butchered antelope on top with the luggage.

At 6 a.m. the bus abruptly stopped again. We groggily looked at our watches and thought, "This is the time that we should be in Itigi, and we're probably half way there!" The mainspring on the bus had broken. Rescue by a passing vehicle on that desolate road was most unlikely. The driver and the passengers built a fire and roasted half the antelope for their breakfast. Fortunately Della and I had packed lunches.

After eating, the ingenious Tanzanians hoisted the bus with a jack and packed in a thick rope to replace the spring. We crawled along, and stops were made every five miles to adjust the substitute spring. The creeping and the stopping were superior to sitting on the road and waiting for help that may never have come.

At noon we came by a tea house, and the passengers and driver went in for tea. Della and I had coffee left in our thermos. When they came out from tea, we expected all of them to climb back in the bus. No? Some came to the bus and fetched the remainder of the antelope; others built another fire to roast that meat. Why they did not build that fire and start the roast before they went in for tea, I will never know.

As we kept on traveling, the rope gave way! Stranded again! Will we never get to Itigi? Nothing daunted, a new substitute was found. Saplings! Experience is a great teacher. The new substitute was an improvement. Checking and adjusting needed to be done only every ten miles.

We arrived in Itigi at about 9 p.m., fifteen hours late and twenty-five hours after leaving Mbeya. Since there were no hotels in Itigi, and since we had not made reservations at the government rest house, we spent another long night in the bus!

In the early morning the driver made us all get off the bus so he could take it for repair. No bus was running from Itigi to Singida until that afternoon. Our food was gone and no food services were available. There was no place to sit except on the dry ground under a tree. We did some reading and a bit of walking. We were exceedingly glad when we saw the bus from Singida come rolling in. At least we now had a cushioned seat to sit on! We arrived in Singida late, late that afternoon, approximately 30 hours late!

As is their habit, the Tanzanians took the ordeal in their stride. We heard no complaining. On Della's and my part, we had the experience and a good story to tell.

CONSCIENCES PRICKED

"'I don't belong here!', said the ax every time I saw it." It was Christian Emphasis Days at the Ruruma Girls' Middle School (RGS), and Rev. Petro Aroni was telling a story from his life.

"Some years ago," he continued, "when I was moved from Ushora Mission Station to Iambi, I took with me an ax and some books that did not belong to me. I got safely away with them, but that ax began talking to me! Every time I saw it, I heard, 'I don't belong here!' 'I don't belong here!' 'I don't belong here!'

"On and on it went, 'I don't belong here!' until it got so much on my nerves and conscience that I could not stand it any longer. I got on my bike and pedaled the 30 miles back to Ushora and returned the ax and the books. I felt much better."

The girls became very quiet and listened very attentively. They began thinking about things that they had taken that did not belong to them.

Rev. Aroni continued, "It was so good to get the Ushora stuff off my mind, but something else kept nagging at my conscience until I gave in to the Holy Spirit and wrote a letter to Rev. Martin Olson. I wrote that I had told him a lie when he asked me if I had any Ushora property with me when he moved me to Iambi. I asked for forgiveness for the lie. As soon as I posted that letter, peace came into my heart."

By this time some of the girls were fidgeting, studying their laps and feet, and bowing their heads. After that session the girls began making confessions and restitutions to the headmistress, Vivian Gulleen, and to me, a teacher on the staff. Some confessed that they had stolen thread and pencils, had told lies, had left school grounds without permission and they had been angry.

Three girls, who came to our attic once a week to get soap for the school, confessed that they had each taken a feed sack. Two returned their feed sacks. The third one told that when she had planned to wear it as a headcloth on Christmas Day, the cloth said, "Don't wear me on the day of Jesus' birth." When she thought about wearing it on Easter, she said, "I was again not able to wear it. The cloth is at home, but when I get there I will send it back."

The school nurse returned three feed sacks and paid for three others. She also went to the Kiomboi Hospital and paid for articles that she had stolen when she worked there. Salome was a witness for her Lord and became a church leader, especially in the women's work.

Many went to Pastor Aroni and to another speaker, Marian Halvorson, for counseling. Some were the only Christians in their home villages and wanted help on how to witness. Others wanted to know how to live a victorious life.

"I have invited Jesus into my heart and to take full control. Now I have real joy and peace," said Miriamu Selemani with her face beaming. She was a Muslim girl, the daughter of a Lyamba Chief. She had attended all the Christianity classes during her four years at RGS even though she had not been required to do so.

"I was a true Muslim to the core. Now that I am a Christian and have so much joy, I don't care if my parents throw me out of our home." Miriamu became a teacher and even came back to teach at RGS. She was truly a witness for Christ.

The confessions and the witnessing continued after the Christian Emphasis Days, especially on Saturday nights after the Bible studies. Time did not allow all who wanted to witness. It was touching to see the girls who sat in the back of the chapel keep moving to the front in order to get a chance to speak. We praised God for this cleansing and revival.

Inez Olson *comes from Hutchinson, KS. She obtained a B.A. from Bethany College, Lindsborg, KS. Before going to Tanganyika she taught in primary school for 10 years and in secondary education for one and a half years.*

She had served in several positions related to the Lutheran Church: as a National Lutheran Council volunteer in an army housing area; as a survey worker for the Augustana Board of Home Missions; and as a parish worker at Immanuel Lutheran Church in Kansas City, MO.

In Tanganyika/Tanzania from 1952 to 1977, Inez filled a number of teaching positions: headmistress of the Ruruma Girls' School, teacher at the Augustana School for missionaries' children, teacher at the Kinampanda Teachers' Training College, and at Mwenge and Tumaini Secondary Schools.

Rounding out her store of many gifts, she served for a time as acting treasurer of the Central Synod of the Evangelical Lutheran Church in Tanzania.

Inez retired in Hutchinson, KS, and is active both in her church and in women's organizations of the Evangelical Lutheran Church in America. She has discovered a latent talent for painting and enjoys many forms of art. She is happiest when kept very busy.

WE LEARNED FROM THE VILLAGE

Marjorie Nishek

"Recess is over—time to come in—class time." It is 10:30 on a typical Monday morning in our home at Tumaini Secondary School in Kinampanda, near Singida.

"Now where are those boys?" I moan, feeling the now familiar nudge of exasperation beginning to form. Nothing was novel about this situation; it happened about three of five school days in the week. Home schooling brought much joy; but is it coincidental that I found my first gray hairs then at the not so old age of 34?

When my husband Wayne and I, and our three children, Douglas, 8, Samuel, 6, and Shoba, 1½, first arrived in Kinampanda at Christmastime in 1974, the number of missionary families in Central Synod had decreased dramatically. In fact, our children were the only missionary kids below high school age in that area. The Augustana School at Kiomboi had closed several years earlier, and the nearest English-speaking boarding school was St. Constantine's, run by the Greek Orthodox Church, located in Arusha, nine bumpy hours to the north.

My husband was called to Tumaini School to teach agriculture to high school students—that was our mission. Little did we realize that the education of our three children would soon become another mission demanding just as much patience, creativity, sense of adventure and yet more patience.

Sam and Doug had begun first and third grade studies in the American International School in Nairobi while Wayne and I took a three-month Swahili course preceding our arrival in Tanzania. Then, with Swahili classes behind us, it was time to get on with the work we had come to do. For our children this meant a new home (in Kinampanda); a new school (The Nishek School with an enrollment of two); and a new teacher (Mom). New friends were yet on the horizon as were numerous unimaginable experiences.

We arrived in Kinampanda to find there was no house for us to live in. But in the true spirit of living in an African village, which almost always means being a member of an extended family, Mary Eddy, the only other LCA (Lutheran Church in America) missionary at Tumaini, opened her house to our family. Mary's husband, Wellington, of the Norwegian Mission, had died of cancer a few weeks previously and Mary said she would welcome our companionship. She turned over two of her bedrooms to us, helped us roll our 22 barrels of household goods into her attic and designated her corner sun room as "The Nishek School." Very fortunately we had received good advice regarding what correspondence materials to order and the first box of "school stuff" arrived right on time, the day after Christmas.

The first day of class arrived. It was January 2, 1975. Like a good teacher (I am a trained teacher, but not in elementary education) I was well prepared. In fact, I had spent hours absorbing the colorful and exciting materials supplied by our correspondence school. I knew our boys, whom we considered to be very bright, would learn quickly and well, and would very soon be way ahead of their scheduled learning activities. "What an advantage," I naively thought, "Doug and Sam can progress at their own speed. We'll finish this year's work in no time."

With multiplication tables for Doug and phonetic words for Sam tacked to the bulletin board, with stories about cheese, peas and chocolate pudding resounding in our heads, and with science experiments taking place in the kitchen, all proceeded well and right on schedule.

That was before our children met the Kinampanda village children.

Somehow word got out that there was a new school at our house. Soon more and more faces appeared at the windows of our school room. Noses and hands were pressed flat against the glass. Dozens of large, dark eyes watched every move we made; but there was no noise. The Kinampanda children did not want to disturb, they only wanted to watch, to see, and to know what our children were doing.

In Tanzania at that time children did not begin school until age eight. Swahili was the language of instruction in most schools in the lower grades. Therefore Kinampanda children of our children's age did not speak any English, and because they were not yet in school, they were free to play most of the day. At the time, the most exciting activity in town was to peer in the school window at the missionary house.

At this point the reader may foresee the beginning of a classic missionary story—"Nishek Missionary School Opens to Entire Village." This did not happen. In fact, quite the opposite occurred.

At first Doug and Sam were enthralled by their new classroom, their new books, their new teacher (smile) and the break-time treats that Mary's cook, Solomon, supplied each morning. And Shoba, not yet two, was also happy with all the attention she was receiving from Maria, an eighteen-year-old girl we hired to care for her during school hours. Maria carried Shoba in a cloth sling on her back as African mothers and older sisters do, as they visited house to house each day interacting with those they met in a casual, typically African manner. She would join her little Tanzanian friends as they imitated the older village children, repeating the intricate dance steps and taking their turn on the goat-hide drum.

Our 9 a.m. to 1 p.m. school day was punctuated with a 15-minute recess at 10:30. That's where our trouble began.

The first time the boys did not respond when I rang the school bell after break I found them with their new friends at a "clay hole" about a mile from the house. Tanzanian children can sit for hours molding animals, village scenes and other figures from clay and water. But the clay must be of good quality and good quality clay can only be found in special locations. The boys learned once you start being creative, you can't stop just because you hear your school bell ring frantically in the distance.

Another day the unplanned extra-curricular activity involved the creation of a very drivable toy lorry (truck) made from flattened tin cans, lengths of wire formed into wheels and bound with strips of rubber cut from an old innertube. Again, this was a community project.

A soccer game could be organized in a minute. Although a real soccer ball did not exist, there was always one that served the purpose, made from strips of fabric or old socks tightly rolled and secured by tree sap.

My days were full of surprises. One day I looked out and saw a large truck-size rubber tire rolling down the slope heading for our house. This in itself was not so amazing as Tanzanian children often roll tires down pathways for fun. But this tire had legs and arms sticking out from both sides as it rolled towards me. As the hillside leveled, the tire slowed and eventually flopped on its side. And what should appear from the inner part of the tire but Doug and his friend, Simioni, Headmaster Mpumpa's son. They had positioned their bodies end to end within the curvature of the tire extending their arms and legs to the sides. "That was a great ride, Mom" exclaimed Doug. "You should try it."

Clay from the special clay hole was transported closer to home via plastic pails carried on the head (this the boys never were able to do successfully, but Shoba learned to carry objects on her head at an early age). The clay was mixed with straw and a little water and patted into wooden brick-shaped molds made by the children. After drying in the hot, dry Tanzanian sun for some days, the children used the bricks and more clay mortar to construct miniature houses, corrals and entire villages. Today Sam is an architect in Boulder, Colorado. I often wonder were the seed for this ability was first planted.

The best treat of all occurred right after the first rains when the flying termites emerged from dormancy. The termites had plump, crispy bodies and butter-like insides. When the rains ceased, the termites would emerge by the hundreds and the children would be ready with their *kopos* (tin cans). They would collect as many termites as possible and then meet at their communal campfire. Out would come the large tin can used for cooking, a little oil and a stirring stick. A canful of termites was dumped into the cooking pot, there would be a momentary sizzling sound and some fortunate termites would escape by crawling up the cooking stick.

The children, being excited and sometimes hungry, did not bother to see if all were "well done." Using leaves or whatever would serve the purpose, they scooped the termites out of the oil and, after a moment of cooling, took in a mouthful even though some of the termites were still wiggling.

I'll never forget the sight of little Shoba, even in competition with the older children, managing to get a handful of termites from the cooking pot to her mouth. Her eyes were big and she was as eager as anyone to share this treat. In the process of jamming as many into her mouth as possible, two termites—not quite cooked—wiggled up her cheek towards her ear. While our beautiful and now much more sophisticated daughter denies this ever happened, I have a precious home movie to prove it with a close-up shot of the escaping termites.

Speaking of termites, I must relate one incident that did not take place during recess. We were invited to Makiungu, an Irish Catholic mission station near Singida, for dinner one New Year's Eve. The three Irish priests and seven Sisters at the Mission liked to celebrate in a more formal way than our family was accustomed to. I knew Mary Eddy and our family would be the only guests, and I also knew the meal would be several courses with multiple knives, forks and spoons set at each place. In preparation for this grand event the kids and I had a practice session at home. "Sit straight, do not slurp your soup, watch others and do as they do," was my motherly advice.

The night of the big dinner arrived and the kids were unrecognizably polite. I was proud of them. The long, lavishly laden table was illuminated by a one bulb lamp hung low over the center of the table near where Sam was sitting.

As is common in Tanzania, a few bugs and this night a few flying termites were circling the single light bulb. One termite decided to check the contents of Sam's plate and alighted on the plate's rim. Sam took note of the situation and looked around the table for guidance on how to handle this turn of events. Finding no example to follow, he nonchalantly plucked the termite by its two wings, popped it into his mouth, delicately withdrew the now bodiless wings and casually wiped the wings on his pant leg under the linen tablecloth. I glanced around the table but only Father Ned had noticed and I saw the twinkle in his eye. The delicious meal continued.

No, the Nishek School did not become a village school. We did not teach the Kinampanda children much. If fact, the opposite happened. The children of Kinampanda Village taught our children more than they could ever learn from the most beautiful, educationally-correct books available.

Today, Doug works for the U.S. Forest Service and has the gift of seeing the beauty and interrelationships of nature through the eyes of a young African boy. Sam, an architect, designs no-nonsense dwellings that blend with the environment in a dramatic way. And Shoba, in the medical field, has the gift of empathizing with those who are hurting and cheering them with her radiant smile. Her friends say she is still number one on the dance floor.

After two years of home schooling, Doug and Sam enrolled in St. Constantine's, the boarding school in Arusha, where they eventually caught up with their curriculum. But I'm certain what our children learned from the village children of Kinampanda was much more sustainable and, in fact, will continue to influence their thoughts and actions throughout their lifetimes.

Marjorie Nishek *and her husband Wayne served as LCA lay missionaries in Tanzania, from 1974 - 1977. Wayne was called to be an agricultural instructor for Tumaini Secondary School.*

In May of 1975, the Central Synod of the Evangelical Lutheran Church in Tanzania turned Tumaini Secondary School over to the government and transferred Wayne and Marjorie to Ihanja. There they helped to open the Ihanja Technical Secondary School at the site which had originally served as a Lutheran hospital and later as a Bible School. Seven students were enrolled that first year. The school has grown steadily and now operates at full capacity.

Wayne and Marjorie completed their work with LCA in 1977 but continued living and working in Arusha for the next four years. Wayne was one of the founders of the Arusha Appropriate Technology Project, and Marjorie worked with a USAID project in the Arusha Regional Office.

Presently the Nisheks reside in Banjul, The Gambia, in West Africa, where Wayne is Director of the U.S. Peace Corps and Marjorie is employed by the American Embassy.

The Nisheks have three children:

Douglas married Laura Absher. They have two children, Heather and Hannah. Doug works for the U.S. Forest Service. Laura is a dietician. The family resides in Bonners Ferry, ID.

Samuel married Dena Bandazian. He is an architect; Dena is a magazine editor. They live in Boulder, Colorado.

Shoba is a Certified Medical Assistant who lives in Coeur d'Alene, Idaho.

ONE OF THE LEAST OF THESE BROTHERS OF MINE

Carol C. Kusserow

"Oh dear! Here comes Ngasak again!" His grizzled white hair and beard contrast sharply with his black face. His baggy clothes and lurching steps identify him immediately. As the old man shuffles up to our front door, I greet him and hand him the usual coins he expects every Friday.

"Ngasak, how would you like to hear some Bible verses this morning?"

He sits down heavily on the front step, grateful to rest awhile. I bring the Swahili Bible and sit with him and read the passage we had read this morning at breakfast.

What is running through his mind? Can he understand the words? Is it pointless to read him God's word, since he has just been drinking? I chide myself for feeling resentful toward him. Many people despise him. Even the children, who normally respect their elders, jeer and poke fun at him as he stumbles by on his way home. Why then should I pay any attention to him? What is it that makes me feel guilty for my impatience with him?

"How is your wife these days? Any better?"

Ngasak pulls himself up to leave. "She's still in bed at home. Those two quilts you gave us are all we have to sleep on."

As Ngasak hobbles away, I remember what Evangelist Edward called over his shoulder to me as he passed by our house two Fridays ago. "Certainly he will sit and listen to you read if you give him money when he comes. But don't expect him to understand the Ten Commandments you are teaching him, much less put them into practice."

Now it is Sunday morning, and Amani Lutheran Church, Maswa, is filling up. There are no benches yet as the church only got its roof two Sundays ago. People come bringing chairs and stools to sit on. There are two rows of cement blocks at the front for the children. The youth choir is singing now, but heads turn to look back. My curiosity gets the better of me. I look back, too. It's Ngasak shuffling in. He doesn't pay attention to the stares or the whispering, but finds his way to the front and sits on a cement block.

Suddenly I feel warm and grateful inside. "Dear Lord, are you working on Ngasak's heart to draw him to you?"

After church Ralph and I greet everyone outside. We take special care to greet Ngasak and invite him to come to worship service again next Sunday. Walking back to the house, Ralph and I make plans to try to get Ngasak into the baptism class that Evangelist Temaeli is teaching. Temaeli will be patient with Ngasak.

Sunday after Sunday finds Ngasak in church. He even gives an offering now. But when he comes to do some weeding for us around the garden, he complains about the instruction class.

"All the others are young people. They don't like it when I can't answer questions. I just hold them back. I don't think I'll attend any more. But I do want to be baptized. I will take the name Reuben when I am baptized."

"I'm very happy to see you coming to church regularly."

"Tomorrow I'll bring my wife to church. She's better. But because she's blind and doesn't understand Swahili, she probably won't want to keep coming."

"Isn't she from Lyamba like you?"

"No, she is of the Sukuma tribe. She never went to school."

"I always see you leading her by the hand, but I thought it was because she was drunk like you! So she's blind is she?"

"Yes, and she's usually sick. As for being drunk—I'm not drunk. I only drink a little. We're social drinkers, you know! Ha! Ha! Ha!"

"Have you met our new watchman? He is a Sukuma man and I think he is attending that instruction class you used to go to."

"Yes, Saluum. I like him. He laughs easily. He says he has many Christians in his family, but he never took instruction for baptism, and now he is getting quite old. He likes to joke a lot."

"I know what you mean about his joking. A couple of nights ago when he came to *Mchungaji* (pastor) for batteries, he said that he needed some new 'stones' for his torchlight, because that's the word the Sukuma people use for batteries. *Mchungaji* reached down, picked up a couple of stones from the ground and handed them to Saluum. What a good laugh he got out of that! Every night since then he has joked with *Mchungaji* about the 'stones' in his torchlight."

"Well, I'm finished with the weeding for today. I should be going home. I'll be back next week to do some more weeding. Please thank *Mchungaji* for giving me a way to earn some money."

I watch him leaving slowly. Yet time has flown. When we first knew him we hardly spoke more than a few words of greeting. Now we can carry on long conversations about all kinds of things. Ngasak is nearly out of sight. I turn back to the house.

Reformation Sunday, October 25, 1992. Sixteen people were confirmed or baptized today. Saluum and Ngasak were among those baptized. Saluum chose the name Timotheo. Ngasak was baptized Reuben.

How fast the time flies! Has it already been three years since we met Ngasak? Today he is part of God's family. Thanks be to God for his infinite patience with each one of us.

Carol C. Kusserow *was born in India in 1938 to Lutheran missionaries, Dr. and Mrs. Virgil E. Zigler. Carol went to boarding school at Kodaikanal, South India. She attended Thiel College, Greenville, PA, then Wittenberg University, Springfield, Ohio, graduating with a degree in music in 1959.*

Carol was married in 1959 to Ralph F. Kusserow, missionary pastor to Malaysia, Singapore and Tanzania. They have three children: Hans, born in 1960, Kurt born in 1963, Timothy, born in 1964. All sons are married and each has two children

Ralph and Carol went to Tanzania in 1984. After language study in Morogoro they lived in Maswa, Shinyanga Region, for 10 years, working in the Sukuma Mission under the former Central Synod, now the Central Diocese of the Evangelical Lutheran Church in Tanzania. The Sukuma Mission is now the East of Lake Victoria Diocese. The Kusserows were assigned to Dar es Salaam in 1994.

ADVENTURES WITH THE GREEN JEEP

Helen Pedersen

I still visualize with fondness that faithful 4-wheel drive Jeep, made available for the church president at that time, my husband Rube. It was a pickup, cab and chassis with large box body, expanded metal (reinforcing iron mesh) and canvas roll-up curtains for privacy or warmth as needed. It made a cozy bedroom at night and kitchen and passenger space by day.

In one year it saw 42 weekend visits to all of the parishes of the Lyamba-Turu areas. A package of gum to be chewed for plugging any pin-hole leak in the gas tank, tinned foods, tool box, rifle, flashlight, and canteen of water made up the emergency supplies stored behind the front seat. There were times when this "green machine" warranted the name "Martin Luther," since it practiced his famous words: "Here I stand, I cannot do otherwise."

STUCK IN BLACK COTTON

"Pray, Helen, that this Jeep doesn't stall," yelled Rube, as he observed black smoke from the exhaust pipe and the engine knocking, wheezing and coughing like someone with severe asthma.

"Rube, will the kerosene you added to the tank get us home tonight?" I asked. Our vehicle was low on gas after four hours of being stuck in a black-cotton mud hole. This particular mud hole was especially obnoxious from smelly deposits left by visiting cattle and goats.

We were moving a teacher to a new place of work, where he would pioneer in the Christian witness of teaching some 60 children in grades 1 and 2. By the time we had his meager furniture and personal effects loaded high—including some on the car roof—it was nearing dusk. The car "track" road became an almost invisible footpath that was to lead us to the village. Suddenly, in the darkness, we saw this questionable mud hole area, and stopped.

As Rube got out to check, the anxious teacher said, "Go through it, Sir! It's not deep! You'll make it just fine!"

Since we often followed the advice of our African co-workers, we locked in the 4-wheel drive, revved that engine and plowed into the mud hole. Alas, it was wider and deeper than predicted! We bogged down, hung up on all four wheels! (Groans all around—I wasn't sure the wheels were even visible!)

Being a dutiful wife, I got out of the Jeep to help, but sank into the mud to mid-calf. Trying to move, I lost one shoe, then lost my balance and fell backward, full length.

"Ruuube, I'm stuck, I can't get up !"

I could almost hear him whisper, "Lord, give me strength," as he pulled me from the smelly mess. Fortunately there was a large hedgerow of min-yara (smooth pencil cactus, grown fifteen feet high) at the edge of the mud hole. It saw a major trimming-pruning as we cut branches to stuff under each wheel and slowly jacked each side up to ground level. The jacking and stuffing was repeated several times, with me as designated driver, and Rube and the teacher as pushers. Finally, we emerged from the muddy mess, found the teacher's house and unloaded his belongings. He was profoundly grateful, and pleased to be at his new place of witness. We were deeply relieved, and weary!

We limped back to Iambi, running on half kerosene. Rube then got ready for the Sunday services - some four hours in length - including communion, child and adult baptisms, preaching and numerous choir selections.

This experience brought to mind the saying about two qualifications of a good missionary: 1) to have a strong sense of humor, and 2) a weak sense of smell!

THE THREE-MEAL EVENING

The sun was high in the sky, and according to the Tanzanians' "clock" it was early afternoon as we boarded the Jeep pickup for a weekend visit to Tulya congregation, one of some fourteen of the Kiomboi parish. Tulya village also had a primary school (grades 1-4) and a small medical clinic, so there were three trained leaders in residence: teacher, evangelist and medical worker. This made for a vital emphasis of the Gospel message: teaching, preaching, healing.

It was a beautiful dry-season day; the narrow auto track road that descended nearly 1,000 feet to the valley area was rough, but passable. The wooded area and open plains gave us the pleasure of observing wildlife - an impala suddenly disturbed in its grazing, the jack-rabbit-sized dik-dik, too busy nibbling new green leaves of nearby bushes to bother with us. The adjacent area also boasted rhino, giraffe and lion.

We reached Tulya in late afternoon. The "bush radio" had been in operation, since we were welcomed by the entire village. We unloaded our bedding and food into a small guest house, a single- room structure made of aluminum roofing. The school teacher welcomed us on behalf of the village and invited us to his home for the evening meal. We accepted with delight and went to his mud-brick, thatch-roofed, three-room house at meal time.

The usual greetings were followed by the custom of all guests washing their hands, using a bar of soap and water poured from a large gourd, and a towel. Water spilled on the smooth dirt floor disappeared quickly. We were seated at a small table, and after offering prayer, the teacher's wife brought the meal: a large platter heaped with rice and delicious chicken parts, with meat sauce poured over it. We were encouraged to keep eating, a task easily accomplished with each one using a large spoon and eating together from the platter.

Just as we were thanking our hosts and leaving, the evangelist appeared and said, "We are expecting you at our home for the evening meal. It is all ready, so come with me." Knowing that only impoliteness would decline such an invitation, we thanked him and followed.

Again the custom of greetings, hand washing and table prayer preceded the bringing of the food, this time a large mound of *ugali* (thick corn porridge, eaten with your fingers), with a side dish of cooked wild spinach. The evangelist ate with us while his wife looked on, ready to increase the portions as needed. We tried to make a good showing of eating enough to please our hosts. (By this time, I had no plans to serve breakfast in the morning!)

Then came the usual expressions of gratitude. They thanked us for giving them a "bit" of our life—the amount of time spent in their home—and we thanked them for their generous hospitality. As we left we were met on the path by the medical worker and I remembered that I had an appointment to visit the clinic the next morning.

After welcoming us again, he said, "Mama and *Bwana*, we have prepared food for you. All is ready and my wife is waiting."

By this time my stomach was "full-term-pregnant" with food and could deliver at any time! But African hospitality is not to be rejected. We followed him to his home. Once more, the custom of greetings, hand washing and prayer, preceded the bringing of food. This time a hand-stone-ground mound of *ugali*, with a side dish of cooked sun-dried fish—the latter with bits of sand from its dry-ground drying rack. What to do? (My alimentary canal was full to the epiglottis!)

But fortune smiled on us, since African hospitality also sometimes included the guests being left alone in the dining area. We sat for a while just looking at the food. Finally, I asked Rube if he had a handkerchief. He produced it and I dug out a substantial amount of the *ugali*, wrapped it in the hanky and stowed it in my large handbag. We nibbled just enough to be able to say "thank-you for the food." Friendship with our hosts remained intact.

When we got back to the Jeep I stowed the *ugali*-filled item under the seat and forgot it! Several days later a strange sour odor filled the cab, and I remembered—and retrieved the little bundle.

Another good missionary qualification was realized: Never refuse an invitation to dinner.

"THOSE TALL, DARK, AND HANDSOME MEN !"

"Helen," called Rube, "I just got word from builder Kapoor Singh that the Faust's new house at Balangida is ready. Let's escort them out there and be their first guests."

"Right on—I'd like that," I replied, and started for the kitchen to prepare food supplies to take along. Bedding was stuffed into our well-worn army duffel bag. Our assistant, Israel, helped bring everything to the Jeep pickup, where Rube did the packing.

It was late afternoon when the church president's (Rube's position) office was closed and we began the sixty-mile trip which included a shortcut across a dry lake bed. Midway in the trip it began to rain and we hoped the lake bottom wouldn't give us trouble. We reviewed the many delays involved in the building of this house. We were keen to witness proof of the claim that it was now ready, since on occasion the Indian builders "stretched" the facts a bit.

The light rain continued, but as darkness fell we crossed the lake bottom without difficulty and finally pulled up to the front door of the house. What front door??! No doors, no windows had been installed—just gaping frames to hold them! All open to the wind and rain!

We were met in the living room by saw horses piled with boards, waiting to be cut and installed someplace. Sawdust and wood shavings littered the floor which hadn't been swept since the concrete was poured and cured. And Hal and Louise Faust had waited so long to see the house completed! We located a bedroom and put our cots and bedding in a corner away from the wind and rain. It was cold!

Several hours later we saw the headlights and heard the unsteady sounds of the laboring engine of the old 5-ton truck, filled with personal and household items, the earthly possessions of the Fausts. They had been stuck enroute, and now, weary and hungry, stopped at the front door of the doorless house. We held a lantern to light up the front steps, and welcomed them to their new home.

Undaunted, they took it all in stride. It seemed to them just an additional but minor challenge as part of living alone in a remote, thorn-tree bush area occupied by the pastoral cattle herders—the Barabaig. We wondered how the Fausts would escape loneliness in the years stretched out ahead of them, in service of the Good Shepherd, caring for the medical, educational and spiritual needs of the Barabaig, and to witness the founding of a new community of believers in the fellowship of the church. We remembered the quiet counsel of an African church leader when commending a worker to a new place of work: "Be sure your hoe and axe are sharp, and remember there will be stones also in that new field."

Since the loaded truck was covered with a tarp, we waited until morning to unload, except for necessary bedding and food. Our single-burner kerosene stove soon had the casserole heated and the coffee boiled. Adding some bread, a plate of cookies, and with a dish towel draped over the saw horse lumber table, we enjoyed a hearty, happy first meal.

The soft glow of the kerosene lantern disguised the disappointing appearance of the unfinished house. Hal and Rube collected waste lumber and wood shavings to build the first fire in the beautiful stone fireplace. The four of us were soon engrossed in thought, enjoying the fire and the shadows it played on the wall.

As I turned around to move away from the fireplace, I suddenly realized we were not alone. Forming a semi-circle behind us stood a group of sandaled, tall, dark and handsome men, draped in loose-fitting long over-the-shoulder "robes," with legs crossed and leaning on their long walking sticks. Curious to see these newly-arrived pale neighbors, they had entered the new house so quietly we were unaware of their arrival.

But clearly they had come also to be our friends. Thus, that first evening in the new house was blest with the presence of a delegation from the people whom the Fausts had come to serve. It was like a confirmation that this work was God's work, and His grace would be utterly sufficient, in times of difficulty and in seasons of joy.

We thought of another qualification of a good missionary: accept what you cannot change, and trust God for patience and courage in unforeseen circumstances.

"GOSSIPING" THE GOSPEL

While on vacation a unique privilege came our way—a visit to a Maasai *boma* (kraal, enclosure for domestic animals). This one was a football-field-size, thick thorn-branch-encircled yard, containing six igloo-shaped huts of stick-and-mortar construction, coated with cow dung-and-mud plaster. As strangers we viewed it as an ideal place for flies, and their attraction to exploring our eyes and mouth. The animal dung aroma, less an annoyance than the flies, reached its peak, we were told, during the heavy rainy season.

Our missionary guide, well-known and warmly welcomed by the kraal dwellers, introduced us to several family members, including the white-haired, stately elder/clan leader. The customary "visitors' gift" to the elder, a colorful quilt made by American church women, brought him obvious delight, and added to the warmth of the welcome we felt.

Following the customary exchange of greetings, one of the wives, named "Luti" (Ruth) invited us to her home, one of the six in the enclosure. We stooped to enter the doorway, noticing a separate enclosure for chickens and baby animals. Bed frames were of tree limb construction, with rope covering the rectangular frame, and covered with cow skins for a mattress. Smaller beds were built into the walls, and served as benches for us to sit. A hole in the roof encouraged exit of smoke from the open fire in the three-stone-triangle "stove."

Our eyes felt the sting from smoke, but the fire also produced a large kettle of boiled tea, with generous addition of milk and sugar. We were handed a pint-sized enamel cup of tea. We knew that accepting her warm hospitality was important.

As we chatted, Ruth told us about her life. Before becoming a Christian believer, she said she was the worst gossiper in the area, disliked by many and shunned by others. She then told how their "church" was in the shade of a large thorn tree, where the good news of God's love was shared. She became a believer, and found a deep joy she had not known before.

"Now my life is different," she said with a broad smile. "I like to say that now I'm 'gossiping' the Gospel!"

Helen Pedersen, *commissioned as a missionary by the Augustana Lutheran Church in 1947, went to Tanganyika, Africa, the following year.*

She served in a mission hospital until 1949 when she was assigned as the first fulltime medical missionary to the Mkalama Leprosy Settlement. In 1952 while in the U.S., she married missionary Rev. Ruben Pedersen (widower with three children) and returned to Africa with the family. She served in medical and evangelism outreach programs for another nine years.

AT HOME IN A PLACE OF CHILDHOOD MEMORIES

Peace L. Finlayson

This was the country I had heard about ever since I was a small child. At that time of my life, my Uncle Lud was a bachelor missionary who would visit us when he was on furlough. I had vivid memories of him seated at the table, cooling and drinking his coffee from a saucer and telling stories about exciting places and unusual happenings in a country then known as Tanganyika. It was to be renamed Tanzania about the time my husband, Dick, 4½-year-old Grace, 3½-year-old Susie, 1½-year-old Todd and I entered the country in 1964. We got off the plane in Moshi, right at the base of snow-capped Mount Kilimanjaro.

Uncle Lud Melander was one of the first Augustana Lutheran missionary pastors, arriving in Tanganyika in 1923. He was something of a medicine man himself in the early days of his ministry, before medical backup was available. As he told it, he provided the Africans with one of two treatments, quinine for symptoms located above the waist and Epsom salts for those complaints located below the waist. He had provided other medical services as well.

After we were settled in Tanzania, Dick was on a bush safari and met an African woman about thirty years of age who had been vaccinated for smallpox. When asked about it she said, "*Mchungaji Melanda* (Pastor Melander) vaccinated me when I was a child."

Uncle Lud married Esther Olson, a missionary teacher in Tanzania. The two of them were widely welcomed by African and missionary alike. Their music and preaching had been refined by decades of experience. Uncle Lud delighted children by playing his violin in such a manner as to imitate wild animals speaking in English and, of course, Swahili.

It was thus with some feelings of familiarity that I began life with my physician husband and three children in Tanzania. After three months of language classes in the small village of Isanzu, we settled in at Kiomboi in central Tanzania. The Kiomboi Mission Station included Augustana School, a boarding school for missionary children; Kiomboi Lutheran Hospital; and Kiomboi Nurses' Training Centre.

The station had a deep well providing good quality water. Electricity was available to the homes of the staff briefly in the morning during radio contact between mission stations, twice a week for a few hours on surgery days and daily from dark until 11:00 p.m. Thus no one bothered to turn off the house lights in the evening. On surgery days we washed clothes, ironed, sewed, used the electric mixer or other electric appliances.

Being on call was far different for Dick than it had been in St. Paul, Minnesota. There were no telephone calls because there were no telephones. The gradual appearance of a dim light outside our bedroom window meant that two or more African nurses were standing there holding a kerosene lamp. Sometimes, when we didn't respond to the light alone, they would call out in a soft voice, *"Daktari!"* It always meant there was a serious medical or surgical problem at the hospital. Little did I imagine that one night I would be the reason that the lights would come on all over the mission station.

It was the day before Thanksgiving. I didn't feel well. I had lost my appetite and had a vague upper abdominal pain. Dick and the other physician at Kiomboi, Dr. Ken Wilcox, followed my condition throughout the day, uncertain as to what the problem was. Towards evening the pain had settled in the right lower portion of my abdomen and could no longer only be observed. The physical signs pointed to the need for surgery. It is fair to say that my two physicians did not easily make their decision to operate. Dick gave me spinal anesthesia and Ken and a nurse did the surgery. During the operation I had difficulty breathing and was given the last of the oxygen supply at the hospital. My blood pressure had fallen temporarily after the spinal was given. Yes, it was a very inflamed appendix and the only one removed at Kiomboi Lutheran Hospital while we were there. I recuperated for about a week in the hospital, very well cared for by the African and missionary staff.

Our lives revolved around Augustana School as the children grew older. We had parents and other overnight guests almost daily because Kiomboi had no hotels. Every Saturday afternoon the school houseparents invited all the Kiomboi missionaries and the guests over for coffee and homemade pastries. There many adventure stories were shared including encounters with wild animals, snakes, etc. It seemed to us that some of the missionaries delighted in telling hair-raising stories, the kind that made you doubt whether you had made the right choice in coming to Africa. Of course, after more time in the country, we had some experiences which we enjoyed telling as well.

In August 1966 the first and second grade teacher became ill and was flown back to the United States. I had my teaching degree and was asked to take over the class. Out of ten first- and second- graders, two were our children, Grace and Susie. Also, we had students from Norway, Denmark, Tanzania and the United States. Martha Malloy, Augustana School housemother, arranged for our family to eat noon and evening meals at the school while I was teaching. Thus we truly became a part of the school family.

My first day in the classroom presented a challenge which I had not anticipated. One of my daughters stood on top of her desk, apparently in an attempt to show me who was boss. I decided that I was and sent her back to our home. It was important that I did not show any favoritism towards my two children. Most of my classroom experiences were like those I had encountered in Minnesota. The different national backgrounds and the fact that these children had traveled all over the world did make for interesting learning experiences.

The school day most of us will not forget was in late March when we learned that some of the children had infectious hepatitis. The mission doctors and nurses instituted measures to prevent the spread of the illness, including the administration of large doses of gamma globulin. As some of our readers know, these injections are very uncomfortable and as a result many of the children and teachers were too sore to sit in school, so classes were canceled for the day.

I received this protective measure, but too late because in five days I was in bed with hepatitis. Aunt Esther heard about my illness and sent many packages of chocolate, but I had no appetite for it. This perplexed our children, but caused no regret on their part because they liked chocolate as much as I usually do. My strength did not return sufficiently to permit me to resume teaching before we left for Minnesota in July.

After coming back to the United States, one of our most asked questions was, "How could you stand being gone at Christmas time?" The answer was easy. Christmas was a most special time at Kiomboi. Because of the lack of commercialism we could stress the real meaning of Christmas as Christ's birth.

It was Christmas Eve. We were about to begin our traditional missionary Christmas Eve progressive dinner when we realized that there would be no electricity. The light plant would not be working because it needed repairs. This year we would burn candles for beauty and also out of necessity.

Just before Christmas someone driving the 260 miles to the larger town of Arusha for supplies had purchased a large frozen turkey. Everyone contributed the remainder of the dinner, including salad at one home, main course with the turkey at another, and then dessert, Christmas carols and reading of the Christmas story at another home. We were one large, extended family with Christ at the center.

On Christmas morning we were awakened to the beautiful sound of the African student nurses singing Christmas hymns outside our window, kerosene lamps illuminating their faces. We quickly dressed and followed them to the early morning Christmas service at Kiomboi Lutheran Church. The church also was lit only with kerosene lanterns. To me the most impressive part of the service was the free prayer that closed the service. I had my eyes closed, and upon opening them realized that night had passed and the light of another day had dawned. What a beautiful reminder that Christ, the Light of the world, had come to be with us.

Peace L. Finlayson *and her husband, Dr. Richard Finlayson, live in Rochester, Minnesota, where Dick practices psychiatry at the Mayo Clinic.*

Their children are Grace DeRoose, a speech pathologist, married with two children; Susan Knutson, in marketing for General Electric Capital Finance, married with two children; and Todd, graduate student in environmental toxicology at the University of Maine.

Peace and Dick lived in Kiomboi, Tanzania, from 1964-1967. At that time Dick was a general practitioner M.D.

THE DIRT PATH

Mary Alice Peterhaensel

It was the first day of school. With butterflies fluttering inside, I walked the 100 or so yards down the hard dirt path from my house on the school compound in the small village of Kinampanda to the small five-room building that was the school. I had two years of teaching experience behind me; but, this was Africa. This was strange and new and different. I walked out of the early morning sun through the open door into the coolness of the classroom. The students rose as a body and stood at attention until I reached the front of the room.

"Good morning, Class," I intoned.

"Good morning, Teacher," they echoed.

"You may be seated," I told them, marveling already at the respect shown teachers here that I never had experienced in the States. The students seated themselves on the benches behind their tables. Thirty-six pairs of eyes stared at me out of thirty-six dark faces, excited, eagerly waiting, anticipating.

Such eagerness I noted as I approached my own little table and chair. I plopped down the books I was carrying and faced the class, at the same time pulling out my chair from under the little table. I noticed the intake of breath, the rising excitement among my students. What was going on? The question was answered as I glanced down at the shed skin of a cobra coiled on my chair. "Mary, remain calm; it's not alive. IT'S NOT ALIVE!" I told myself, heart racing, adrenaline pumping. Somehow I found my voice, reached down, picked up the skin.

"Does this belong to anyone? Did anyone lose a snakeskin?" I heard my weak, shaky voice asking lamely.

Sheepish smiles appeared throughout the room along with furtive glances. We, students and teacher alike, dissolved into all-out laughter, the kind that goes on and on. I had passed my first test.

Many times I walked that dirt path, both by day and night. In the early morning at sun-up, five days a week, I jogged down the path to rouse the girls from their dorm for *mchaka-mchaka*, (morning exercise). We would do a few calisthenics to warm up and then run around the campus. We ran along the edge of the escarpment, the sun just coming up and shining on Mt. Hanang, an extinct volcano in the far distance, then on the valley below, on a ribbon of river, shimmering, stretching across the valley floor.

No sign of the lions we had heard the night before, though at times animals could be seen in the distance or impala and duikers grazing right below us at the foot of the escarpment. Such beauty spread out below never ceased to thrill me.

We ended our run at the school dining hall, where with a wave of farewell, the girls left me for breakfast. I, then, walked home for my own breakfast, contemplating the beauty of God's world and feeling refreshed and ready to begin the day.

One night I walked the path to the school. The teachers took turns checking on the students during the evening hours from 7:00-9:00, the compulsory time for them to do their homework. It was also the only time that the generator was on to provide electricity so that the students could see to study.

That night it was my turn to ensure that the students were working and to answer any questions they might have. I hurried toward the school in the dark with my trusty torch (flashlight) lighting the path in front of me. I heard nothing except the sound of the generator, but suddenly before me I saw the glow of two yellow eyes reflected in the light of my torch. I stopped. The hyena five feet in front of me also stopped. There was no fear, only amazement at this sudden strange encounter. We stared at each other for a moment. Then the spotted beast turned tail and loped off in the direction it had come. At the same time, fear made its entrance; and I wheeled, running back up the path toward my house and shelter, away from bone-crushing jaws. Will a hyena attack an adult human being? I still don't know.

Another time, I took the dirt path toward the school in the warm sun of a Saturday morning. My mind was far away, thousands of miles away, in the States where my fiancé was doing his seminary internship. The long distance between us was heart-wrenching at times. Letters and once-in-awhile photos, and rarely a reel-to-reel tape were our means of contact with each other. My contemplation was interrupted, and I was abruptly brought back to the present by laughter beside the path. A group of girls, my students, called out to me.

"Teacher, time to learn Swahili." I had been getting together with several of the girls on Saturday mornings for conversational Swahili. During the week at school the students were allowed to speak only English, so we had chosen Saturday mornings off by ourselves. I groaned, knowing how tired the session would make me, and knowing that on this particular morning I would much rather be thinking about Martin in Chicago.

"*Mwalimu* (teacher), you did not see us. We had to call you."

I sighed. "I was thinking about the man I am to marry."

"Oh, tell us about your *mchumba*! (fiancé)" they exclaimed. "Is he handsome? Have you met him? Do you love him?" The questions came pouring out as we all climbed into the big ebony tree by the side of the path, as was our custom for these sessions. Sheltered among the leaves we talked, with my halting and incorrect Swahili being corrected with much giggling.

"Has the bride price been set?" I was asked. "How many cows and goats must he pay?"

"It will be many," another answered for me, "because Americans are rich."

"How old is he? Are you his first wife? How many children do you want? Where will you live? What will your house be like?" The questions came thick and fast and were hard to answer, and not only because of my inadequate knowledge of Swahili. How does one explain the American way of life to those who have no concept of it?

When we decided to get married at Kinampanda Lutheran Church and my fiancé had come to Tanzania over his Christmas vacation for the wedding, he was asked some of those same questions by the men. When asked about the bride price, he jokingly said he would give some large number of cows and goats; but his comment was taken seriously. "*Pole sana, Bwana.* (I'm so sorry, Sir.) It is a very high price." Then he would have to explain.

Among the last times I walked down that path was when I went to check with the school cooks to see how the planned wedding dinner was coming. The school year was finished; the students had gone to their homes, and the place was bare and empty. But, the cooks were busy, preparing the goat that had been purchased for the occasion and the ostrich that one of our missionaries, who was a hunter, had bagged. There were pounds and pounds of rice.

My housemate, Alpha, and I had baked the three-tiered wedding cake. The limes had been squeezed for the punch. The borrowed wedding gown had arrived in a missionary barrel and was a perfect fit, and the bridesmaids' dresses had been made. Flowers made from flamingo feathers had been brought from Lake Nakuru in Kenya. All was in readiness.

I walked down the path once more, that December morning, to the church to say my vows, and again on the arm of my new husband to the dining hall for the reception. I then walked back up the path for the last time to enjoy the post-reception dancing performed for us by the African villagers.

I stepped from the path into the Land Rover that would take us the 40 miles to Singida for our wedding night and on to other points of interest as we celebrated Christmas and our honeymoon. I left Tanzania a week and a half later and have not had the opportunity to return, but even today I still travel that dirt path in my mind and heart.

Mary Alice (Bagshaw) Peterhaensel *grew up in Huntingdon, PA. From 1968-1969 she was a missionary at Kinampanda, Tanzania, teaching English and related studies, first at Mwenge Secondary School in Singida, then at the new school started at Kinampanda, Tumaini Secondary School.*

She is a graduate of Juniata College and was a Latin/English teacher, and later, from 1980-1986 taught English as a Second Language, and was in immigration and naturalization counseling and refugee resettlement. From 1986-1990, she and her family were missionaries in Monrovia, Liberia.

She is the mother of three children: Erin, married and a missionary in South Korea; Karl, married and living in Arizona; and Benjamin, adopted in Liberia, at home.

She is a 1996 graduate of Gettysburg Lutheran Seminary, and on October 1, 1996, became pastor of Bethlehem Lutheran Church in Falconer, New York.

Mary Alice, with her son Benjamin, share the parsonage with a cat, two brightly-colored anoles, two green iguanas, a corn snake, a ball python, and a boa constrictor.

EXPECT THE UNEXPECTED

Ruth J. Spragg

As usual, the alarm sounded at 5:00 a.m. However, this would prove to be anything but a usual day. We flicked on the solar lights that Scott, my husband, had installed upon our arrival nine years earlier at Ihanja Technical Secondary School in central Tanzania. I washed my hair in the cold tap water flowing down from the attic storage tank which was filled from the school windmill located in the valley below.

Our school is owned by the Evangelical Lutheran Church of Tanzania, Central Diocese. It is a boarding school consisting of 160 boarding students, 22 bumpy miles of unpaved roads from the nearest town, named Singida. Day students living with families near the school campus increased the total number of students. Ihanja village is peaceful, picturesque. Two tall, stately palm trees wave in the wind to welcome anyone approaching the main gate of the school.

Pressed with duties at the school, we didn't always have time to enjoy the beauty all around us. In the course of our time at the school, I had served as English and Bible teacher and school health nurse, providing care day or night for both students and staff and families. I was very grateful for the local government dispensary two miles down the road, even though they were often out of medications.

At least they had some excellent trained medical assistants or nurses, able to diagnose and if necessary, to refer to a hospital. There was the government district hospital in Singida, a one-hour drive each way depending on road conditions, or the Catholic Hospital at Makiungu, an equal distance in a different direction, past boulders and rock formations reminiscent of Garden of the Gods in Colorado. We preferred the latter choice as the Sisters and doctors demonstrate Christ-like compassion and concern. That is where we ourselves went with any major health problems.

However, in recent months I had been released from nursing duties, which were then undertaken by a Tanzanian medical assistant. At this point I became full-time school librarian, assisted by a young Swedish wife whose husband was teaching at the school. The past week had been very busy. Before the two-week Easter break, we had every student return each borrowed textbook. Books are very desirable to students who try different tricks to achieve personal possession. During room inspection, one student was found to have stolen and hidden books in his mattress!

Then this past weekend was the Student Christian Fellowship Easter Conference held at the College of Development in Singida. Scott and I had each taught a seminar. Mine was on prayer, given in my stumbling Swahili. Starting to learn Swahili in my 50's and not really gifted in languages (three years of high school Latin didn't help a bit!), I never felt satisfied with my fluency during the almost- twelve years spent in Tanzania.

This day dawning was Monday after Easter, April 12, 1993. We were planning to drive to Dar es Salaam, via Dodoma about 125 miles southeast. I was anticipating relaxing and enjoying the ever-changing scenery with those stately baobab trees, ancient sentinels that always prompted me to wonder about the stories they might tell! Or perhaps it might be glimpses of the Barabaig people, a colorful nomadic tribe right out of the *National Geographic* pages. What was anticipated and what happened proved to be two different things.

The first day we had planned to travel as far as Dodoma, on unpaved roads with all kinds of holes, thick mud or deep sand, depending on the rains. It would be no joy ride for the driver. Scott would have to give his full attention to the roads much like those of his youth in the Nebraska Sandhills.

Soon dressed, sitting at the kitchen table, reading the Bible, writing in our journals, we spent time with the Lord.

Our prayer time was cut short as we planned to pray more in the car during the five to seven hours it might take us to reach our destination. There had been no rain for the past two or three weeks. We really needed more rain for the corn crop which was beginning to curl from the dry weather. However, on our trip we preferred not to get rain which could bog down the big trailer trucks, called lorries (British influence), as they wallow out huge ditches in the road, often blocking traffic and passage of the smaller vehicles. Buses have the same effect.

At 7 a.m. our battery-operated shortwave radio pierced the stillness to inform us of world events on VOA (Voice of America) but no weather advisement or prediction. We had to be prepared for whatever God allowed weatherwise.

While the world news filled the air, Scott stirred the oatmeal on the kitchen gas stove. I quickly finished packing snacks and thermos, drinking water and necessities for the trip. We hastily ate our usual breakfast of oatmeal and bananas. We bade farewell to our Tanzanian day guard and gardener.

Surprisingly early, we pulled away from the school gate at 7:30 a.m. (daylight now) unaccompanied by anyone else. The sky was overcast, promising some coolness. Would it rain?

We didn't anticipate seeing any wild animals, although we would be delighted if we did! The road going directly south promised the possibility of seeing some dikdik, very small antelope, that occasionally dart out of the bush. Elephants in the dry season might pass this way at night in search of water. No more rhinoceroses. They had been numerous in this area until fifteen or twenty years before our arrival.

I felt sorry for poor Joshaphat, one of our young guards. Joshaphat's pretty wife had some impacted, swollen wisdom teeth that defied extraction by a medical assistant in a nearby village. He and his family were planning to accompany us to Dodoma, the new capital, where we hoped there was an expatriate oral surgeon still practicing. They were prepared to go as far as Dar es Salaam if necessary. However, Joshaphat canceled their "reservations" at the last minute as his children developed fever and rashes. God had plans for them as a family and for us. It was really best that we would be alone, as we were to learn later in the day.

The steamy old port city and former capital, Dar es Salaam, was to be our final destination which we thought would be reached by the next day. There we could get a burned-out electric motor from the school workshop rewound. This was the main objective of our safari.

We traveled south on a fairly smooth earthen road not used by lorries. We drove past occasional traditional homes built of poles plastered with mud and covered with sod roofs, or homes built of adobe bricks and perhaps covered with metal roofs.

On that road we went fairly close to Rehema's adobe brick home built by her, her husband and growing family. Rehema, illiterate, in her 30's, had brewed local beer and embraced the Muslim faith, being born into it. However, this was changed through the prayers and visits of two missionary women. Rehema came to love the Lord Jesus. She would attend church whenever she could and would grasp every word to swell her joyful faith.

Every year Rehema and her husband worked hard to plant and tend their crops but this year the rains were stopping too soon. They were about out of food. She walked for six miles to her own home village, for fruit to carry and sell to villagers and expatriates in her attempt to provide for her family. We gave help, yet always tried to discourage overdependency on us with consequent loss of her dignity. She would keep account and try to repay us whenever they got ahead financially.

Soon we connected with the main "highway" and prayed alternately as we thought of things to discuss with the Lord in conversational prayer (Scott kept his eyes open at the wheel).

We played tapes on the car cassette player. We munched our cinnamon rolls and lunch, stopping along the road for breaks. On this road, it's not possible to drink coffee without a stop!

Before we knew it, five uneventful hours had passed. We were in Dodoma sooner than expected. Why not travel on and reach Dar es Salaam before dark at 7 p.m.? The sun was shining now. We felt good about continuing on. Without passengers to consider, we were unimpeded. We headed straight east on the fairly new tarmac (asphalt) highway, such a joy for us after the rough roads of the interior! What a scenic route! From the higher plateaus of central Tanzania, about 5 000 feet elevation, we gradually descended to the low-lying coastal region.

By about 4:00 p.m., we were at Morogoro, halfway point to Dar es Salaam. This is where we had attended language school at the Junior Seminary and where we first tried our new language skills in the open market. It is where we had many struggles and yet many happy memories as we bonded with other expatriates from the States, Germany, Norway, Sweden, Denmark and other parts of Europe. It was our introduction to Tanzanian culture.

As Scott filled the fuel tank with diesel at Morogoro, an Asian man nodded his head towards the blackened sky out east and remarked, "They are having very heavy rains in Dar." He had just come from there. No matter! With our trustworthy Landcruiser we had proven over all kinds of terrain and in all kinds of conditions these past two years, we felt we could make it to Dar without any problems. We had been unable to call from Dodoma to make reservations at the Embassy Hotel in Dar. Somewhere we would find a lodging place.

This was our last stretch of tarmac, older and in places more broken up. I pulled out our address file with names of many family members and friends to whom we write two or three times a year. We began to pray over their needs.

There were different crafts placed along the roadside waiting for buyers: chairs made of saplings, wooden giraffes and figurines, Maasai bead necklaces. We evidently didn't regard some of the wrecked vehicles along a newly-paved section of highway until our return trip homeward a week later.

About 60 miles west of Dar we noticed a light sprinkle. The tarmac glistened some. I wished Scott would slow down more but didn't say anything. He is an excellent driver. We often joked that after all these years in Tanzania he could probably compete in the Kenyan Marlboro auto races! I put down the address book and quietly prayed. We had begun the day, as we always did, with prayer for God's safety which we never take for granted.

Suddenly, I instinctively grasped the grab bar on the dash, leaned forward and cried out, "Lord God! Jesus!" We were fishtailing all over the road! The front wheel touched the shoulder on my side (I think!) and for an instant it seemed we would straighten out. But, no, we began to pick up speed as the car swished around in reverse position. Then we were in a forward position heading with lightning speed for the right side of the road and into tall grass and gravel.

My mind thought, "We'll never make it! We're about to enter heaven this very minute!" We continued on our collision course which ended about as abruptly as it started, stopped as by a giant hand. The car tipped over onto the passenger side. My head was down but both our bodies were held securely in the seat belts. I heard tinkling glass and felt some things in the car change position. I thought, "Oh, our beautiful car!" We waited for an instant or so before moving. Miraculously, we were both unscathed and intact!

Scott struggled to open his door, directly overhead. Helpful, kind Tanzanians were there to force the door open and to pull us out to the solid ground.

It wasn't long before another expatriate motorist stopped at the scene and took command of the situation. He organized the Tanzanian bystanders to throw their weight together to get our disabled vehicle back on it wheels. One of the tires was flat. Our new friend seemed in a hurry. We never did learn his name. He agreed to phone a couple of numbers in Dar es Salaam to summon help, for friends to come and get us. In a moment, he was gone.

Later another passing motorist heading for the city agreed to try these same two numbers.

We quickly assessed the damages. With the flat tire and a punctured, crushed radiator, our car was non-drivable. Apparently we had nosed down as though to flip over onto the top.

People began to disappear.

Sitting inside the car, we straightened out some of the disarray within the car and within our shaken selves. Amazing that no side windows were broken! The windshield was shattered but in place. The seat belts were such a blessing, preventing our being thrown out.

Many other things seemed divinely arranged on this eventful trip: no other passengers, no cars near us, and no pedestrians on either side of the road! Praise God! But there were more "coincidences" to come as God proved His faithfulness.

Alone, we sat in our crunched car waiting for our friends from Dar es Salaam, but they never came. We did not know that thieves had tampered with the phone lines, then demanded large prices to re-connect. However, God had His own rescuers on the way.

As darkness fell, we sought refuge in the nearby home of the village Party Chairman who informed us that it wasn't safe to stay in the car. There was the possibility of thieves on the prowl, ready to do anything to get a car like ours, even if only for the parts which would bring good prices.

Nine p.m. came but still no friends. Surely they should have arrived long ago! We sat there in a darkness penetrated by the flickering of a kerosene lamp casting eerie shadows. As we carried on a conversation in Swahili, we could hear cars passing. Then it happened that one car stopped off the road, near ours. Fear gripped me. Voices approached. Were they calling, "Spragg?" Sure enough, God's rescuers had arrived! But not the ones we expected!

The rescue vehicle was driven by a Pakistani, a Singida business man who was late in trying to reach Dar es Salaam. We had been in his home less than two weeks earlier to watch a video tape! It was the beginning of a friendly relationship with this delightful, warm-hearted Muslim family! He said that as they passed our car, pulled off the road, someone in his car called out, "Is that Spraggs' car?" He lost no time in turning around to check it out, What a joy to see a friend eager to help!

Being the aggressive type, he took charge to ensure security for our car by quickly recruiting local "guards," to be paid the next day. He then squeezed us and limited luggage into his already crowded car. But as he tried to turn his malfunctioning car from the middle of the highway, it stalled. Seeing headlights approaching from both directions and fearing another accident, Scott yelled for me to get out of the rescue car, They wouldn't be able to see us. Was our rescue to end with another accident?

But Praise God! Before I could get out, somehow the ailing vehicle did start, though the lights were very weak. We headed east on the proper side of the road, just creeping along. Finally, as we got closer to the city, there was a spacious, well-lit service station on our left. It was there that we pulled over while one of our riders, an Asian youth, was able to get under the hood to facilitate a better electrical connection. Again, praise God!

With brighter lights and a more responsive car, we were soon at the Embassy Hotel where they had a comfortable room available for us at 11 p.m. We crawled into bed but I did not really sleep. That nightmarish, wild ride kept playing and replaying in my mind's eye all night long.

Morning came and Scott, through the help of friends, delivered the car to a government-owned garage for repairs. One week later, we were graciously granted transport home in a Central Diocese car. The burned-out motor did get rewound. We learned that the new stretch of tarmac which had caused our accident (and many more!) had lost its thin stone cover, intended for traction, when the asphalt was applied. With a little moisture, it became a very slick, lubricated surface. Later this section was resurfaced properly.

It's so amazing that our car was repaired in time for us to meet our daughter and friend in Nairobi one month later for their three-week visit. Normally, few available spare parts and poor mechanics complicate speedy repairs.

Meanwhile, God had graciously led Joshaphat to another local medical assistant who successfully extracted those troublesome, painful wisdom teeth.

We constantly marvel at God's faithfulness to us and to others in His family. Also, God faithfully taught us more about Himself through this unforgettable safari.

Ruth J. Spragg *was born in June of 1931 in Kingston, NY. She graduated from Syracuse University in 1953 with a BS degree in nursing. Thereafter, she moved to the midwest where she assumed various jobs in nursing but finally settled into teaching student nurses.*

In July, 1969, she married Scott Spragg, a widower, and became the mother of his three children. During the first years of marriage, Ruth concentrated on the roles of being a wife and a mother, but later when her husband returned to the university to study for his teaching credentials, she also did some nursing.

In February, 1984, she accompanied her husband on a missionary assignment to a church-owned technical secondary school in a very rural area near Singida, in Tanzania. While at the school Ruth volunteered as school health nurse, English teacher, Bible teacher and school librarian. She remained at the school for ten years and then moved closer to Singida town as she followed her husband in a change of work.

They lived there until retirement in September of 1995 when they returned to their home in Ankeny, Iowa. From there she engages in work at her church and in short-term overseas missionary work along with her husband.

I'LL BE YOUR MAMA / BABA

Lois Swanson

"Two telegrams just came for you, Lois. Do you want me to wait while you open them?"

"Yes," I replied, fearing the worst news that my Mom had just died, yet knowing that if she had, she was now safe in Jesus' arms after a long battle with cancer.

Esther Oberg waited while I opened the first telegram which said: "Mom's condition not good, keep praying!" By now I was trembling, for I was quite sure what the second one said. Sure enough, it was as I had anticipated, for it read: "Mother went home to Jesus at 10 p.m. Sunday." My brother, Allen, had sent the two telegrams ten hours apart from California, where he was on a study leave from Taiwan. I was so grateful he was at home at the time for this was the death of my first parent and I was 10,000 miles away.

Being so far away from family at a time like this made me question: "How will I cope now?" You see, I was still a fairly new missionary and had always dreaded the idea of being overseas should one of my parents die. In fact, it was this very thought that had kept me from going to Tanganyika earlier in my life. I found it difficult to deal with the idea of a parent dying when I would be so far away. This was 1968, prior to the high tech age.

It was apparent that I could not make it home for the funeral, but I decided to try to make a telephone call the next day to talk to my Dad and see how he was doing. What a relief to hear his voice and know that the Lord was guiding him through this time of sorrow.

I soon discovered that the news of my Mom's death quickly reached the "bush radio" and before the day was over a number of my Tanzanian friends had walked out to Kititimu, three miles from the city of Singida, to share Scripture verses and songs of comfort. I shall never forget that day nor the week that followed, for many Tanzanians came to my home or the office to comfort me, bringing me gifts of fruit, vegetables, eggs or sugar cane. Each one shared God's Word with me. and many sang beautiful Swahili hymns of comfort. My missionary co-workers also were a great blessing to me at that time, as they came to my home and shared God's Word. And of course, the Lord Jesus was my greatest source of comfort.

One thing I shall never forget from that time were the words of a recently baptized, elderly, uneducated woman from a nearby village, who, when she saw me the following week at church, said to me: "Don't feel sad, I'll be your Mama!"

From that day on, and for the next 22 years, this Christian Turu lady took the role of my mother. She visited me as I visited her. She never failed to greet me at church by asking, "How's my daughter doing today?"

I'd always reply, "Mama, I'm doing fine! Thank you for being my spiritual mother!"

When she died, I wept, for she had truly played a mother's role, bringing comfort when I needed it and continuing to encourage me throughout our days together. How beautiful to be one in Christ!

Ten years after my mother died, my father became very ill. By now, technology enabled my family to contact me very quickly, so I was able to arrange for an immediate return home. I was with my dad for just six days. Then the Lord called him to his eternal home. I remembered my Tanzanian friend who had become my "Mama," but would there be a Tanzanian man who would become my "Baba?"

I returned to Tanzania after one month in America, to be greeted and visited by many. I was greatly blessed by these visits as I had been ten years earlier. And once again the Lord comforted me through Christian Tanzanians and missionary friends.

About two weeks after I returned to my work, a Tanzanian pastor who had been in the USA after my mother's death and had met my dad, came to me and said: "I'm so sorry to hear about your father's death. But fear not, I will be your Baba!"

It had happened again! Now I had both a Tanzanian Mama and Baba! Isn't it wonderful how the Lord provides at just the right time? From these experiences I realized how true Jesus' words were as found in Mark 10:29-31:

"Jesus said, 'Truly I tell you, there is no one who has left house or brothers or sisters or mother or father or children or fields, for my sake and for the sake of the good news, who will not receive a hundredfold now in this age—houses, brothers, sisters, mothers...' "

THEY'VE COME, THEY'VE COME !

"How about starting a Sunday School for the missionary and other expatriate children here in Singida town?" asked some of the parents of these children. It sounded like a great idea, since there were American, British and Indian children whose parents worked in government positions or served as missionaries.

And so the little Sunday School class was born in 1959. Since it met on Friday afternoons, the name was changed to English Church School Class. Friday was chosen as the class period day because there wasn't room for the class to meet in the small Singida Lutheran Church on Sunday.

Helen Pedersen, who became the first teacher, was often on *safari* (trip, itinerary) with her husband on Sundays; thus the logical day was Friday. The time? 5-6 p.m., for by then the children would be through with their last school class. They went to school until 4 p.m., so there would be time to go home for a cup of tea or juice before going to class in Helen's dining room.

The class was well received by the children and I was privileged to teach it whenever Helen was absent.

In 1961, the year of independence for the country of Tanganyika, many of the expatriates in government and paristatal positions began to turn over their work to Tanzanians and return home. Consequently, most of the children in the class left also, leaving behind a handful of missionary and expatriate children. By March 1962 there were even fewer children in the class which was now in my care, for Helen and her husband had moved to another position.

Among the children left were two Indian Christian boys whose father was an accountant for the local Internal Revenue Office. Reju and Rajews' parents came from South India where the Christian Church is strong; thus the boys were well grounded in the Christian faith. They were also very concerned for the many Hindu and Muslim Indian children in Singida who didn't know Jesus. This deep concern surfaced one day when the class was talking about how Jesus wants each one of us to be a missionary. Reju enthusiastically said, "Aunty Lois, next week I'm going to bring my Hindu friends to Church School!"

I was, of course, thrilled to hear this little boy's response to the lesson; thus I encouraged him to do so. Of course I eagerly awaited the following Friday's class. When it was time to begin that day, Reju walked in, a bit downhearted. He greeted me with the words: "Aunty Lois, they'll come next time!"

The next Friday and the next Friday and the next Friday came and went. Each time it was the same response—his Hindu friends would come, but not yet! Still Reju never gave up. He was determined that his Hindu friends should also know about Jesus!

My home-leave year was to commence in June and I wanted so much to see the Hindu children come to class, but May arrived without a sign of them. I kept praying for a breakthrough and knew Reju and his brother also prayed about these children.

It was my last Friday to teach before I was to return to America for a year. As I prepared the room for my class that day, I felt sad that there were so many Hindu and Muslim children in town who did not know about Jesus, and seemingly had no desire to learn about Him. "Lord," I prayed, "please help Reju not to become discouraged in his work for you, for you know how hard he's tried during the past three months to get his friends to come."

As I placed the lesson sheets with the crayons on the table, I heard an enthusiastic voice call out, as Reju flew into the room, "Aunty Lois, *they've come, they've come!*" Reju was so excited he was jumping up and down as he repeated his beautiful words.

"Where are they?" I asked. With a big smile he replied, "Oh, they're standing outside, but they are afraid to come in!" Together we walked to the door and to my utter amazement there were 10 Hindu Indian boys and girls from the ages of 6-12. I couldn't believe my eyes, for I knew their parents would not come into our church, yet they had allowed their children to come to our office for the English Church School class! What a miracle this was!

From 1962 until I retired in 1995 I worked with these children every Friday evening. Some of the first students sent their own children to the class during my last ten years in Singida.

Another miracle that came forth was that these Hindu children brought their Indian Muslim and Sikh friends to class, something that could not have happened if the Hindu children's love for Jesus had not become meaningful. To have watched these precious little ones grow in their love for Jesus, was one of my deepest joys while working in Tanzania. To see their big brown eyes sparkle as they sang, *"Oh, how I love Jesus, because He first loved me,"* is a memory I'll cherish the rest of my life.

Today many of these "little ones" are now adults, living in the USA, Canada, England, India and Pakistan. I keep in touch with some of these precious people, who though they have not become professing Christians, still hold a love for Jesus in their hearts, encouraging their own children to go to a Sunday School at a nearby church. Reju has a high position in India. He still loves and serves the Lord, working and praying to bring little ones into God's fold.

THE UNFORGETABLE CHRISTMAS

"Would you be able to take a guest for Christmas?" Marian Halvorson asked me. "She's an East German professor's wife who felt she needed to get away from the cold of Germany's winters due to her severe case of arthritis. I'm sure you'll like her and will learn much from her," she concluded.

It was my year to be in Tanzania for Christmas. Thus I had planned to be doing the usual entertaining of Tanzanian co-workers, the European community of Singida area, the English Church-School class students and families and my neighbors' children.

"Well," I thought, "it would be great to have someone help me with these activities." It took a lot of time to do all the necessary baking for the some 75 or so guests who would be coming the week prior to Christmas. There was also the house decorating plus the end-of-the-year work at the office which always kept us busy.

With all these thoughts circulating through my mind, I immediately agreed that I would host this woman for two or three weeks. It was with great anticipation that I awaited her arrival the first week of December.

I shall never forget the day she arrived with only one suitcase plus a big cardboard box containing two cats and all that they would need for their survival in Singida.

It was a great joy to get to know this dear woman. Often her stories about life in East Germany at that time (1975) brought tears to my eyes, especially when she told how she felt she had to get away from cold Germany because of the excruciating pain she had, and for which there was very little medical help for her back home. She had left behind her professor husband who was not allowed out of the country due to his position. Thus she had struck out on her own.

She was a wonderful help during the week prior to Christmas, making many German Christmas goodies. When the guests came, she readily shared about her faith in the Lord Jesus. She enjoyed the Europeans, Indians, Tanzanians and Americans who came to celebrate the beautiful season of Christmas.

As each one of them shared about his/her faith, she was blessed as I was. Especially were we blessed when we closed with devotions and each one sang "Silent Night" in his/her national language. Sometimes it sounded like another Pentecost as some five to six languages were used at the same time to sing this beautiful Christmas carol which has been translated into so many languages of our world.

Christmas Eve found our Immanuel Lutheran Church bursting at the seams as some 1000 people tried to get into a church built to seat 700 people comfortably. My guest was so amazed to see such a large turnout and commented often that it was hard to believe so many people could come freely to church in Tanzania.

When we returned home I prepared some coffee, then we sat down in the living room to enjoy the soft Christmas music on tape in the glow of the Christmas tree lights and candles. It was a very reverent time as we sat in silence recalling memories of past Christmases of our lives, wishing somehow we could be together with our families at that moment. But I'm sure she realized, as I did, that even though Christmas is "family time," when the Lord calls you to serve Him in an area, He provides for you by giving you other families that take the place of your blood-related family.

Before going to bed, we decided to sing some favorite Christmas carols. We proceeded to the piano and the first song sung was *"O Tannenbaum..."* She sang it in German. When we finished, I asked her if she had another favorite carol. Immediately she said, *"Stille Nacht,"* to which I commented, "That's my favorite carol also."

"Silent Night, Holy Night,...Glories Stream From Heaven Afar,
Christ, The Saviour is Born"

As memories of past Christmases with our families flowed into mind and heart, our tears seemed to be saying, "Christmas is family time, and of all carols, *Silent Night* brings back family memories and binds people together as no other carol can." Because of Christ, we were one large family, united in him no matter what our ethnic background.

Lois Swanson *began life in Duluth, MN. After high school she attended and graduated from the parish workers' course at the Lutheran Bible Institute in Minneapolis, MN and served as a parish worker in north Minneapolis for four years.*

In 1958, after completing an orientation course for missionaries at the School of Missions in Chicago, she was commissioned by the Augustana Lutheran Church for missionary service in Tanganyika, where she served from 1958 to 1995.

Her first term's assignment was as secretary to the president, treasurer and education secretary of the Augustana Lutheran Mission. In her second term she was secretary to the education secretary and began to do parish work in the Singida Lutheran Church. This was predominantly youth and children's work, an area dear to her heart.

Lois lived at the hub of great change. Through her work with the church, she was administratively involved in:

Government: Tanganyika Territory won independence from England in Dec. 1961 and became the nation of Tanganyika.

Tanganyika united with the Island of Zanzibar in 1964 to form a new nation which took the name of Tanzania.

Church: The mission field of the Augustana Lutheran Church in U.S.A. became a self-governing church called the Lutheran Church of Central Tanganyika (LCCT).

The LCCT joined other newly formed Lutheran Churches in Tanganyika to form the Evangelical Lutheran Church in Tanganyika (ELCT); the LCCT became the Central Synod of ELCT.

Church government changed in favor of an episcopal structure at about the same time the nation's name changed to Tanzania. The ELCT now stood for the Evangelical Lutheran Church in Tanzania; the Central Synod of ELCT became the Central Diocese of ELCT. The leaders' designations likewise changed, e.g. from president to bishop.

In her secretarial role, Lois supported all these changes; yet she also found energy for Youth and Christian Education work in the Diocese. She served as the Regional Director of the Tanzania Students' Christian Fellowship from 1990-1995.

In retirement she lives in Duluth, MN.

HELP AT THE FOOT OF THE CROSS

Alice Turnbladh

It had been a busy day. I had just extinguished my kerosene lamp and was ready to crawl into bed when I heard a voice at the door saying, *"Hodi! Hodi!"* I quickly slipped on my housecoat and went to the window to see who needed me. It was full moon, and in its bright light I could see three men standing at the door. They were tall and slender, wearing russet-colored robes slung loosely over the shoulder; each carried a long spear. In the background I could see four men carrying a patient on their version of an "ambulance" which consists of an animal skin fastened to two poles, the ends of which are carried by four men. Behind them was a group of eight men who came along to take their turn in carrying the patient.

I recognized these people as being from the Barabaig tribe and I knew that they had traveled a long distance from home. The spokesman of the group, who was the only one who could speak Swahili, said, "We have brought an elderly lady who has been ill for several days; she is coughing constantly and has a high fever. Will you please help us?"

I dressed hurriedly and joined them on the short walk to the hospital. As we walked along I asked him, "When did you leave home?"

"We left home yesterday morning," he replied, "We have never been here before, so we were not sure which route to take. We knew the general direction and some of the villages through which we would be passing; we asked for directions as we traveled along. And then someone told us that as we neared Iambi we would see a hill on which had been erected a white cross. He explained that the hospital is at the foot of the cross and there we would find help.

"And so tonight," he continued, "as we saw the cross gleaming in the bright moonlight, we knew that we had arrived at the place where she would be helped."

The patient was very ill with pneumonia, but responded well to the antibiotic which was ordered for her. During her twelve-day stay at the hospital, Pastor Simeon Petro, our local pastor, had several opportunities to share the Word of God with this group of Barabaig. They had not heard of Jesus before and were very interested in the Gospel message. So the seed was first planted there at the foot of the cross.

When they left us to return to their homes, they expressed the hope that someone would come and live among them and teach them more about Jesus. Some time later a mission station was started in their area, with a church, a primary school and a dispensary. Pastor Harold Faust and his wife, Louise, were the first missionaries in the land of the Barabaig.

BIBLE STUDY AT THE PRISON

The man walking toward the Kiomboi post office seemed familiar some-how, but he was walking so slowly, pausing from time to time for a short rest. Who was he? I should know him!

I was waiting for Eliasafi, the hospital maintenance man, to pick me up after finishing a number of business errands at the Kiomboi *boma* (government offices). As the man drew near, I could see: Oh, of course I knew him! It was Yakobo Ntundu, long-time evangelist from Ruruma Mission Station.

Soon he was sitting beside me on the bench. In his hand he carried a worn Bible and a hymn book. After we had exchanged greetings, I asked him, "What brings you to Kiomboi today?"

Then he explained, "Every Wednesday at 10 o'clock I have a Bible Study for the inmates of the local jail. The Chief of Police always sends a car to fetch me, but yesterday he sent a messenger to tell me that there would not be a car available for today, so he would cancel my class for me."

"So what did you do? Did you walk here from Ruruma? That's six miles!" And, I added mentally, he is no longer a robust young man.

"I know. But I kept thinking about the prisoners. I know how much they look forward to my visit and the class each week—there aren't many people who visit them—so I decided I would get up early this morning and walk over here," he replied earnestly.

"But look at your swollen feet! And barefoot?" I felt concerned.

"It's true, they are very swollen and I can't wear my shoes. There are some deep cracks on the soles of my feet so it is painful to walk very far. But I have taken it slowly, rested frequently and here I am. It is almost time for my class to start."

"What are you studying?" I queried.

"We are studying the Gospel of John," he replied. "Last week we started with Chapter 10 where Jesus tells them that He is the Good Shepherd. The men were very interested and could relate to this as they had all been shepherds of sheep and goats when they were younger. Today we will start with verse 11 and I am eager to share with them again how Jesus, the Good Shepherd, gave His life for the sheep.

"And in this section Jesus tells them that there are some sheep who are not yet in the fold who must be brought in. There is a prisoner whose name is Mpinga; he has led a wicked life and he thinks that there is no forgiveness for him. Please pray especially for him that today he will hear the Shepherd's voice and come into the fold."

He looked at his watch and said, "Now I must be on my way. Pray that God will use me to bring the joy of salvation to these men."

As he shuffled off toward the prison on his sore feet, I thanked God for this man who had heard God's call, had answered it so many years ago and had served so faithfully in sharing the good news of salvation in Christ.

ELBOW GREASE

It was 4 o'clock and I had just finished teaching my last nursing class for the day. When I returned to the school office, I found Miss Lilie, the director of nurses, waiting for me. "There has been a bus accident about nine miles from here," she said, "and they are bringing all of the injured passengers to us for treatment. Almost all of our beds are full now and Dr. Shabhay would like to have the storeroom emptied and cleaned so that we can set up some extra beds there. Could you please get some of the students to help you get it ready?" I assured her that we would get busy on it right away.

I hurried back to the classroom and found that David was washing the blackboards, Seth was sweeping the floor. I explained the situation to them and that I needed their help immediately. I said to David, "Please go to the Central Supply Room and get two brooms, two brushes, two buckets, some soap, cleanser and some cleaning cloths. It will take a lot of elbow grease to get the storeroom ready in a hurry. Seth and I will empty the room while you are gone."

It was not long before David was back with the supplies which I had requested. He had a puzzled look on his face as he said, "I have brought all of the things from the Central Supply Room, but where do I get the elbow grease?"

Alice Turnbladh *was born at Sebeka, MN and went to school there through high school. She is a graduate of the Lutheran Bible Institute in Minneapolis, MN and the Swedish Hospital School of Nursing, also in Minneapolis, and became a registered nurse. Alice served in the U.S. Army Nurse Corps for two years. Called and commissioned by the Augustana Lutheran Church, she went to Tanganyika in October, 1949 and was stationed at Iambi Hospital. During her first furlough she attended the Sister Tutor course at the Royal College of Nursing in Edinburgh, Scotland, gaining her Sister Tutor certificate in 1955.*

She served as Nurse Tutor in charge of Kiomboi Nurses' Training Centre from 1956 to 1976.

Alice returned to the U.S.A. in January, 1976 and resides in Alexandria, MN.

A TANZANIAN WOMAN'S TOUCH

Gloria Cunningham

My husband heard the tapping first. He reached over and shook me awake. "Gloria, someone's at the window. It's most likely another hospital trip." I looked at the luminous hands of our clock. It was just after 4 a.m. The local people here at Gendabi Mission in the center of Tanzania knew that if there was a medical emergency, I as a nurse could be awakened quickly, even in the middle of the night, just by tapping on our bedroom window.

I opened the window to find a small woman who would speak only in a whisper. I sensed urgency in her voice. "Mama, can you help me? I need to talk with you now!" She used the word "Mama," because this is how most married women are addressed.

"Come around to the door and I'll let you in," I said in Swahili. As she came in, I scanned her face. I recognized her and knew that she lived nearby. She was clutching a small bundle close to her breast. "What's this?" I inquired. Her apprehension was apparent as she nervously unwrapped the bundle. When she finally spoke, she explained that she had delivered this baby at home just a few hours earlier.

"But look, something is wrong with his mouth! My baby can't suck! When the women who helped me noticed the misshapen face, they fled from the room. I was so afraid! Then when I was sure that everyone was asleep, I slipped out secretly with my baby and ran here."

Taking the child in my arms, I saw a perfect baby except for a large split in the upper lip that disfigured the child's face. Gently probing inside the mouth, I felt the cleft in the palate that was preventing the child from sucking. I looked at the mother and then even before she said it, I understood the fear that gripped her heart. "Mama, what am I going to do? They'll take my baby away!"

In the Mbulu and the Barabaig culture in this remote pastoral region around Gendabi, any child born with a malformation is not considered to be a whole human being. In a non-Christian family, such an infant is considered unfit to survive. The newborn is carried into the forest at night and left in a ravine. By morning the child is gone, usually taken by a hyena or a leopard.

Although not yet a Christian, this mother had often come to the worship services at the church. She had heard that Christians do not give up their infants even when they have deformities. She had heard how these children had been helped. Now, filled with fear, she was desperate to save her child from the fate in the forest. "Is there any way you can you help me, Mama?" she implored once again.

The deeply troubled look of anxiety etched on her face, caused me to remember my own feelings of deep anxiety a dozen years earlier. Then wanting to reassure this young mother that we would certainly help her in every way possible, I smiled and said, "Look, you have a beautiful baby! I'm sure that with surgery the baby's lip and the opening in the roof of the mouth can be corrected and made normal! We'll help you take the baby to the hospital. But first, there are other things we must do." Her look of desperation softened.

"Will the child be able to suck?" she inquired.

"Of course, but it will take time before that happens," I explained. "Please stay here with us until the sun comes up. I'll show you how to feed the baby with a dropper. Then all of us must go together to your house to talk with your husband and other members of the clan about the child."

Before leaving for the mother's home we prayed together. We asked God to prepare the hearts of her husband and clan to allow the necessary time for the surgery and healing to take place so that they could accept the child.

A typical Mbulu dwelling, the home was semi-hidden, dug back into the hillside, with only the windowless front wall visible. As we were approaching, we heard a shrieking and the wailing of women's voices. Fighting my own fears, I kept appealing to God to prepare a way for this baby to be rescued. There at the entrance to the home we saw the women swaying with their cries. When they caught sight of us, one came running. Instantly she turned and accused the young mother, "She has the child!"

In the Mbulu culture, a person who does something wrong can be openly criticized by neighbors and relatives. The wrongdoer, in exceptional cases, can be driven out from the community. As the crowd gathered around us, the wailing ceased. One of the women began to pray to *Lo'a,* a female deity. These Cushitic-speaking people have a difficult language, and I had no understanding of what they were saying. Presently the three of us, with the baby still in the mother's arms, were escorted by one of the elders to a nearby tree. "Sit here and wait!" was his abbreviated command.

"Please listen to us! This child can be made well, completely whole again, by surgery at the hospital!" Ray and I were frantic to convince him.

"We'll consider that possibility," he responded unexpectedly. We waited with apprehension in our hearts.

I knew that those who had helped the mother during delivery could be placed under *Metemani*, a curse of temporary ostracism, an asbsolute quarantine for a whole year. If nothing happened to the clan during that period, the ominous danger is considered to have passed and the *Metemani* curse would be lifted.

After a lengthy debate, the elders decided that the mother could place her baby in the care of a Christian relative until the child would be taken to the hospital for the needed surgery. "The child can be returned to the mother only if the surgery you say is possible proves successful!" one of the elders declared curtly.

I was elated with their decision. I was confident that the doctors at Dareda Hospital would skillfully accomplish their work of reconstruction, making this child whole.

Many months later, the child was returned to an exceedingly happy and deeply devoted mother. "Look, he's perfect, as if he had been born that way!" she exclaimed.

My heart joined with this mother in pure delight and an outpouring of thankfulness to God.

And once again I remembered how I, too, had been prayed for, encouraged and helped by another mother, a Tanzanian mother, when I was still a young new missionary.

When we had first arrived in Tanganyika in 1956, our placement was at Kiomboi, a large mission station that included a hospital, the nurses' training center, a church, several missionary homes and the Augustana School for missionary children, grades one through eight. Ray's first assignment was to be principal of Augustana School.

This was to only be a temporary post. It eventually stretched into twenty-three months, until the Board of World Missions could locate and send permanent replacements. Ray was also housefather and I the volunteer housemother and boarding supervisor. The forty-six kids were a joy, but our schedule was hectic. The never-ending cycle of tasks, even with the invaluable aid of our Tanzanian helpers, kept Ray and me on our feet roughly sixteen hours a day. Even the remaining eight hours of the night we were "on call" for any children who were physically sick or just plain homesick.

The months passed. Ray and I rarely had a day off to be together with our small daughter, Diane, as a family. I was also eight months pregnant with our second child and feeling stressed by the demands of the work at the school.

Yet, in spite of this quandary, memories of happy times ring clear of those days at Augustana School. There were lots of fun times, parties and picnics, and Sundays were always very special with the Kiomboi missionary family joining the children for dinner at the school. The youngsters enriched and enlivened our lives with their wit and humor, mischief and frolic, and helpful and thoughtful ways.

It happened very suddenly, without any warning. I awoke in the middle of the night to find myself hemorrhaging profusely. I knew immediately that I was experiencing a life-threatening complication of pregnancy that requires urgent surgical intervention.

I shouted, "Quick, Ray, run and get Dr. Vi!" Dr. Viola Fischer was one of our missionary doctors who lived near the school. Within a short time, I was at the hospital being prepared for a Cesarean section. Dr. Vi later told me, "You had a great deal of blood loss, and at one point we were unable to get your blood pressure. For a moment we even thought we'd lost you!"

A few hours later when I had recovered from the anesthesia, I was filled with happiness to learn that we had a five-pound baby boy. We named him David. But our bliss was short lived. Ray gently took my hand in his and tearfully told me, "Our David is having difficulty breathing. Dr. Vi says there is uncertainty whether he can survive."

David died later that evening. I was devastated. I doubted the goodness of God. Inside, I was silently screaming, "God, why would you bring me all the way to Africa to let our child die? And why would you let me almost die?" I was emotionally shattered, bitter and angry. I retreated into myself.

The school children wrote me loving notes of concern. The missionary family rallied around me with prayers and words of comfort, but no words could touch me.

Missionary wives volunteered to help at the school. A month earlier a single-lady missionary had been called to work at the school. Despite all the caring people who surrounded me, this painful time in my life became a valley experience, and my lack of faith deepened that valley. Even after several months, I was despondent and sad. Then God sent me some special messengers.

One afternoon, Mrs. Manase Yona, wife of the African pastor at Kiomboi Church, and two of her friends came to visit me. Love shone in Mrs. Yona's eyes as she shared her compassion and honesty with me. "We have seen that your heart is very heavy. We have been praying for you."

They talked with me about the child we had lost and who was now buried in the church cemetery just behind the school. Mrs. Yona closed her eyes in a moment of thought. "You know," she said, measuring her words carefully, "almost every African mother has lost a child, and some have lost two or three and even more. We feel your pain." I felt a lump in my throat and my eyes began to smart.

"All mothers feel deeply grieved when they lose a child. You have been grieving, and that is needed for a time. Grieving does not mean that you lack faith," she declared. "The three of us have been praying for you. We believe that now God has something else for you to do. When the time comes for you and your husband to move to another mission station, God will show you opportunities to share in the medical work. There is a tremendous need for child health clinics in the outlying villages, training women in basic health care and pre-natal care for expectant mothers. You will be able to encourage and assist other mothers to have healthy children."

Like a flash of light, her words had touched my heart. "Oh God...help!" Great pain-racked sobs, tears of healing, and then my pain was eased. God had shown his presence and love for me through these special messengers. I felt at peace for the first time in many months. At that moment, when these three women so tenderly ministered to me, I comprehended the reality of the truth that mission is a two-way bridge: we bring—we receive.

We did not say goodbye at the door. I had learned from the Africans a wonderful neighborly custom called *kusindikiza* (to accompany a visitor part way). So following their way, I walked out the door with my guests. Then together we strolled for a couple of blocks toward their homes before parting with the words, *"Kwa heri ya kuonana!"* (God bless you, till we meet again!)

Months later, Ray and I moved from the school at Kiomboi to Isanzu, a distant station in a very rural area. Ray was appointed to be the district missionary pastor and I volunteered to be the nurse at the mission health center. Early on, it became apparent to both of us that it was impossible to preach the gospel without also reaching out to heal and to teach, and during special need, to provide transportation and food.

One day someone called, *"Hodi! Hodi!"* (May I come in?) At the door stood a man and woman who looked like strangers to this area, because they were unusually tall in stature and dressed wholly in black clothing.

"Karibuni!" (Welcome!) We exchanged several kinds of greetings before beginning our main conversation. I would sound unfriendly and impatient if I did not continue to greet properly, as is the African custom. I inquired, "Where have you come from? Where is your home?"

"We're from way out in Sukumaland. We're so tired! We've been walking since sunrise yesterday across the dusty Sukuma plains and today we had to cross through the Sibiti River and come up the escarpment here to Isanzu.

We've heard that here there are Christians and that we can find *Dawa ya Mungu* (God's medicine). My wife is very sick! Please help us!"

"Come, sit here and tell me about your wife."

"My wife has been sick for a very long time. She has had many pregnancies, but she has no children!"

I looked over at his wife, her head bowed and her eyes turned to the floor. I could feel her anguish. In African society, a woman without a child is considered a failure. Children are so very important to the family's security and social status, that having no children carries a tragic cultural stigma.

"Please, *Bwana* (Sir), wait in this other room while I talk with your wife," I said in Swahili.

"But my wife does not speak Swahili," he said.

"Oh! Well, there's a friend of mine in the village who speaks your Sukuma language. Please go with my husband to ask her to come and help us."

A short time later, as we three women sat at the dining room table, I said to the stranger, "Mama, what is your name?"

"My name is Senida," she replied in her language, with my friend translating for me.

"Senida, are you pregnant now?"

"Yes, but I fear that the child is not alive. I have produced *only soundless* babies. Why should this happen to me? I am frightened that the spirits of my ancestors are angry with me and causing me this trouble. Do you have medicine that can help me?"

It didn't take long to find one major problem. Both Senida and her husband had syphilis. Other tests showed that Senida was six months pregnant, but was anemic and had malaria. But the good news was that the child she carried was alive!

Senida stayed on at the Health Center where she received penicillin therapy, a proper diet and other medications. The village woman who knew Senida's language would often come to talk with her about Jesus. She explained how God's Word, God's medicine, could free her from her fears and the superstitions that kept her in bondage. Senida reflected on these things. She began coming to the worship services at our church. It would take faith, belief and commitment on Senida's part.

Three months later, in the delivery room, it was a euphoric Senida who heard the cry of her newborn infant, her first living child. "My child is alive! The curse is gone! My child is alive! Praise God!"

As I rejoiced with her, my heart flooded with warmth and thankfulness, especially for Mrs. Manase Yona and her friends. Those remarkable Tanzanian women had touched my life during a difficult and perplexing time, inspiring in me new faith, implanting new hope and igniting a new sense of challenge.

Gloria Flesness Cunningham *was born May 27, 1928, and grew up in Minneapolis, MN. After graduating from Central High, she attended Lutheran Bible Institute. She is a graduate of the School of Nursing, Lutheran Hospital, Moline, Illinois, and a R.N.*

In 1956, her husband, Pastor Ray Cunningham, Jr., and Sister Jean Myklebust, an R.N., were commissioned together at Grand View Lutheran Church, Des Moines, IA, to serve as missionaries in Tanganyika. Gloria and Ray traveled with Sister Jean to East Africa.

While at Augustana School, Kiomboi, Gloria held a full-time position as housemother and boarding supervisor for missionary children.

During the rest of her years in Tanzania, Gloria was involved in maternal and child health clinics and in public health outreach to surrounding villages. She was on call for emergencies and ambulance service. Together with a Tanzanian colleague, they established a home visitation program that combined evangelism and health teaching. During the three-year severe drought in Tanzania, 1973-1975, Gloria assisted in transporting and distributing famine relief food at Gendabi.

Ray and Gloria served for twenty-seven years in Tanzania, living at Kiomboi, Isanzu, Isuna, Balangida Lelu and Gendabi, all in rural central Tanzania, then at Mbaga-Manka in the Pare Mountains of northern Tanzania.

From 1988 to 1994, Ray and Gloria were in Uganda, East Africa, serving as International Partners and Project Developers, with Habitat for Humanity International.

The Cunninghams have four children: Diana, Patricia, Mary and Steven. Steve has returned to Tanzania and is serving as a pilot with the Flying Medical Service, Arusha. The Cunningham's first grandson, David, now in college, is interested in mission service.

Ray and Gloria are retired and make their home in Lakewood, CO. Gloria says of her years in Tanzania, "I have journeyed in a beautiful land among gracious people. I am both humbled and thrilled that I had the opportunity to be a part of God's mission in Africa."

MEN AS TREES WALKING

Pauline Swanson

The beating of drums and the wailing of mourners was heard from a nearby sun-dried brick home as the family and friends were grieving over the loss of a loved one. The length of the death dance depends on the status of the deceased person. The bereaved family of an animist may even hire professional mourners to perform the death dance for several days and nights.

The contrast between the death and grieving process for an animist and a Christian is quite pronounced. The family and friends of a Christian person, while mourning their loss in their hearts, sing hymns emphasizing the Resurrection Hope during the service at church and as they walk from the church to the cemetery and back home. What a contrast!

I often thought of this contrast as I walked from my home to the hospital, passing the primary school. In the morning I would hear the sounds of fifes and drums as the children marched around the school buildings, At other times I would hear them singing: *"I Have Decided to Follow Jesus."* How these children loved to sing; their voices were loud and strong as they harmonized on this beautiful chorus. What a joy it was to see and hear these young people sing of their desire to follow our Lord!

"I came to church this morning because I remembered my Savior," said *Yohana* (John). "I have literally been raised both physically and spiritually from the dead," he added.

Yes, this former patient who had come to our hospital without any knowledge of our Lord, had been treated for his ailment and also had come to know the Lord during his stay there. As the custom was, when a person becomes a Christian and is baptized (whether a child or an adult) he/she is given a Christian name to replace the clan name given at birth. When the evangelist suggested that he take the name "Peter" he replied: "No, that name is too heavy. I want to be called Yohana." So that's what he was named at his baptism. Now Yohana was a new person in Christ.

"I can see trees walking!" shouted *Yakobo* (Jacob), another patient, as he walked outside of the hospital a few days after his cataract eye surgery.

I was reminded of the passage in Mark 8:24 telling of Jesus touching the blind man's eyes and that man making a similar statement. This was the beginning of Yakobo's healing process of sight restoration. What a thrill it was for him to progressively regain his eyesight as the days went by. For the staff it was gratifying to hear him express his joy and thanksgiving both for his sight as well as for his renewed faith in God's healing power.

A BARABAIG BLESSING

Each day when I made rounds in the women's ward I would greet with a smile a woman from the Barabaig tribe. We had no other method of communication since she didn't know any Swahili or even the Lyamba language which most of our patients spoke. She had had surgery and had been in the hospital for quite awhile. On the day of her discharge from the hospital, she met me at the door with her usual big smile. She removed one of the many bracelets from her arm and gave it to me. Then she took my hand, spit into the palm and closed my fingers over my palm.

"Ugh," I thought to myself. Sometime later when I told a fellow missionary who worked with that tribal group about this experience, she said that this was the way their tribe expressed their deepest gratitude for help received. There had been no verbal exchange, but her actions spoke louder than words!

In many and various ways we were privileged to see and hear that many were receiving physical healing and that they also heard and received the Gospel, the good news of God's love.

MOTHER MARY'S TRANSPORTATION

"Come to the courtyard for the Christmas pageant!" announced the hospital evangelist. Some of the patients and their families weren't sure what Christmas was all about. They were soon to find out.

Tanzanian Christians love the Christmas story and especially acting out this miracle of God's coming to earth. Many of the Tanzanians are born actors, are very ingenious and love to perform. During Christmas week the hospital staff always presented the Christmas story in pageant form for the patients and their relatives who accompanied them to the hospital to cook and help care for them.

The shepherds wore hospital bedspreads for their cloaks and carried hot water bottles at their sides as canteens for their long journey. The angel choir, draped in muslin hospital sheets, sang: *"Gloria in Excelsis Deo"* in Swahili. Mother Mary holding the baby Jesus (a newborn from our maternity ward), came riding in on a brand new bicycle with Joseph at her side!

Following the Christmas pageant, an old man came forward and asked one of the missionaries: "Who is this Jesus that I've heard about? I'd like to see him and shake his hand." Thus, there was another opportunity to introduce the Gift of Christmas, Jesus Christ, by sharing the miracle of the Christmas story.

A MEMORABLE PALM SUNDAY

It was Palm Sunday. "Let's go to the *shamba* (orchard) for a picnic!" These words were met with approval by my colleagues and in a short time we single workers had a picnic supper prepared which included fresh fruit from the *shamba*. Having had plenty of rain this season, the fruit was sweet and juicy. I remembered another year when due to lack of rain there was not one drop of juice in any of the oranges, lemons or grapefruit.

The path through the shamba was lined with tall, stately date palm trees. These had been planted many years ago and were believed to be on the path which the early slave traders had followed.

While enjoying our picnic supper, our eyes feasted on God's beautiful creation. Besides the citrus fruit trees and palms, there were bamboo, eucalyptus, as well as various native flowers.

Since it was the night of full moon, the moon arose in the east at the same time as the western sky was brilliant with the colors of the setting sun. It was a sight never to be forgotten!

On our way home from the picnic, we stopped by the Augustana School for a concert given by the missionaries' children. It included hymns and various classical selections concluding with the very fitting song: "The Palms."

As we left the school, walking home by the light of the full moon, we all agreed that this had been a perfect conclusion for our Palm Sunday observance!

AN INTERRUPTED HALLOWE'EN PARTY

"Hodi!" then again, *"Hodi, hodi!"* (a loud shout, in lieu of a knock).

My heart almost stopped. What now? Together with the Augustana School students, and staff and all others on the station, I had been anticipating the Augustana School Halloween party. My costume was all laid out on my bed and the party was to begin in minutes. The Tanzanian nurse at the door was on evening duty at the hospital. "You are needed immediately," she stated.

I dressed quickly in my uniform rather than in my costume, hurried out the door, and joined Dr. John Hult (our missionary doctor) on the road to the hospital. All my thoughts of the Halloween party crumbled.

This patient had been brought to the hospital by a typical "bush ambulance," which is a rope bed turned upside down, with a canopy fashioned by a blanket tied to each leg of the bed. The blanket served as protection from the hot sun for the patient. The ambulance was being carried by four men, accompanied by other men who would take their turn carrying as needed. *Ukende* (Grace) had been ill for six days at home before the ambulance trip started.

"It's a bowel obstruction," Dr. John decided. "The only way she can possibly survive is to do surgery immediately. After all this time, it's still very touchy as to the outcome of the surgery."

The Tanzanian surgical staff was called and soon the instruments were boiling on the Primus stove (small Swedish-made kerosene stove) while I was preparing Ukende for the surgical procedure. The repair of the bowel obstruction proved to be a long and tedious operation. We realized that her condition was critical and doubted that she would survive the night. We left her in the care of the Tanzanian night nurse and also her relatives who had accompanied her from home.

When I made rounds the next morning, I was startled and thrilled to see Ukende sitting up in her bed: "May I have some *uji* (porridge)?" she asked.

A few minutes later Dr. John arrived and asked me: "What time did she die?" He, too, was most amazed and thankful to find Ukende alive and already on her way to recovery. Again, we had witnessed a miracle of God's healing power!

Pauline Swanson *grew up in Two Harbors, MN. She graduated from the Bethesda Lutheran Hospital School of Nursing in St. Paul in 1945 and from the Lutheran Bible Institute in Minneapolis, MN, in 1948; she returned there for the Missions course during a furlough.*

In 1949 she was commissioned by the Augustana Lutheran Church, to go to Tanganyika (now Tanzania) to serve as a missionary nurse.

During all of her three terms she was stationed at Kiomboi Hospital and served in various capacities, including teaching and supervising students and staff on the wards, and in the surgery and obstetrics departments. Her last assignment was that of matron of the hospital.

After returning to the USA in 1965, she worked as an instructor at a hospital school of nursing and later as staff development director at a large nursing home in Minneapolis.

She is enjoying her retirement years by being involved in various volunteer activities, including in her church, the World Mission Prayer League, the Nurses' Christian Fellowship, the Arthritis Foundation and Bible Study Fellowship.

CHURCH—"YEA, GOD!"

Annette Stixrud

COREY'S MILK SISTER

Late at night was an unlikely time for someone to knock on our door in Kiomboi, Tanzania. My husband Neal had been called to be principal of Augustana School, a school for missionary children, situated in this small East African village. "*Mchungagi* Kitundu" (Pastor Kitundu), I heard my husband exclaim. "*Karibu!*" ("Come in!") Our pastor had come because his wife was ill and unable to nurse their new baby. Our son, Corey, was about six months old at the time. Did we have a bottle so they could feed her?

"No," I said. "I nurse Corey and don't have a single bottle. But I could come and nurse the baby."

Thus began a new venture in my life as a wet nurse. For several days, *Luti* (Swahili for Ruth) nursed first at her mother's breasts and then I nursed her until she was full. She became Corey's milk-sister and my milk-daughter. In this life we become extended family in a variety of ways, largely without our choosing. I will always feel physically, emotionally, socially and spiritually linked to little Luti and her family. And yet, aren't we all, through baptism, God's extended family in the world?

Years later, our family visited the Kitundu's in Kiomboi. Luti was a charming, intelligent young woman who was attending the seminary at Morogoro. We took a picture of Corey and his milk-sister, but unfortunately it was ruined as we went through the customs check at the airport. It would be nice to have that picture, but the blessing of that experience is at a heart level where I have a "picture" that is indelible.

A new couple came to teach at Augustana School and were upset that the school children were expected to worship in the local African church. The service was in Swahili or the tribal language of Lyamba, and the usual length of service from two to three hours. They felt it was hypocritical to "make" children participate in a service in a language they did not understand. I pondered over this and felt they were right. I didn't understand very much Swahili and even less Lyamba, and it seemed pointless. Talking this over with Neal ended up with, "Annette, if that is the way you feel, then don't go to church." He was non-judgmental about my attitude and continued to take the children and attend church.

"I can worship at home," was my stand on this issue, "in a language I can understand."

Several weeks went by. Each Sunday it felt a bit more painful as Neal and the children walked to church. One day I heard my three-year-old Lindsey singing a song made popular by the Medical Mission Sisters called *God Loves a Cheerful Giver, Give it All You've Got!*

That's exactly right! Worship is about giving God praise. . . . in any language! Mine was an attitude problem. I was looking at church from the wrong perspective. The next Sunday, I went to church and it was amazing what happened to my heart and my ears. I understood the Swahili for the first time, but more importantly why I go to church. To this day, while I am happy to attend an English service, it really doesn't matter. Worship is beyond language. *"And a little child shall lead them."*

When Corey was five I remember him saying, "Going to church is like saying, *"Yea God!"*

THE PANCAKE SUPPER

When we were sent to Tanzania there was a feeling that the school and government were at odds with each other. In an effort to make friends with government people, Neal and I worked in the evenings to learn Swahili and would practice on anyone willing to struggle through with us. After being in Kiomboi for almost a year, we attended the local *Saba Saba* Day (a Tanzania patriotic holiday) celebration. Neal met a man who had just arrived to take over the running of the local government office, Henry Nyirenda. Neal conferred with me quickly to see if it would be okay to invite Henry to dinner.

"Of course," I said, and the two agreed on a day the next week.

The day came and I was not feeling well at all! It was all I could do to change diapers and feed the kids and lie on the couch and watch them play. My house needed to be cleaned and I had to come up with something for dinner. Slowly, I managed to straighten things up but couldn't even think of food without becoming more nauseated. Early afternoon came, the kids were down for a nap, Neal was at school. "What can I possibly do, Lord? ... Pancakes?" I thought, "it isn't much, but I think I can manage that."

Neal arrived home late, and Henry was there only minutes later. The two talked and it was obvious that Henry enjoyed the conversation as well as getting to know Lindsey and Corey. Eventually, sick as I felt, we sat down to dinner. Neal prayed and thanked God for Henry's presence with us. As we were beginning to eat I noticed two tears running down Henry's face. "Oh, dear," I thought, self-conscious about the menu, "maybe it's the pancakes?"

"I'm sorry, Henry, is something wrong?"

"Well," he said. "I have been in Kiomboi several weeks now and you are the first people that have been hospitable to me. I am thankful." So was I. Did Augustana School have any further "government" problems? Not to our knowledge, and Henry remains a friend to this day.

When we remember that the act of inviting the stranger and welcoming him in, is what we are called to do, God is there.

Annette Foege Stixrud *graduated from Pacific Lutheran University in Tacoma, Washington and taught first grade for three years in Bellevue, WA. During that time she married her college sweetheart, Neal. They moved to Vancouver, WA, in 1964 in order for Annette to complete a nursing degree before going to the mission field.*

In 1968, as missionaries for the Lutheran Church in America (LCA), Annette, Neal, and their children, Lindsey and Corey, moved to Tanzania, East Africa, to serve at the Augustana School for missionary children.

The Stixruds returned to Eugene, Oregon in 1973, where Annette worked for Community Health and Social Services in Lane County. She conducted immunization clinics and health screenings and counseled low-income senior citizens.

From 1977 to 1986, the Stixruds, once again serving as missionaries with the LCA, worked at Kodaikanal International School in Tamil Nadu, India. Some of Annette's time was spent as teacher, student ombuds-person, and principal's secretary, but the majority of her efforts lay outside the confines of the school, working with village health workers. Annette also spent six months working with Mother Teresa's Mission- aries of Charity, at Shishu Bhavan Orphanage in Madras.

In January 1987, Annette and Neal were seconded from the Evangelical Lutheran Church in America (ELCA) to serve with the Coptic Orthodox Church in Cairo, Egypt. Annette worked in development programs for women and nursery school children. Along with another R.N., she developed health materials for Egyptian children. Annette completed her M.S. in Health Education from the University of Oregon in 1989, before traveling to Alexandria, Egypt, to serve as Elementary Principal at Schutz American School for the 1989-1990 school year.

Since returning to the U.S., Annette has taught Health Careers at Beaverton High School and is presently the Program Director for Northwest Parish Nurse Ministries, a non-profit organization located in Portland, OR.

GOD'S PROMISES—FULFILLED

Jeanne Ward

I was filled with mixed emotions: of being frightened, excited and sad. Frightened because of not knowing what lay ahead and feeling that I wasn't prepared or capable. But I was confident that God had called us and that He had promised to be with us.

It was September 1954. My husband Bob and I, together with our two little ones, Kristine, two years, and Daniel, nine months, were ready to sail from New York on the Queen Elizabeth II, on our way to Tanganyika, East Africa. That was the exciting part.

I was sad because saying goodbye to my mother had been very difficult. She turned away and wouldn't—or couldn't—say goodbye. Perhaps it reminded her of when she had left Norway at the age of 19 to emigrate to America and didn't return to visit Scandinavia until 45 years later. She wasn't ready to let me go and to trust us into God's care. She thought Bob was taking me to the other end of the world and that she wouldn't see me again.

I was comforted as I claimed God's promise found in Matthew 28:20b, *"…and remember, I am with you always, to the end of the age."* My translation read, *"even unto the end of the world."*

After three months of language study at Mgori Mission Station as guests of Rev. Les and Ruth Peterson, we were assigned to serve at Isanzu Mission Station. Isanzu was located at the northern edge of our mission field. We were often alone at the station while the two missionary nurses who also lived at Isanzu were on duty at the Mkalama Leprosarium, nine miles away.

Because I was also a registered nurse, I was quite often called out during the night to our dispensary. We had an excellent midwife, Eliwandisha. A call for me to come at night meant that there was an emergency.

One night I was awakened by a loud: *"Hodi! Hodi!"* (the African vocal way of knocking at the door.) A voice said, "Eliwandisha is calling you, she needs your help. Come quickly!"

This particular time I grabbed my obstetrical book, a kerosene storm lantern as well as my flashlight and quickly ran with the messenger. I prayed all the way to the dispensary.

Upon examination of the patient, I found a foot presenting in the delivery, and my heart started pounding faster.

"Lord," I prayed, "I haven't had midwifery training. I should have taken that course I was offered by the Lutheran Hospital at Moline, Illinois sometime ago—*Please help me!*"

I flipped through the pages of the book and was so thankful that I had brought it along. I found the reference: Footling, Breech Presentation. With the help of a flashlight and a lantern and *the Lord,* I succeeded in following the procedures and delivered a healthy baby! I gave a great sight of relief, and through some tears I murmured, "Thank you Lord. You promised me that—*'I can do all things through him who strengthens me.'* " (Phil. 4:13)

It was Sunday morning. The children, Kris and Dan, wanted to go to Sunday School and take their two-year-old sister Kathy with them. Later someone came and asked if I knew where my children were. I said, "Yes, they went down to Sunday School."

"Hapana, Mama! Njoo, uwaone!" ("No, Mama, come see where they are!") He pointed down towards a rock which we called Bulldog Rock, a mammoth bolder which was quite a distance from our house. There up on the top of the rock stood all three children dressed in their Sunday best clothes. I yelled at them, "Don't move until I get there!"

I got them down safely and praised the Lord for His guardian angels who had watched over them.

I was often alone with the children while Bob was away on evangelistic foot safaris, or building schools, making trips to Singida, or hunting. One Sunday afternoon a lot of thunder and lightning was threatening us with a heavy rain storm. I ran out to check the pigs and baby chickens and quickly returned to the house. I entered through the main back door. Maria, the young girl working for us, was attending a youth meeting at the church. She had just run up to the house to ask if she could borrow a rain coat.

I walked through the kitchen out to the side porch. As I reached up to get the rain coat that was hanging on a nail, a huge bolt of lightning struck, hitting the big tree adjacent to the porch. It was so broadly spread out that it also hit the palm of my hand knocking me to the floor. I don't recall how long I lay there, but as I got up I heard Maria sobbing and crying, *"Mama, Mama amekufa!"* ("Mama, Mama has died!")

I went to her and put my arms around her saying *"Mimi nipo sawasawa, Maria, namshukuru Mungu."* ("I'm all right, Maria, so I thank God.")

The house smelled from burned-out wires. I quickly checked out the children who had been napping and they were all safe.

The top of the tree that had been struck was totally gone. The big yard light that had been attached lower down on the tree had completely disintegrated, leaving no trace. Had I entered the back door one minute or even a few seconds later, I undoubtedly would have been killed. God was watching over me and fulfilling His promise in Isaiah 52:12, *"For the Lord will go before you and ... will be your rear guard."*

When we returned from our first furlough in August 1959, we were assigned to serve at the Barabaig Mission Station to fill in for Rev. Hal and Louise Faust while they went home on leave.

One morning when I got up and walked into the hallway, I smelled a strong odor of kerosene. Just then Joel, our little two-year-old, came from the living room crying and reeking from kerosene. I picked him up and ran into the living room. There I found a tiny kerosene lamp called a *"koroboi"* by the fireplace with its top missing. It had been left within Joel's inquisitive reach and he had taken a drink from it. How much? I didn't know!

I ran with him into the kitchen and quickly mixed up milk and egg whites and got him to swallow some before he became semi-comatose. Hindsight told me that I should not have tried to make him vomit after swallowing kerosene. We were very far from a hospital and I prayed again for the Lord's help. I carried Joel to his crib, placed him on his side and kept watch. Within the hour he awakened and started retching and vomiting, filling the room with the smell of kerosene. He was all right! No kerosene had gotten into his lungs.

"Thank you, Lord!" I cried out, "for your promise fulfilled." *"He will command his angels concerning you, to guard you in all your ways. On their hands they will bear you up."* (Ps. 91:11-12)

In December 1967, there was a measles epidemic at Isanzu. It took the lives of several children. Both our Joel, 10 years old, and Heidi, 5, contracted the disease. They both also had the complication of pneumonia. Heidi's temperature hovered around 105° for several days in spite of receiving penicillin shots. On the fifth day, which was December 24, her temperature rose to 105.6° and yet no rash appeared. She then started vomiting a brownish fluid that looked as it was flecked with blood. I was frantic! We called our hospital station, Kiomboi, on our inter-station radio and were told by a doctor that we had better bring Heidi there. Because recent heavy rains had caused the Ndulumu River to rise, it would be necessary to drive the long way around, a trip of at least four hours.

"Lord, what should we do?" was our prayer as the family gathered around the Christmas tree. "You've asked us to call upon you at all times and in all situations."

Bob and I were led to stay at Isanzu and not try to make that long trip with such a critically ill little girl.

I continued with tepid sponges throughout the night and at 5 a.m. on Christmas day Heidi's fever broke and the measle's rash erupted. What a glorious Christmas dawning! Two days later she was well enough for me to bring her out to the front porch so that she could watch her brother Dan blow out the candles on his birthday cake.

Yes, the Lord's angels were there bearing us up and again He *"was our rear guard."*

Our children were the main part of my life those first years in Tanganyika. The Lord blessed us with three more beautiful children and I had to trust them all to His loving care as they played outside in "the bush" and climbed the rocks and trees surrounding our station.

For seven years we made many bush safaris and lived in tents as we witnessed among the nomadic hunting tribe called the Tindiga. They are a click-speaking people of short stature who are related to the Hottentots of South Africa. The tribe is very small in number. Being a docile and shy people they would always run and hide when they heard us coming. I remember them peeking out from behind trees until they felt it was safe to approach us.

The Tindiga moved about the bush country following seasonal availability of roots and seeds and searching for places to harvest wild honey. They also looked for the seeds of the baobab tree, berries, and wild animals which the government allowed them to hunt as food with their poison-tipped arrows. They liked to live on hilltops in order to see animals or even human intruders. Their homes were small igloo-shaped grass huts easily and sparsely put together. They moved frequently. They neither planted crops nor herded domestic animals. Clothing for the men was a loin cloth and for the women animal skins, but the clothing customs were changing as the Tindiga came into closer contact with neighboring tribes.

Our younger children went with us on our bush safaris while the older ones were away at boarding school. Sometimes during school vacations the whole family went together on safari into the bush. Heidi was about eight weeks old when she made her first trip into Tindiga-land with us. I kept her in a little car bed covered with mosquito netting. No harm ever came to any of the children by taking them along and I think they were an asset to our witness. They always enjoyed playing with their little Tindiga friends in our camps.

One place that we visited even had a swimming hole, much to the delight of the children! The weather could be very hot and dry. Several times during the heat of the day we had to move our camp chairs around following the shade cast by a lone baobab tree.

342 / TOUCHED BY THE AFRICAN SOUL

The tsetse flies were always around, but we would especially encounter them while driving through the bush in our car. We had to keep the car windows closed which made it unbearably hot inside the car. Our daughter Kathy tried in vain to make a netting for the windows so she could keep them open. However, after only a few minutes, the netting would get ripped off by a thorn bush. Those were the times that made our children not too happy on visits to the "Digas." Tsetse fly bites sting and for some people can even cause severe swelling and redness around the bite. It is also possible to contract sleeping sickness (Trypanosomaiasis) from the bite of an infected fly.

I was able to use my nursing abilities and set a time each day for sick call when we were in camp. I made certain that the dispensing place was a distance from our tents and our cooking area. This was done as a preventative health measure out of concern for all of us on our visits.

It was always a joy for me to gather a group of Tindiga and play songs and gospel messages for them in their own language. This was made possible by playing small records made by Gospel Recording Inc. which three women from this mission had recorded when they visited us. We shared the need of a Saviour and the gospel messages wherever we camped. We also ate with the Tindiga, prayed with them, fellowshiped with them around their fires, and loved them very much.

Our big joy was the day, after about four and a half years of witness, when a large group of eighty Tindiga was baptized and brought into God's family of believers. The joy of that day was saddened for me, however, when I saw a man, Sha Kitundu, go up for communion with his wife. The Tindiga usually are monogamous, but this man had had two wives. Before he could be baptized he was told that he had to choose only one and he had chosen the younger one. My heart went out to his former first wife.

As I look back, the Lord was teaching and preparing us through all our experiences in Tanzania, for His future plan for our lives. Those experiences of evangelism, nursing, and bush pioneer mission work helped in later years when we served Him reaching out to the Samburu, a nomadic cattle herding tribe in northern Kenya.

I am thankful for all our past memories, pleasant and unpleasant. During those fifteen years in the Central Synod in Tanzania, our trust was in the Lord and He remained faithful. He sustained me through many bouts of malaria and amoebic dysentery as well as through other trials and tough situations.

There was the sadness in sending our children off to boarding school, when at that time we knew it was best for them. I held back the tears when we said good-byes to Kristie, our first to leave. Then I turned around and saw her standing there with tears running down her cheeks. It broke my heart and then my tears broke loose. To this day I get a lump in my throat when I recall some of those Kiomboi school experiences.

We had our frailties and our failures, but the Lord was always in control. There were challenges every day, prayers poured out, prayers answered and strength given beyond our own. *"And my God will supply every need of yours according to His riches in glory in Christ Jesus."* (Phil. 4:19).

We planted, and we watered where others had planted, but it was God who caused the growth. Holding on to God's many promises and supported by many faithful prayer partners, we counted it a privilege to serve our Lord and be co-workers along with the Tanzanians and all the other missionaries serving Him in what began as the Augustana Lutheran Mission, in central Tanganyika.

"Go therefore and make disciples of all nations, baptizing them in the name of the Father and of the Son and of the Holy Spirit, and teaching them to obey everything that I have commanded you. And remember, I am with you always, to the end of the age." (Matthew 28:19-20).

Jeanne Ward *was born in Balaton, MN, July 1, 1926. She graduated from Swedish Hospital School of Nursing, Minneapolis, MN, 1948.*

With her husband, Rev. Bob Ward, Jeanne served twenty-one years in Tanzania—at Isanzu Mission Station for fifteen years (except for one year at Barabaig Mission Station), then lived six years in Arusha where Bob was Audio-Visual Director for the Evangelical Lutheran Church of Tanzania.

Returning to Africa, they served in Kenya under the World Mission Prayer League. For six years they served the Evangelical Lutheran Church of Kenya in Nairobi at Uhuru Highway Lutheran Church. The last ten years before their retirement in 1992, they began a new work among the Samburu people in Kenya's Northern Frontier District.

PICTURES

Kiomboi Hospital, student nurses and nursing staff, 1975.

The 30th anniversary of the mission at Ruruma.

Kijota Church.

Kijota Church interior with central altar and seating for 1000 people.

Missionary Family 1961.

All teachers.

Missionary Family 1961.

"The great day of Freedom" December 9, 1961.

Risky roads.

Guess who has the right-of-way?

The charm and beauty of Africa. Symbol of Tanzania.

Mt. Kilimanjaro, 19 340 ft. A mountain top experience.

The medical work, looking for malaria parasites.

Grandmother and granddaughter, midwife, and nurse,
"each in her own time".

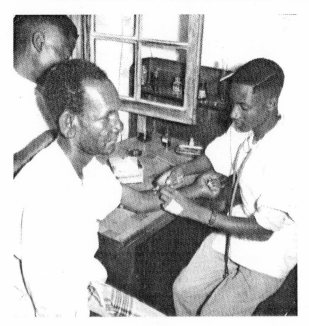

Outpatient Clinic.

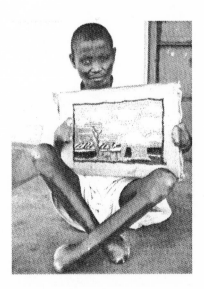

Daudi (David) "Teach me to sew."

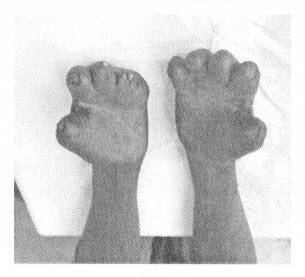

Thankful.

A touch of love.

Basket weaving.

Pastor Manase Yona, first African president of Lutheran church of central Tanzania, his wife and daughters.

"Who is the greatest in the Kingdom of Heaven?"

Literacy work.

The 4 R's Learning to read right side up.

Outreach to the Barabaig.

Transporting a sick person.

Outreach to the Tindiga.

Quiet Waters Publications
Other titles related to *Touched by the African Soul:*
(for prices and order information visit our web site at
www.quietwaterspub.com):

Daktari Yohana
By John Hult
This book is a compilation of stories, which grew out of the author's four
years as a medical missionary to Tanzania from 1957-1961. John Hult is the
husband of Adeline Lundquist Hult, one of the contributors to *Touched by
the African Soul.* If you love Africa, you will enjoy this book.
ISBN 0-9663966-5-0

Miracle At Sea
By Eleanor Anderson
In 1941 about 140 American missionaries had embarked on the ill-fated
Egyptian liner Zamzam, including Mrs. Danielson with her six children who
planned to join her missionary husband in Tanzania. The vessel was sunk
by a German raider off the African coast. Eleanor Anderson, one of the
surviving Danielson daughters, tells the story of the events leading up to the
sinking and of the family's miraculous rescue.
ISBN 0-9663966-3-4

On Our Way Rejoicing
By Ingrid Hult-Trobisch
Ralph Hult, one of the first American missionaries to Tanzania, was a
passenger on the *Zamzam* as well. After returning to the US, he set out for
Tanzania the following year, where he died unexpectedly. His daughter,
Ingrid Trobisch, tells the story of what happens when God takes away the
father of ten children. A whole family is called to service and sent into the
world. The story surges with movement, partings and reunion, sorrows and
joys, adventure and romance, shining courage, and above all, the warm love
that knits together a large Christian family.
ISBN 0-9663966-2-6

I Loved A Girl
By Walter Trobisch
'Last Friday, I loved a girl—or as you would put it, I committed adultery.'
This deeply moving story of a young African couple has become a worldwide classic with its frank answers to frank questions about sex and love. Its
tremendous success led Walter and Ingrid Trobisch to leave their missionary post in Cameroon and start an international ministry as marriage and
family counselors.
ISBN 0-9663966-0-X

The Adventures Of Pumpelhoober
By David Trobisch, illustrated by Eva Bruchmann

"A Pumpelhoober is someone who has bad luck. I, too, often have bad luck, and that is why everyone calls me Pumpelhoober. My father is German and speaks German, my mother is American and speaks English but with my luck I was born in a country in Africa, where everyone speaks French." This humorous children's book tells the story of a missionary family in Africa from the perspective of a nine-year-old.

ISBN 0-9663966-4-2

I Married You
By Walter Trobisch

Set in a large African city, this story covers only four days in the life of Walter and Ingrid Trobisch. Nothing in this book is fiction. All the stories have really happened. The people involved are still living today. The direct, sensitive, and compassionate narrative presents Christian marriage as a dynamic triangle.

ISBN 0-9663966-6-9

Printed in the United States
1152500004B/88-117